Making Schools More Effective
New Directions from Follow Through

EDUCATIONAL PSYCHOLOGY

Allen J. Edwards, Series Editor
Department of Psychology
Southwest Missouri State University
Springfield, Missouri

In preparation:

Patricia A. Schmuck and W. W. Charters, Jr. (eds.). Educational Policy and Management: Sex Differentials

Phillip S. Strain and Mary Margaret Kerr. Mainstreaming of Children in Schools: Research and Programming Issues

Ronald W. Henderson (ed.). Parent-Child Interaction: Theory, Research, and Prospects

Published

W. Ray Rhine (ed.). Making Schools More Effective: New Directions from Follow Through

Herbert J. Klausmeier and Thomas S. Sipple. Learning and Teaching Concepts: A Strategy for Testing Applications Theory

James H. McMillan (ed.). The Social Psychology of School Learning

M. C. Wittrock (ed.). The Brain and Psychology

Marvin J. Fine (ed.). Handbook on Parent Education

Dale G. Range, James R. Layton, and Darrell L. Roubinek (eds.). Aspects of Early Childhood Education: Theory to Research to Practice

Jean Stockard, Patricia A. Schmuck, Ken Kempner, Peg Williams, Sakre K. Edson, and Mary Ann Smith. Sex Equity in Education

James R. Layton. The Psychology of Learning to Read

Thomas E. Jordan. Development in the Preschool Years: Birth to Age Five

Gary D. Phye and Daniel J. Reschly (eds.). School Psychology: Perspectives and Issues

Norman Steinaker and M. Robert Bell. The Experiential Taxonomy: A New Approach to Teaching and Learning

J. P. Das, John R. Kirby, and Ronald F. Jarman. Simultaneous and Successive Cognitive Processes

Herbert J. Klausmeier and Patricia S. Allen. Cognitive Development of Children and Youth: A Longitudinal Study

Victor M. Agruso, Jr. Learning in the Later Years: Principles of Educational Gerontology

The list of titles in this series continues on the last page of this volume.

Making Schools More Effective
New Directions from Follow Through

EDITED BY

W. RAY RHINE

Department of Behavioral Studies
School of Education
University of Missouri
St. Louis, Missouri

With a foreword by
EDWARD F. ZIGLER

1981

ACADEMIC PRESS
A Subsidiary of Harcourt Brace Jovanovich, Publishers

New York   London   Toronto   Sydney   San Francisco

ACADEMIC PRESS, INC.
111 Fifth Avenue, New York, New York 10003

United Kingdom Edition published by
ACADEMIC PRESS, INC. (LONDON) LTD.
24/28 Oval Road, London NW1 7DX

Library of Congress Cataloging in Publication Data
Main entry under title:

Making schools more effective.

   (Educational psychology)
   Includes bibliographies and index.
   1. Socially handicapped children--Education--
United States. 2. Project Follow Through.
3. Compensatory education--United States.
I. Rhine, W. Ray. II. Series.
LC4091.M26   371.96'7   81-4901
ISBN 0-12-587060-4

PRINTED IN THE UNITED STATES OF AMERICA

81 82 83 84   9 8 7 6 5 4 3 2 1

For
All those individuals who worked
to make Follow Through a success

Project Follow Through is an im-
mensely important milestone in the
search for more varied and better
ways to educate children, disadvan-
taged or not. We now have a clear
precedent for change in public
school education.

> [McCandless, B. R., & Evans,
> E. D. *Children and youth: Psy-*
> *chosocial development.* Hins-
> dale, Ill.: Dryden Press, 1973.
> Pp. 448–449]

Contents

Part I
Introduction

1
An Overview

W. RAY RHINE

5

Behavior Analysis Model *155*

EUGENE A. RAMP AND W. RAY RHINE

6

High/Scope Cognitively Oriented Curriculum Model *201*

DAVID P. WEIKART, CHARLES F. HOHMANN, AND W. RAY RHINE

7

*Bank Street Model: A Developmental–
Interaction Approach* *249*

ELIZABETH C. GILKESON, LORRAINE M. SMITHBERG, GARDA W. BOWMAN,
AND W. RAY RHINE

Part III
The Impact of Follow Through

List of Contributors

Numbers in parentheses indicate the pages on which the authors' contributions begin.

WESLEY C. BECKER (95), Division of Developmental Studies, College of Education, University of Oregon, Eugene, Oregon 97403

GARDA W. BOWMAN (249), Bank Street College of Education, New York, New York 10025

DOUGLAS W. CARNINE (95), Division of Special Education and Rehabilitation, College of Education, University of Oregon, Eugene, Oregon 97403

RICHARD ELARDO (25), Division of Early Childhood Education and Elementary Education; Division of Educational Psychology, Measurement, and Statistics; and the Early Childhood Education Center, University of Iowa, Iowa City, Iowa 52242

SIEGFRIED ENGELMANN (95), Division of Special Education and Rehabilitation, College of Education, University of Oregon, Eugene, Oregon 97403

ELIZABETH C. GILKESON (249), Bank Street College of Education, New York, New York 10025

IRA J. GORDON* (49), School of Education, University of North Carolina, Chapel Hill, North Carolina 27514

* Deceased

GORDON E. GREENWOOD (49), College of Education, University of Florida, Gainesville, Florida 32611

CHARLES F. HOHMANN (201), High/Scope Educational Research Foundation, Ypsilanti, Michigan 48197

EUGENE A. RAMP (155), Department of Human Development, University of Kansas, Lawrence, Kansas 66044

W. RAY RHINE (3, 25, 49, 95, 155, 201, 249, 291, 325), Department of Behavioral Studies, School of Education, University of Missouri—St. Louis, St. Louis, Missouri 63121

LORRAINE M. SMITHBERG (249), Bank Street College of Education, New York, New York 10025

LEILANI M. SPENCER (25), Florissant Valley Community College, St. Louis, Missouri 63135

WILLIAM B. WARE (49), Division of Human Development and Psychological Services, School of Education, University of North Carolina, Chapel Hill, North Carolina 27514

DAVID P. WEIKART (201), High/Scope Educational Research Foundation, Ypsilanti, Michigan 48197

Foreword

This volume merits careful attention by all those individuals who want to help improve the nation's schools. For many reasons, this book represents an important contribution to a growing body of literature on the utilization of the social sciences in intervention research to strengthen educational programs. The content of the various chapters illustrates that reports of applied, problem-focused research can be well-organized, informative, and interesting to read. Detailed descriptions of Follow Through educational models reveal how researchers used the resources of the social sciences and much practical knowledge gained from their own extensive experience in schools to plan, implement, and evaluate their innovative approaches for educating economically disadvantaged children. Reading this book encourages feelings of optimism that in the years ahead advances such as those accomplished in Follow Through may be used to enhance greatly the educational and life opportunities of children from low-income families and indeed for all children.

In the mid-1960s, the consensus in America supported a war to eliminate poverty. But how was this formidable task to be accomplished? Numerous causes for poverty could be cited—including powerful economic, political, and cultural forces that tended to perpetuate the status quo. Even the educational system appeared to be contributing to inequality of opportunity. According to the American ethos, education was expected to serve as the great equalizer of the population. Indeed, education had been the means for acculturating and assimilating the disparate immigrant groups when they arrived at this country's shores. Americans felt justified in believing that equality of education opened to each and every individual the door to unlimited opportunities for wealth, prestige, and the good life in general. But the nation no longer could overlook the glaring fact that certain ethnic, racial, and rural groups were excluded from access to the American dream. These groups remained poverty stricken from generation to generation. Although many causes might be implicated in the continuing plight of economically disadvantaged children, the failure of the educational system to meet their needs could no longer be ignored.

Why was the educational system unable to educate children of the poor? The system as a whole did not seem to be at fault, as it appeared to be successful in meeting the needs of many children. Perhaps, then, the cause lay in economically disadvantaged children themselves. It was known that these children entered school with inadequate cognitive skills, as compared to their more affluent peers. Thus, many individuals concluded that the initial deficiencies of disadvantaged children prevented them from performing as well as other children in the regular educational program. This reasoning appeared to explain why students from low-income backgrounds had lower levels of academic skills than their peers when they completed their school experience and, therefore, why they could not compete effectively for jobs. When the problem of poverty was represented in this manner, the solution appeared to require a preschool intervention program to increase these children's cognitive and social skills, so they might profit as much as other children from the educational opportunities provided in school. Then, when poor children completed their formal schooling, they, too, would be eligible for high-level jobs and careers—and thus the vicious cycle of poverty would be broken.

In a simplified manner, this account describes the type of thinking that led to the development of Head Start and eventually to Follow Through. A more lengthy description of events that supported the initiation of these two projects is presented in Chapter 2 of this volume. Many individuals expected the students who received the benefits of both Head Start and Follow Through to acquire momentum that would propel them into a more optimal course of development. Then, the children were expected to sustain this new desirable trajectory of development during the remainder of their school attendance and during their adult years. Also, a central goal of Follow Through was to discover "what works best" in the education of poor children.

During the past 15 years, I frequently have expressed support for Head Start and have observed with interest the evolution of Follow Through. My views about the accomplishments and significance of Head Start have been stated in many publications, including a recent volume entitled, *Project Head Start: A Legacy of the War on Poverty* (New York: Free Press, 1979), which I co-edited with Jeanette Valentine. My initial contact with Follow Through was in the summer of 1967, when I served as a member of the national Follow Through Advisory Committee. The individuals in that group made a number of recommendations about the structure and functions of the new project. Ray Rhine and his colleagues completed this volume to describe the results of their participation in Follow Through and its implications for education, research, and social policy. Taken together, these two books contain much needed information about the history and performance of Head Start and Follow Through, as well as the future prospects for improving educational and life opportunities for children and their families who participate in these projects.

Follow Through was planned to be both a large-scale ecological study on the effects of a variety of educational models for economically disadvantaged children and an attempt to extend the benefits of compensatory education for these children as they advanced through kindergarten and the primary grades. The model sponsors who were selected to participate in the project differed in their visions of the goals of education and the methods for attaining them. In this volume, the authors of chapters on five Follow Through models share with us the knowledge they gained from more than a decade of experience in implementing their approaches, including successes, failures, and suggestions for improving the implementation of the models. Without a doubt, the accomplishments of each model described in this book are impressive. Throughout the chapters on the various models, the achievements of Follow Through are seen in the documentation of marked improvement in children's reading, mathematics, and language skills; an increase in children's feelings of self-esteem and other motivational, affective characteristics; and an increase in parents' educational skills, teaching ability, and involvement with their children.

Two prominent features of Follow Through are the use of scholars to develop educational interventions and the planned variation of the interventions. These features were designed into the project so educators, researchers, and citizens could decide eventually which educational approaches provide the greatest benefits to students and their families. Therefore, a large part of the discussion about these approaches focuses on the problem of evaluating each model fairly and comprehensively. Because the original intent in Follow Through was to compare various educational models, evaluation is an important issue. But reviewing the outcomes of evaluation studies reported in this volume does not compel readers to conclude that one model is superior to all others. The results of a number of evaluations indicate that each model has its merits and value.

Therefore, the true winner of any contest that may have occurred in Follow Through has been the nation as a whole. One important result of Follow Through is that the nation now has an array of educational programs that have been proven to be effective in teaching economically disadvantaged children.

Although the issue of which model provides the most gains to children and their families is a difficult one to resolve, the book does answer the question of "what works best" for children. What works best is continuity of high-quality educational experiences. Economically disadvantaged children, like all children, develop optimally so long as they receive the attention of caring and able persons who are committed to providing educational programs that are adapted to children's needs. The children appear to gain in proportion to the amount of time they spend in such an environment. After they leave this optimal environment, their further development usually is not maintained at the same level.

A number of investigators have reported that children are unable to maintain all the gains they achieve in Head Start and Follow Through when they leave these programs. Some individuals have construed these findings as contrary to the original expectancies for these programs and, therefore, as evidence that the programs have failed. However, perhaps what is faulty is the conception of economically disadvantaged children as substandard individuals who, after their achievement levels are made commensurate with other children, can be processed efficiently through the remainder of their school experience by the machinery of the regular school system. But accumulating evidence suggests that it is unreasonable to expect disadvantaged children to sustain and build upon their gains from short-term compensatory programs unless they receive continued support from an optimal environment. This may be the most important lesson from Head Start and Follow Through.

This lesson has profound theoretical and practical implications. Head Start and Follow Through were developed during the 1960s when the notion of "critical periods" in children's development was widely accepted. Many researchers were attempting to discover critical periods during which particular interventions would guarantee children's optimal future development. Underlying the concept of critical periods is the belief that development proceeds as a series of propulsive events. According to this position, children who receive proper stimulation during a critical period are hurled in the correct developmental direction, and they require little further guidance in order to arrive at their appropriate developmental destination. Furthermore, appropriate experiences during the next critical period serve to propel children to the next developmental landmark. In contrast, the results of Head Start and Follow Through suggest that continuity of support and guidance over the years, not critical periods of special stimulation, may be the true basis for optimal development. Head Start and Follow Through also demonstrate that children attain developmental success when their families, schools, and communities provide consistent and integrated patterns of experience. This continuity of experience is required not only across time but also across social institutions.

Continuity of experience is essential in efforts to encourage more successful developmental patterns among economically disadvantaged children. Throughout the development of advantaged children, their total environment is characterized by complementary cultural values and experiences. Disadvantaged children who attend compensatory programs do not have the benefit of such continuity. Although their parents and part of the community also may be involved in these programs, much of the remainder of their environment lacks a consistent emphasis on academic values and the skills that are necessary for success in school. Moreover, when they leave these special programs, the children typically enroll in other school programs that are less stimulating. If children are unable to sustain their developmental gains in Head Start and Follow Through, the reason may be that the gains are not reinforced during subsequent stages of growth. The writers of this book and sponsors of other Follow Through models have demonstrated that high-quality educational interventions for children from low-income backgrounds can be designed to achieve and maintain developmental gains over prolonged periods of time. The clear message from Follow Through is that such programs should be extended as required during the whole developmental period of the economically disadvantaged child.

Head Start and Follow Through were developed to answer the question, "Why do economically disadvantaged children fail to benefit from the American system of equal educational opportunity?" However, the results of these projects have raised questions about the correct conception of equal educational opportunity. The outcomes of Follow Through indicate clearly that the ideal of equal educational opportunity does not imply that all children must proceed along the same educational path. Rather, educators should recognize the individual needs of children and provide teaching–learning experiences that enhance each child's development toward his or her full potential. Only when this ideal becomes a reality will the nation achieve its dream of equal educational opportunity for all.

EDWARD F. ZIGLER
Sterling Professor
Department of Psychology
Yale University

Preface

The national Follow Through Project is a unique longitudinal experiment in education that has been funded by the United States Office of Education (USOE) since 1967. The federal government has invested almost one billion dollars to assist educators and parents in local school districts to create a variety of new model program approaches for educating children in kindergarten and the primary grades. The program sponsors, or developers, who are researchers in child development and education in either universities or educational laboratories, perform key responsibilities in Follow Through. They and their staffs provide much of the expertise, supervision, and leadership for generating and refining the model programs through many developmental cycles. Each sponsor's approach is constructed around a distinct, coherent set of ideas about child development and education.

The purpose of the present volume is to describe the origins and unique characteristics of Project Follow Through, and to present cohesive descriptions of five of the most visible and widely implemented models. Follow Through is a landmark in the history of American education because it represents an important advance in the use of empirical and systematic methods to develop and evaluate educational programs. The results and implications are increasingly recognized as a timely contribution to the national debate on contemporary educational issues such as the purpose of education in our society, accountability, "return to basics," parent participation, and both preservice and in-service education of teachers. Furthermore, the project already has affected educational policies at federal, state, and local levels, as well as curriculum reform, evaluation research, institutional change, and the teaching of large numbers of children. Indeed, Follow Through may contribute eventually to significant change in education at all levels.

This book represents the first serious effort to organize and communicate comprehensive knowledge about educational alternatives developed in America's most extensive longitudinal research and development project in education. The contributors are social scientists, most of whom either have served as sponsors of the educational models described in this volume or have planned and supervised the construction of the models. Their experiences in the project represent a major source of original information on the uses of the social sciences in large-scale intervention research to design more effective educational programs.

This volume is intended for all researchers, practitioners, and policymakers who are concerned with the improvement of education. It will be useful especially to individuals in educational psychology, developmental psychology, educational leadership, curriculum studies, evaluation research, school psychology, and community psychology. The book illustrates how researchers used theories about child development, results of empirical investigations, and research skills to bridge the gap between knowledge and practice in education. These scientists–professionals may serve as role models for growing numbers of students who are preparing to enter careers that will require a blend of scholarly and practical knowledge.

The contents of this book also will be useful to classroom teachers, curriculum specialists, school administrators, and others who have responsibilities for educating children in the nation's schools. The descriptions of the innovative approaches to curriculum and evaluation, and the supplementary sources included among the references, contain much information that may be applied to the education of children. In addition, educational policymakers, planners, and administrators at federal, state, and local levels of government, many of whom already have some knowledge on Follow Through, will find the information about the various models to be pertinent and helpful in their efforts to provide effective educational services for America's children.

The volume is composed of nine chapters arranged in three parts. The first two chapters (Part I) acquaint readers with the major characteristics of Follow Through. In Chapter 1, Rhine explores the significance of Follow Through, explains the circumstances that influenced the preparation of this book, and summarizes each of the chapters on the model programs that are descibed in Part II. In Chapter 2, Rhine, Elardo, and Spencer review the beginnings of Head Start and other events that led to the initiation of Follow Through, and they examine the project's two guiding strategies— "planned variation" and "sponsorship." A number of conceptual systems that may be used to compare similarities and differences among the Follow Through models also are discussed, followed by a presentation of the guidelines that authors used to select and organize the information included in Chapters 3 through 7.

The next five chapters (Part II) contain descriptions of Follow Through models. Greenwood, Ware, Gordon, and Rhine, the authors of Chapter 3, discuss the *Parent Education Model.* The goal of this approach is to establish a new partnership between school personnel and parents who work together to create new learning opportunities for children and parents in homes and schools. In Chapter 4, the characteristics of the *Direct Instruction Model* are presented by Becker, Engelmann, Carnine, and Rhine. The core of this model is the DISTAR instructional materials, which were developed through the use of methods and research findings from behavioral psychology to improve instruction in basic academic skills. Ramp and Rhine describe in Chapter 5 the use of applied behavior analysis to construct the *Behavior Analysis Model.* Classroom teachers use a variety of behavioral procedures in this approach to help students gain at least one year of academic achievement for each year they are enrolled in school. In Chapter 6, Weikart, Hohmann, and Rhine discuss the *High/Scope Cognitively Oriented Curriculum Model.* This approach is derived from developmental theory, in part Piagetian, and the focus is on helping children develop the underlying cognitive processes and formal knowledge systems that they use to acquire and organize information. In Chapter 7, the distinctive features of the *Bank Street Model: A Developmental-Interaction Approach* are portrayed by Gilkeson, Smithberg, Bowman, and Rhine. The intent in this model is to adapt instruction to the growth patterns of each child in supportive and intellectually stimulating learning environments.

In the last two chapters (Part III), Rhine examines the impact of Follow Through by focusing on a number of issues that have emerged from more than a decade of planned variation research in the project. In Chapter 8, the pattern of effective cooperation among many participants in Follow Through is presented as a promising mechanism for improving educational services and generating knowledge about major concerns in the current national debate on education. In addition, selected issues in evaluation, implementation, and knowledge diffusion about exemplary educational programs are discussed. In Chapter 9, the focus is on the implications of events in Follow Through for using the social sciences to ameliorate social problems, followed by some concluding comments about the production of literature on problem-focused research conducted in large-scale intervention projects.

A major reason for organizing this volume was to increase the amount and variety of public information about Follow Through. Previously, public attention on the project had focused primarily on discussions about the planning, management, and outcomes of the national longitudinal evaluation. Many of the issues in that evaluation were examined in the May, 1978, issue of *Harvard Educational Review*. But a balanced appraisal of Follow Through also requires information from other sources, including the sponsors' experiences in program implementation and the results of their own evaluation research. The content of the present volume illustrates a variety of uses of the social sciences in problem-focused research. Thus, this book is an addition to the list of previous publications by Academic Press on the principles, methodology, and evaluation of intervention research.

Producing the final drafts of the manuscripts was a lengthy process involving frequent communication between the editor and the other authors. The editor worked with the representatives of each model to develop chapters that included essential information about the models within the format and guidelines that all contributors had accepted. Implementing the plan for completing the five chapters on the Follow Through models required that the editor also participate as an author in planning and completing each of those chapters.

For many practical reasons, the coverage in this volume was restricted to five Follow Through models. The editor and the other authors sincerely hope that the publication of this book will encourage others to publish materials about the models developed in Follow Through.

Acknowledgments

The generous efforts of many individuals were necessary in order to complete this volume. The authors maintained their commitment and enthusiasm through numerous iterations of the manuscripts for the chapters. Special appreciation is expressed to Richard Elardo and Edward J. Barnes. Elardo, my former colleague in the School of Education at the University of Missouri–St. Louis (UMSL), is now Associate Professor of Early Childhood and Elementary Education, Educational Psychology, Measurement, and Statistics, and Director of the Early Childhood Education Center at the University of Iowa. He helped solve some difficult conceptual and organizational problems encountered during the early stages of the completion of the volume. Barnes, late Deputy Director of the National Institute of Education (NIE), strongly supported the preparation of the book. He made many constructive responses to early versions of the prospectus before his sudden death in 1975.

Other individuals who helped in a variety of ways include: Lois-Ellin Datta, NIE; John A. Emrick, John A. Emrick Associates, Los Altos, California; Cyrus Rubeck, National Diffusion Network (NDN) of the USOE; Joseph S. Wholey, Deputy Assistant Secretary for Evaluation in the office of the USOE Assistant Secretary for Planning and Evaluation; Rosemary Wilson, Director of the national USOE–Follow Through Project, and Pat

Gore, a staff member of USOE-Follow Through. Throughout the endeavor, several members of the editorial staff of Academic Press provided encouragement and perceptive consultation. William F. Frazen, Dean of the UMSL School of Education, supported the completion of the volume by providing advice and essential logistical support. Appreciation also is expressed to Patricia A. Martin, Susan L. Stassi, and Erma J. Young, secretaries in the UMSL Department of Behavioral Studies, for their gracious, goodhumored support and technical assistance.

Finally, grateful recognition is due to the thousands of professional educators, parents, and children whose participation in local Follow Through programs made possible the accomplishments reported in this book.

Part I
Introduction

The future of our society is in no small way dependent upon the results produced by this creative and complex project [Follow Through].

> [EVANS, E. D. *Contemporary viewpoints on early childhood education.* Hinsdale, Ill.: Dryden Press, 1973, p. 96.]

Follow Through is a comprehensive project that represents a compromise between the rigor of a highly controlled and tightly designed laboratory experiment with the popular and politically appealing feature of community participation and local control.

> [RIECKEN, W. H., & BORUCH, R. F. (Eds.). *Social experimentation.* New York: Academic Press, 1974, p. 19.]

W. RAY RHINE   **1**

An Overview

Making Schools More Effective

Copyright © 1981 by Academic Press, Inc.
All rights of reproduction in any form reserved.
ISBN 0-12-587060-4

The three purposes of this chapter are (a) to discuss the significance of Follow Through as a large-scale venture in educational research; (b) to explain the circumstances that created a need for this volume; and (c) to present brief descriptions of the five Follow Through models portrayed in Chapters 3, 4, 5, 6, and 7.

Significance of Follow Through

During the early 1960s, the Congress enacted legislation designed to improve educational and life opportunities for children from low-income backgrounds. This historic legislation stimulated many attempts to link the interests and resources of school personnel, parents, and social scientists in a common cause to make schools more effective. But the results often failed to evoke enthusiasm because such attempts were generally nonexperimental, brief in duration, or limited to tinkering with existing procedures. Follow Through is an exception: it is a longitudinal intervention study designed to promote fundamental change in education and conducted within a research and development framework. In the pursuit of their goals, the federal administrators of the project employed many social scientists, molded a social intervention study in education, developed new resources for changing educational environments, and authorized a national longitudinal evaluation. Each of these four characteristics is discussed in this section.

SOCIAL SCIENTISTS IN FOLLOW THROUGH

When Follow Through began in 1967, the social sciences were riding a crest of public acceptance and encouragement. Government agencies were recruiting social scientists to help explore the usefulness of a variety of domestic social programs. Prominent United States congressmen, including then Senator Mondale, were supporting the creation of a national foundation to stimulate the growth of the social sciences. The prestigious National Academy of Science recommended that professionals in these disciplines devote more effort toward adapting practical applications of their knowledge to a broad range of social problems. In this heady atmosphere, the planners of Follow Through developed a structure for utilizing social scientists in a variety of functions.

Social scientists had major responsibilities in all phases of Follow Through—planning the project, administering it, designing and implementing programs, reviewing and critiquing the total effort, and evaluating outcomes. The disciplines represented in the project included education, psychology, sociology, anthropology, economics, political science, systems analysis, and policy research. Many social scientists chose to participate in Follow Through because they wanted to explore the usefulness of their disciplines in a large-scale social intervention project. Psychology was represented by a large contingent, including Wesley C. Becker, Urie Bronfenbrenner, Ira J. Gordon, Robert D. Hess, Jerome Kagan, Eleanor E. Maccoby, and Sheldon H. White. Included in the long list of organizations that contracted to provide social science expertise were the following: Abt Associates, Inc., Biodynamics, Inc., Educational Testing Service, National Opinion Research Council, National Training Laboratories, Social Science Research Council, Stanford Research Institute, several regional educational laboratories, and a number of universities.

A SOCIAL INTERVENTION STUDY IN EDUCATION

The intent of those who designed Follow Through was in line with recommendations that Campbell (1969), McGuire (1969), Rossi (1970), Rivlin (1971), Rossi and Williams (1972), and Riecken and Boruch (1974) expressed in their writings on planned intervention. Campbell explained how an "experimenting society" might employ the findings and methods of the social sciences to analyze and solve social problems. McGuire recommended more theory-oriented research on real-world problems in their natural settings. Rossi advocated intervention studies in which researchers developed and evaluated not one or a few models for a problem area but a full range of alternative approaches. Rivlin contended that social action projects and rigorous investigation were not opposed and that the two activities should be conducted simultaneously. Riecken and Boruch emphasized that planned approaches to social action should employ a strategy of "designed variation" to accumulate useful information. The writings of these authors provided a policy framework for more effective utilization of the social sciences that appeared to include three essential components: (a) Social scientists should be encouraged to analyze a target area and design a variety of pilot approaches to the problem; (b) these pilot studies should be refined through several iterations of a program development cycle, which includes planning, implementation, evaluation, and revision, in order to identify their strengths and weaknesses on a small scale before any one program is enacted on a large scale; and (c) information about attempts to utilize the social sciences should be disseminated within the academic and professional communities to promote discussion, criticism, and recommendations for improvement.

Follow Through represents important progress in performing social intervention studies in education. The individuals who worked in the project successfully used a unique set of concepts and operations, especially "planned variation" and "sponsorship," which illustrate the means for implementing the recommendations cited in the preceding paragraph.[1] Planned variation and sponsorship refer to the development of a variety of approaches to childhood education through the cooperative efforts of qualified social scientists, educators, and parents in local school districts. The characteristics of planned variation and sponsorship were described briefly in the preface and will be presented in greater detail in the next chapter.

In 1968, the administrators of Follow Through enthusiastically described the project as probably the most important social research effort in America.[2] Indeed, Follow Through was a serious attempt to improve upon the "scatter gun" approach to social intervention that was prevalent in the early 1960s by formulating a more systematic methodology for conducting and evaluating social experiments. Many social planners in the federal government believed that if the twin strategies of sponsorship and planned variation proved successful in Follow Through, they also might be applicable to a whole spectrum of social problems, whether in education, mental health, housing, income maintenance, or prevention and/or treatment of crime, alcoholism, or drug abuse.

NEW RESOURCES FOR
CHANGING EDUCATIONAL ENVIRONMENTS

Longitudinal studies in education are rare, and even more rare are those that have continued for more than a decade. During the years since 1968, Follow Through evolved into a comprehensive effort to change educational environments. The project derives its strength from the following resources: long-term relationships between schools and program sponsors, integrated initiatives for change, theory-based approaches to instruction, and effective methods for staff development in school settings.

---

[1] Riecken and Boruch (1974) present an excellent discussion on the differences between an experiment and a quasi-experiment and the appropriate uses of each in social intervention research. In quasi-experiments, such as Project Follow Through, participants are not randomly assigned to treatment and comparison groups. Indeed, random assignment of students in applied educational research is extremely rare. Some authors (Campbell & Boruch, 1975) have argued strongly for the advantages of generating more true experiments in educational intervention research. But other authors (Wisler, Burns, & Iwamoto, 1978) have questioned whether the use of random assignment of students in school settings may be such an atypical occurrence that the effects probably would weaken the internal validity of the research.

[2] In discussions of Follow Through in this volume, the term *project* refers to the national USOE–Follow Through Project; the term *program* refers to the educational programs developed by sponsors, educators, and parents in local communities. In addition, the terms *model, approach, model program,* and *model program approach* are interchangeable. Similarly, the terms "community" and "site" are used interchangeably to refer to the locations in which Follow Through programs were developed.

Long-Term Relationships between
Schools and Program Sponsors

In order to maintain continuity in the work performed at the various Follow Through sites, the United States Office of Education (USOE) encouraged individuals in local communities and program sponsors to work together for the duration of the project. School districts and sponsors are funded separately, thus avoiding a superior–subordinate relationship. In addition, both the school district and the sponsor are funded at a local site, or neither is funded. Thus, these policies provide considerable inducement for the participants to use cooperative, rather than competitive or power-oriented, strategies to resolve disagreements and conflicts before they become disruptive.

Integrated Initiatives for Change

Efforts to improve educational environments usually have been piecemeal, thus preventing the development of a "critical mass" required to support and sustain a broad-gauged strategy for change. Consequently, attempts to improve education often have consisted of "single-shot" approaches in which teachers used new materials or instructional techniques in a single subject area such as reading or math. Other examples of single-shot strategies to improve education are the following innovations: arrangements for grouping students, such as team teaching or nongraded classes; behavioral objectives; learning centers; and computer-assisted instruction. In contrast, school personnel and program sponsors in Follow Through have combined many innovative strategies, as well as extensive parent and community involvement, in integrated longitudinal efforts to improve educational programs.

Theory-Based Approaches to Instruction

Another characteristic that makes Follow Through a potent force for comprehensive change in education is that the model sponsors are guided by cohesive sets of ideas about children's development and learning in school settings. These ideas provide a source of direction, or "design guidance," for generating the materials, teaching-learning interactions, record keeping, and evaluation procedures that make up the day-to-day pattern of educational activities in classrooms. In addition, researchers are able to formulate hypotheses, conduct research, and use the results to improve educational services. By pursuing theory-based approaches to changing school environments, the sponsors attain a high level of integration and coordination among their activities in program development, staff development, and program evaluation. Furthermore, each set of ideas can be adapted to conditions in local communities in ways that maintain the integrity of the sponsor's general plan.

Effective Methods for Staff
Development in School Settings

Staff development programs in schools typically consist of courses offered by universities and colleges, workshops provided by professional consultants, or educational programs for parents. These are often of short duration and seldom linked to other elements of the school program. The professors who provide the staff development experiences usually have no continuing relationships with the school personnel or parents who receive their services. Similarly, the faculty members who provide the preservice training for students preparing to enter careers in education have little or no contact with them after they become practitioners. Thus, there are few opportunities for continuous, reciprocal exchange of information and ideas among the various levels represented by professors, school personnel, parents, and children.

In contrast, the network of linkages that exists among individuals in each Follow Through program encourages mutual communication at all levels. The participants work together in a continuous developmental process that makes it possible for them to learn about and refine educational programs through the results of experience and to develop coherent, reciprocal connections between educational theory and practice. Consequently, school personnel, parents, and students are able to see evidence of their success in influencing and shaping the implementation of a sponsor's model. These dynamic networks of linkages among participants in Follow Through models are among the primary reasons that sponsors have been able to develop coordinated approaches for changing and improving the ways in which individuals communicate with each other and work together in school environments. These accomplishments seldom are possible within the pattern of static relationships described in the preceding paragraph.

THE NATIONAL LONGITUDINAL EVALUATION

Most of the evaluation research reported in this book is drawn from the sponsor's own evaluations of their models. However, any report on Follow Through would be incomplete unless it included information on the national longitudinal evaluation. Therefore, the rapid growth in the scope and size of this evaluation and additional knowledge about it are discussed in this subsection. More commentary and critique on the national evaluation are presented in the next section of this chapter, as well as in the ensuing chapters.

In 1968, the administrators of Follow Through awarded contracts for longitudinal evaluation was weighted excessively toward measuring cognitive, academic learning objectives. The sponsors who advocated direct instructional methods generally favored the inclusion of many academic achievement items in the evaluation. From their perspective, the primary purpose of Follow Through should be to develop more effective techniques for teaching children the traditional skills in spoken language, reading, spelling, writing, and arithmetic. Conversely, other sponsors believed that the educational needs of children required the development of new curriculum content, which incorporated both cognitive and affective objectives. They sought to produce positive changes in self-concept, curiosity, and attitudes toward learning as ends in themselves as well as means for improving students' rates of learning in academic subjects. They insisted that appropriate instruments for measuring change in those areas should be selected or developed and included in the evaluation (Rhine, 1973a).

In response to the strong pressures for change, the administrators of Follow Through increased the number of model sponsors and greatly expanded the scope of the national longitudinal evaluation. Following a series of meetings at Menlo Park in the summer of 1969, they authorized initiatives to develop new approaches to measurement in several areas, including institutional change, classroom environments, and affective or noncognitive characteristics of children. One of the new approaches, parent interview techniques, was developed jointly by the USOE, the Stanford Research Institute, and the National Opinion Research Center. These interviews were administered during the 1969–1970 school year to approximately 15,000 families located in 49 communities.

The evaluation procedures produced an enormous amount and variety of data during the first 4 years of Follow Through. The number of students included in the basic evaluation sample increased from 17,500 in 1968 to 55,000 in 1972. During 1972, approximately 2200 people were employed in developing, printing, and shipping 10 tons of test materials and in collecting, coding, analyzing, and storing data in a computerized data bank. The 1968–1969 data bank contained approximately 65,000 card images; the number of card images increased to over 500,000 in the 1969–1970 data bank and to over 1,000,000 in the 1970–1971 bank.

In the spring of 1972, a panel consisting of Follow Through administrators and their consultants reviewed the rapid escalation in the scope, size, and cost of the evaluation. The members of the panel concluded that all possible questions could not be addressed by the evaluation, and that steps must be taken to control and reduce its cost. Their recommendations included the following: (a) The basic test battery should consist of the Metropolitan Achievement Test series for measuring

evaluation services to three organizations: the Stanford Research Institu
Biodynamics, Inc., and the National Training Laboratories. The ma
component in the total evaluation plan for the first year was
administration of a basic survey of language and number skills, which c
sisted primarily of items drawn from the Metropolitan Readiness Test a
the Lee–Clark Reading Readiness Test. Near the beginning and end of
school year, achievement tests were administered to samples of pupil
most of the 780 experimental classrooms and to many students in a la
number of non-Follow-Through comparison classrooms. In addition,
short form of the Stanford–Binet and a supplementary test consistin
items recommended by the program sponsors were administered t
smaller sample of children (Rhine, 1973a).

In July, 1969, the federal perspective on the significance of Fo
Through and the important role of evaluation in the project was expre
in an interoffice memo by Lewis Bright, Associate Commissioner in
USOE. He wrote, "We must take every precaution to insure that we ar
open to criticism with respect to the management as well as the subst
of the evaluation of this complex experimental program." He further s
that the Follow Through evaluation was the most costly single evalu
study in education ever financed by the federal government. In fact, t
million allocated for that purpose in fiscal 1970 was larger than the
amount allocated for the evaluation of all federal educational progra
fiscal 1969. In fiscal 1971, the allocation for the longitudinal evalu
rose to $6 million. Eventually, the total cost exceeded $40 million.

As might be expected in such a large project, stakeholder grou
Follow Through quickly became polarized on many issues. In policy r
meetings conducted in 1968 and 1969 in Washington, D. C., Atlant
at Menlo Park and Pajaro Dunes in California, the representatives
various stakeholder groups differed sharply on many matters, includi
definition of project goals and the criteria acceptable for evaluatio
example, representatives of ethnic minority groups strongly criticize
they perceived as a "pupil-change model" for implementing and eva
Follow Through. They contended that, if the evaluation results prove
disappointing, some individuals might interpret such findings as e
of racial inferiority rather than as evidence of the failure of the p
They argued that a "social-system change model" would be a mor
tive framework for generating responses to both the educational n
children and the broader concerns of parents for social justice and
of local institutions that affected their lives. Their top priority, the
was to define and measure the institutional changes that were nece
increase parents' participation in decisions about the operation of s

Other critics, including some model sponsors, argued that the academic skills, the Raven's Progressive Matrices for testing ability in abstract problem solving, and the Coopersmith Self-Esteem Inventory and Intellectual Achievement Responsibility Scale for assessing the affective domains of self-concept and locus of control, respectively; (b) both the amount of data collected and the frequency of data collections should be reduced; and (c) the collection of data and analyses of data should be assigned to separate organizations with data collection retained by SRI and data analyses conducted by Abt Associates, Inc. (McDaniels, 1975).

Efforts to analyze and interpret the massive amount of data collected in the national evaluation have been fraught with difficult problems, and reanalyses of these data and debate over interpretation of the results may continue for many years. Readers who wish to review the original sources of information on the design and results of the longitudinal evaluation are referred to the following technical reports: Rhine (1971), Sorensen (1971), Emrick, Sorensen, and Stearns (1973), Cline (1974), and Stebbins, St. Pierre, Proper, Anderson, and Cerva (1977). Other pertinent sources of information on this evaluation include Sorensen (1969), Bereiter and Kurland (1978), House, Glass, McLean, and Walker (1978), and Kennedy (1978). In addition, Chapter 4 in this volume, written by Becker, Engelmann, Carnine, and Rhine, includes a summary and critique of the national longitudinal evaluation, and commentary on that evaluation is included in other chapters as well. The characteristics of the national longitudinal evaluation and the controversy that has surrounded it are discussed in the next section of this chapter.

Need for This Volume

The decision to organize this volume evolved over a number of years. Following the completion of a postdoctoral research fellowship at Stanford University, the editor of this book was employed from 1968 to 1971 by the Stanford Research Institute as a senior research psychologist in the national longitudinal evaluation of Follow Through. During that period, he worked as a task leader in the evaluation and participated in most of the major meetings on policy and implementation of the national longitudinal evaluation. One of his major responsibilities was to organize and supervise a large pilot study on the selection and development of instruments for measuring the noncognitive characteristics of children (Rhine, 1971).

After Rhine accepted a university faculty position in the fall of 1971, in the Behavorial Studies Department at the University of Missouri at St. Louis, he maintained his interest in Follow Through by publishing papers and organizing four symposia on the project. Two of these symposia were presented at meetings of the American Psychological Association in 1971 and 1973, and two others were presented at meetings of the American Educational Research Association in 1972 and 1974. The participants in these symposia explored a number of topics, including issues in the evaluation of childhood education programs, utilization of the social sciences in a pluralistic society, social experimentation in education, and lessons derived from the Follow Through experience. Under the auspices of a grant from the National Institutes of Mental Health (MH–26055–01), Rhine also continued the work he began at the Stanford Research Institute on the measurement of noncognitive characteristics of children. A number of papers and publications have resulted from this work (Rhine & Spaner, 1973, 1974, 1976; Rhine & Spencer, 1975).

During the editor's conversations with colleagues who also had worked in Follow Through, he noted that many of them expressed the following concerns: (a) The general public had limited access to information about Follow Through; (b) public discussions about Follow Through were focused almost entirely on the results of the national longitudinal evaluation; and (c) the unique perspectives of the model sponsors were not being communicated effectively to practitioners in education, members of the academic community, and decision makers at various levels of government. Each of these three concerns is discussed here.

LIMITED INFORMATION ABOUT FOLLOW THROUGH

Early in the history of Follow Through, the administrators decided to limit the dissemination of information about the project to a small number of participants who had decision-making responsibilities. The administrators succeeded in providing the sponsors with a relatively protected period of time in which to develop their models. They also were able to prevent the confusion that might have been created by premature and inaccurate conclusions about the status of the Follow Through experiments. But one undesirable effect of that policy is that publications on the project have been limited to a small number, even though it has been in operation for more than a decade.

During the period from 1968 to 1973, one book and three chapters were published on Follow Through, and there have been only a few additional publications on the project since 1973. Maccoby and Zellner (1970) wrote a small volume that contains brief descriptions of the conceptual bases for most of the 13 original Follow Through models.[3] Bissel (1973), Rhine

[3] A total of 13 sponsors initiated Follow Through models during the 1968–1969 school year. Subsequently, 10 additional models were incorporated into the project. All current Follow Through models, the addresses of the sponsoring institutions, and the number of communities served by each model are presented in Appendix A. The number of communities served by the

(1973a),and Soar and Soar (1972) published chapters, each dealing with some facets of the national longitudinal evaluation. Rivlin and Timpane (1975) edited a volume on Follow Through that focuses primarily on issues in policy research. Their book contains selected papers that were presented at a conference entitled "Planned Variation in Education," which convened in April, 1973, at the Brookings Institution in Washington, D.C. Gordon and Breivogel (1976) edited a volume that contains descriptive information on various components of the Parent Education Model. Some writers presented selected results from the national longitudinal evaluation (Becker, 1977; Kennedy, 1978; Rhine & Spencer, 1975; Stallings, 1975). The May, 1978, issue of the *Harvard Educational* Review contains four articles that explore the national longitudinal evaluation. Among the publications cited in this paragraph, only those authored by Gordon and Breivogel (1976) and Becker (1977) contain extensive information about Follow Through models, and only Becker's article contains results from a sponsor's evaluation. Clearly, there is a need for more published information on the sponsors' models, including the results of the evaluations they performed on those models.

EXCLUSIVE ATTENTION TO THE NATIONAL LONGITUDINAL EVALUATION

Even though the dissemination of information on Follow Through was restricted, a number of individuals were able to obtain some knowledge on the national longitudinal evaluation. Not surprisingly, their interest in the project focused on the outcomes of that evaluation, rather than on a careful examination of the details of the work performed in the various models, with which they had little or no acquaintance. The public fascination with the national longitudinal evaluation is due in part to the controversy that has surrounded it throughout the history of Follow Through. Krulee (1973) and Rhine (1973a) documented the primary source of this controversy as the intense competition among, and sometimes within, stakeholder groups to influence policy decisions.

The logistical problems encountered in conducting the national evaluation of Follow Through were enormous, but the greatest challenge was to formulate an effective, representative decision-making process for accommodating the strong disagreements among the participants. Early in the history of Follow Through, it became apparent that the task of improving

---

models is indicated by the number following the name of each model. Models that have been discontinued are not included in the list. These models and the sponsoring institutions include the California Process Model (California State Department of Education), DARCEE (George Peabody College), the Parent Implementation Model (AFRAM Associates, Inc.), and the Role-Trade Model (Western Behavioral Sciences Institute).

educational opportunities for children from low-income backgrounds could not be accomplished in isolation from the social, ethnic, and other group tensions that existed in the larger society. In social intervention research, the recurring problems, confrontations, and stress cannot be resolved simply by eliminating one or more stakeholder groups from participation. The "politicization of evaluation research" that occurred in Follow Through and in other large-scale social intervention projects during the late 1969s and early 1970s has been described by Weiss (1970, 1972), Williams (1971), Rossi and Williams (1972), and Rhine (1973a, 1973b).

The struggles for control of policymaking and expenditure of funds in Follow Through often were converted into dramatic, emotional arguments on methodological and design issues in evaluation research. Many of the core issues and concerns were so personal, divisive, and inflammatory that they could not be expressed and dealt with openly and directly. Consequently, the conversion of these issues and concerns into arguments on methodological and design problems in evaluation research appeared to make practical compromises more likely. Without the arena of the national longitudinal evaluation in which these differences could be expressed and debated, it might have been impossible to conduct a project such as Follow Through. From this viewpoint, the controversy on evaluation served as a safety valve that prevented a total breakdown in communication among stakeholder groups and permitted the work of the project to continue. Thus, the national evaluation was not only an exercise in scientific research, but also an exercise in political craftsmanship and compromise.

Disagreements over the choice of instruments for the national evaluation have emerged in part from ambiguities about the purpose of Follow Through. The USOE–Follow Through project administrators stated in 1968 that they were not planning to conduct a "horse race" to pick the best model, but rather a developmental endeavor to construct alternative models of childhood education. However, the administrators' use of results from the national evaluation to compare and rank the performance of the various models appeared to reinforce the perception that the purpose of the project was to "pick a winner." This view received further confirmation when the national evaluation was restructured in 1972. Emrick (1978) stated that in fact there were two evaluations—one conducted before 1972 to assist program development and another conducted after 1972 to identify the best performer(s).

The national longitudinal evaluation of Follow Through has stimulated much discussion and evoked a range of responses among researchers. The multitude of results from this evaluation have been presented in detailed technical reports prepared by researchers employed at the Stanford Research Institute and Abt Associates, Inc. No brief summary of these results is presented here, due to the complexities involved in describing the many sets of alternative analyses and results and to the large number of qualifications attached to each set. Most of the points that have emerged in debates on the national evaluation were presented in several articles published in the May, 1978, issue of the *Harvard Educational Review*. For example, the criticisms stated by House *et al.* (1978) included the following: Many model-specific objectives were not measured by instruments employed in the national evaluation; the psychometric characteristics of some instruments were inadequate; the instruments were unfair to some sponsors' models and biased in favor of others; different methods for aggregating data (pupil, class, and school) yielded different results; and inappropriate statistical analyses were performed on the data.

Detailed responses to the criticisms stated in the preceding paragraph are contained in the articles written by Anderson, St. Pierre, Proper, and Stebbins (1978) and Wisler *et al.* (1978). These authors agreed with a few of the stated criticisms, but rejected most of them on the grounds that they were ill conceived and not supported by the full range of available evidence. For example, they acknowledged that the Follow Through evaluation suffered from a number of problems that resulted from decisions made by the federal administrators of the project during the period from 1968 to 1971. But they argued that most of these problems were characteristic of all large-scale evaluations of educational projects conducted during the decade from 1968 to 1978, and therefore were not peculiar to the evaluation of Follow Through.

Anderson *et al.* (1978) and Wisler *et al.* (1978) also agreed that for a variety of reasons it was not possible to develop an evaluation test battery that could be used to assess the whole array of model sponsors' stated goals and objectives. But they contended that the instruments employed in the national evaluation were the best available a decade ago and that no better ones have been developed. They also stated that the instruments used to evaluate Follow Through represented a strong consensus among parents, educators, tax-payers, and legislators on important traditional objectives of schooling. Therefore, they reasoned that the use of these instruments to evaluate outcomes of all models was appropriate, regardless of whether the instruments measured the specific objectives stated for a particular sponsor's model. According to Stebbins *et al.* (1977), the instruments represented the "best compromise between the need for accountability and the difficulty of measuring sponsors' diverse goals and objectives [p. 35]." Readers who wish to delve more deeply into the fine points of the debate on the national longitudinal evaluation are referred to the sources of information identified at various places in this chapter and other chapters in this volume.

It is not yet possible to make a final statement about the merits of the national longitudinal evaluation of Follow Through. However, most informed observers probably would agree that the evolution of this evaluation was influenced strongly by the remarkable explosion of growth in the amount of knowledge about program evaluation research during the past decade. Indeed, the national evaluation of Follow Through contributed in many ways to the rapid accumulation of this knowledge. In order to appreciate the innovative character of the national evaluation of Follow Through, one only need recall that when the project began in 1968 the evaluation of educational programs often was limited to the administration of academic achievement tests at the close of a period of instruction.

The linking of educational research and strategies for social change in Follow Through necessitated a far broader perspective on evaluating the impact of educational programs. Consequently, some notable initiatives in the evaluation of Follow Through were the following: inclusion of non-cognitive characteristics of children and attitudes of parents as legitimate variables in the evaluation of educational programs, strong encouragement for the development of classroom observation scales and a process orientation to research on education, an exploration of quasi-experiments in education as a useful source of information in policy research, and the application of many new statistical techniques to analyze evaluation data. To be sure, not all the initiatives begun in the evaluation of Follow Through were continued to a successful conclusion. Nevertheless, these initiatives produced a rich yield of information that is likely to influence the field of program evaluation research for many years to come (Cooley, 1978; Cooley & Lohnes, 1976; Schiller, Stalford, Rudner, Kocher, & Lesnick, 1980; Wholey, 1979).

One major effect of the debate on the national longitudinal evaluation of Follow Through has been to underscore the absence of information on the results of the model sponsors' evaluations of their own programs. The individuals who prepared the Abt Associates' technical reports on the longitudinal evaluation, and others who studied these reports carefully, acknowledge that the results of that evaluation may not provide an adequate basis for making definitive comparisons among the various Follow Through models. In a paper delivered to the meeting of the American Educational Research Association, Anderson (1977) stated, "Our results [from the Abt reports] do not constitute a comprehensive evaluation of the national Follow Through endeavor [p.1]." He also said, "Much of the existing evidence on the worth and consequence of Follow Through intervention lies outside our data base. . . . Other evaluation reports, including the self-evaluations of the sponsors, can come closer than we to providing a complete catalogue of all that has been good and bad, effective and ineffec-

tive about Follow Through in its decade of development and trial [p. 2]."
Similarly, Kennedy (1978) stated that the issue of the choice of instruments
for evaluating Follow Through models is crucial. That author wrote, "The
data suggest that different conclusions could be drawn as a function of the
choice of outcome measures. . . . apparent negative outcomes from the national evaluation may not mean that the model failed, but simply that it
emphasized different outcomes at the expense of those outcomes which
were measured in the national evaluation [p. 11]." It seems reasonable to
conclude from these statements that the public discussions about Follow
Through will remain radically incomplete as long as there is a scarcity of
information about the Follow Through models, and especially until the
results of the sponsors' evaluations of their own programs become
available.

Many individuals who knew about the multifaceted character of Follow
Through were disappointed that the public discussion on the project appeared to center on the pursuit of answers to narrow, summative questions
such as, "Was Follow Through a success?" or "Which Follow Through
model is the best?" As noted previously in this section, debates on these
questions produced heated exchanges on the correct interpretation of the
outcomes of the national longitudinal evaluation; however, few individuals
appeared to comprehend either the full range of activities that had occurred
in the sponsors' programs or the knowledge that had been accumulated
through these endeavors. Thus, an expenditure of more than half a billion
dollars and an immense number of work hours invested by the participants
appeared to be contributing little to the advancement of knowledge about
the education of children or the utilization of the social sciences in problem-
focused research.

A number of concerned observers of Follow Through concluded that
steps should be taken to increase public understanding of the accomplishments and heuristic issues represented in the various Follow
Through models. They hoped that the results of the sponsors' work could
be assimilated into the mainstream of thought about childhood education
and intervention studies. These persons perceived the project as a bold
experiment, a first step toward the scientific exploration of alternative approaches to childhood education, but not as an effort that necessarily
would culminate in the selection of *one best approach to educating all
children.* Consequently, these individuals believed that public discussions
about the project would be more useful if they centered on broad, open-
ended, formative questions such as "Why do some models work better than
others?" "What can be done to make models work better?" "What conditions facilitate the successful implementation of models?"and "How can the
knowledge obtained by the model sponsors and other researchers in Follow

Through be used to guide future research in education and other social problem areas?"

UNIQUE PERSPECTIVES OF THE MODEL SPONSORS

A large and complex endeavor like Follow Through can be viewed from many perspectives, including those of members of Congress, planners, administrators, school personnel, parents, and the evaluators who performed the national longitudinal evaluation. Individuals in each of these groups have perceptions that stem from their particular responsibilities and vested interests. Similarly, the program sponsors and their staff members have a unique set of perceptions about the Follow Through experience and its meaning.

The sponsors prepared many technical reports about their work for administrators of agencies that provided funding, but these reports rarely were disseminated in large quantities and they seldom were refined for publication in journals read by other researchers and practitioners. Like most researchers who participate in social intervention studies, the sponsors have felt stressed and sometimes overwhelmed by the strenuous requirements for productivity in a highly politicized, pressure cooker situation. Unfortunately, the preparation of manuscripts for publication in journals read by researchers and practitioners often has a low priority among individuals who engage in problem-focused research. One important reason is that those who fund these activities seldom provide encouragement or reward for such publications. Thus, the time required for preparing high-quality manuscripts usually must "come out of the writer's hide." Consequently, the quantity of literature about activities and accomplishments in problem-focused research is limited and seldom impressive.

Because the number of publications about program operations in large-scale problem-focused research projects is small, the first public information on such efforts often is provided by individuals who evaluate the projects. The entire substance of developmental research endeavors may be quickly telescoped and distorted in the predictable controversies that erupt over the instruments employed to collect data, sampling techniques, data analysis procedures, interpretation of results, and a host of other scientific and political issues. Pleas for attention to the knowledge gained through the planning and implementation process go uncomprehended and unheeded because few individuals are informed concerning the details of that work. And there are typically few, if any, publications that state how the work contributes to the advancement of knowledge. By default in these circumstances, evaluators usually become the spokesmen for the entire effort. Unfortunately, they are not the individuals who constructed and supervised the program operations, and they may know very little about the work they evaluate. Their knowledge often is limited primarily to the issues pertaining to the selection of outcome measures, collection and analysis of data, and interpretation of results. The purpose of these statements is not to criticize evaluators, who often receive more than their share of harassment, but rather to describe a bottleneck in the dissemination of information concerning the planning, implementation, and accomplishments of problem-focused research.

The model sponsors in Follow Through also recognize the importance of evaluation, but their perspective is that of program developers who are interested in using information about the processes and outcomes of learning and instruction to improve educational services. They view their work within a broad framework, which includes such dimensions as reasons for their participation in the project, scientific rationale for the work performed, implementation procedures, results of their own evaluations, and lessons that may be derived from the total effort. In fact, these dimensions serve as the guidelines for the five chapters presented in Part II of this volume.

For a number of reasons, problem-focused research generally has evoked little enthusiasm from academicians, who sometimes refer to it as a mindless activity that contributes little to the accumulation of useful knowledge. But when it is performed well, problem-focused research requires not only high levels of dedication, sustained energy, tolerance for ambiguity, and a thick skin, but also expertise in conceptual and methodological areas and political sophistication. The contributors to this volume believe that such research is a legitimate activity for social scientists and one that can be of great benefit to society.

Brief Descriptions of Five Follow Through Models

The brief descriptions of five Follow Through models presented here are intended to serve as advance organizers for the more detailed discussions contained in Chapters 3, 4, 5, 6, and 7.

PARENT EDUCATION MODEL—CHAPTER 3

The primary focus in this model is on the relationships between home and school, rather than on the classroom instructional process, and on improving home learning opportunities for children and their parents. Parents and teachers are expected to become working partners, and parents are encouraged to become involved in many areas of educational decision making. The advocates of this approach do not prescribe a specific curriculum or classroom organization, but they do recommend teaching styles that are applicable to home and school. One of the sponsor's most important functions is to train parent educators, who serve as links between home and school. The teachers, parent educators, and parents cooperate in developing home learning tasks. The parent educators teach these enrichment tasks to mothers who then teach them to their children. The researchers who work in this model have developed a number of new instruments for assessing program effects, particularly the effects on parents and parent educators. These new instruments include a number of observation procedures for collecting evaluation data.

DIRECT INSTRUCTION MODEL—CHAPTER 4

This model is based on methods and research from behavioral psychology and on Seigfried Engelmann's contributions to the logic of program construction. The aim is to teach basic skills that are believed to be essential for intelligent behavior. Using modern learning principles, the sponsor designed nine DISTAR instructional programs (three each in reading, arithmetic, and language) that contain carefully sequenced daily lessons. Children are taught by the teachers in small groups. The teachers present the learning tasks, use signals to coordinate group or individual responses, reinforce correct responses, and quickly correct mistakes that occur in children's learning. Students are expected to achieve positive self-concepts as by-products of good teaching and their achievement of competence in academic skills. The instruments employed to evaluate the effects of the model on children's learning include both criterion-referenced tests and normative tests of academic achievement. The authors of Chapter 4 also present an extensive critique of the national longitudinal evaluation.

BEHAVIOR ANALYSIS MODEL—CHAPTER 5

The motivational system employed in classrooms includes positive teacher attention for appropriate student behavior, ignoring inappropriate behavior, and the absence of any form of corporal punishment. Teaching teams composed of a lead teacher, a paraprofessional, and one or two parents provide children with small-group and individual instruction. Teaching activities are conducted concurrently in reading, math, spelling, and handwriting. Teachers are not required to use a specific curriculum, but the instructional materials must meet certain stated criteria. The academic progress of each child and the amount of instructional time actually allotted to each academic area are closely monitored. The quality control system consists of the following four components: a computerized curriculum feedback system called Continuous Progress Assessment, Annual Achievement Testing, Annual Consumer Evaluation, and the Educational Audit. The focus of the sponsor's approach to evaluation is on students' performance on academic achievement tests and levels of consumer satisfaction among both adults and students.

HIGH SCOPE COGNITIVELY ORIENTED CURRICULUM MODEL—CHAPTER 6

Following Piaget, the child's intellectual development is believed to occur in a series of sequential stages. The direction of children's development is toward increasing understanding and use of more abstract and complex relationships among things, people, and events in the environment. Children are expected to generate much of their own learning by engaging in self-selected activities. These activities require them to use a wide range of educational materials that are provided in classrooms. Teachers ask open-ended questions, not to determine whether children are thinking and solving problems in "the right way," but to encourage children to learn how to examine and critique their own thinking. The sponsor believes that most conventional measures of children's learning are inappropriate for measuring the processes and outcomes of this model. Consequently, new instruments have been developed for performing "generative" and "process" assessment of children's learning in a number of areas, including interpersonal relationships and productive language.

BANK STREET MODEL: A DEVELOPMENTAL-INTERACTION APPROACH—CHAPTER 7

Teachers in this model seek to provide experiences and information that stimulate children's capacities for knowing, thinking, and feeling. The rationale for the model consists of concepts drawn from a number of theorists, including Dewey, Freud, and Piaget. Children are expected to achieve competence in intellectual, affective, social, and physical areas of development. Teachers are expected to achieve competence in creating a vital curriculum that is developmentally and sequentially sound. The central theme in curriculum building is the organization of integrated learning experiences based upon intensive study of each child's abilities, interests, and developmental needs. The staff development program includes creative experiences, child study, diagnostic teaching of academic skills, and problem solving. Parents are encouraged to teach their children and to participate in educational decision making, programs of self-development, and community action groups. The sponsor's evaluation of this model consists of three parts: Program Analysis, Child Assessment, and Evaluation of Program Outcomes.

The purpose of Chapter 1 has been to present an overview of Follow Through, including some central issues that emerged during a decade of large-scale intervention research in education and broad-gauged perspectives on five representative educational models. The role of the federal government in the initiation of Follow Through, some distinctive characteristics of the project, similarities and differences among Follow Through models, and the structure and content of the chapters that comprise Part II of this volume are explained in the next chapter.

References

Anderson, R. B. *The effectiveness of Follow Through: What have we learned?* Paper presented at the annual meeting of the American Educational Research Association, New York, April 1977.

Anderson, R. B., St. Pierre, R. G., Proper, E. C., & Stebbins, L. B. Pardon us, but what was the question again?: A response to the critique of the Follow Through evaluation. *Harvard Educational Review*, 1978, 48, 161–170.

Becker, W. C. Teaching reading and language to the disadvantaged — what we have learned from field research. *Harvard Educational Review*, 1977, 47, 518–543.

Bereiter, C. A., & Kurland, M. *Were some Follow Through models more effective than others?* Paper presented at the annual meeting of the American Educational Research Association, Toronto, Ontario, Canada, March 1978.

Bissel, J. S. Planned variation in Head Start and Follow Through. In J. S. Stanley (Ed.), *Compensatory education for children, ages 2 to 8*. Baltimore: Johns Hopkins University Press, 1973. Pp. 63–101.

Campbell, D. T. Reforms as experiments. *American Psychologist*, 1969, 24, 409–429.

Campbell, D. T., & Boruch, R. F. Making the case for randomized assignment to treatments by considering the alternatives: Six ways in which quasi-experimental evaluations in compensatory education tend to underestimate effects. In C. A. Bennett & A. A. Lumsdaine (Eds.), *Evaluation and experiment: Some critical issues in assessing social programs*. New York: Academic Press, 1975. Pp. 191–296.

Cline, M. G. *Education as experimentation: Evaluation of the Follow Through planned variation model: Early effects of Follow Through*. Cambridge, Mass.: Abt Associates, 1974.

Cooley, W. W. Explanatory observational studies. *Educational Researcher*, 1978, 7, No.9, 9–15.

Cooley, W. W., & Lohnes, P. R. *Evaluation research in education*. New York: Irvington Publishers, 1976.

Emrick, J. A. *Validity of Follow Through measures: A critique and reply*. Paper presented at the annual meeting of the American Educational Research Association, Toronto, Ontario, Canada, March 1978.

Emrick, J. A., Sorensen, P. H., & Stearns, M. S. *Interim evaluation of the national Follow Through program, 1969–1971*. Menlo Park, Calif.: Stanford Research Institute, 1973.

Gordon, I. J., & Breivogel, W. G. (Eds.). *Building effective home/school relationships*. Boston: Allyn & Bacon, 1976.

House, E. R., Glass, G. V., McLean, L. D., & Walker, D. F. No simple answer: Critique of the Follow Through evaluation. *Harvard Educational Review*, 1978, 48, 128–160.

Kennedy, M. M. Findings from the Follow Through planned variation study. *Educational Researcher*, 1978, 7, No. 6, 3–11.

Krulee, G. K. *An organizational analysis of Project Follow Through, final report*. Evanston, Ill.: Northwestern University, 1973. (ERIC Document Reproduction Service No. 093446)

Maccoby, E. E., & Zellner, M. *Experiments in primary education: Aspects of Project Follow Through*. New York: Harcourt, Brace, Jovanovich, 1970.

McDaniels, G. L. Evaluation problems in Follow Through. In A. M. Rivlin & P. M. Timpane,

(Eds.), *Planned variation in education.* Washington, D. C.: Brookings Institution, 1975. Pp. 47–60.

McGuire, W. J. Theory-oriented research in natural settings: The best of both worlds of social psychology. In M. Sherif & C. W. Sherif (Eds.), *Inter-disciplinary relationships in the social sciences.* Chicago: Aldine, 1969. Pp. 21–51.

Rhine, W. R. *Issues in noncognitive measurement: Interim report on Project Follow Through 1969–1971.* Menlo Park, Calif.: Stanford Research Institute, 1971, 403 pp.

Rhine, W. R. Strategies for evaluating Follow Through. In R. M. Rippey (Ed.), *Studies in transactional evaluation.* Berkeley, Calif.: McCutchan Publishing, 1973. Pp. 157–180. (a)

Rhine, W. R. *Follow Through: A model for utilizing the social sciences for solving social problems.* Paper presented at the annual meeting of the American Psychological Association, Montreal, Quebec, Canada, August 1973. (b)

Rhine, W. R., & Spaner, S. D. A comparison of the factor structure of the Test Anxiety Scale for Children among lower- and middle-class children. *Developmental Psychology,* 1973, *9,* 421–423.

Rhine, W. R., & Spaner, S. D. *Application of factor analysis to the study of school fearfulness.* Paper presented at the annual meeting of the American Psychological Association, New Orleans, September 1974.

Rhine, W. R., & Spaner, S. D. *Developing measures of affect for young children.* Final report to the National Institutes of Mental Health (MH 26055–01). St. Louis, Mo.: University of Missouri, St. Louis, 1976.

Rhine, W. R., & Spencer, L. M. Effects of Follow Through on school fearfulness among Black children. *Journal of Negro Education,* 1975, *44,* 446–453.

Riecken, H. W., & Boruch, R. F. (Eds.). *Social experimentation.* New York: Academic Press, 1974.

Rivlin, A. M. *Systematic thinking for social action.* Washington, D. C.: Brookings Institution, 1971.

Rivlin, A. M., & Timpane, P. M. (Eds.). *Planned variation in education.* Washington, D. C.: Brookings Institution, 1975.

Rossi, P. H. No good idea goes unpunished: Moynihan's misunderstanding and the proper role of social science in policy making. In L. A. Zurcher & C. M. Bonjean (Eds.), *Planned social intervention.* Scranton, Penn.: Chandler Publishing, 1970. Pp. 74–84.

Rossi, P. H., & Williams, W. (Eds.). *Evaluating social programs: Theory, practice, and politics.* New York: Seminar Press, 1972.

Schiller, J., Stalford, C., Rudner, L., Kocher, T., & Lesnick, H. Plans for Follow Through research and development. Interdepartmental memorandum, National Institute of Education, Washington, D. C., October, 1, 1980.

Soar, R. S., & Soar, R. M. An empirical analysis of selected Follow Through programs: An example of a process approach to evaluation. In I. J. Gordon (Ed.), *Early childhood education* (seventy-fifth yearbook of the National Society for the Study of Education). Chicago: University of Chicago Press, 1972. Pp. 229–259.

Sorensen, P. H. *Problems in the evaluation of Follow Through projects.* Paper presented at the annual meeting of the American Educational Research Association, Los Angeles, February 1969.

Sorensen, P. H. *Longitudinal evaluation of selected features of the national Follow Through Project.* Menlo Park, Calif.: Stanford Research Institute, 1971.

Stallings, J. A. Implementation and child effects of teaching practices in Follow Through classrooms. *Monographs of the Society for Research in Child Development,* 1975, *40,* (7–8, Serial No. 163).

Stebbins, L. B., St. Pierre, R. G., Proper, E. C., Anderson, R. B., & Cerva, T. R. *Education as experimentation: A planned variation model. Vol. IV–A: An evaluation of Follow Through.* Cambridge, Mass.: Abt Associates, 1977. (Also issued by the U. S. Office of

Education as *National evaluation: Patterns of effects,* [Vol. II-A of the Follow Through planned variation experimental series].)

Weiss, C. A. The politicization of evaluation research. *Journal of Social Issues,* 1970, *26,* 57–68.

Weiss, C. A. *Evaluating social action programs.* Boston: Allyn & Bacon, 1972.

Wholey, J. S. New directions for Follow Through. Interdepartmental memorandum, U. S. Office of Education, Washington, D. C., December, 14, 1979.

Williams, W. *Social policy research and analysis: The experience in the federal agencies.* New York: American Elsevier, 1971.

Wisler, C. E., Burns, G. P., & Iwamoto, D. Follow Through redux: A response to the critique by House, Glass, McLean, and Walker. *Harvard Educational Review,* 1978, *48,* 171–185.

W. RAY RHINE
RICHARD ELARDO
LEILANI M. SPENCER **2**

Improving Educational Environments: The Follow Through Approach

Making Schools More Effective

Follow Through began as a part of the federal initiative in compensatory education. Therefore, a brief history of the increasing involvement of the legislative and executive branches of government in education, particularly in Head Start, will serve as a helpful preface to the description of the particular characteristics of Follow Through. This chapter also contains descriptions of the two key implementation strategies employed in the project—planned variation and sponsorship. Next, some conceptual schemes for comparing the similarities and differences among Follow Through models are described. The chapter concludes with a statement of the guidelines that the authors followed in completing chapters on the five Follow Through models described in Part II.

Origins of Follow Through

In 1964, the Economic Opportunity Act (EOA) and its amendments provided for a broad range of projects intended "to mobilize the human and financial resources of the nation to combat poverty in the United States [Public Law 88–452, 1964]." The federal policy on childhood education that emerged from that legislation was influenced strongly by the results of research on the effects of environment on intellectual development during the early years of growth (Bloom, 1964; Hunt, 1961). The results of many studies indicated both the plasticity of intellectual growth among young children and the extremely rapid rate at which they may acquire knowledge during the preschool years. Nevertheless, many preschool children failed to acquire the cognitive skills necessary for success in kindergarten and the primary grades. Consequently, early childhood appeared to be a crucial time for intervention to prevent the personal and social ills associated with the recurring cycle of inferior education, inadequate coping behavior, and poverty. Expressed first in Head Start, the federal policy on childhood education reflected a consensus among child development researchers and educators that the quality of children's early educational experiences could either encourage or destroy their potential for growth.[1]

The first group of Head Start preschool programs were planned during the winter of 1965, and they became operational in the following summer. More than one-half million children enrolled in 6- or 8-week preschool sessions designed by local representatives of school systems, churches, and community action agencies. The results of evaluation studies on the effects of Head Start began to appear in 1966. The comparisons of the performance of children who attended Head Start with those who did not in-

[1] Zigler and Valentine (1979) present a comprehensive account of the history and accomplishments of Head Start.

dicated that participation in the preschool programs produced measurable gains in cognitive and affective areas. However, the outcomes of those studies also indicated that the advantages that children achieved through Head Start largely disappeared during the first year of their attendance in regular grade classrooms (Cicirelli, Cooper, & Granger, 1969; Horowitz & Paden, 1973; Ramsey, 1968; Wolff & Stein, 1967). Some individuals concluded that Head Start had failed, but the majority view was that an additional support system should be provided for the graduates of Head Start and similar preschool programs when they enrolled in regular grade classrooms.

During the latter part of 1966 and early in 1967, Sargent Shriver, Director of the Office of Economic Opportunity (OEO), President Lyndon Johnson, and others succeeded in generating political support for a new comprehensive project to maintain and strengthen the benefits of preschool education for children when they enrolled in kindergarten and the primary grades. In impassioned rhetoric Shriver stated, "The readiness and receptivity they [the children] had gained in Head Start has been crushed by the broken promises of the first grade." President Johnson, in his State of the Union address in January, 1967, urged that Congress amend the EOA to authorize the extension of the benefits of Head Start into kindergarten and the primary grades. He recommended, "We should strengthen the Head Start program, begin it for children 3 years old, and maintain its educational momentum by following through in the early years [*Congressional Record*, vol. 113, 1967, p. 37]." In another message, President Johnson requested the Congress to "preserve the hope and opportunity of Head Start by a 'follow-through' program in the early grades. . . . to fulfill the rights of America's children to equal educational opportunity the benefits of Head Start must be carried through to the early grades [*Congressional Record*, vol. 113, 1967, p. 2882]." Several weeks later the Congress agreed to amend the EOA by enacting Public Law 90–92. Section 222 /a/ of this bill established a project "to be known as Follow Through focused primarily on the children in kindergarten or elementary school who were previously enrolled in Head Start or similar programs designed to provide comprehensive services and parent participation activities . . . which the Director finds will aid in the continued development of children in their full potential."

In March, 1967, the USOE and the OEO sought assistance in conceptualizing the new project by forming a National Follow Through Advisory Committee, which was chaired by Dr. Gordon J. Klopf, Dean of the Faculties of Bank Street College of Education. The members of the committee designated task forces in the following areas: personnel and staff development, guidance and psychological services, instruction, research and evaluation, state assistance, family and community services, and health services. The reports of these task forces and the legislation enacted by the Congress provided the basis for the preliminary Follow Through guidelines.

Those individuals who planned the initial version of Follow Through expected that it, like Head Start, would both provide a wide range of health, psychological, and educational services and grant a high degree of local autonomy in the development of programs. Indeed, the administrators of Follow Through expected to receive $120 million in the fall of 1968 to launch a major project that would provide services for about 200,000 children and their parents. To prepare for that large effort, they began a $2.8 million dollar pilot project involving approximately 3000 children in 40 school districts during the 1967–1968 school year. But the original plan for Follow Through was not implemented for two reasons: First, the financial requirements for conducting the Vietnam War appeared to oppose the launching of new large-scale social service projects; and second, many persons had concluded that the effectiveness of new domestic initiatives should be explored on a small scale before they were implemented on a large scale. When the actual funding of Follow Through was set at a total of $15 million for the 1968–1969 school year, the planners began in the fall of 1967 to redesign the goals of the project.

Late in 1967 and early in 1968, the USOE conducted three series of meetings concurrently in Washington, D.C., to organize the revision of Follow Through. In one series, a group of academicians including Urie Bronfenbrenner, Donald M. Baer, Robert D. Hess, Halbert B. Robinson, and Robert L. Thorndike focused on social science research pertaining to issues in childhood education. In other meetings, 25 persons who had gained recognition for planning, describing, and initiating new approaches for educating young children presented information about their work. In the third series of meetings, representatives of local, state, and federal education agencies, as well as the OEO, agreed on procedures for selecting local communities and school districts for participation in Follow Through. The consensus of those meetings generally supported the implementation of two key strategies, *planned variation* and *sponsorship*, to develop Follow Through as an experimental, longitudinal project for evolving and studying many alternative approaches to educating young children.

In January, 1968, 13 sponsors were selected to begin program development activities in the 1968–1969 school year (USOE, 1969). During a 4-day meeting in Kansas City, Missouri, in late February, 1968, the sponsors described their models to the representatives of 90 local school districts that had been selected for participation in Follow Through. The purpose of the meeting was to encourage the representatives from each district to choose a particular approach that they wished to implement in their schools. Most of the 40 school districts that had participated in the pilot project during the previous year chose a sponsor, but some maintained a "self-sponsored" status in order to develop their own programs. As a condition for participating in the project, each of the 50 newly selected districts was required to select a sponsor. The working relationship between sponsors and local communities began shortly after the sponsors negotiated agreements with the USOE and local boards of education to develop their programs. The members of each sponsor's staff then began training teachers, procuring materials, and selecting pupils for their classrooms.[2]

Planned Variation

Most of the distinctive characteristics of Follow Through flow from the core concept of planned variation, which is a statement of intent to develop a range of alternative approaches to educating young children. The pursuit of that objective within a research and development framework represented a major policy innovation in the federal approach to improving educational programs (Cohen & Garet, 1975). The notion of planned variation developed over a period of several years. A group of individuals consisting of planners in the federal government, persons in the educational establishment, and members of the academic community had become intrigued with the possibilities for utilizing the social sciences to develop more effective methods of education. The implementation experiences in Head Start and the assimilation of information from theories and research about the development and education of children were necessary precursors of such a programmatic effort. When the smaller-than-expected funding for Follow Through required fundamental changes in its objectives, influences from many sources converged to support the selection of planned variation as the raison d'être for the project.

Many of those who favored the planned variation strategy for Follow Through hoped that it would produce more systematic and coordinated methods for developing educational programs. In the operation of Head Start, persons in local communities were encouraged to exercise a high degree of autonomy over program development, a feature that contributed to the enormous public and political support for the project. That policy also served to generate many different programs for educating young children, but researchers often reported that those preschool programs

[2] More detailed accounts of the origins and history of Follow Through are presented in Krulee (1973), Rhine (1973b), Elmore (1976), and Haney (1977).

were difficult to evaluate because they lacked conceptual clarity and clear definition of independent and dependent variables. Thus, although Head Start programs generally were a political success, researchers frequently characterized them as lacking in rigor. Perhaps the most serious consequence of the general approach to program development in Head Start was that the frequent absence of adequate quality control prevented the accumulation of knowledge that was needed to improve future programs.

Most of the problems encountered in Head Start had been predicted in 1965–1966 by the researchers who participated in planning the project. They knew that a collection of theories about child development and the accumulating results of empirical studies provided a framework within which experts were beginning to engage in stimulating discussions about alternative approaches to childhood education. But they also recognized that there were strong differences of opinion about how those theories and research findings should be used to construct instructional procedures and program operations. Moreover, efforts to derive coherent curriculum designs, instructional procedures, and materials from existing knowledge were in a primitive state.

Under those circumstances, many researchers believed that Head Start should commence in 1965 as an experimental pilot project to systematically develop preschool education programs, which, when proven effective, could be implemented on a large scale (Williams & Evans, 1972). But there were strong political pressures for Head Start to bypass the experimental pilot phase, to disperse authority for the development of educational programs among citizens in local communities, and to develop quickly into a large-scale national service project. The situation induced conflicting feelings among academicians who were participating in planning Head Start. Many of them correctly perceived that the results of the brief summer preschool programs in Head Start were likely to be less than what was hoped for. But they also were impressed by the cogent political arguments for moving quickly in favorable circumstances to establish a national intervention project in early childhood education.

The comments of some social scientists who participated in planning Head Start expressed their feelings of being awed and overwhelmed by the political pressure to quickly develop Head Start as a "showcase operation." For example, Williams and Evans (1972) recalled that the basic idea of Head Start—to break the power of poverty by improving the education of children—was "too good." Because Head Start had such strong political appeal, it quickly became the primary symbol of the War on Poverty. McDill, McDill, and Sprehe (1972) remembered that a combination of "staggering suddenness and monumental resources" rapidly escalated Head

Start from the status of a concept on the planners' drawing board to a large-scale, national project providing services to one-half million children. Caldwell (1972) stated, "It was as though there existed an unverbalized fear that if one dared suggest that too much was being expected, it would remove the opportunity to make even a small beginning. So we all surfed on the excitement and hoped we would not drown in our own foamy rhetoric [p. 57]."

According to McDill, McDill, and Sprehe (1969), the use of uncoordinated initiatives of persons in local communities to develop Head Start preschool programs reflected a "try everything philosophy (or, perhaps more accurately, try anything) [p. 45]," apparently in the hope that if enough program approaches were tried, some of them might work. But the preliminary results of that experience suggested that successful efforts to develop effective educational programs required more than public participation and sincere desires to help children.[3] Many informed observers became convinced that subsequent attempts could become more rigorous, systematic, and productive through intensive utilization of findings and research methods from the social sciences.[4]

Reflecting the thoughts of a large number of persons who had followed the events of Head Start closely, the White House Task Force on Child Development (USDHEW, 1968) concluded that existing programs should be strengthened in order to obtain the kind of knowledge needed to improve educational programs for children. Consequently, the Task Force recommended that federal educational projects should adopt a policy of "planned variation" for the purpose of promoting systematic efforts to develop a range of approaches to childhood education under a variety of school and community conditions. Specifically, the Task Force recommended that officials in the USOE select a variety of educational strategies that were consistent with plans for a major project for educational variation and evaluation. Similarly, McDill et al. (1972) concluded from their observations of Head Start that a variety of approaches to educating

[3] Lazar, Hubbell, Murray, Rosche, and Royce (1977) reported that the results of their study conducted during 1976–1977 revealed that children who had attended Head Start programs during the 1960s were placed less frequently in special education classrooms and more frequently at grade levels appropriate for their chronological age, as compared to children who had no experience in Head Start or a similar preschool program.

[4] The recommendations for a planned approach to experimentation in education were in line with suggestions by a number of writers on social experimentation, cited previously in Chapter 1, who were advocating increased utilization of the social sciences for seeking solutions to social problems. For example, Campbell (1969) urged that the federal government pursue "an experimental approach to social reform," a policy that would encourage "alternative reform efforts [pp. 409–410]."

children should be carefully planned and tested. "It appears to us," they stated, "that no other strategy can hope to extricate compensatory education from the confusion in which it now struggles [pp. 182–183]."[5]

Other developments within both the federal bureaucracy and the educational establishment also supported the implementation of a more' systematic, theory-based approach to the development of educational programs in Follow Through. In October, 1965, the Bureau of the Budget issued Bulletin No. 66–3, establishing the Planning, Programming, Budgeting System (PPBS) within all federal departments and agencies. PPBS was a modification of the cost–benefit model that the Rand Corporation had developed in the early 1960s to strengthen the quantitative basis for decision-making processes within the Department of Defense. Among those agencies that had responsibilities for administering a host of new educational programs in the public schools, the effect of introducing PPBS was to intensify efforts to establish more rational, data-based approaches to making decisions about those programs. Thus, PPBS created an urgent need for larger amounts of policy research, developmental activities, and evaluation research of the sort that social scientists could perform.

About the same time that social scientists were increasing their participation in the federal bureaucracy, they also were forming close working relationships with the educational establishment. Due to a greater emphasis upon the social sciences in the education of practitioners, these individuals were becoming more interested in the details of approaches to learning and instruction such as those proposed by Barbara Biber, Jerome S. Bruner, John B. Carroll, Arthur W. Combs, Ned A. Flanders, Robert M. Gagné, Robert Glaser, and others. In addition, many practitioners were beginning to explore the relevance of knowledge about classroom instruction and child development for both the development of new forms of curricula and the analysis of existing programs. Practitioners and social scientists collaborated in the development of a number of new, experimental curricula (Bereiter & Engelmann, 1966; Cazden, 1968; Deutsch, 1967; Gordon, 1967; Resnick, 1967; Stendler-Lavatelli, 1968; Weikart, 1967). Furthermore, many social scientists were beginning to reorient the focus of their research away from laboratory studies aimed exclusively at the construction of theory and toward studies designed to develop more effective methods for teaching children basic skills in arithmetic, language development, reading, and spelling.

The increasing rapprochement between educators and social scientists

---

[5] In 1969, a number of Follow Through models, including the five described in this volume, were adapted to the needs of preschool children enrolled in Head Start classrooms. Datta (1975) described the Head Start Planned Variation (HSPV) experiments.

during the mid-1960s also was reflected in the content of many volumes published during those years. For example, the 1960 yearbook of the National Society for the Study of Education (NSSE) on learning and instruction scarcely listed the names of psychologists in its index. In contrast, the 1964 NSSE yearbook contained many references to the writings of Hull, Skinner, Spence, Tolman, and others. In addition, many chapters in the yearbook were written by experimental psychologists and other social scientists. Included among the many volumes that signaled the increasing linkage between the social sciences and practitioners in education were the following: *Early Childhood Education Rediscovered: Readings* (Frost, 1968), *Learning Research and School Subjects* (Gagné & Gephart, 1968), and *Early Education: Current Theory, Research, and Action* (Hess & Baer, 1968).

Sponsorship

The decision to implement planned variation in Follow Through was accompanied by a number of discussions on the operational form that the policy would take. One group of policy advisers recommended the identification and systematic variation of a set of structural characteristics of schools and classrooms, such as pupil–teacher ratio, teacher experience and ability, socioeconomic composition of students, and participation by parents and other paraprofessionals in school activities. Another group contended that the purpose of planned variation should be to develop a range of alternative curriculum approaches. The proponents of the first strategy argued that their plan would extend the results of previous research on the effects of differences in characteristics of educational environments on pupil performance, which had been studied by Coleman, Campbell, Mood, Weinfeld, Hobson, York, and McPartland, (1966). They also believed that, as compared to differences in curricula, differences in structural characteristics of schools were less likely to be affected by variations among teachers and more likely to be implemented consistently across many classrooms. In addition, it was argued that the effects of differences in structural characteristics of schools would be easier to evaluate. Although the first proposal had certain advantages, the final decision was to select a group of "program sponsors" and encourage them to develop innovative educational models that would be representative of the existing range of conceptual orientations to childhood education.

The USOE chose a group of 13 sponsors, primarily social scientists, to develop and evaluate a variety of program models. These sponsors shared the following characteristics: (a) They had established themselves as effective advocates of integrated sets of beliefs about teaching and learning; (b) they had achieved successful experiences in translating their beliefs into practical applications in school classrooms; and (c) they had shown indications that, if given a developmental period of several years, they could construct a theory-based, comprehensive program, including teaching methods and curriculum materials, for use with children in kindergarten and the primary grades and their parents.

The sponsors contracted with the USOE to design, implement, and monitor their models through long-term, cooperative relationships with school districts located throughout the country. Some sponsors agreed to work with as many as 20 school districts; others agreed to work with as few as 6.[6] Most of the sponsors and their staffs were based at colleges, universities, or regional educational laboratories.

Consistent with the intent of the planned variation strategy, the program sponsors derived their instructional models from the whole spectrum of philosophies about the growth and education of children and from the results of empirical research on child development. For example, the sponsors derived their basic principles from the following diverse sources: the writings of behavioral, cognitive–developmental, psychoanalytic, and humanistic psychologists on child development; the results of research on classroom instructional processes; and lessons from their own experiences as researchers and educators. Consequently, each sponsor advocates a particular set of beliefs about the education of young children that distinguishes each model from all the others.

The purpose of models in education, as in other fields, is to make possible the conceptualization and study of complex phenomena. The models in Follow Through are integrated sets of ideas about optimal conditions for teaching and learning. Each model incorporates some of the complex processes involved in education, but it is not possible for any single model to include all of those processes. Sponsorship involves the use of models for performing several essential functions: (a) The models provide tentative explanations, or sets of hypotheses, about teaching and learning; (b) they serve as guides for generating educational goals and objectives, prescribing instructional procedures and materials, and conducting research; and (c) the models serve as frameworks within which the sponsors continually use the results of their evaluation research to modify and elaborate the components of models and to improve instructional procedures, materials, and program evaluation.

---

[6] The locations of communities in which Follow Through models have been implemented are indicated in Figure 2.1. The communities that adopted the five models described in this volume are listed in Appendix B.

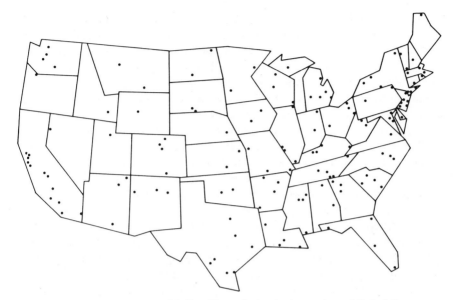

FIGURE 2.1.   *Locations of Follow Through sites in the continental United States.*

Most of the sponsors focus their models primarily upon changing the behaviors of teachers and students in classrooms; others direct their programs primarily toward changing the behavior of parents and children in their homes. Among those sponsors who aim to change what happens in classrooms, some advocate that teachers present a highly structured curriculum and that they use a variety of verbal and token reinforcement systems to motivate children to learn basic language and number skills. They believe that the mastery of academic skills will strengthen the children's sense of competence and self-esteem, which will produce positive attitudes toward school attendance.

Other sponsors who also focus on changing classroom environments contend that children often fail in school because they are alienated from the traditional techniques and goals of classroom learning. The members of this group doubt that basic skills can be taught effectively unless the children feel secure and confident in the classroom and develop positive attitudes toward learning. They favor methods of instruction that incorporate the particular interests and needs of each child. Those sponsors prefer that teachers use instructional methods that establish open, responsive learning environments. They believe that their approaches encourage children to learn from peers and engage in self-directed learning activities, such as exploratory and discovery learning.

All sponsors are required by law to include parents as significant partners in the administration, policymaking, and decision-making activities of Follow Through programs through local organizations known as the Policy Advisory Committee (PAC). But the sponsors are permitted, even encouraged, to vary in the methods that they employ to involve parents in the education of their children. Some sponsors choose to direct their greatest efforts toward designing learning environments in homes that effectively support the teachers' instruction in classrooms. Those sponsors have a special interest in working directly with the parents, especially the mother or other primary caretaker of the child, in order to improve instructional methods and materials for the child in the home environment.

The sponsors link their basic beliefs about education to different concepts and strategies for designing curricula, providing in-service training for teachers, and encouraging parents to participate in the education of their children. Among the five sponsors represented in this volume, the range of distinctive approaches to formulating curricula is indicated by the following descriptive terms: teacher-directed programmed instruction, process curriculum, behavior analysis, child-initiated learning, and cognitive–affective integration. To prepare teachers to implement their model programs, each sponsor developed in-service training and support systems that were much more comprehensive than traditional approaches to in-service training. Some of the new roles that sponsors advocate for teachers are denoted by these phrases: travelling teacher role, clinical supervision, small-group instruction, contingent reinforcement, interdisciplinary team approach, and application of Piagetian tasks and concepts. Some terms that sponsors use to indicate their distinctive approaches to fostering parent participation are parents teaching at home, parent educators, home visiting cycle, teaching assistants, paraprofessional aides, dialogue with parents, and linkage between teacher and parent. The definition and significance of the descriptive phrases stated in this paragraph can be communicated and understood best within the context of the statements that authors make about the Follow Through models described in Chapters 3, 4, 5, 6, and 7.

Similarities and Differences among Follow Through Models

The educational models that comprise Follow Through may be thought of as forming an educational mosaic, an example of "diversity within unity." Both integration and diversity among models are represented because planned variation and sponsorship result in both similarities and differences in the basic features, stated philosophies, and actual practices of the various models. It should be expected that in any well-designed approach to studying a variety of educational approaches the participants probably will agree on a number of goals, even when the approaches are based upon diverse belief systems and research traditions. Furthermore, the differences in beliefs among academicians and educators about the growth and education of children provide a fertile environment for developing and comparing educational alternatives.

The integration that characterizes the total Follow Through project has been encouraged by the following sources of influence: First, all models were adaptations to the social, political, and academic trends that characterized the 1960s; second, all models have been subjected to intensive scrutiny through evaluation procedures conducted by the sponsors, the national longitudinal evaluation, and sometimes by local school districts; and third, all models share the following set of broad educational goals stated by Maccoby and Zellner (1970):

1. Since children's education must begin at their point of readiness to learn, their entry capabilities should be assessed in some manner and programs should be adapted to the results.
2. Instruction of children should be individualized to the extent possible, a goal that may be pursued through individual or small-group instruction.
3. Children, from whatever background, will learn the essentials of a curriculum when conditions for learning are favorable. Failure to learn results from faulty materials and techniques of instruction, not from inadequacies within the child.
3. Program goals should be sufficiently clear to provide direction and consistency in educational planning, curriculum delivery, and evaluation.
4. There are a "core" of school-appropriate behaviors that all children should acquire, including attentional responses, capacity for task orientation (versus disruptiveness or distractibility), and motivation to learn academic concepts.
5. In any educational program, attention to children's affective development is necessary because they will acquire self-confidence, positive self-esteem, freedom from fear, and a generally positive attitude toward school and self only when they have primarily successful experiences in learning.

A fourth source of influence for integration among Follow Through models is that they may be compared and contrasted on the different sets of relevant psychological and educational dimensions that are represented in the six conceptual systems that are described here.

MACCOBY AND ZELLNER (1970)

These authors analyzed the conceptual origins of many Follow Through models and concluded that they could be grouped into four broad categories. Their *first category* includes models in which sponsors use principles of contemporary learning theory and behavior modification techniques for shaping children's behavior in classrooms. Teachers in these models establish precise behavioral objectives, provide systematic strategies for the presentation of academic material, and reinforce children for desired behavior. The *second category* includes those models whose sponsors encourage and support the stage-related evolution of cognitive structures and processes that are believed to be required for logical thought. Sponsors of these approaches differ from those in the first group by preferring less precision in the statement of educational objectives and more child-initiated activities in classrooms. Proponents of models in the *third category* contend that approaches to education that emphasize the use of process learning and problem solving are more likely to produce self-actualization, healthy self-concepts, and the ability to make intelligent choices. Another important goal is to encourage children's natural exploratory interests by providing a wide range of age-appropriate materials and experiences in a loosely organized, nurturant, and responsive atmosphere. Advocates of models in the *fourth category* identified by Maccoby and Zellner share a belief in client-controlled approaches to education in which parents and educators cooperate to develop educational services that are responsive and accountable directly to members of the community. Educators who favor this orientation seek to facilitate curriculum designs that are adapted to policy- and decision-making processes within the community.

Maccoby and Zellner's four categories have value for classifying Follow Through models, but some writers have criticized their system as an oversimplification of the similarities and differences that actually exist among programs in Follow Through. For example, Glaser and Resnick (1972) state that although Maccoby and Zellner's system "appears to work reasonably well with respect to motivation and incentives, it does not seem to adequately represent the variety of empirical and theoretical bases for content selection of the various programs [p. 220]." Glaser and Resnick also believe that the four category system "is incapable of adequately describing the work of those who seek to apply behavioral analysis to Piagetian and related tasks in the course of defining curriculum, nor does it account for all varieties of language and perceptual development emphases [p. 220]."

GORDON (1968, 1972)

Gordon's method for comparing Follow Through programs differs markedly from Maccoby and Zellner's emphasis upon conceptual origins.

Are the sponsor's views based on empirical research results as well as on a set of philosophical principles?

Are there specific sources that have been especially influential in shaping the sponsor's beliefs about the growth and education of children? That is, have specific theorists, research results, books, published articles, or other sources been particularly influential?

How much emphasis is placed on accommodating the instructional program to individual differences among children?

What are the characteristics of educational environments that favor the optimal development of children's potential for learning? What circumstances are likely to oppose optimal development?

Have the sponsor's experiences in Follow Through or the results of recent developments in theory or research tended to change, modify, or strengthen the views that guided the initial work in Follow Through?

THE WELL–IMPLEMENTED MODEL

The purpose of this section is to describe the instructional and implementation procedures that the sponsor is currently advocating. Each model has passed through many stages of development, and the authors will describe some of the major conceptual and/or operational changes that have shaped the current status of their programs. The questions and statements that guided the selection of material for this section are the following:

Describe the teaching techniques and materials that are derived from the sponsor's basic beliefs.

What are the most important skills, competencies, and attitudes that students are expected to acquire through their participation in the model?

How are the parents involved in the instruction of their children in the classroom, home, or community?

Is there a specialized language, or terminology, that members of the sponsor's group use to communicate with each other about the model?

Does the sponsor advocate systematic, external reinforcement of students, or is there a belief in intrinsic, or autotelic, sources of motivation? Or are both sources believed to be important?

Does the sponsor seek to influence interactions between cognitive and affective domains in learning? Are specific teaching procedures recommended to achieve such interactions?

Are learning tasks carefully sequenced for each student, or does the sponsor expect students to have some initiative in planning and implementing their own learning experiences? Are elements of both approaches included in the model?

It was adapted from the recommendations for analyzing instructional programs made in 1968 by the Association for Supervision and Curriculum Development (ASCD). Those recommendations focus on descriptions of, and interrelationships among, the following: cognitive and affective goals of instructional programs, biosocial characteristics of pupils, and features of instructional settings. Descriptions of instructional programs are expected to include specific statements about program goals and the relationships among the characteristics of instructional techniques, pupils, and program goals.

WEIKART (1972)

This author proposed that childhood education programs may be grouped according to both the teachers' characteristic role (initiate versus respond) and the pupils' characteristic role (initiate versus respond) in the classroom. Teachers' initiating behaviors include planning and completing lessons, projects, or activities; responding behaviors include observing the children, meeting their needs, and helping them interact with others and with classroom materials. Children initiate when they select and manipulate objects, involve themselves voluntarily in classroom activities, or plan their daily programs; they respond when they listen to the teacher, follow instructions, and answer questions. Weikart's 2 × 2 matrix yields the following four possible categories of childhood education programs: *programmed curricula*, *child-centered curricula*, *open-framework curricula*, and *custodial care*. Weikart's matrix will be discussed further in Chapter 6 of this volume.

EMRICK, SORENSEN, AND STEARNS (1973)

Evaluation researchers at the Stanford Research Institute categorized Follow Through models into five groups on the basis of sponsors' preferred approaches to working with children and their families. Sponsors of models in the first group, the *structured academic* approaches, stress behavioral objectives, careful sequencing of learning experiences, and a consistent use of reinforcement procedures. Sponsors of the *discovery* approaches, which comprise the second group, emphasize the importance of intrinsic motivation, exploration, and discovery in educational environments that are responsive to children's initiatives. In the third group are the *cognitive discovery* approaches, in which sponsors focus on stimulating the growth of cognitive processes through a variety of teaching procedures. *Self-sponsored* approaches, designed by individuals in local school districts, and *parent-implemented* approaches, which share a strong commitment to high levels of parent participation, comprise the fourth and fifth groups, respectively.

STEBBINS, ST. PIERRE, PROPER, ANDERSON, AND CERVA (1977)

Evaluation researchers at Abt Associates classified Follow Through models into three categories on the basis of the sponsors' stated goals and objectives. The *basic skills* category included those models in which the focus was on teaching academic skills in reading, arithmetic, spelling, and language. The *cognitive–conceptual* category contained models in which the primary intent was to develop the more complex learning-to-learn and problem-solving skills. The *affective–cognitive* category was composed of models in which sponsors' purposes were primarily to build positive self-concepts and attitudes toward learning, and secondarily to strengthen learning-to-learn skills. Among the five models described in this volume, the Direct Instruction and Behavior Analysis Models were placed in the basic skills category, the High/Scope Cognitively Oriented Curriculum Model and the Parent Education Model in the cognitive–conceptual category, and the Bank Street Model: A Developmental–Interaction Approach in the affective–cognitive category.

PARKER AND DAY (1972)

These authors formulated a comprehensive structure for comparing and contrasting childhood education programs on five criteria. The *first criterion* pertains to the question of which formal theory, or theories, of child development and/or results of empirical research influenced the conceptualization of the program. The *second criterion* consists of the following three characteristics of stated goals and objectives: the degree to which they are stated in operational terms that lend themselves to objective evaluation, their breadth across the various areas of child learning and development, and whether the curriculum is process- or content-oriented. The focus of the *third criterion* is on the implementation qualities, or the format, of the curriculum and the organizational qualities that may be observed in the classroom. Parker and Day's *fourth criterion* is the extent to which intrinsic or extrinsic sources of motivation are believed to influence pupils. The *fifth criterion* for conceptual analysis is the program's capability for "exportation," or successful implementation in environments that may differ markedly from the one in which it was formulated initially.

The six conceptual systems described here represent different perspectives for viewing the Follow Through models. None of these systems incorporates all criteria on which the models may be compared, and some criteria are represented in most of the six systems. Taken together, they represent the range of criteria that may be used to discriminate among different approaches to childhood education.

Guidelines f

Each of the chapters in Part II is divided into the fol
(a) Overview; (b) Origins; (c) Rationale; (d) The Well-Ir
(e) Evaluation; and (f) Lessons Learned. Most of the
chapters is allocated to sections c, d, e, and f. This par
tains lists of suggestions that were formulated to guide
selection of material for inclusion in their chapters.
questions and statements was to provide an advisory s
authors could use to select information that wou
describe their models within the recommended format
to make comparisons among the models. However, a
quired to respond to each question or statement, and th
to formulate additional guidelines of choice if doing s
state the most salient information about their model.

The purpose of this section is to introduce and br
content of the chapter.

This section contains background information or
generated the model, including a description of forma
have occurred before the beginning of Follow Through
cludes some comment about the host institution.

The purpose of this section is to describe the princi
findings that comprise the sponsor's rationale for the n
how these are used to guide program development, t
tion activities. The guidelines for this section include

1. What are the sponsor's basic beliefs about the de
   cation of children? For example, does the spc
   theory of growth and development, a belief in t
   nate, structural qualities, an emphasis upon the p
   vironment and learning experiences, or an inter
   the contributions of heredity and environment?
2. Is the sponsor's conceptual framework locate
   behaviorist, cognitive developmental, humanisti
   tradition, or does it consist of an eclectic set o
   from two or more of these frameworks?

8. Does the sponsor have specific recommendations for classroom management, record keeping, and so forth?

EVALUATION

This section contains the following information about the sponsor's approach to program evaluation: (a) sponsor's views about the purpose(s) of evaluation; (b) characteristics of the students, parents, teachers, or others included in the evaluation; (c) instruments and procedures employed to collect data; (d) statistical methods used to analyze data; and (e) interpretation of the results. The questions and statements that guided the preparation of this section are the following:

1. What purposes are evaluation procedures intended to serve? Are the data employed by students in self-evaluation procedures, made available to teachers, used to verify the implementation of the model, made available to parents, or used for other purposes?
2. Describe as carefully as possible the characteristics of students in the Follow Through, and non-Follow-Through comparison, classrooms.
3. What are the psychometric characteristics of the instruments employed in the data collection? That is, what information is available on the reliability and validity of the instruments, norm groups, or other psychometric properties?
4. Describe the data collection procedures.
5. Was it necessary to construct new instruments in order to measure important outcomes of the model?
6. Are data available from sources other than the sponsor's evaluation? Is it possible to compare results from the sponsor's evaluation with results from the national longitudinal evaluation?
7. Describe the data analysis techniques employed in the evaluation research.
8. What conclusions about the effectiveness of the model are supported by the results of the evaluation research? Are there possible alternative interpretations of the data?

LESSONS LEARNED

The authors were requested to reflect upon their entire experience in Follow Through and to derive statements that they believe will help others who may wish to conduct similar experiments in the future. They also were encouraged to indicate the implications of their work for the improvement of childhood education. Furthermore, they were asked to state suggestions that may be useful to those individuals who decide to implement innovative educational programs in local school districts.

The descriptions of the five models included in Part II illustrate the diversity of approaches that are represented in Follow Through. Each of these models has been developed over a period of many years; however, the sponsors will continue to refine their models by making appropriate changes in goals, instructional procedures, materials, and methods of evaluation. Consequently, some statements made about the models discussed in this volume may be changed or modified later in the light of subsequent information.

The descriptions of the five Follow Through models in Part II are presented in the following order: Parent Education Model, Direct Instruction Model, Behavior Analysis Model, High/Scope Cognitively Oriented Curriculum Model, and Bank Street Model: A Developmental–Interaction Approach. Each chapter is preceded by an outline of the contents. All chapters on models are approximately the same length, but the chapter on the Direct Instruction Model is somewhat longer than the others because it contains a description of the structure and results of the national longitudinal evaluation of Follow Through. Readers who wish to obtain additional information about Follow Through models may direct their inquiries to the sponsors listed in Appendix A.

References

Bereiter, C., & Engelmann, S. *Teaching disadvantaged children in the preschool.* Englewood Cliffs, N. J.: Prentice-Hall, 1966.

Bloom, B. S. *Stability and change in human characteristics.* New York: John Wiley & Sons, 1964.

Caldwell, B. Consolidating our gains in early childhood. *Educational Horizons,* 1972, *50,* 56–60.

Campbell, D. T. Reforms as experiments. *American Psychologist,* 1969, *24,* 409–429.

Cazden, C. B. Some implications of research on language development for preschool education. In R. D. Hess & R. M. Baer (Eds.), *Early education: Current theory, research, and action.* Chicago: Aldine, 1968. Pp. 132–142.

Cicirelli, V. G., Cooper, W., & Granger, R. *The impact of Head Start: An evaluation of the effects of the Head Start experience on children's cognitive and affective development.* Athens, Ohio: Westinghouse Learning Corporation and Ohio University, 1969.

Cohen, D. D., & Garet, M. S. Reforming educational policy with applied social research. *Harvard Educational Review,* 1975, *45,* 17–43.

Coleman, J. S., Campbell, E., Mood, A., Weinfeld, E., Hobson, C., York, R., & McPartland, J. *Equality of educational opportunity.* Washington, D. C.: U. S. Government Printing Office, 1966.

Datta, L. E. Design of the Head Start planned variation experiments. In A. M. Rivlin & P. M. Timpane (Eds.), *Planned variation in education.* Washington, D. C.: Brookings Institution, 1975. Pp. 79–99.

Deutsch, M. (Ed.). *The disadvantaged child.* New York: Basic Books, 1967.

Elmore, R. E. *Follow Through: Decisionmaking in a large-scale social experiment*. Unpublished doctoral dissertation, Harvard University, 1976.

Emrick, J. A., Sorensen, P. H., & Stearns, M. S. *Interim evaluation of the national Follow Through program, 1969–1971*. Menlo Park, Calif.: Stanford Research Institute, 1973.

Frost, J. L. (Ed.). *Early childhood education rediscovered: Readings*. New York: Holt, Rinehart, & Winston, 1968.

Gagné, R. M., & Gephart, W. J. (Eds.). *Learning research and school subject*. Itasca, Ill.: Peacock, 1968.

Glaser, R., & Resnick, L. B. Instructional psychology. In P. H. Mussen & M. R. Rosenzweig (Eds.), *Annual review of psychology* (Vol. 23). Palo Alto, Calif.: Annual Reviews, 1972. Pp.207–276.

Gordon, I. J. *A parent education approach to provision of early stimulation for the culturally disadvantaged. Final report to the Fund for the Advancement of Education*. Gainesville, Fla.: University of Florida, 1967.

Gordon, I. J. (Ed.). *Criteria for theories of instruction*. Washington, D. C.: Association for Supervision and Curriculum Development, National Education Association, 1968.

Gordon, I. J. An instructional theory approach to the analysis of selected early childhood programs. In I. J. Gordon (Ed.), *Early childhood education* (75th yearbook of the National Society for the Study of Education). Chicago: University of Chicago Press, 1972. Pp. 203–228.

Haney, W. *The Follow Through evaluation: A technical history* (Vol. 5). Washington, D. C.: Office of Education, U. S. Department of Health, Education, and Welfare, 1977.

Hess, R. D., & Baer, D. M. (Eds.). *Early education: Current theory, research, and action*. Chicago: Aldine, 1968.

Horowitz, F. D., & Paden, L. Y. The effectiveness of environmental intervention programs. In B. M. Caldwell & H. N. Ricciuti (Eds.), *Child development research* (Vol. 3). Chicago: University of Chicago Press, 1973. Pp. 331–402.

Hunt, J. M. *Intelligence and experience*. New York: Ronald Press, 1961.

Krulee, G. K. *An organizational analysis of Project Follow Through, final report*.Evanston, Ill.: Northwestern University, 1973. (ERIC Document Reproduction Service No. 093446)

Lazar, I., Hubbell, V. R., Murray, H., Rosche, M., & Royce, J. *The persistence of preschool effects*. Final Report: Grant #18–76–07843 to the Administration for Children, Youth, and Families, Office of Human Development. Washington, D. C.: U.S. Department of Health, Education, and Welfare, September 1977.

Maccoby, E. E., & Zellner, M. *Experiments in primary education: Aspects of Project Follow Through*. New York: Harcourt, Brace, Jovanovich, 1970.

McDill, E. L., McDill, M. S., & Sprehe, J. T. *Strategies for success in compensatory education: An appraisal of evaluation research*. Baltimore: Johns Hopkins University Press, 1969.

McDill, E. L., McDill, M. S., & Sprehe, J. T. Evaluation in practice: Compensatory education. In P. H. Rossi & W. Williams (Eds.), *Evaluating social programs: Theory, practice, and politics*. New York: Seminar Press, 1972. Pp. 141–185.

Parker, R., & Day, M. Comparisons of preschool curricula. In R. Parker (Ed.), *The preschool in action*. Boston: Allyn & Bacon, 1972. Pp. 466–508.

Ramsey, W. Z. Head Start and first grade reading. In J. Hellmuth (Ed.), *Disadvantaged child* (Vol. 2). New York: Brunner/Mazel, 1968. Pp. 289–298.

Resnick, L. B. Design of early learning curriculum. Working paper 16. Learning Research & Development Center, University of Pittsburgh, 1967.

Rhine, W. R. *Follow Through: A model for utilizing the social sciences for solving social problems*. Paper presented at the annual meeting of the American Psychological Association, Montreal, Quebec, Canada, August 1973. (a)

Rhine, W. R. Strategies for evaluating Follow Through. In R. M. Rippey (Ed.), *Studies in transactional evaluation.* Berkeley, Calif.: McCutchan Publishing, 1973. Pp. 157–180. (b)

Stebbins, L. B., St. Pierre, R. G., Proper, E. C., Anderson, R. B., & Cerva, T. R. *Education as experimentation: A planned variation model. Vol. IV–A: An evaluation of Follow Through.* Cambridge, Mass: Abt Associates, 1977. (Also issued by the U.S. Office of Education as *National evaluation: Patterns of effects* [Vol. II–A of the Follow Through planned variation experimental series].)

Stendler-Lavatelli, C. A Piaget-derived model for compensatory preschool education. In J. L. Frost (Ed.), *Early childhood education rediscovered: Readings.* New York: Holt, Rinehart, & Winston, 1968. Pp. 530–544.

U.S. Department of Health, Education, and Welfare. *Summary report of 1968 White House Task Force on Child Development.* Washington, D.C.: U.S. Government Printing Office, 1968.

U.S. Office of Education. *Follow Through program approaches, 1969–1970.*Washington, D.C.: U.S. Office of Education, 1969.

Weikart, D. P. (Ed.). *Preschool intervention: Preliminary report of the Perry Preschool Project.* Ann Arbor, Mich.: Campus Publishers, 1967.

Weikart, D. P. Relationship of curriculum, teaching, and learning in preschool education. In J. C. Stanley (Ed.), *Preschool programs for the disadvantaged: Five experimental approaches to early childhood education.* Baltimore: Johns Hopkins University Press, 1972. Pp. 22–66.

Williams, W., & Evans, J. W. The politics of evaluation: The case of Head Start. In P. H. Rossi & W. Williams (Eds.), *Evaluating social programs: Theory, practice, and politics.* New York: Seminar Press, 1972. Pp. 247–264.

Wolff, M., & Stein, A. Head Start six months later. *Phi Delta Kappan,* 1967, *48,* 349–350.

Zigler, E., & Valentine, J. (Eds.). *Project Head Start: A legacy of the War on Poverty.* New York: Free Press, 1979.

Part II
Descriptions of Five Follow Through Models

These innovations, known as Follow Through, did much to establish alternatives in curricula for young children.

> [EVANS, E. D., & McCANDLESS, B. R. *Children and youth: Psychosocial development* (2nd ed.). New York: Holt, Rinehart & Winston, 1978, p. 379.]

Follow Through is a unique pattern of teaming outstanding models of early childhood education with school systems to implement planned variations throughout the country. The concept of an external, accountable agency working with the school and parents is a successful device for change.

> [GORDON, I. J. *Human development: A transactional perspective* (3rd ed.). New York: Harper & Row, 1975, p. 153.]

GORDON E. GREENWOOD
WILLIAM B. WARE
IRA J. GORDON
W. RAY RHINE 3

Parent Education Model[1,2]

[1] Preparation of this chapter was supported by USOE Grant G007701619, but no endorsement of its contents by the federal government should be inferred.

[2] On behalf of the other contributors, Greenwood and Ware want to express appreciation to the editor, W. Ray Rhine, for conceptualizing this volume. He also worked diligently with all the other authors to complete the chapters on Follow Through models, and he is as much their author as we.

49

Overview

The Parent Education Model is the Follow Through approach developed by Ira J. Gordon and his associates at the University of Florida's Institute for the Development of Human Resources (IDHR), which is an interdisciplinary research and development organization within the College of Education. The main thrust of the model is to improve the education of young children by helping their parents become more effective teachers at home and by encouraging parents and classroom teachers to become working partners in behalf of children. The designers of the model believe that the family and the school are the two most important and enduring sources of learning for children. Furthermore, they believe that children's success in school and in later life depends at least as much, if not more, on their experiences at home than it does on their experiences at school. Indeed, school personnel can exert an important, constructive influence upon children, and teachers should continue their efforts to improve instructional programs in classrooms. Nevertheless, educators are more likely to accomplish their goals for students when they encourage parents to see themselves as having significant responsibilities and capabilities for educating their own children.

This chapter contains information on how the Parent Education Model evolved from previous intervention research with preschool infants and their mothers, as well as from a broad range of concepts and research results on child development. In the section on implementation, the authors identify the components of the model and how they function in a local school district. The next section is devoted to a description of a variety of innovative approaches to evaluation and some representative results. In the last section, some lessons gleaned from the work in Follow Through are stated, along with their implications for increasing parents' participation in the education of their children and for educational policy decisions at federal, state, and local levels.

Origins

In 1966, the Fund for the Advancement of Education provided grant support for Gordon's proposal to develop an innovative early educational intervention program for mothers from low-income families and their infants. This approach was a response to research results that supported the following general conclusions: *(a)* Mothers influence the rate of children's development in intellectual as well as in personal and social areas; *(b)* children from poor families often fail in school because they are not taught essential cognitive skills during the preschool years; and *(c)* there is a strong link between educational failure and the condition of poverty. Gordon hypothesized that if mothers from poor families could learn to teach their children more effectively during the preschool years, these children would be better prepared to succeed in school. Hopefully, the children who benefited from participation in this educational program ultimately would be able to break the entrenched cycle of low levels of educational achievement in school, occupational failure characterized by unemployment or sporadic employment in unskilled jobs, and chronic poverty and dependency in adult life.

The initial studies were designed to provide answers for four central questions. First, "Can parent educators be recruited and trained to work with parents and their children in home settings?" Second, "Will parent educators be accepted by mothers, and will they be able to sustain long-term working relationships with the mothers?" Third, "Will this form of intervention enhance the cognitive development of children?" And fourth, "Can the results, if they are encouraging, be disseminated in a form that will enable individuals in other communities to develop similar parent education programs?" The outcomes of the studies, completed in November, 1967, provided positive answers to all these questions.

Gordon and his coworkers believed that the home should serve as a basic learning center; consequently, they formulated teaching strategies, games, and other learning activities for use by mothers in their homes. It was expected that becoming more effective teachers of their children would enhance the mothers' feelings of competence, self-esteem, and sense of personal control over the outcomes of interactions with their children and life situations in general. Women from low-income backgrounds were employed to teach mothers from similar backgrounds the techniques for stimulating infants' development. These instructional activities thus created a new occupational role, the *parent educator* (sometimes called the *home visitor*).

The favorable recognition that the infant stimulation program received during its first year encouraged Gordon and his group to prepare a grant proposal to continue their work. The proposal, entitled "Early Child Stimulation through Parent Education," was subsequently funded by the Children's Bureau of the United States Department of Health, Education, and Welfare (HEW) for a period of 2 years beginning in July, 1967. The investigators constructed a demonstration and outreach program in which they used the information acquired during their previous studies to provide a range of services for mothers located in 12 counties in the area surrounding Gainesville, Florida.

Early in 1968, the planners of Follow Through expressed an interest in extending Gordon's approach to parents of older children enrolled in kindergarten and the first three grades. Gordon and his colleagues at IDHR soon were invited to develop their parent educator approach as a Follow

Through model. During the 1968–1969 school year, the Parent Education Follow Through Model was implemented in six communities. The program reached its largest size during the 1974–1975 school year, when it was conducted in the 11 communities listed in Appendix B and served a total of 7008 children enrolled in 48 schools and 282 Follow Through classrooms.[3]

Gordon E. Greenwood, William B. Ware, and Gordon have had a lengthy involvement in the Parent Education Model. Greenwood was codirector and chief administrator of the model from 1973 to 1977. Ware began his association with the model in 1969 and was codirector in charge of evaluation from 1973 to 1976. Gordon was the guiding force in the development of the model and served as director from 1968 to 1973. In addition, he served as director of IDHR from 1966 to 1977. Prior to his sudden death in 1978, Gordon was Dean of the School of Education and Kenan Professor at the University of North Carolina, Chapel Hill.

Rationale

The rationale for the Parent Education Follow Through Model is derived from a large and growing fund of research about the effects of children's home environments on their later performance in school. Some of these studies were published prior to the initiation of the model in the summer of 1968; others were published later. The purpose of this section is to summarize the results of representative research on how competence among children is influenced by (a) socioeconomic status; (b) infant stimulation; (c) home environments versus school environments; and (d) characteristics of parenting behaviors and home environments.

EFFECTS OF SOCIOECONOMIC STATUS

During the period from the early 1940s to the mid-1960s, behavioral scientists used global indicators of socioeconomic status (SES), such as parental occupation, income, education, and location of residence, to describe home environments. Generally, studies of SES effects revealed that middle-and lower-class parents differ in their beliefs about proper methods for rearing children, and that middle-class students perform better than lower-class students on tests of academic achievement, mental ability, and language development. The results of this research suggested a possible link between styles of parent–child interaction in homes and levels of children's success in school (Caldwell, 1964; Deutsch, 1973).

One problem in the use of SES indicators in studies of behavior was that they were structural variables and thus represented only in a general way

---

[3] The sponsor's home offices for the model were moved to the University of North Carolina at Chapel Hill in July, 1977. The current director of the Parent Education Model is Patricia P. Olmsted, who can provide additional information about the model on request.

the differences that actually existed in the home learning environments of children from different social class groups. Consequently, such studies could not identify the specific psychological variables that are linked to the differences in children's performance (Deutsch, Katz, & Jensen, 1968). Perhaps that is why the use of SES indicators rarely accounted for more than 25% of the variance in children's behavior (Bloom, 1964). Nevertheless, the results of the SES studies helped to focus attention upon the inequalities in educational opportunities that exist for children in different social class groups, and these studies prepared the way for many of the studies described in the remainder of this section.

INFANT STIMULATION

In the mid-1960s, several influences supported the development of a small number of intervention programs for stimulating the cognitive development of infants. For example, the SES studies described in the preceding section documented the poor performance of lower-class children on a variety of measures as compared to middle-class children. Also, a growing body of research indicated the importance of development during the period of infancy (Bloom, 1964; Hunt, 1961). In addition, the civil rights movement contributed to strong political support for social action programs designed to improve the educability of infants and young children from low-income homes.

Project Head Start and a number of other projects for stimulating infants' cognitive development were created in 1965. A few years later, the results of the Westinghouse Report (Cicirelli, Cooper, & Granger, 1969), a major evaluation of the effects of Head Start, indicated that children's rate of cognitive development accelerated during their attendance in Head Start classes but slowed after they enrolled in the regular grades. Discussions on this finding led to two major policy decisions: (a) to initiate Project Follow Through for the purpose of preserving children's positive gains in Head Start; and (b) to increase the number of programs for stimulating growth and development during infancy. Involving parents in the education of their children is one of the clear trends that emerged and grew stronger during the development of programs for stimulating infants' cognitive development. The benefits of parent participation were documented by Bronfenbrenner (1975), who concluded that parent participation in intervention programs leads to better results.

HOME ENVIRONMENTS VERSUS
SCHOOL ENVIRONMENTS

Some investigators compared the relative influence of the home and the school on children's levels of success in school. Coleman et al. (1966) assessed the effects of many variables on children's academic achievement in a study that included approximately 600,000 students in grades 1, 3, 6, 9, and 12 in 4000 schools. The results strongly supported two major conclusions: (a) Variations among students in levels of academic achievement are determined primarily by their family backgrounds (social class), and traditional measures of the quality of a school's staff, curricula, and physical facilities account for a comparatively small amount of the differences among students; and (b) the strong relationship between the economic and educational characteristics of families and students' levels of academic performance increases as the children progress through elementary school. Coleman, Campbell, Mood, Weinfeld, Hobson, York, and McPartland (1966) stated,

> The sources of inequality of educational opportunity appear to be first in the home itself and the cultural influences surrounding the home; then they lie in the schools' ineffectiveness to free achievement from the impact of the home, and in the schools' cultural homogeneity which perpetuates the social influences of the home and its environs [pp. 73–74].

Two investigators in England also compared the influence of parents and schools on the development of competence among children, and their results strongly support the conclusions stated in the Coleman Report. Douglas (1964) reported that measures of parents' interest in and involvement with their childrens' education accounted for four times as much of the variation in children's scores on intelligence and achievement tests than did measures of the quality of the schools the children attended. Similarly, the results of Moore's (1968) longitudinal study among English children indicated that these children's scores on tests of reading ability at age 7 and on tests of mental ability at age 8 were correlated with ratings of toys, books, experiences, and language stimulation provided for the children by home visitors when the children were 2½-years-old.

The results of three more recent studies also support the general conclusion that home variables are more important than school variables in determining the level of academic achievement that children attain through their studies. Mosteller and Moynihan (1972) reanalyzed the data from several large studies and concluded that variation in schools "have little effect upon school achievement [p. 21]," and they urged consideration of methods "to alter the way in which parents deal with their children at home [p. 43]." In the second study, Jencks, Smith, Acland, Bane, Cohen, Gintis, Heyns, and Michelson (1972) reanalyzed data from several sources, including the original data collected by Coleman *et al.* (1966). They contended that the most important elements in determining children's capabilities when they leave school are the capabilities and advantages that they bring to school from their homes, and that even if education could be reformed to insure that all schools were equal in quality, inequalities in children's performance probably would continue. Finally, Coleman (1975) analyzed data from achievement tests in literature, reading, and science collected from children age 10–14 years living in Chile, England, Finland, Italy, Sweden, and the United States. He stated that for "all three subjects, the total effect of home background is considerably greater than the direct effect of school variables [p. 381]."

Taken together, the results of many studies have both confirmed and strengthened the belief that more attention should be given to the development of strategies for helping parents become more effective teachers of their own children. In the following section, the authors summarize some studies in which investigators identified and analyzed teaching and learning processes in parent–child interactions that appear to account for the observed differences in children's later performance in school.

CHARACTERISTICS OF PARENTING BEHAVIORS AND HOME ENVIRONMENTS

During the 1960s, researchers began to study parent behaviors and home environments in different social classes. These process-oriented studies differed from the earlier structurally oriented (SES) studies in the following ways: (a) Independent variables were identified more specifically; (b) direct observation and/or laboratory procedures often were employed to obtain data; and (c) some studies were designed to investigate the influence of parents' teaching behaviors on their children's academic performance in school.

Two researchers interviewed mothers to identify variables in home environments that produce differences in children's levels of mental abilities and school achievement (Davé, 1963; Wolf, 1964). They studied the effects of the quality of language that parents modeled for children, including the language styles they used in a variety of situations, the extent to which they emphasized correct usage of language, and the encouragement and opportunities they provided for children to enlarge their vocabularies. Other dimensions of interest to the investigators included parents' child-rearing practices, patterns of reinforcement, expectancies for children's educational attainment, the stability and mobility of the family, physical surroundings of the home, and so forth. Wolf (1964) stated that the correlation of .69 between his ratings of the intellectual environments of homes and children's scores on intelligence tests indicated nearly three times as much variance explained, as compared with typical correlations of approximately .40 between SES indicators and intelligence test scores.

Other investigators reported results that appeared to support the findings stated in the preceding paragraph. For example, Hess and Shipman (1965) and Hess, Shipman, Brophy, and Bear (1968) used direct observation techniques in laboratory settings to examine the relationships between mothers' teaching styles and their children's performance. They reported that many dimensions of maternal teaching behaviors were correlated with their children's scores on standardized reading achievement tests and grades assigned by teachers. In another study, Rupp (1969) found that among first graders in Holland, those who performed well had parents who provided greater amounts of cognitive stimulation in the home, including reading aloud, playing table games and word games, providing educational toys and books, as well as both encouraging and answering "why" questions. These parents also were more likely to participate in school functions, encourage their children to attend school regularly, serve as educators of their own children, teach them preschool skills, and accompany them to places and events that were interesting. Rupp suggested that the home visit was a viable technique for changing and improving the quality of home learning environments for many children. Finally, Miller's (1975) 4-year longitudinal study revealed significant correlations between children's scores on reading achievement test scores in the third grade and such maternal language variables as mean sentence length, adverb range, verb elaboration, and complex verb preference.

In 1966, Bettye M. Caldwell and her colleagues began to develop the Home Observation for Measurement of the Environment (HOME), and they employed this instrument in a number of studies to analyze the characteristics of learning environments provided in homes (Caldwell, Heider, & Kaplan, 1966). For example, Elardo, Bradley, and Caldwell (1975) administered both the HOME and the Bayley Scales of Infant Development to 77 infants who were 12 months of age, and they administered the Stanford–Binet Intelligence Test to these same infants when they reached age 3. The correlation of .58 between the infants' HOME scores and their scores on the Stanford–Binet accounted for nearly three times as much variance as the correlation of .32 between infants' scores on the Bayley tests and the Stanford–Binet, and it was higher than correlations typically reported between either social class or parental education and IQ scores. Van Doorninck, Caldwell, Wright, and Frankenberg (1975) reported that infants' HOME scores at age 12 months were better predictors of their level of success in the primary grades than was the infants' social class or whether they had attended an early childhood center. The HOME also has been used to study language development (Elardo, Bradley, & Caldwell, 1977), to evaluate the effects of training programs for parents (Hamilton, 1972), and to detect developmental delay in young children (Bradley & Caldwell, 1977).

In this section, the authors summarized selected research in order to indicate important progress toward identifying the variables in parent–child interaction that account for observed differences in school performance among children. This research evolved from the early SES studies of differences among parents and among children to the more recent and more sophisticated studies of process variables in parent–child interaction. Continued progress in identifying these variables may assist investigators to develop more effective intervention techniques for helping parents improve their abilities to prepare their children for success in school and in later life.

The Well-Implemented Model

The purpose of this section is to describe some key components of the Parent Education Model and how they operate when it is well-implemented. In the first part, the authors present an overview of the home–school relationship, including modes of participation by parents, parent educators, and classroom teachers. The second part contains a description of the home visit cycle. The third part includes information on methods for developing home learning tasks. Finally, the fourth part contains a description of the characteristics of the delivery and quality control systems.

OVERVIEW OF THE HOME–SCHOOL RELATIONSHIP

During the past two decades, increasing numbers of educators recognized the need for more effective patterns of cooperation between parents and school personnel (Gordon & Breivogel, 1976). The elements of a new partnership between home and school emerged in many federally funded programs such as Head Start and Follow Through. In some instances, parent educators established new linkages between parents and teachers; in others, decision-making processes in the schools were decentralized in order to involve parents more directly as partners in the education of their children. The individuals who designed the Parent Education Model identified a number of modes of participation in school-related activities for parents, parent educators, and classroom teachers. These modes are described next.

Modes of Participation by Parents

The six modes of participation by parents in the Parent Education Follow Through Model are represented in Figure 3.1. First, parents are supported in their efforts to teach their own children more effectively at home. Most of them want their children to become well educated, but they often need support to accomplish their goal. Second, many parents participate as paid

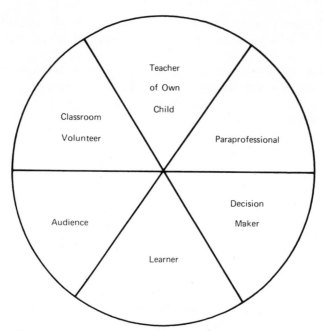

FIGURE 3.1. *Parental roles in parent involvement (from Gordon, I. J., Olmsted, P. P., Rubin, R. I., & True, J. H.* Continuity between home and school: Aspects of parent involvement in Follow Through. *Paper presented at meeting of Society for Research in Child Development, Atlanta, April 1978).*

paraprofessionals who function as parent educators. Third, parents become involved in the Policy Advisory Council (PAC) in order to influence the formulation of policies and decisions on how schools should educate their children. In the fourth and fifth modes of participation, parents observe events that occur within schools, meet with school personnel and come to know them as people, and participate in a wide range of activities to acquire new information and skills. Finally, parents both gain much and contribute much through their participation as aides and volunteers in classrooms (Gordon, 1970; Gordon & Breivogel, 1976; Gordon, Olmsted, Rubin, & True, 1978).

Modes of Participation by Parent Educators

Parent educators are employed by school systems to work a 40-hr week and they adhere to school policies concerning attendance, punctuality, calling in when delayed, and so forth. They devote one-half of their time to conducting home visits and the other half to performing duties at school (see Figure 3.2), including participation in inservice education. Two parent educators are assigned to a classroom, and the primary responsibility of

Teacher		1.0 HOUSEKEEPING	Parent	
1 2 3 4 5			1 2 3 4 5	

Teacher	**Parent**
1 2 3 4 5	1 2 3 4 5

1.0 HOUSEKEEPING
1. Dusts, cleans, etc.
2. Helps children with clothing
3. Arranges furniture
4. Keeps order (babysitting)
5. Posts bulletin board
6. Takes monitoring responsibility
(bus, lunch, snacks, lavatory, recess)

2.0 CLERICAL
1. Collects monies
2. Collects papers
3. Takes attendance
4. Duplicates materials
5. Distributes materials
6. Fills out routine reports
7. Gives tests
8. Maintains inventory
9. Maintains instructional material file
10. Keeps records

3.0 MATERIALS
1. Locates materials
2. Makes bibliography
3. Sets up displays
4. Sets up demonstrations
(prepares materials)

4.0 INSTRUCTION
4.1 Teaching
1. Tutors child
2. Organizes play activity
3. Selects materials
4. Develops materials
5. Teaches total group
6. Teaches small group
7. Disciplines
8. Organizes group for instruction
9. Makes judgments
4.2 Planning
10. Plans, organizes meetings
11. Plans bulletin board
12. Plans lesson
(small group, large group)

5.0 EVALUATION
1. Grades papers
2. Makes anecdotal records
3. Uses Systematic Observation Schedule
4. Organizes case study
5. Evaluates materials
6. Makes tests
7. Interprets test results

FIGURE 3.2 *Teacher aide instructional activities (from Soar, R. S., & Kaplan, L.* Taxonomy of classroom activities. *Gainesville, Fla.: University of Florida, 1968 [mimeo]).*

each is to visit one-half of the homes represented by the children enrolled in that classroom. For example, if there are a total of 28 children in the classroom, each parent educator will conduct 14 home visits per week. One home visit will usually require between 30 and 60 min to complete.

Parent educators are typically mothers from low-income families. Procedures for screening, interviewing, and selecting applicants were formulated jointly by the members of the PAC and the program director in each community. The majority of parent educators are women who possess at least a high school diploma, and they are paid employees (Greenwood, Breivogel, & Olmsted, 1974). Men have served but few as parent educators, have continued in the position for as long as a year. Since much of the parent educator's work is with parents and school personnel, the ability to communicate with adults is as important as the ability to work effectively with children. Parent educators also should be able to follow orderly procedures in preparing and filing the necessary reports and to exercise good judgment in social relationships. Each parent educator receives extensive preservice and in-service training.

Modes of Participation by Classroom Teachers

The training and work experiences of most teachers prepare them to teach only in self-contained classrooms where there are no other adults. But teachers in the Parent Education Model are expected to function as facilitators for the work of the parent educators, as team leaders for the instructional process in classrooms, and as linkage agents between groups of parents and the school. Consequently, they participate in preservice and in-service training to acquire new managerial skills and new attitudes. Most teachers adapt to these more complex role behaviors and report that they enjoy the expanded range of opportunities for new experiences and professional growth.

Teachers and parent educators work cooperatively to analyze information, select learning activities, and develop strategies for teaching these activities to mothers and their children. Parent educators often learn the instructional methods that they use in homes by teaching children individually and in small groups under the teacher's supervision in the classroom. In addition, teachers help parent educators acquire knowledge about individual differences in learning styles among parents and children and about adapting instructional methods to these differences. Occasionally, teachers may accompany parent educators during the home visits to acquire a fund of shared experiences as a basis for their discussions in planning sessions. Through visits in homes, teachers may strengthen their relationships with families, encourage mothers to participate as decision makers through the PAC and as volunteers in classrooms, and help parents obtain health, financial, or other services. In the role of team leader in classrooms, teachers supervise the activities of parents who volunteer to participate as aides in the instructional process.

Problems may occur during the implementation of the Parent Education Model. For example, the responsibilities of each adult participant in the classroom may not be clearly defined or may not be understood even when they are. In addition, even though most teachers state that the new procedures make their teaching more interesting and productive, some may feel that their responsibilities are too complex and demanding. Other problems may occur in the attempt to balance the requirements of parent participation against the requirements of the legislation, traditions and administrative practices, certification standards, and other factors that are important in the operation of the public schools. The approach to resolving conflicts is to encourage the adults who participate in activities in classrooms to engage in bimonthly conferences to discuss their concerns. Of course, they also have other opportunities to engage in spontaneous discussions.

HOME VISIT CYCLE

The most important procedure for establishing the home–school relationship in the Parent Education Model is the home visit. A brief description of a typical home visit cycle will illustrate how parents, teachers, and parent educators work together as three equal partners to create challenging educational environments that are appropriate to the needs and abilities of each child. The three phases in the home visit cycle are described below.

In *Phase I*, the teacher and the parent educator begin the home visit cycle by reviewing information about the child that is based on their observations of the child's behavior in the home and school. In particular, they discuss the results of the last home visit and any problems that may have occurred. The parent's comments are often a useful source of information about the child's capabilities or preferences for activities. After a thorough discussion concerning the child, the teacher and the parent educator agree on an appropriate learning activity that will be presented to the parent and child at home. This activity will either be selected from existing tasks in the home learning activity library, or an appropriate one will be constructed. The teacher and parent educator also agree on ways to present the activity to the mother in the home. They analyze the Desirable Teaching Behaviors (DTBs), a list of teaching strategies (Gordon & Breivogel, 1976) that is presented later in this section, and select the DTBs to be used in the teaching of the learning task. Often, the teacher demonstrates a technique for teaching the mother how to perform the activity in the home and then engages in a role-playing session in which the parent educator practices the technique while the teacher takes the role of the mother.

In *Phase II*, the parent educator goes to the home at a scheduled time. She informs the parent about the child's progress in school and encourages the parent to comment on the results of the learning activity that was demonstrated in the home during the previous visit. Did the child enjoy performing the activity? Did members of the family join in the activity with the child? Did the child want to perform the task spontaneously without urging from the parents? As the mother's comments are recorded in the Parent Educator's Weekly Report (PEWR) (Gordon & Breivogel, 1976), she also is encouraged to ask questions and suggest ways for improving the activity and adapting it to both the child's abilities and circumstances within the home. Obtaining and incorporating the parent's thoughts, feelings, and skills in the process of teaching the child ensures that the parent maintains a high degree of control over what happens in the home visit cycle.

The parent educator presents a new learning activity, explains its purpose, and helps the mother perform it. The presentation may include both demonstration and role playing to ensure that the parent understands the basic pattern of the activity and that she can teach it to her own child. During the role playing, the parent and parent educator may alternate in the role of the child. The parent also is encouraged to state ways in which the activity might be modified and adapted to the child's interests and abilities and to the general context of the family. Parents are encouraged to ask questions about the activities, and parent educators cooperate with the parents to develop learning activities that are stimulating and enjoyable for all members of the family.

In *Phase III* of the home visit cycle, the mother teaches the task to her child. If the parent educator has done her job well, the mother will teach the child in the manner that the parent educator taught her. Much of the parent educator's efforts are directed toward helping mothers use the following set of Desirable Teaching Behaviors (DTBs):

1. Before starting an activity, explain what you are going to do.
2. Before starting an activity, give the learners time to familiarize themselves with the materials.
3. Ask questions that have more than one correct answer.
4. Ask questions that require multiple-word answers.
5. Encourage learners to enlarge upon their answers.
6. Encourage learners to ask questions.
7. Give learners time to think about problems; don't be too quick to help.
8. Help learners become able to make judgments on the basis of evidence rather than by guessing.
9. Praise learners when they do well or take small steps in the right direction.

10. Let learners know when their answers or work are wrong, but do so in a positive or neutral manner.

DEVELOPING HOME-LEARNING TASKS[4]

Home learning tasks serve several purposes. They support the development of children's intellectual skills that are necessary for success in school. They also strengthen the bond between parents and children by giving them opportunities to interact in recreational learning activities. The children can share their activities with older and younger siblings. The activities also encourage children to develop and refine a number of physical and social skills that they use at home or in school. Learning tasks are not "homework," nor are they remedial work assigned to just a few children. They can be enjoyed by all children enrolled in Follow Through classrooms.

Home learning tasks are more likely to be successful when they are based on children's interests and include materials that are readily available in their homes. Ideas for these home learning tasks may originate from parents, parent educators, teachers, a curriculum committee, or a curriculum specialist. Persons in each local community develop a library of tasks that can be used by any Follow Through teacher. Any particular task may be appropriate for many children, or just a few. A task is effective when it meets the following criteria:

1. The directions for the task are clear.
2. The parent educators, parents, and children understand why they are performing the task.
3. The task can be taught in different ways and children can perform it in different ways.
4. The materials employed in the task are readily available in the home.
5. Children do a lot of talking, describe objects, state reasons, ask questions, and generally make many "why," "what," "where," and "how" statements.
6. Children enjoy performing the task.

[4] Readers may obtain additional information about the planning and implementation of home learning tasks from the following sources: Breivogel, W. F., Greenwood, G. E., & Sterling, D., *Training of teachers, parent educators, members of the PAC, and administrators in the Florida Parent Education Follow Through Model,*Education Professions Development Act Final Report (OEG-0-70-1817), Gainesville, University of Florida, 1973; Gordon, I. J., & Breivogel, W. R., *Building effective home/school relationships*, Boston, Allyn & Bacon, 1976; Shea, J., & Hoffman, S., Extending the curriculum: Home learning tasks, *Theory into Practice*, 1977, *16*, 2–6.

7. Children recognize quickly that they have gained new knowledge and feel good about it.
8. Children generate new activities from their experience in performing the task.

DELIVERY AND QUALITY CONTROL SYSTEMS

Faculty members in the Institute for Development of Human Resources (IDHR) designed systems for delivering services and maintaining quality control in the Parent Education Model. These systems permitted the maximum, flexible use of IDHR's personnel and provided for a continuous flow of information to and among the faculty. One faculty member, called a liaison officer, was assigned to each community, and that person became knowledgeable about and responsible for the program development needs in that community. The entire IDHR faculty comprised a panel of consultants who provided assistance to local communities in all phases of program development. In each community, a faculty person visited 2 days each month during the school year to provide needed help. Faculty members who were not liaison officers were involved throughout the year in numerous staff meetings and planning sessions conducted on the campus of the University of Florida in Gainesville. Currently, technical assistance is provided jointly by members of the faculty at the University of Florida and the University of North Carolina at Chapel Hill. Many parents, parent educators, teachers, curriculum specialists, and school administrators have participated in summer workshops conducted on both campuses.

Another purpose of the delivery and quality control systems was to encourage local communities to develop and use their own resources. Members of the IDHR faculty conducted summer workshops, in-service training sessions, and monthly visits in which they worked to strengthen the capabilities of teachers, parent educators, parents, administrators, and local Follow Through staff persons to implement the model. The faculty resource person typically spent about half of the time allotted for each visit in the homes of parents to observe, assess, and improve the delivery of program services by parent educators.

In this section, the authors presented an overview of the major components of the Parent Education Model, including a description of the home–school partnership, some new roles for parent educators and classroom teachers, methods for developing learning tasks that are presented to mothers and their children during home visits, and procedures for delivering program services and maintaining quality control over these services. The next section contains information on the evaluation of the impact of the Parent Education Model on individuals who participated in it.

Evaluation

The selection of the home–school partnership as the primary intervention strategy clearly distinguishes the Parent Education Model from other Follow Through models. The sponsors of many models have made commendable progress in encouraging parent involvement, but they are interested chiefly in events that occur in classrooms. In contrast, the major concern of Gordon and his associates was to help parents strengthen their abilities to teach children at home in order to improve their performance in classrooms. Thus, the program operations and goals of the Parent Education Model have a markedly different focus, as compared to other Follow Through models. Consequently, the evaluation of the unique features of the Parent Education Model required the development of many new instruments. The three major parts of this section contain descriptions of (*a*) the general orientation to evaluation; (*b*) the extensive effort to develop new instruments for measuring program effects; and (*c*) some representative evaluation results.

ORIENTATION TO EVALUATION

The first priority was to obtain information from evaluation research that would be useful for improving the quality of program implementation, particularly in the area of home visits. Accordingly, much effort was directed toward obtaining and utilizing evaluation results to help parents improve their ability to teach their children at home and to help parent educators improve the performance of their responsibilities in both homes and schools. Thus, the approach to evaluating the Parent Education Model was designed to provide useful information about the performance of parents, parent educators, classroom teachers, and children. Members of the sponsor's staff, teachers, and others used the evaluation results to learn from both their successes and misdirected efforts in order to make continuous progress in improving the design and implementation of the model.

DEVELOPING NEW INSTRUMENTS

The attempt to develop new approaches and instruments for evaluating the Parent Education Model began during the 1968–1969 school year and continued through the completion of the 1974–1975 school year. Table 3.1 contains a list of instruments that were employed to assess program effects on parents, parent educators, teachers, and children. Inspection of Table 3.1 reveals that during the first 2 years, the major emphasis was on evaluating the performance of parent educators and classroom teachers. The emphasis on evaluating parent educators continued throught most of

TABLE 3.1
Instruments/Procedures Employed to Collect Data[a] in the Parent Education Model (1968–1976)

	1968–1969	1969–1970	1970–1971	1971–1972	1972–1973	1973–1974	1974–1975	1975–1976
I. Parents								
A. How I See Myself			S	S	S	S	S	S
B. Home Environment Review	A	A	A	A	A	A		
C. Mother as Teacher			S					
D. Parent Education Cycle Evaluation				S	S	S		
E. Interview Schedule to Assess Attitudes toward Model				S	S	S		
F. Vertical Diffusion					S	S	S	
G. Volunteering				S	A	A	A	A
H. Parent Response Report					S	S	S	
I. Desirable Teaching Behavior Identification Task								
II. Parent educators								
A. Parent Educator Weekly Report	A	A	A	A	A	A	A	A
B. Taxonomy of Classroom Activities	A	A	A	A	A	A	A	A
C. How I See Myself	A	A	A	A	A			
D. Social Reaction Inventory	A	A	A	A	A	A		
E. Questionnaire to Assess Change in Parent Educators				A				
F. Desirable Teaching Behavior Identification Task					A	A	A	A

III. Teachers						
A. Purdue Teacher Opinionaire	A	A	A	A		
B. Teacher Practices Observation Record	A	A				
C. Reciprocal Category System	A	A				
D. Taxonomy of Affective Behavior	A	A				
E. Taxonomy of Cognitive Behavior	A	A				
F. Taxonomy of Classroom Behavior	A	A	A	A	A	A
G. Planning Home Visits & Building/Selecting Tasks	A		A		A	A
IV. Children						
A. Children's Self-Social Constructs Test	A	A				
B. I Feel-Me Feel		A	A	A		
		S	S	S		
C. Cincinnati Autonomy Test Battery		A	A			
D. Average Daily Attendance/Average Daily Membership (ADA/ADM)	A	A	A	A	A	A

[a] A = Administered in all communities; S = Administered in selected communities

the data collection period, but the evaluation of classroom teachers was not assigned a high priority after the first 2 years. Beginning in the 1970–1971 school year, more emphasis was placed on evaluating the performance of parents, and much attention was directed toward evaluating the participation and contributions of parents during the next 4 years. Generally, the instruments were administered for data collection either in *all* ten Parent Education Model sites (A) or in *selected* sites (S), which always numbered five or less.

REPRESENTATIVE EVALUATION RESULTS

It is not possible to summarize in this chapter all the research that evaluators performed on the Parent Education Model. Thus, the authors selected representative groups of studies to illustrate the range of approaches to evaluation, and they are presented below separately for parents, parent educators, classroom teachers, and children.[5]

Evaluation of Parents

Parents who participate in the Parent Education Model are expected to acquire information, skills, and attitudes that help them contribute more effectively to the education of their children. The extent to which these parents were assisted to develop new competencies was established by obtaining answers to two key questions: (a) Do parents who participate in the Parent Education Model become more effective teachers of their own children? (b) Do parents of children enrolled in the Parent Education Model volunteer to perform activities in classrooms, attend meetings of the PAC, and make decisions on the education of their children? Data pertaining to each question are presented in the following sections.

Do parents who participate in the Parent Education Model become more effective teachers of their own children? Evaluators pursued three approaches to obtain answers to this question: They (a) analyzed children's

---

[5] More space is devoted to reporting evaluation results for parents, as compared to the other three groups, for several reasons. First, although the federal guidelines for Follow Through emphasize the importance of parent involvement, there generally has been little effort to evaluate the contributions and performance of parents. Second, positive changes in parent behavior constitute a cluster of crucial, specific goals in the Parent Education Model, and success in achieving these goals is necessary in order to accomplish desired changes in the behavior of students. Third, due to the increasing resistance that classroom teachers expressed to the intensive evaluation of their performance during the period from 1968 to 1970, the sponsor decided reluctantly to reduce the effort in that area. Finally, the primary responsibility for evaluating the academic performance of children in classrooms was assigned to the Stanford Research Institute (SRI) in 1968 and was later assigned jointly to SRI and Abt Associates, Inc. The technical reports produced by these two organizations contain data that pertain to the Parent Education Model, and these findings are summarized briefly later in this section.

home-learning environments, (b) studied the manner which parents teach their children in laboratory settings, and (c) investigated "vertical diffusion" effects on the performance of younger children in families. The results of evaluation studies in each of these three areas of investigation are presented next.

1. Analyses of children's home learning environments. Garber (1970) extended previous work by Wolf (1964) and developed the Home Environment Review (HER). The HER has been used to analyze selected environmental process characteristics of children's home learning environments that are believed to encourage academic achievement. The HER is composed of nine sections, and each section consists of two parts. The first part of each section is a semistructured interview schedule that contains a number of questions. The parent educator administers these questions and any follow-up questions to the parent, who is usually the mother, and makes a written record of the responses. After the parent educator leaves the home, she reviews the record and completes the second part of each section, a rating scale on which the score may range from a low score of 1 to a high score of 5.

The nine areas of the home environment that are assessed by the HER, and a brief description of each, are as follows:

a. Expectations for Child's Schooling: highest level of schooling the parent expects the child to complete.
b. Awareness of Child's Development: extent of the parent's knowledge about the child's strengths and weaknesses and how they may be linked to the child's level of success in school.
c. Rewards for Intellectual Attainment: consistency of the parent's use of reward and punishment in teaching the child.
d. Press for Language Development: strength of the parent's effort to help the child develop correct language skills.
e. Availability and Use of Supplies for Language Development: extent to which books, magazines, newspapers, and reference materials are available to the child in the home.
f. Learning Opportunities Outside the Home: degree to which the parent provides learning experiences for the child in situations outside the home.
g. Materials for Learning in the Home: extent to which paper, pencils, and other materials are available to stimulate the child's learning experiences in the home.
h. Reading Press in the Home: frequency with which the parent uses library books and other reading materials to teach the child at home.
i. Parent's Trust in the School: degree to which the parent trusts school personnel and believes that they will treat the child fairly.

Researchers employed the HER in a number of studies. For example, Garber and Ware (1970, 1972) performed two studies to examine the interrelationships between the characteristics of children's home learning environments and their scores on other instruments that measure intellectual development. In their first study, the HER was administered in the homes of white, first grade children who were enrolled in Parent Education Follow Through classrooms. They reported moderate correlations between scores on the HER and these children's scores on the Peabody Picture Vocabulary Test (PPVT). In their second study, Garber and Ware administered the HER in the homes of 67 Mexican American and black 4-year-olds who were enrolled in Head Start classrooms. The purpose of the study was to examine some methodological characteristics of the HER and to explore the interrelationships between scores on the nine subscales of the HER and children's scores on Caldwell's Preschool Inventory (PSI).

Packer and Cage (1972) employed the HER to compare the home learning environments of children ($N = 541$) in large urban communities and children ($N = 541$) in small rural communities. All the children were enrolled in Parent Education Follow Through classrooms during the 1970–1971 school year, and the data were collected in a pre/post design near the beginning and end of the school year. The authors reported that the pretest scores of mothers in the large urban communities were significantly higher than those in the small rural communities on each of the nine HER Scales. The largest initial differences occurred on HER Scales 2, 4, 6, 8, and 9. Mothers in small rural communities made large gains during the school year on HER Scales 3 and 5. The gain scores for the two groups were virtually the same on HER Scales 1 and 7.

Greenwood, Breivogel, and Bessent (1972) analyzed data obtained from a total of 2282 parents. The HER was administered in a pre/post design during September and May of the 1970–1971 school year. Each parent had enrolled a child in a Parent Education classroom. The investigators reported that the comparison of the pre- and postscores revealed that from 30 to 36% of the parents had higher post test scores on six of the HER scales. These six scales, in the order of gains from highest to lowest, were 7, 8, 6, 2, 9, and 5. The results of these studies support the conclusion that participation in Follow Through may improve the home environments of families in areas assessed by the Home Environment Review.

2. Studies of parents teaching their children in laboratory settings. Ten Desirable Teaching Behaviors (DTBs) were listed previously in this chapter. Patricia P. Olmsted and her coworkers developed the Parent Education Cycle Evaluation (PECE) instrument to study how frequently parents use DTBs in teaching their children. The instrument has been developed through a number of phases over a period of several years. The

early work was inspired by the results of research on parent teaching styles conducted by Hess *et al.* (1968). In the current form of the PECE, parents are videotaped while they teach their children a matching faces activity and a book-reading activity. Parents select a comfortable method for teaching their child and they take as much time as needed to teach the tasks. Two observers view videotapes of the teaching sessions independently and record how frequently each parent uses the DTBs. The observers then compare their frequency counts and resolve any differences between them by jointly observing the tapes a third time to establish a consensus. The index of interobserver agreement is calculated by dividing the number of agreements by the total number of observations, and researchers attempt to maintain that index at levels of .80 or higher.

Two studies were conducted to compare groups of Follow Through and non-Follow Through mothers on their use of DTBs in teaching their children. Olmsted and Ware (1976) administered the PECE to a total of 24 Follow Through mothers and 24 non-Follow Through mothers located in two communities. The data were analyzed with a 2 × 2 factorial design in which the number of times parents used the DTBs served as the dependent variable. The results of a multivariate analysis of variance indicated that in both communities Follow Through mothers used the DTBs more frequently in teaching their children than did non-Follow Through mothers ($F = 2.26$, 7 and 78 *df*, $p < .05$). In further analyses, Olmsted (1977) compared the use of DTBs among one group of mothers who had participated in the Parent Education Model for at least one year to the use of DTBs among another group of comparable mothers who had never participated in the model. The results indicated that the mothers who had participated in the model used an average of 24.0 DTBs, as compared to an average of 14.5 DTBs for those who had not. This difference was statistically significant ($F = 4.35$, 1 and 105 *df*, $p < .05$).

Further analyses of the data from Olmsted's study revealed a relationship between the number of DTBs used by mothers and the performance of children on the Total Reading and Total Mathematics subtests of the Stanford Achievement Test. The results indicated that the number of DTBs used by parents correlated with the children's scores on achievement tests of both Reading ($r = .50$, $p < .001$) and Math ($r = .35$, $p < .05$). Thus, the results of studies using the PECE support the conclusions that parent educators were successful in increasing the use of DTBs among Follow Through mothers and that the use of DTBs by mothers appeared to have a positive effect upon children's levels of academic achievement.

3. Studies of vertical diffusion effects on the performance of younger children in families. When parents improve their ability to teach their own children, they also may use these skills to teach younger children in

the family. The term *vertical diffusion* designates this phenomenon, and it refers to the diffusion, or spreading, of the positive effects within the family to improve the performance of other children. The first evidence of vertical diffusion effects was presented by Klaus and Gray (1968), who reported that the younger siblings in families participating in the DARCEE Preschool Program had significantly higher scores on the Stanford-Binet than their counterparts in families that were not participating. Gilmer (1969) found that younger siblings in families that participated in DARCEE performed significantly better ($p < .001$) on a test that measured the contents of the DARCEE program when their mothers were committed to obtaining the benefits of the program. Gilmer, Miller, and Gray (1970) reported similar results from their study, which was performed over a period of 2 years. In a review of the results of the DARCEE program of research, Gray (1971) emphasized the importance of both the involvement of the total family in children's preschool education and the vertical diffusion concept.

Evaluators working in the Parent Education Model also performed a number of studies of vertical diffusion effects. For example, Ware, Organ, Olmsted, and Moreno (1974) studied the vertical diffusion phenomena in one community in which the Follow Through Parent Education Model, Head Start, and Home Base programs were implemented. (Home Base is a program in which paraprofessionals make weekly home visits to the homes of preschool children ranging in age from 8 mo to 4 years and provide a comprehensive range of instructional and informational services to the mothers whose children are enrolled). In the fall of 1972, a total of 86 children who were entering Head Start classrooms were classified into one of four groups: (a) children whose older siblings and mothers had participated in Follow Through and who themselves had participated in Home Base; (b) children whose older siblings and mothers had not participated in Follow Through, but who themselves had participated in Home Base; (c) children whose older siblings and mothers had participated in Follow Through, but who themselves had not participated in Home Base; and (d) children whose older siblings had not participated in Follow Through and who themselves had not participated in Home Base.

The revised edition of the Preschool Inventory (PSI) was administered to each of the 86 children. The PSI mean scores for the four groups were compared using analyses of covariance for group differences in SES, ethnicity, and age. This procedure yielded a significant F-ratio ($F = 3.46$, 3 and 77 df, $p < .05$), thus indicating the presence of at least one significant effect. More detailed comparisons between sets of adjusted mean scores were completed with Dunnett's Test. The only statistically significant difference among the four mean scores was obtained in the comparison between the Follow Through–Home Base group (Group 1), which had a mean score of

47.5, and the group of children who had no contacts with either Follow Through or Home Base (Group 4), which had a mean score of 39.6. The children in Group 1 had participated directly in Project Home Base and their older siblings had participated in Follow Through. Thus, the combined influence of these two programs had the most positive effect upon raising the level of skills assessed by the PSI.

Another noteworthy finding was obtained in the comparison of children from Group 3 with those in Group 4, whose mean scores on the PSI were 45.5 and 39.6, respectively. The mean difference failed to reach levels of statistical significance ($p > .05$), but the magnitude of the difference was nevertheless impressive. The children in Group 3 had not participated directly in Follow Through, but they apparently reaped benefits from the positive influences associated with their older siblings who had been enrolled in Follow Through. Generally, the results appeared to support the conclusion that mothers' participation in Follow Through had a substantial, positive effect on their ability to teach younger children. The researchers who reported these results stated that studies of vertical diffusion effects offered a promising approach to assessing the effects of family-centered programs of intervention.

The results of other studies by Moreno (1974) and Kinard (1974) also support the conclusion that vertical diffusion effects occur when parents are actively committed to participation in the Parent Education Model. These effects appear to result from positive changes in the parents' ability to teach their children at home, with the result that younger children in the family may receive even greater benefits than the older target children. The results of a number of studies suggest that parents must participate in the model about 2 years before the maximum positive effects of that participation are reflected in the improved academic performance of their children.

Do parents of children enrolled in the Parent Education Model volunteer to perform activities in classrooms, attend meetings of the PAC, and make decisions on the education of their children? The lack of parent involvement in education appears to be a major reason for the poor academic performance of many children. This problem was underscored by the following results reported by Greenwood et al. (1972) from their study of a total of 2282 parents of children enrolled in Parent Education Model classrooms during the 1970–1971 school year: (a) Only 22% of these parents had visited schools attended by their children; (b) only 6% of them had talked to the principal; and (c) only 7% of them had volunteered to participate in classroom activities.

For a number of reasons, including the results reported in the preceding paragraph, members of the sponsor's staff increased their efforts to encourage parents to participate in school activities during the 1973–1974 school year. For example, improvements were made in the procedures for collecting data on parents who volunteered for activities such as teaching, keeping records, and developing materials. Previously, this information was obtained from parents' self-reports that parent educators recorded in the PEWR protocols. In the fall of 1973, that data collection procedure was revised by constructing a Classroom Volunteer Sign-In Form and maintaining copies of that form in each classroom. Parents who volunteered to participate in classroom activities recorded their names, the names of their children, and the amount of time they actually spent in performing the activities. These data were useful in documenting the number of families that were represented by at least one volunteer during the school year. The results for 5 school years are presented in Table 3.2. Inspection of these data reveals (a) different levels of volunteering among parents in various communities; and (b) a general pattern of substantial improvement over the 5-year period in the proportion of families represented by at least one volunteer.

Data reported more recently by Gordon et al. (1978) also indicate that during the 4-year period from 1974 to 1977, the percentage of parents who volunteered in Follow Through classrooms increased substantially. These authors also reported an overall pattern of improvement in the frequency of parents' attendance at meetings of the PAC that focused on topics such as hiring of personnel, writing proposals, and reviewing actions taken by parents to support the future funding of their local Follow Through classrooms. In addition, parents also increased their participation in other activities such as attending Graduate Equivalency Diploma (GED) classes and making educational decisions.

Recently, ethnographic case studies were initiated in seven selected project sites to study the impact of the Parent Education Model upon schools

TABLE 3.2
Proportion of Families Represented by at Least One Classroom Volunteer

Site	1973–1974	1974–1975	1975–1976	1976–1977	1977–1978
1	—	.45	.62	.51	.76
2	.45	.72	.60	.67	.90
3	.29	.29	.27	.28	.36
4	.23	.39	.34	.49	.85
5	.42	.41	.39	.59	.80
6	.47	.64	.70	.62	.90
7	.32	.47	.33	.31	—
8	—	.61	.96	.68	.71
9	.43	.41	.38	.50	.56
10	.19	—	—	.84	.51

and the communities they serve and upon the career development of parents, paraprofessionals, and professionals. The data-gathering techniques employed in these case studies include focused and nondirective interviews of individuals in local communities, structured observations, and examination of unprocessed information from the extensive files of longitudinal data. Gordon *et al.* (1978) stated that the information gained in these ethnographic studies indicates that the benefits of the Parent Education Model have (*a*) helped many poor families become self-sufficient by providing jobs, education, and training; and (*b*) influenced the development of a number of new programs that provide needed services for preschool children, prenatal care for expectant mothers, services for the deaf, home visits for adolescent students, and other services for parents. In addition, many parents have become more active in their efforts to influence decisions made by local school boards and county commissions, and some who entered local elections were elected as members of school boards. Gordon (1978) stated that parents become better informed consumers of medical, dental, social, and psychological services and more effective advocates for improved delivery, integration, and coordination of these services.

Evaluation of Parent Educators

The primary function of parent educators is to make home visits. In classrooms, parent educators are expected to engage in meaningful activities that contribute both to the education of children and to their own professional growth. Hopefully, through their participation in the Parent Education Model, parent educators will acquire more positive feelings toward themselves and others. The questions and discussion presented below contain illustrations of some procedures employed to evaluate the peformance of parent educators.

What proportion of planned home visits are completed by parent educators? The primary source of information about home visits is the Parent Educator Weekly Report (PEWR) that parent educators complete after each home visit. A similar instrument was developed and used previously in the infant stimulation programs (Gordon, 1969). Over the years, the PEWR evolved into a multipurpose instrument that contains a large number of items. When a parent educator completes a PEWR, she records essential information about the task presented, the previous task and the child's reaction to it, participation by other members of the family in the instruction of the child, a description of important events that occurred during the home visit, decisions that were agreed upon, and so forth. The questions that comprise the total PEWR scale are reported by Gordon and Breivogel (1976).

Data from the PEWR have been used to calculate the total number and frequency of home visits. During the 1971–1972 school year, a total of 144,573 home visits were completed in 8654 homes, or an average of 16.7 visits per home. In 1972–1973, a total of 169,713 home visits were completed in 9392 homes, or an average of 18.1 visits per home. Beginning in the 1973–1974 school year, the primary objective was to complete at least 75% of planned home visits for at least 80% of the participating families. The results obtained during a 5-year period are shown in Table 3.3. There was a marked increase in the percentage of completed home visits from 1973–1974 to the following year, and a smaller increase in 1975–1976. A moderate increase occurred in 1976–1977, followed by a levelling off in 1977–1978, with eight of nine communities reporting results at or above the stated goal.

What activities do parent educators perform in classrooms? Soar and Kaplan (1968) developed the Taxonomy of Classroom Activities (TCA) to obtain information about the activities that parent educators perform in classrooms. In completing the TCA, observers record tallies to represent the behaviors and responsibilities that parent educators perform. Observation of many parent educators revealed that their duties in classrooms could be classified into the five categories presented in Figure 3.2. Typical behaviors are listed in each of the five categories. The TCA has been used to collect data since 1971. Observations are made on many occasions throughout the school year. The proportion of time spent in instructional activities is estimated by dividing the total number of "instructional tallies" by the total number of tallies. During 1971–1972, the TCA was administered in six programs. The results suggested that teachers spent 59% of their time in instructional activities; parent educators spent 28% of their time in similar activities. The data for 1972–1973 showed that 66% and 31% of the observed activities of teachers and parent educators, respectively, were instructional in nature. Beginning in 1973–1974, data were col-

TABLE 3.3
Proportion of Families Receiving at Least 75% of Planned Home Visits

Site	1973–1974	1974–1975	1975–1976	1976–1977	1977–1978
1	.49	.56	.53	.91	.96
2	.18	.59	.64	.93	1.00
3	.29	.54	.61	.86	.87
4	.10	.72	.83	.97	.97
5	.25	.62	.79	.88	.86
6	.20	.60	.72	.88	.89
7	.08	.22	.34	.55	—
8	.20	.52	.69	.96	.97
9	.23	.33	.53	.73	.76
10	.38	.81	.23	.98	.91

lected in nine programs. The proportion of instructional activities performed by parent educators in each community are shown in Table 3.4. Examination of the trend over the years suggests that efforts to increase the frequency of instructional activities in classrooms among parent educators were successful.

Is there an increase in feelings of "internal" locus of control and self-esteem among parent educators? Through their work, parent educators were expected to gain not only new skills, but also more confidence in their abilities to control the consequences of their own behavior and higher levels of self-esteem. The Social Reaction Inventory instrument was developed by Bilker (1970) to measure locus of control, and the How I See Myself (HISM) instrument was developed by Gordon (1966) to measure self-esteem. In a pre- and posttest design, both instruments were administered to all parent educators in the fall and spring during the 1971–1972 and 1972–1973 school years. The comparisons of parent educators' pre- and post- mean scores on the Social Reaction Inventory produced mixed and inconclusive results, which will not be summarized here. The HISM instrument purports to measure dimensions of self-esteem such as feelings of interpersonal adequacy, social attractiveness, competence, and so forth. The analyses of the 1971–1972 data revealed a significantly higher posttest mean score on the competence scale ($t = 3.84$, 376 df, $p < .01$). The MANOVA analyses performed on the data for 1972–1973 revealed that generally the posttest mean scores for that year were significantly higher than pretest mean scores ($F = 2.42$, 4 and 424 df, $p < .05$), but none of the univariate follow-up tests yielded significant results. Other analyses of data from the HISM revealed that all posttest mean scores in the spring of 1973 were higher than those for the spring of 1972, but none of the univariate mean differences was statistically significant (Greenwood, Gordon, Ware, Olmsted, & Kirkpatrick, 1972).

TABLE 3.4
Proportion of Instructional Activities Performed by Parent Educators

Site	1973–1974	1974–1975	1975–1976	1976–1977	1977–1978
1	.09	.38	.59	—	.82
2	.10	.57	.66	—	.89
3	.10	.41	.38	—	.66
4	.13	.65	.57	—	.47
5	.17	.54	.69	—	.82
6	.24	.60	.62	—	.86
7	—	.66	.63	—	—
8	.17	.59	.61	—	.82
9	.12	.62	.70	—	.70
10	.20	.38	—	—	.56

Evaluation of Teachers

The role of the classroom teacher was described previously in the section entitled "The Well-Implemented Model." During the 1968–1969 and 1969–1970 school years, evaluation researchers devoted a major effort to assessing the performance of teachers, including the development of five new observation instruments (See Table 3.1, Teachers: B, C, D, E, and G). A plan was devised for training parent educators to administer the observation instruments in classrooms and for communicating information obtained through these procedures to teachers. The plan appeared to have the potential for focusing the attention of both teachers and parent educators on significant components of the model and fostering cooperation between them in performing instructional and other activities in classrooms and homes. However, these hopes were never fully realized, because many teachers objected to the notion of being "evaluated" by paraprofessionals. Consequently, the observations were discontinued after the completion of the 1969–1970 school year. The effort did have some valuable payoff, however, since Soar and Soar (1972) used several of these five observation instruments in their comparative study of selected Follow Through programs.

In addition to the observation scales indicated in the preceding paragraph, other procedures also were employed to evaluate the performance of teachers. For example, the Purdue Teacher Opinionaire was administered to teachers from 1968 to 1972. Data from that instrument provided helpful information concerning teachers' perceptions and feelings about their participation in the Parent Education Model. Beginning in the 1972–1973 school year, each Follow Through teacher was requested to submit a schedule that indicated when the teacher would meet with parent educators during the school year to plan and select home teaching tasks and to plan home visits. The purpose of this procedure was to insure that each teacher spent at least 1½ hr per week in these activities with each parent educator. Random checking procedures indicated that the schedules were implemented as planned about 80% of the time. Finally, Cline (1974) reported the results of analyses of data on teacher attitudes obtained through the national longitudinal evaluation. He stated that teachers in the Parent Education Model placed a greater value on involving parents in the education of children than did teachers in other Follow Through models or teachers in non-Follow-Through comparison classrooms.

Evaluation of Children

Improving the performance of children is the ultimate goal of those persons who designed the Parent Education Model. Intensive evaluations of the model's effectiveness in improving the affective and cognitive development of children enrolled in Parent Education classrooms were conducted by researchers employed by the Stanford Research Institute and Abt Associates, by persons in many local school districts, and by members of the sponsor's evaluation staff. Some of the procedures employed and the findings are summarized briefly here.

Affective Domain. A number of investigators have attempted to measure the impact of Follow Through models on the affective characteristics of children. For example, Cline (1974) analyzed data collected in the national longitudinal evaluation and concluded that levels of achievement motivation and internal locus of control were higher among children enrolled in Parent Education classrooms, as compared with the scores of children enrolled in non-Follow-Through classrooms. Efforts by members of the sponsor's evaluation staff to measure children's self-concept and regularity of school attendance produced mixed results. Yeats and Bentley (1970) developed the I Feel-Me Feel (IFMF) instrument to measure children's self-concept, and data were collected over the 3-year period from 1971 to 1974. But the results have been inconclusive, and the general experience with the instrument has not been encouraging. Llabre, Ware, and Newell (1977) reported that the psychometric characteristics of the IFMF instrument appeared to be different for children in different ethnic groups. They were unable to replicate the original factor structure reported by Yeats and Bentley (1971) in any of the ethnic groups included in their study. Furthermore, the factor structures identified in various ethnic goups were not comparable. Consequently, no data from the IFMF instrument are reported here.

The difficulties encountered in attempts to measure the self-concepts of young children are typical of problems that usually occur in attempts to measure affective characteristics among primary-age children. In fact, there are few reported instances of successful measurement of self-concept, or other affective characteristics, among children between the ages of 5 and 8 years. Most of these attempts have led to nonsignificant results and/or to severe instrumentation problems (Coller, 1971; Shavelson, Habner, & Stanton, 1976).

Members of the evaluation research group hypothesized that if children enjoyed their attendance in Parent Education Follow Through classrooms, they might attend school more frequently than comparable children in regular school programs. Therefore, during the 1975–1976 school year, comparative attendance data were collected in a total of seven communities that implemented the Parent Education Model. The ratio of Average Daily Attendance to Average Daily Membership (ADA/ADM) was calculated separately for Follow Through and non-Follow-Through groups in each community. In five of the seven communities, children's attendance records were better in Parent Education Follow Through classrooms than in comparison classrooms, but none of the mean differences was statistically significant.

Cognitive Domain. Data pertaining to the cognitive attainments of children enrolled in Parent Education classrooms are presented in a number of sources, including many lengthy technical reports on the results of the national longitudinal evaluation and reports prepared by members of the Parent Education evaluation staff. Some representative findings from these sources are presented here.

1. Results from the national longitudinal evaluation. Researchers employed by Abt Associates, Inc. (Cline, 1974; Stebbins, St. Pierre, Proper, Anderson, & Cerva, 1977) stated that their analyses of data from the national longitudinal evaluation indicated that the Parent Education Model produced positive results in raising the achievement levels of children. However, these writers also stated that the characteristics of children enrolled in Parent Education Follow Through classrooms differed in a number of ways from those enrolled in non-Follow-Through comparison classrooms. For example, the Follow Through children had lower initial scores on readiness tests when they entered kindergarten, they represented fewer intact families, and their families had lower levels of income. Generally, it appeared that the children in Parent Education classrooms were substantially more disadvantaged than those in comparison classrooms. Researchers attempted to implement statistical controls for these initial differences, but McLean, Ware, and McClave (1976) and others have demonstrated that analysis of covariance techniques may produce misleading results when the initial differences between groups are large. It was also difficult to document the extent to which a number of other effects, such as vertical diffusion, may have influenced the outcomes of comparisons between Follow Through and non-Follow-Through children.

Several groups of researchers analyzed data from achievement tests administered during the national longitudinal evaluation of Follow Through in order to make comparisons among various models. For example, House, Glass, McLean, and Walker (1978) reported the results of two analyses of these data in which increases in pupil achievement test scores were compared across 13 Follow Through models. In one study, the Parent Education Model ranked third and in the other study it ranked fourth. The Parent Education Model was 1 of 9 models included in Kennedy's (1978) analyses of achievement test data from the national evaluation. It was also 1 of 8 models included in Bereiter and Kurland's (1978) analyses of these data.

Each of the four studies identified in the preceding paragraph produced a set of results that differed from the others. In some instances the differences were great, in other instances they were small. Some of the differences in the results appear to have emerged from the different analytic techniques and covariates employed in the various studies. In addition, data deleted from analyses conducted in some studies were incorporated in analyses performed in other studies. Furthermore, the data from the national longitudinal evaluation may be grouped according to communities, schools, classes, or individual pupils. Consequently, the units of analysis employed were not the same in all studies. Apparently, a definitive analysis of the data from the national evaluation has not yet been performed, and it may be quite some time before such an analysis is possible. The controversies that have surrounded the national longitudinal evaluation of Follow Through are described elsewhere in this volume and will not be repeated here. Readers who wish to delve more deeply into the complex issues associated with the national evaluation should consult the sources cited in the two preceding paragraphs, as well as appropriate sources cited by other authors in this volume.

2. Reports prepared by members of the sponsor's evaluation staff. In 1972, evaluators in the Parent Education Model began to attempt some coordination with local school districts in the collection of achievement test data. One alternative was to select a single test battery and administer it to children in each of the 10 Parent Education sites. But there were practical limits to the amount of testing that could be performed without disrupting the educational process in classrooms. Because there was already an intensive program of testing, evaluators were reluctant to add an additional burden on teachers and children in Parent Education classrooms. Consequently, they attempted to use data from existing testing programs in local school districts. But that decision produced a number of problems for the evaluation staff, because various districts provided data from different test batteries that were administered at different points in time. Furthermore, these data were expressed in bewildering combinations of raw scores, scaled scores, percentile ranks, and stanines. In addition, some school districts were administering outdated tests, and others were using tests that were inappropriate for the grade level of children who were tested. After much effort, some of these problems were resolved, but then it became evident that school personnel in many communities were unable to identify and/or administer tests to a sample of comparable non-Follow-Through children. Due to the difficulties encountered in the attempts to use achievement test data collected by local school districts, none of these results are reported here.

The evaluation researchers also completed a number of analyses of data collected in "within group" designs to determine whether children's scores on achievement tests might be linked to the completion of planned home visits. The procedure was to conduct a series of regression analyses on data collected in two communities. Posttest data were regressed on pretest data, socioeconomic status of the child's family, sex, and number of home visits completed, with the number of completed home visits entered last.

Among kindergarten children, analyses of data collected from one community failed to establish the hypothesized link, but analyses of data collected from the second site yielded positive results ($F = 5.88$, 1 and 82 df, $p < .05$). Among first grade students, separate regression analyses of data obtained from the two communities supported the conclusion that the number of completed home visits made a unique contribution to explaining mean differences in children's achievement test scores. The relationships in both these studies were statistically significant at the .05 level. Similar results were achieved in two studies of students enrolled in second and third grade classrooms, respectively. In both studies, the relationships were significant at the .05 level (Ware & Llabre, 1977). Thus, these results support the conclusion that the completion of planned home visits is a vital link between instructional activities in the homes of children and their academic success in classrooms.

In summary, this section contains descriptions of a range of approaches to evaluating the performance of parents, parent educators, teachers, and children who participated in the Parent Education Model. There were no precedents for evaluating a home–school partnership approach to educating children when Follow Through began. Consequently, it was necessary to develop a large number of new instruments and procedures in order to study the processes and outcomes of the model. Many of these yielded information that was useful for guiding program development activities, but some did not. The knowledge gained from experiences in program implementation, instrument development, and evaluation is presented in the hope that it will be helpful to others who wish to explore the enormous potential that exists when parents participate as full partners with school personnel in the education of children.

Lessons Learned

The purpose of this section is to summarize three sets of conclusions derived from experiences in Follow Through. These conclusions pertain to (a) the support for parent participation in education; (b) the roles of individuals who participate in intervention research to improve education;

and (c) the procedures for implementing large-scale educational research
projects.

SUPPORT FOR PARENT PARTICIPATION
IN EDUCATION

When Gordon and his colleagues began in the early 1960s to emphasize
the contributions that parents can make to the education of children, they
were almost alone in advocating this approach. Now, there is increasing
support at federal, state, and local levels for participation by parents in
education. Thus, they are pleased with the results of their efforts to serve as
a catalyst for promoting public awareness and acceptance of the opportunities and necessity for involving parents in the education of children.

Evidence of the burgeoning support for parent participation in education
can be seen in many recent developments. Parent involvement procedures
similar to the ones developed in the Parent Education Follow Through
Model are being enacted in a number of educational programs funded at
federal and state levels of government. For example, the guidelines for
Titles I, III, V, and VII of the Elementary and Secondary Education Act
(ESEA) have required the formation of parent advisory committees for
many years. Recently, the role of these committees has been more clearly
defined, expanded, and strengthened. Official federal policies also have
strongly supported meaningful participation by parents in Head Start programs, especially those in Home Start.

On July 7, 1978, the United States Office of Education issued a Request
for Proposals (RFP) on the topic, "Study of Parental Involvement in
Various Programs." The stated purpose of the RFP (number 78-79) was to
invite proposals that "take a broader view of parental involvement and
seek to describe the wide variability in activities in which parents can participate in the educational process with a view toward identifying those activities or combinations of activities which would seem to have the greatest
benefits [p. 1]." The four projects targeted for study in the RFP were Title I
of ESEA, the Emergency School Aid Act, the Bilingual Project of ESEA
Title VII, and Project Follow Through. (The contract was awarded to the
Systems Development Corporation.) In another noteworthy development at the national level, the Parent-Teacher Association recently expanded its efforts to involve parents in educational decision-making activities,
including evaluation.

In addition to favorable developments at the national level, many states
have enacted legislation that mandates increased parent participation in
schools. Florida, Hawaii, Colorado, and Maryland are among the states in
which legislators have mandated the establishment of school advisory committees in school districts (Greenwood, Breivogel, & Jester, 1977). Since the

Parent Education Model was developed at the University of Florida, the members of the IDHR have been especially interested in legislation and programmatic developments that have encouraged greater parent participation in Florida. In 1973, legislators in Florida authorized the formation of school advisory committees at the local district level (Florida Statutes, Chapter 73-338). In addition, they enacted the Early Childhood Education Act (Florida Statutes, Chapter 75-284), which requires school districts to plan and implement early childhood and basic skills development programs that involve parents as teacher aides, parent volunteers, foster grandparents, and paraprofessionals. The most important provision of the Act advocates the use of parents in the classroom and for home visitations and parent education in order to strengthen the role of the family and the home in the education process and to develop a cooperative relationship between the family, the home, and the school.

In 1978, a Select Committee appointed by the Florida legislature recommended that "the legislature should empower school advisory committees to participate in the selection of school principals and to help develop criteria for the selection of school level personnel [Cunningham, 1978, prologue, p. 10]." The Select Committee Report also recommended the formation of a statewide school advisory committee and the appropriation of funds to be made available to school districts to assist them in improving their school advisory committees. Other attempts currently are being made to increase effective involvement of parents in a number of educational programs in Florida, including the Florida Migratory Child Compensatory Program and the Health and Rehabilitative Services Program. Many other examples of encouraging progress in implementing approaches that embody the objectives of the Parent Education Model could be cited to support the conclusion that *the notion of involving parents in education has clearly come of age.*

ROLES IN EDUCATIONAL INTERVENTION RESEARCH

In order to be successful, intervention research performed in schools requires the cooperative participation of parents, school personnel, and other local citizens. Some comments about the roles that individuals in each of these groups can fulfill are presented here.

Role of Parents

Efforts to involve parents are more likley to be successful when parents are included at the beginning of such attempts in writing proposals and selecting key personnel. When this happens, parents know that their contributions are valued and both school personnel and other local citizens know that parents will have a significant voice in all phases of decision making. The most successful Parent Education Model programs have been those in which parents have had a major role in selecting the participating school administrators and teachers. It is difficult for many school personnel to initially accept parents as full partners and decision makers in education. But most school personnel do learn eventually to trust parents and to welcome, indeed to actively seek, their participation in the education of children. Furthermore, this acceptance and trust is extended to parents at all socioeconomic levels. Such relationships in no way oppose the prerogatives of school boards and school administrators to make decisions that are necessary, even when those decisions may not be entirely supported by parents. In addition, members of school boards, teachers, school personnel, and sponsors of Follow Through models should state their positions on issues and enter into discussions with parents in order to explain their perceptions of the options for solving problems and the probable consequences of each option for decision making. Efforts to involve parents as educational decision makers are time consuming, but the rewards are great.

Roles of Teachers, Principals, and Local Citizens

Many initial expectancies for the performance of teachers were unrealistic. For example, it was assumed that teachers could quickly adapt their knowledge and experience to the instruction of parent educators or parent volunteers in correct procedures for teaching learning tasks to parents during home visits. In addition, it was thought that teachers who learned the criteria for developing good home learning tasks would be able to generate many new learning tasks on their own initiative. In fact, both assumptions were wrong. Consequently, in-service training procedures were developed to instruct teachers on how to conduct planning sessions with parent educators and how to use the Desirable Teaching Behaviors as guides for developing and teaching home learning tasks. Even then, the Parent Education Cycle (teacher presents a learning task to the parent educator, who teaches the task to a parent, who teaches the task to the child) sometimes contained "slippage," and tasks were not delivered to children as originally intended. The consultants provided 2 days of in-service training per month, but this approach was more successful among those teachers and parent educators who had previously attended summer workshops lasting 2 to 3 weeks.

Efforts to implement the Parent Education Model were far more efficient when leaders in school systems and local communities were openly supportive. Effective relationships with members of school boards, superintendents, assistant superintendents, directors of other federally funded programs, and school principals are necessary to the success of intervention programs such as Follow Through. Persuasion and effective communication with community leaders are also essential. Face-to-face contacts with them, dissemination of information through local media, and presentations to meetings of civic organizations should begin early in the program and continue in a systematic fashion.

The school principal is the person who can contribute the most facilitation or obstruction to the development of an innovative educational program. Generally, the implementation of the Parent Education Model proceeded more smoothly when the rank of local program coordinators was higher than that of principals of schools in which Parent Education classrooms were conducted. When the rank of project coordinators was below or equal to that of principals, persuasion or appealing to a higher ranking administrator appeared to be the only methods for overcoming opposition from principals. The tension points included such issues as whether parent educators would be permitted to complete planned home visits or required to perform duties exclusively in classrooms.

IMPLEMENTING LARGE-SCALE EDUCATIONAL RESEARCH PROJECTS

Some lessons derived from the Follow Through experience may be used to improve the implementation of large-scale projects in educational research. Planners and administrators of such projects at federal and state levels may wish to consider the five suggestions stated here in their current and future efforts to improve educational opportunities for children.

1. All project services should be made available to all children in target schools. Funds and services in some federally funded educational projects have been allocated for only part of the children enrolled in target schools and classrooms. This policy appears to be unwise, since some children in a classroom may appear to benefit more than others from the program. According to the Follow Through guidelines, some comprehensive services could be provided only to qualified children from low-income families, but there was no such restriction on providing instructional services. Consequently, the same instructional services were provided to all children enrolled in all Parent Education Follow Through classrooms. For example, parent educators visited the homes of all children enrolled in these classrooms. This approach contributed to positive perceptions and constructive interactions among parents and school personnel and encouraged them to accept and support the model.

2. Open decision-making processes should be practiced. Members of the sponsor's staff maintained a central focus for program development in each local project, but they also encouraged continuous input from other par-

ticipants. The flow of information was sustained by disseminating written reports, including evaluation reports, and by conducting regular meetings and informal briefings. Programs were modified through open decision-making processes on matters pertaining to the statement of program objectives, the formulation of letters of agreement, and the discussion of issues and problems in evaluation. Conferences were conducted at the University of Florida, and frequent communication was maintained among persons in local communities, liaison officers, and consultants.

3. Participants in local programs should become increasingly autonomous. The concepts of planned variation and sponsorship guided the implementation of education intervention research in Project Follow Through. Within this framework, the sponsor has a dual responsibility as instigator and facilitator to assist individuals in local communities in conducting their programs. When the sponsor's function is performed well over a period of several years, individuals in local communities should develop the ability to operate their Parent Education programs independently. It is difficult to clearly define either the time required or the developmental stages in this maturing process, but there are observable cues that signal progress toward maturity.

The route that individuals travel and the time they require to reach autonomy in conducting a Parent Education Model program probably will be unique in each community, because real differences in attitudes, resources, and general circumstances exist among communities. For example, initial attitudes toward home visits, in-service training, evaluation activities, participation in the PAC, parent volunteering, and so forth differ greatly from one community to another. These differences also may become linked to the effects of unanticipated local problems, including teacher strikes, court-ordered busing, and natural disasters such as tornadoes, and floods. Due to these and other complexities, an educational model cannot be implemented in precisely the same way in different communities. Furthermore, the characteristics of mature programs are likely to differ from one community to another.

Most Follow Through sponsors attempted to use the same implementation patterns in each community they served. However, none of the sponsors suspected in 1968 that Follow Through would operate for more than a decade, and plans were made on a year-to-year basis. If funding had been provided for a period of several years, perhaps the sponsors could have conducted a needs assessment prior to the implementation phase in each community. They could have used this information to vary patterns of implementation according to the characteristics of each community. Such an approach might have encouraged individuals in each community to achieve autonomy more quickly, and members of the sponsors' staffs would have felt less pressure to implement the same "pure intervention model" in all their project communities. Nevertheless, some implementation dimensions in the Parent Education Model, such as the requirement that two parent educators in each classroom make weekly visits to the homes of children, must be uniform in all communities. To what extent should individuals in local communities be encouraged to vary implementation patterns, and to what extent should model sponsors seek to maintain the same implementation patterns in all communities they serve? Such issues will doubtless continue to evoke much discussion in large-scale efforts to conduct social intervention research.

4. Sponsorship and planned variation are effective strategies for improving the nation's schools. One of the most important characteristics of Follow Through is the notion that model sponsors who are based in universities and regional educational laboratories can work effectively with school systems that adopt a particular sponsor's model for improving educational opportunities for children. Because local school districts must agree to accept the Follow Through guidelines, including the regulations concerning Policy Advisory Committees and other facets of model implementation, the model sponsors have been required to function as "institutional change agents." Under the best of circumstances, changing educational institutions is difficult work with uncertain outcomes. It is especially difficult for individuals who are part of an educational institution to change that institution. The model sponsors are insiders in the sense that they accepted responsibilities to work with local educators, but they are outsiders in the sense that their offices are located elsewhere. This arrangement appears to be a promising way to accomplish desirable changes in schools. The possibilities for effecting these changes might be further enhanced if local education agencies agreed to make a financial commitment when they accepted the project guidelines.

Two other lessons about sponsorship may be derived from the Follow Through experience. The first lesson is that the group that can be most effective in developing and implementing a longitudinal intervention model is the group that originates the model. If another group of individuals had been asked to implement a model originated by one of the Follow Through sponsors, the results would probably have been less productive. Thus, in future large-scale research efforts, those who originate innovative models should also be the ones who implement them. The second lesson is that the policy of separate funding for model sponsors and school systems is a wise one. Under these circumstances, sponsors and school systems are more likely to work together on an equalitarian and cooperative basis during the implementation process.

5. Effective procedures for evaluating educational programs can be

developed. Many new evaluation instruments may have to be developed in order to support the implementation of an innovative educational model. There has been substantial progress in developing new instruments for evaluating processes and outcomes in some areas of the Parent Education Model, but difficult problems have been encountered in attempts to develop instruments in other areas. More intensive efforts to develop good instruments are required in order to measure children's affective processes and higher-order cognitive processes of the sort identified by Piaget and others. Existing instruments in these areas are generally unsatisfactory, and attempts to develop alternatives were generally unsuccessful. Nevertheless, additional attempts should be made.

Three other important lessons about evaluation may be stated briefly. First, school administrators will support research activities in schools, if they believe that the results may be useful. Second, it is difficult to collect comparison data in evaluation research. Even when non-Follow-Through classrooms were available, strong administrative support often was necessary in order to actually collect the data. Third, paraprofessionals may perform some types of data collection, such as the administration of the Parent Educator's Weekly Report (PEWR). However, graduate students, substitute teachers, or other individuals not directly involved in implementation should be employed when the data collection procedures require high levels of reliability and/or interobserver agreement.

In conclusion, the Follow Through experience yielded many lessons, including a profound respect for the difficulties that confront school personnel and parents in their efforts to improve education. There is much good will in both groups, but also much misunderstanding and suspicion between them. One of the most important accomplishments of the Parent Education Model is that it provided school personnel and parents a unique opportunity to interact under the aegis of the model sponsor. The combination of planned variation and sponsorship in Project Follow Through represents a powerful approach to changing school environments, especially when it is linked to an understanding of the age-old lessons that meaningful changes in education usually occur slowly, are sometimes painful, and always must be accomplished one step at a time.

Acknowledgments

Many individuals contributed to the accomplishments of the Parent Education Follow Through Model during the past decade. The work would not have been possible without the participation of thousands of parents, parent educators, teachers, and administrators in 11 school systems. In addition, large numbers of dedicated faculty and staff members at the

University of Florida and the University of North Carolina at Chapel Hill made essential contributions. Most of all, the Parent Education Model is the expression of the genius and leadership of Ira J. Gordon, an inspiring and innovative national leader in education. His untimely death in 1978 caused a deep sense of loss among all those who knew of his unique contributions, but he is missed especially by all those individuals who worked with him and loved him.

References

Bereiter, C. A., & Kurland, M. *Were some Follow Through models more effective than others?* Paper presented at the meeting of the American Educational Research Association, Toronto, Canada, March 1978.
Bilker, L. M. *The social reaction inventory.* Gainesville, Fla.: University of Florida, 1970.
Bloom, B. S. *Stability and change in human characteristics.* New York: Wiley, 1964.
Bradley, R. H., & Caldwell, B. M. Home observation for measurement of the home environment: A validation study of screening efficiency. *American Journal of Mental Deficiency,* 1977, *81,* 417–420.
Bronfenbrenner, U. Is early intervention effective? In B. Z. Friedlander, G. M Sterrett, & G. E. Kirk (Eds.), *Exceptional infant,* (Vol. 3). New York: Brunner/Mazel, 1975. Pp. 449–475.
Caldwell, B. M. The effects of infant care. In M. L. Hoffman & L. W. Hoffman (Eds.), *Review of child development research* (Vol. 1). New York: Russell Sage Foundation, 1964. Pp. 9–88.
Caldwell, B. M., Heider, J., & Kaplan, B. *The inventory of Home Stimulation.* Paper presented at the meeting of the American Psychological Association, New York, September 1966.
Caldwell, B. M., & Richmond, J. The children's center — A microcosmic health, education, and welfare unit. In L. Dittman (Ed.), *Early child care: The new perspectives.* New York: Atherton, 1968. Pp. 326–358.
Cicirelli, V. G., Cooper, W., & Granger, R. *The impact of Head Start: An evaluation of the effects of the Head Start experience on children's cognitive and affective development.* Athens, Ohio: Westinghouse Learning Corporation and Ohio University, 1969.
Cline, M. G. *Education as experimentation: Evaluation of the Follow Through planned variation model. Volume II–A: Early effects of Follow Through.* (Final Report. OEC-0-72-5221.) Cambridge, Mass.: ABT Associates, Inc., 1974.
Coleman, J. S. Methods and results in the IEA studies of effects of school on learning. *Review of Educational Research,* 1975, *45,* 355–386.
Coleman, J. S., Campbell, E., Mood, A., Weinfeld, E., Hobson, C., York, R., & McPartland, J. *Equality of educational opportunity.* Washington, D.C.: U.S. Government Printing Office, 1966.
Coller, A. R. *The assessment of self-concept in early childhood education.* Urbana, Ill.: ERIC Clearinghouse in Early Childhood Education, 1971.
Cunningham, L. L. *Improving education in Florida: A reassessment.* Tallahassee, Fla.: Joint Committee on Public Schools of the Florida Legislature, 1978.
Davé, R. J. *The identification and measurement of environmental process variables that are related to educational achievement.* Unpublished doctoral dissertation, University of Chicago, 1963.
Deutsch, C. P. Social class and child development. In B. M. Caldwell & R. N. Ricciuti (Eds.), *Child development* (Vol. 3). Chicago: University of Chicago, 1973. Pp. 233–282.
Deutsch, M., Katz, I., & Jensen, A. R. *Social class, race, and psychological development.* New York: Holt, Rinehart, & Winston, 1968.

Douglas, I. W. *The home and the school: A study of ability and attainment in the primary school.* London: MacGibbon & Kee, 1964.

Elardo, R., Bradley, R. H., & Caldwell, B. M. The relation of infants' home environments to mental test performance from 6 to 36 months: A longitudinal analysis. *Child Development,* 1975, *46,* 71-76.

Elardo, R., Bradley, R. H., & Caldwell, B. M. A longitudinal study of the relation of infants' home environments to language development at age three. *Child Development,* 1977, *48,* 595-603.

Garber, M. *The home environment review.* Gainesville, Fla.: Institute for the Development of Human Resources, 1970.

Garber, M., & Ware, W. B. *A relationship between measures of the home environment and intelligence scores.* Paper presented at the meeting of the American Psychological Association, Miami Beach, September 1970.

Garber, M., & Ware, W. B. The home environment as a predictor of school achievement. *Theory into Practice,* 1972, *11,* 190-195.

Gilmer, B. R. Intra-family diffusion of selected cognitive skills as a function of educational stimulation. *DARCEE Papers and Reports,* 1969, *3,* 1-4.

Gilmer, B. R., Miller, J. O., & Gray, S. W. Intervention with mothers and young children: A study of intrafamily effects. *DARCEE Papers and Reports,* 1970, *4,* 11-13.

Gordon, I. J. *Studying the child in school.* New York: John Wiley & Sons, 1966.

Gordon, I. J. *Early child stimulation through parent education.* (Final Report to the Children's Bureau, Department of Health, Education, and Welfare, PHS-R-306.) Gainesville, Fla.: University of Florida, 1969.

Gordon, I. J. *Parent involvement in compensatory education.* Urbana, Ill.: University of Illinois Press, 1970.

Gordon, I. J. *What does research say about the effects of parent involvement on schooling?* Distinguished lecture presented at the meeting of the Association for Supervision and Curriculum Development, San Francisco, March 1978.

Gordon, I. J., & Breivogel, W. G. (Eds.). *Building effective home/school relationsips.* Boston: Allyn & Bacon, 1976.

Gordon, I. J., Olmsted, P. P., Rubin, R. I., & True, J. H. *Continuity between home and school: Aspects of parent involvement in Follow Through.* Paper presented at the meeting of Society for Research in Child Development, Atlanta, April 1978.

Gray, S. W. Children from three to ten: The early training project. *DARCEE Papers and Reports,* 1971, *5,* 3-7.

Greenwood, G. E., Breivogel, W. G., & Bessent, H. Some promising approaches to parent involvement. *Theory into Practice,* 1972, *11,* 183-189.

Greenwood, G. E., Breivogel, W. F., & Jester, R. E. Citizen advisory committees. *Theory into Practice,* 1977, *16,* 12-16.

Greenwood, G. E., Breivogel, W. F., & Olmsted, P. P. *A study of changes in parents employed as paraprofessionals in a home intervention Follow Through program.* Paper presented at the meeting of the American Educational Research Association, Chicago, April 1974.

Greenwood, G. E., Gordon, I. J., Ware, W. B., Olmsted, P. P., & Kirkpatrick, P. K. *Assistance to local Follow Through programs.* (Annual Report, OEG - 0-8-522394 - 3991). Gainesville, Fla.: University of Florida, 1972.

Hamilton, M. L. Evaluation of a parent and child center program. *Child Welfare,* 1972, *51,* 248-258.

Hess, R. D., & Shipman, V. C. Early experience and the socialization of cognitive modes in children. *Child Development,* 1965, *36,* 869-886.

Hess, R. D., Shipman, V. C., Brophy, J. E., & Bear, R. M. *Cognitive environments of urban preschool children.* Chicago: University of Chicago Press, 1968.

House, E. R., Glass, G. V., McLean, L. D., & Walker, D. F. No simple answer: Critique of the Follow Through evaluation. *Harvard Educational Review,* 1978, *48,* 128–160.

Hunt, J. M. *Intelligence and experience.* New York: Ronald Press, 1961.

Jencks, C., Smith, M., Acland, H., Bane, M. J., Cohen, D., Gintis, H., Heyns, B., & Michelson, S. *Inequality: A reassessment of the effects of family and schooling in America.* New York: Basic Books, 1972.

Kennedy, M. M. Findings from the Follow Through planned variation study. *Educational Researcher,* 1978, *7,* 3–11.

Kinard, J. E. *The effect of parent involvement on achievement of first and second siblings who have attended Head Start and Follow Through programs.* Unpublished doctoral dissertation, Florida State University, 1974.

Klaus, R., & Gray, S. The early training project for disadvantaged children: A report after five years. *Monographs of the Society for Research in Child Development,* 1968, *33,* (4, Serial No. 120).

Llabre, M. M., Ware, W. B., & Newell, J. M. *A factor analytic study of the self-concept of children in three ethnic groups.* Paper presented at the meeting of the National Council of Measurement in Education, New York, April 1977.

McLean, J. E., Ware, W. B., & McClave, J. T. *How analysis of covariance can yield misleading results in educational experiments — A Monte Carlo study.* Paper presented at the meeting of the American Statistical Association, Atlanta, March 1976.

Miller, G. W. Educational opportunity and the home. *Longman sociology of education.* London: Longman Group, 1975.

Moore, I. Language and intelligence: A longitudinal study of the first eight years. *Human Development,* 1968, *11,* 1–24.

Moreno, P. R. *Vertical diffusion effects within black and Mexican-American families participating in the Florida parent education model.* Unpublished doctoral dissertation, University of Florida, 1974.

Mosteller, F., & Moynihan, D. P. *On equality of educational opportunity.* New York: Random House, 1972.

Olmsted, P. P. *The relationship of program participation and parental teaching behavior with children's standardized achievement measures in two program sites.* Unpublished doctoral dissertation, University of Florida, 1977.

Olmsted, P. P., & Ware, W. B. Effects of a parent education program on parental teaching program. Gainesville, Fla.: University of Florida, 1976.

Packer, A. B., & Cage, B. N. Changing attitudes of mothers toward themselves and education. *Theory into Practice,* 1972, *11,* 163–170.

Rupp, J. C. *Helping the child to cope with school.* Groningen, Netherlands: Wolters-Noordhoof, 1969.

Shavelson, R. J., Habner, J. J., & Stanton, G. C. Self-concept: Validation of construct interpretations. *Review of Educational Research,* 1976, *43,* 407–441.

Soar, R. S., & Kaplan, L. *Taxonomy of classroom activities.* Gainesville, Fla.: University of Florida, 1968. (mimeo)

Soar, R. S., & Soar, R. M. An empirical analysis of selected Follow Through programs: An example of a process approach to evaluation. In I. J. Gordon (Ed.), *Early childhood education, 1972 National Society for the Study of Education Yearbook.* Chicago: University of Chicago Press, 1972. Pp. 229–259.

Stebbins, L. B., St. Pierre, R. G., Proper, E. C., Anderson, R. B., & Cerva, T. R. *Education as experimentation: A planned variation model. Vol. IV-A: An evaluation of Follow Through.* Cambridge, Mass.: Abt Associates, 1977. (Also issued by the U.S. Office of

Education as *National evaluation: Patterns of effects*, [Vol. II-A of the Follow Through planned variation experiment series].)

Van Doorninck, W. J., Caldwell, B. M., Wright, C., & Frankenberg, W. K. *The inventory of Home stimulation as a predictor of school competence.* Paper presented at the meeting of the Society for Research in Child Development, Denver, April 1975.

Ware, W. B., & Llabre, M. M. *Multiple regression studies of parental program variables and measures of children's achievement.* Unpublished manuscript, University of Florida, 1977.

Ware, W. B., Organ, D., Olmsted, P. P., & Moreno, P. R. Vertical diffusion in a family-centered intervention program. *Childhood Education*, 1974, *51*, 111–115.

Wolf, D. M. *The identification and measurement of environmental process variables related to intelligence.* Unpublished doctoral dissertation, University of Chicago, 1964.

Yeats, P. O., & Bentley, E. L. I Feel-Me Feel. Atlanta: Supplementary Education Center, 1970.

Yeats, P. O., & Bentley, E. L. *The development of a non-verbal measure to assess the self-concept of young and low-verbal children.* Paper presented at the meeting of the American Educational Research Association, New York, February 1971.

WESLEY C. BECKER
SIEGFRIED ENGELMANN
DOUGLAS W. CARNINE
W. RAY RHINE **4**

Direct Instruction Model [1]

[1] Preparation of this chapter was supported by USOE Grant GOO7507234, but no endorsement of its content by the federal government should be inferred.

Parts of this chapter are summarized from Becker (Ed.), *Review of Research on Direct Instruction*, a book in preparation.

Overview

The Direct Instruction Model is based on the belief that children can be taught competencies more rapidly if teachers are provided with well-planned educational procedures, including pretested curriculum materials. The teachers in the model use small-group, face-to-face methods of instruction to present carefully sequenced, daily lessons in reading, arithmetic, and language. Siegfried Engelmann employed modern learning principles and advanced programming strategies (Becker, Engelmann, & Thomas, 1975b) to construct these programmed lessons in reading, arithmetic, and language, which are published by Science Research Associates (SRA) under the trade name DISTAR©. Each lesson was carefully field-tested to ensure that the materials were effective in helping low-performing children attain stated teaching objectives.

Currently, teachers in thousands of classrooms fail to teach basic skills to many low-performing children because the basal programs in use require language skills above those the children possess when they enter school (Bereiter, Note 1). The best way to meet the educational needs of such children, many of whom are from low-income backgrounds, is to design school programs that start with the entry skills in a way that permits the low performers to catch up with their more advantaged peers. The data presented in this chapter indicate that this goal has been accomplished in Direct Instruction Follow Through classrooms.

The purpose of this chapter is to describe the Direct Instructional Model and to summarize the results of much evaluation research on its effects. The events that preceded the implementation of the model in Follow Through are stated briefly. Next, the empirical foundations for the theory of instruction and the programming principles that have been used to develop the recommended educational procedures and the DISTAR materials are explained. Then, the basic components of the model are presented, followed by a summary and discussion of results obtained from both the sponsor's evaluation of the model and the national longitudinal evaluation of Follow Through. The outcomes of these evaluations are the basis for recommending fundamental changes in priorities and directions for American education.

Origins

The Direct Instruction Model represents a blend of Engelmann's interest in teaching basic skills to preschool children and Wesley C. Becker's interest in applying knowledge from contemporary learning theories and behavioral psychology to improve education. In addition, Carl A. Bereiter made important contributions through his work on the acceleration of intellectual development among preschool children. Bereiter's work during the early- and mid-1960s focused on teaching the preskills that enable young children to be successful in kindergarten and the primary grades.

An important precursor to the Direct Instruction Model was the Bereiter-Engelmann preschool that was established at the University of Illinois at Urbana in the mid-1960s. The preschool was based on the assumption that all children could be taught and that lower-performing children could catch up with their more advantaged peers if their instructional programs were designed to teach more academic skills in less time. Bereiter and Engelmann's work was directed toward identifying skills that should be taught to children and developing a coherent program to teach those skills (Bereiter, Note 1).

The preschool program that Bereiter and Engelmann formulated provided 2 hr of direct instruction per day. The evaluation of two groups of 4- and 5-year-olds produced very promising results (Bereiter & Engelmann, 1966; Engelmann, 1968; Bereiter, Note 1). Engelmann's contributions to those studies came to the attention of the planners of Follow Through in the USOE, and they later invited him to participate in the project.

Becker, a research psychologist who had interests in the child–clinical area, became dissatisfied in the early 1960s with traditional approaches in clinical psychology and directed his efforts toward building a behaviorally oriented approach. He and his associates performed functional studies of the maladaptive behaviors of children and adults and of the variables that caused and maintained those behaviors (Becker, Zipse, & Madsen, 1967; O'Leary, O'Leary, & Becker, 1967). These investigations were followed by a series of studies performed in classrooms (Becker, 1973; Becker, Carlson, Arnold, & Madsen, 1968; Becker, Madsen, Arnold, & Thomas, 1967; Madsen, Becker, & Thomas, 1968; O'Leary & Becker, 1967; Thomas, Becker, & Armstrong, 1968). The results of that research revealed that teachers could be taught to employ behavioral methods for reducing and eliminating the maladaptive behaviors of children who previously were sent out of the classroom for someone else to "therapize."

Becker and Engelmann began working together at the University of Illinois at Urbana in the fall of 1967, after Bereiter had moved to the Ontario Institute for Studies in Education. The Direct Instruction Model and the members of its staff were moved to the University of Oregon in 1970. Becker's contributions to the Direct Instruction Model included the following: (a) helping parents teach their children more effectively; (b) training teachers to employ behavioral principles (Becker, Engelmann, & Thomas, 1971, 1975a); (c) using criterion-referenced tests to assess students' progress; (d) monitoring teacher's progress through biweekly reports; and (e) applying computer technology to the evaluation and management of a project involving 9000 children each year. Engelmann's contributions to the model included (a) expertise in designing instructional programs and teaching strategies; (b) tough-minded realism about school systems; and (c) skills in training teachers "how to do it."

The third contributor to this chapter, Douglas W. Carnine, joined the project at its inception as a field supervisor and manager. He also helped Engelmann prepare the DISTAR arithmetic program. During the early years of Follow Through, he completed his doctoral degree at the University of Utah. At the same time, Carnine gained much experience in training teachers in Direct Instruction methods and developing an extensive program of experimental studies on teaching processes and programming principles. Some of this work is summarized in the next section of this chapter. Carnine is now the director of the University of Oregon Direct Instruction Model.

Rationale

The Direct Instruction Model is built upon two basic premises: (a) that the rate and quality of children's learning in the classroom is a function of environmental events; and (b) that educators can increase the amount of children's learning in the classroom by engineering carefully the details of students' interaction with that environment. When these details are chosen and sequenced according to a rational plan, efforts to improve the rate at which children learn are likely to be successful. The purpose of this section is to describe the theoretical and research foundations of the model. This information is presented in two parts: (a) sources of knowledge, and (b) design of the DISTAR curriculum.

SOURCES OF KNOWLEDGE

The knowledge that has been utilized in the construction of the Direct Instruction Model was derived from three primary sources: (a) empirical behavior theory; (b) logical analysis of concepts and tasks; and (c) logical analysis of the use of resources in classrooms. After the model was designed and implemented, programmatic research was conducted to verify or refute the premises of the model. Some results of these empirical investigations are reported in the description of principles and procedures that is presented later in this section.

Empirical Behavior Theory

Contemporary behavioral psychology represents an important source of knowledge that educators can draw upon to enhance children's learning. Detailed presentations of behavior theory approaches are available in a number of texts (Becker *et al.*, 1971, 1975a, 1975b; Ferster & Perrott, 1968; Honig, 1966; Millenson, 1967; Reynolds, 1968; Salzinger, 1969; Skinner, 1938, 1953, 1968). The basic principles of behavior that influenced decisions about the design of the model include reinforcement, conditioned responses, stimulus control, prompting, shaping, punishment, extinction, and fading. Information about these principles is readily available in the texts cited above and will not be reviewed here.

The designers of the Direct Instruction Model followed behavioral principles in three major areas of development. First, they used techniques such as prompts, fades, corrections, discrimination training, and chaining verbal responses in constructing the DISTAR programs. Second, behavioral principles were employed in developing teaching procedures for eliciting and maintaining students' attention, securing their responses, dispensing reinforcers, and so forth. Third, those individuals who designed the model were guided by behavioral principles in activities such as organizing classrooms and prescribing management procedures for regulating the verbal behavior of teachers and students, monitoring students' academic progress, and using praise and other reinforcers to encourage students to acquire desirable behaviors.

Logical Analysis of Concepts and Tasks

The logical analysis of concepts and tasks has contributed much information that Engelmann has employed in designing the DISTAR programs. The prerequisite for designing efficient educational programs is to identify the structural relationships that exist among concepts and tasks. This information is utilized for teaching students to generalize and transfer what they learn in order to increase their capabilities for solving problems. For example, *hot-cold*, *wet-dry*, and *long-short* are sets of polar concepts that share a common characteristic: they are two-member groups. Therefore, if you know that something does not have one characteristic, it must have the other. Concepts also may be organized into various kinds of hierarchical structures to illustrate the characteristics they share. For example, collies are dogs, dogs are mammals, mammals are animals, animals are living things, living things are things, and so forth. The analysis of structural relationships, as described by Becker et al. (1975b, p. 146), provides information that is necessary for designing common procedures for teaching related concepts and for specifying the discriminations among them that are most important to practice.

It is also possible to perform logical analyses of the complexity of the tasks used to teach concepts. Those concepts that can be taught with simpler tasks should be taught first. For example, a teacher may teach the object concept *ball* by stating the prompt, "This is a ball," and next pointing to a ball and asking, "What is this?" In order to teach the object property concept *yellow*, the teacher may state the prompt, "This ball is yellow," then point to the ball and ask, "What color is this ball?" The second task is more complex, because it requires that the student possess knowledge about the object concept *ball*, the property class *color*, and the property *yellow*. The tasks employed to teach concepts about object relations such as *larger than*, events such as *falling*, and causal relations such as *the teacher let go and the ball fell* become increasingly complex.

Another approach to analyzing the complexity of tasks is required in order to teach problem-solving operations. The procedure used to solve a problem is analyzed into its component parts and the components are pretaught before they are employed in the more complex task. The approach to identifying components must be thoughtful. The objective is to identify the minimum set of "building blocks" that can be used to help students perform the maximum number of tasks. An efficient analysis will include the full range of problems to which the component tasks might be applied.

Logical Analysis of the Use of Resources in Classrooms

The resources available in classrooms are limited, and the pressures for their use are often conflicting. The designers of the Direct Instruction Model had to confront the question of how to use these limited resources to produce the greatest educational benefit for students. The results of logical analyses of the potential benefits and costs of alternative choices in the use of resources influenced decisions on many issues, including the choice of small-group rather than individualized instruction; the use of paraprofessionals rather than employment of more teachers; the placement of the top priority on academic instruction rather than play, art, music, or some other activity; and the use of scripted presentation of lessons rather than permitting teachers to choose their own instructions. The results of research peformed in recent years on relationships between methods of teaching and learning outcomes, which have been reviewed by Rosenshine (1976), have confirmed the wisdom of many decisions that were made many years ago on the basis of logical analyses of the requirements for successful teaching and learning in classrooms.

DESIGN OF THE DISTAR CURRICULUM

The design of the DISTAR curriculum materials can be described in a number of ways. For example, Becker *et al.* (1975b) present a technical description aimed at persons who possess a detailed knowledge of operant learning principles. In this chapter, the description of the principles underlying the design of the DISTAR materials follows the more recent formulation by Engelmann and Carnine (Note 2). The discussion in this section is presented below in three parts: (*a*) teaching for generalization; (*b*) teaching strategies that change with time; and (*c*) teaching strategies for different classes of tasks.

Teaching for Generalization

In designing the DISTAR programs, the primary goal was to teach skills that students could generalize. Thus, objectives were analyzed into sets of related problems that children could solve by using a common strategy, and concepts were identified that could be taught as *general cases.* Students have learned a general case when, after having been taught some members of a general case set, they can identify all members of the set. The teaching of general cases differs greatly from the teaching of *linear–additive sets*, in which each member must be taught separately (Becker & Engelmann, 1976; Wittgenstein, 1958). This difference can be illustrated with an example from reading. If you teach a set of sounds, blending skills, and say-it-fast skills to instruct students in word-reading (decoding) skills, the students should be able to read thousands of words that they were not taught during the teaching process. This efficiency in teaching is made possible because the students were taught a strategy for decoding words, or what may be called a general case. In contrast, if teachers use a sight-word method, the students probably will learn only the words they are taught, because they will have been taught not a general case, but a linear–additive set. Consequently, what students learn when they discriminate one word does not necessarily help them to discriminate the next word.

Teaching Strategies that Change with Time

The DISTAR programs in reading, arithmetic, and language are the core around which the rest of the model is constructed. Certain general principles have been followed in assembling the tasks that comprise these materials. The teaching and task requirements of these tasks shift along a number of dimensions as students advance from kindergarten through the third grade. These changes and adaptations occur along the six dimensions that are described as follows:

1. The first shift is *from overtized to covertized* problem-solving strategies. When teachers use an overtized problem-solving strategy, they make every step in the strategy explicit to the children. They first prompt learners to perform every step required to solve a particular type of problem, a practice that is called *forward-chaining*. Since each child must make an overt response at each step, the teacher can identify the exact skills in a strategy that the learner may have difficulty in mastering. Eventually, the strategy is covertized, and the teacher no longer requires an overt response at each step. Some of the children's responses at many steps may no longer be observable. It is possible that only the answer will be overt. Covertization provides an essential link between the work that students perform under close supervision by the teacher and other work that they perform independently.

2. The second shift is *from simplified contexts*, in which teachers emphasize the relevant features of a task when they introduce a discrimination to students, *to complex contexts*, in which students must make applications of knowledge in a variety of settings characterized by a wide range of irrelevant detail.

3. The third shift is *from providing prompts to removing those prompts*. This process is called *fading*. Early in instruction, the teacher may use prompts, which are modified examples or special wordings, to focus the learner's attention on relevant features. Later, these prompts are faded.

4. The fourth shift is *from massed practice* during the acquisition of new skills *to distributed practice,* and a gradually decreasing amount of practice, when students incorporate these skills into more complex applications. The massed practice is designed to bring about mastery learning; the distributed practice aids retention of what has been learned.

5. The fifth shift is *from immediate feedback* by teachers early in instruction *to delayed feedback* by teachers as learners become more capable.

6. The sixth shift is *from an emphasis on the teacher's role as a source of information to an emphasis on the learner's role as a source of information.* As learners increase their repertoire of skills, the teacher's role changes from that of a provider of new information to that of a guide who assists the learner to use information previously acquired. The learner must decide how to apply previously learned skills and information in a variety of problem-solving situations.

Teaching Strategies for Different Classes of Tasks

To further explain the principles underlying the design of the DISTAR programs, it is necessary to explain the approach to teaching four important classes of learning tasks: (a) teaching basic concepts; (b) teaching systematically related concepts; (c) teaching rules; and (d) teaching cognitive operations.

Teaching Basic Concepts The approach to teaching basic concepts relies heavily on the use of positive and negative examples. The following principle is crucial to the design of tasks used to teach basic concepts, indeed all tasks: *The presentation should be capable of evoking only one interpretation.* If a presentation can evoke several possible interpretations, students may learn an interpretation other than the one intended by the teacher. The use of examples in teaching concepts and sets of concepts is explored in the following four parts: (a) design of positive and negative examples, (b) sequencing examples, (c) number of practice examples required, and (d) principles for teaching sets of basic concepts.

1. Design of positive and negative examples. An application of the "only one interpretation" principle is illustrated in Figure 4.1, which contains positive and negative examples for teaching the discrimination *on*. The pair of examples from teaching set *a* illustrates a minimum difference between positive and negative examples of *on*. In set *a*, the number of possible interpretations of *on* is few because the number of differences between the positive and negative examples is small. In contrast, the pairs of examples in set *b* through *e* differ in several ways, and thus lend themselves to a much greater number of possible interpretations. If only example *e* was presented, a student might make the interpretation that *on* means a block, something not held in a hand, horizontally positioned objects, and so forth. None of these interpretations are possible from the presentation of set *a*.

In order to ensure that a set of examples evokes only one interpretation, the teacher must not only present pairs of positive and negative examples that are minimally different, but also must select a range of positive and negative examples in which irrelevant characteristics are varied.

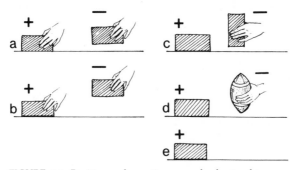

FIGURE 4.1 *Positive and negative examples for teaching* on.

2. Sequencing examples. Several principles are followed in sequencing examples, two of which are described here. The first principle is: *Sequence minimally different positive and negative examples of a concept (those most alike) adjacent to each other or present them as a pair of examples.* Sequencing minimally different examples in this way increased learners' perception of the relevant features of concepts (Granzin & Carnine, 1977). The second principle for sequencing examples is: *Generate positive and negative examples by changing a single stimulus (a dynamic presentation), rather than presenting a series of discrete stimuli (a static presentation).* Carnine (Note 3) reported faster acquisition and higher transfer scores among preschoolers who were taught the concepts *diagonal* and *convex* through a dynamic as compared to a static presentation.

3. Number of practice examples required. Because there are individual differences among learners, it is not possible to state a specific number of examples that should be used in teaching a concept to all students. A mastery learning approach, in which examples are presented until the student reaches a specified performance standard, helps to deal with this variable. A mastery criterion should be set lower when the task involves labeling, since the likelihood of reaching criterion through guessing is lower. A more rigorous criterion should be used when tasks require a "yes" or "no" answer.

4. Principles for teaching sets of basic concepts. A number of additional principles are followed in teaching sets of concepts, such as identifying letters by their sounds, prepositions, sentence types, and so forth. The first principle is: *The concepts in a set should be introduced cumulatively, so that two members of the set are introduced and practiced until they are mastered.* The new concepts are added to the set, one at a time. Carnine (1976) reported that preschoolers mastered six letter–sound correspondences in fewer trials when the letters were introduced cumulatively rather than simultaneously. The second principle for teaching a set of concepts is: *Concepts that are more useful to the learner (generate more applications) or are easier should be introduced earlier.* Carnine and Carnine (1978) reported that decoding consonant–vowel–consonant (CVC) words is easier than decoding CVCC words, which in turn is easier than decoding CVCC words. The third principle is: *The members of a set that are similar to each other either in stimulus features or response requirements, such as* **b** *and* **d**, *should be separated in the program as far as possible, given other constraints.* Increased response similarity clearly makes paired associate learning more difficult (Feldman & Underwood, 1957; Higa, 1963; Underwood, Runquist, & Schultz, 1959). The designer of instructional programs also may employ a fourth principle, which is: *Review previously introduced related concepts.* Of course, reviewing every previously intro-

duced concept would be too time consuming, so the programmer must save time by constructing a review set that includes troublesome members (those defined by high error rates during field testing), recently introduced members (those probably not yet mastered), members not reviewed recently, and finally, members that are highly similar to the new member.

Teaching Systematically Related Concepts Two concepts are systematically related if several examples of the first concept can be transformed through a standard procedure into examples of the second concept. For example, the concepts *singular nouns* and *plural nouns* are systematically related because the singular nouns, *dog, hat,* and *elephant,* can be transformed into plural nouns by following a standard procedure, which is adding *s* to produce *dogs, hats,* and *elephants.* Systematically related concepts should be introduced after the student has learned the simpler set of concepts.

Teaching Rules Rules often describe a relationship between two concepts. For example, in a rule that states, "The hotter an object becomes, the more it expands," the two key concepts are *hotter* and *expands.* Rules are taught in three stages of decreasing structure: rule repetition, simple applications, and complex applications. For the rule, "The lower you eat on a food ladder, the more protein goes directly to you," the learner first repeats the rule to ensure information retention. The simple applications follow the wording of the rule: "Beans are lower on the food ladder than hamburger. Which food gives more protein directly to you?" The students indicate that beans would provide more direct protein. Complex applications do not use the words from the rule, so the item would not state that beans are lower on the food ladder. The student must use the information in the application item to draw an inference about whether beans are lower on the food ladder and then draw a second inference that beans provide more direct protein than hamburgers. The teacher asks, "Which food gives more protein directly to you, peanuts or fried chicken?" The student answers, "Peanuts." The teacher asks, "How do you know?" and the learner answers, "Peanuts are lower on the food ladder." The last question tests whether the learner applied the rule in arriving at an answer.

Teaching Cognitive Operations In the Direct Instruction Model, the principles and procedures for teaching basic concepts, systematically related concepts, and rules often serve as the building blocks for teaching cognitive operations, which are sequences of steps used to solve problems of a given type. Students use cognitive operations when they solve a wide range of problems, including algebraic equations, analogies, long division problems, and so forth. Initially, the steps of a cognitive operation must be made overt, both to show students the relevant steps and to provide a basis for teacher feedback as the students attempt to complete each step.

The designer of instructional programs first selects a problem appropriate for an operation, such as $9 - 2 = \square$ in simple subtraction, and then generates a list of minimally different problems, which might include $9 + 2 = \square$, $9 - 3 = \square$, and $9 - \square = 2$. The minimally different problems alert the designer to the operation's range of application. Constructing operations that take into account these minimally different problems sets the stage for transfer, enabling the student to use variations of the operation for working the minimally different problems. After the minimally different problems have been listed, a teaching procedure is designed for each aspect of the problem identified by the minimal difference. After a teaching question, or set of questions, has been identified for each pair of minimally different problems, the separate procedures are combined to create the overtized cognitive operation. The range and structure of the examples to which the operation applies also must be made explicit.

A specification of the cognitive operation and the range and structure of the examples is the starting point from which the designer constructs a series of lessons for teaching the operation. These lessons for teaching a cognitive operation proceed through two major instructional stages: (a) teaching component skills and (b) covertizing cognitive operations.

1. Teaching component skills. Component skills consist of the basic concepts, related concepts, and rules that make up a cognitive operation. Component skills are pretaught in modules and clusters. A module is the simplest possible instructional unit. A cluster is a sequence of modules. For example, a cognitive operation for simple subtraction includes this cluster:

> Teacher points to $- 2$ and says, "Read it." The student reads, "Minus 2." Teacher points to $- 2$ and asks, "What do these symbols tell you to do?" The student replies, "Make two minuses." The teacher then instructs the student to make the minuses. This cluster is composed of two modules in which the teacher says, "Read it," and "What do these symbols tell you to do?"

In preparing students to learn a cognitive operation, those individuals who design instructional programs first identify the clusters that make up the operation and next identify the modules that make up each cluster. The next step is to construct teaching procedures for the modules and clusters, select examples for them, and finally sequence the modules and clusters along with their corresponding examples. This process of identifying, sequencing, and selecting examples for modules and clusters defines the component skill stage.

2. Covertizing cognitive operations. The other major stage in teaching a

cognitive operation is covertization, the process in which students learn to solve applications with little direction from the teacher. As stated previously, covertization is the process of moving the learner from a highly structured, overtized operation to an unstructured, covertized context in which the learner completes steps without direction or assistance from the teacher. The operation also is covertized in the sense that the learner may complete several steps without making any observable responses.

Covertization begins after the learner's responses are consistently correct during the application of an overtized operation. Covertization can occur through any of three procedures: (a) A step is dropped from the overtized operation; (b) several steps are replaced by a more inclusive instruction; or (c) several steps are chained together so that the learner no longer responds after each step, but rather produces a chain of responses following the chained steps. Prompting and fading are employed in teaching component skills and covertizing cognitive operations.

In this section, the purpose has been to briefly describe how research methods were utilized to generate and apply knowledge from several sources to develop effective educational programs for young children. The formulation of rational, direct, programming procedures for teaching cognitive operations is a complex activity that requires, in all phases, careful attention to detail. Consequently, it is difficult to convey the full variety and breadth of intellectual skills that can be taught through direct instruction procedures within the limited amount of space available. Readers will obtain a more comprehensive understanding of the Direct Instruction Model by examining other publications cited in this chapter, by reading the DISTAR programs themselves, and by reading the descriptions of implementation procedures and evaluation data that are presented in the remainder of this chapter.

The Well-Implemented Model

The Direct Instruction Model has the following eight basic components: (a) a focus on academic objectives; (b) additional "teachers" in classrooms; (c) structured use of time; (d) scripted presentation of lessons; (e) efficient teaching methods; (f) careful training and supervision; (g) monitoring of progress; and (h) active parent involvement. Each of these components is discussed in more detail here.

A FOCUS ON ACADEMIC OBJECTIVES

The DISTAR programs in reading, arithmetic, and language are the heart of the Direct Instruction Follow Through model. Each contains objectives for three curriculum levels. A brief overview of the goals of these nine programs follows.

Reading

In DISTAR Reading I and II, teachers focus first on decoding skills and then on comprehension skills. The students learn decoding skills by advancing through the following programmed steps: (a) reading individual sounds; (b) blending those sounds into words; (c) reading regular sound words; (d) reading common irregular words (e.g., *is, said, was*); (e) reading sentences; (f) reading irregular word families (e.g., *hop–hope, bit–bite, rat–rate, hopping–hoping,* and so forth); and (g) reading less common irregular words. The comprehension skills include literal comprehension, following instructions, and remembering what was said (statement repetition). In DISTAR Reading III, the children learn to read to obtain new information and to use that information. Most Reading III stories have a science base, which permits the presentation of rules or information that students can use to solve problems in astronomy, muscle function, or measurement. After Lesson 60, most students read on their own initiative and complete workbook assignments individually rather than work in groups. The students who complete Reading III may use more advanced textbooks, if they are taught the new vocabulary and concepts that are in them.

Arithmetic

Students who complete DISTAR Arithmetic I first learn basic addition and subtraction operations and their related story-problem forms through a problem-solving approach. Then the children memorize number facts to speed up the process and to prepare themselves to solve more elaborate problems. In Arithmetic II, the students are introduced to multiplication and fractions. They receive further instruction in addition, subtraction, and in a variety of measurement concepts pertaining to time, money, length, and weight. The students also learn to derive unknown facts from known facts and to solve more complex story problems. In Arithmetic III, the students receive instruction in algebra, factoring, and division, as well as continued practice in addition, subtraction, multiplication and division.

Language

Teachers use DISTAR Language I and II materials to teach object names, object classes, object properties, and relational terms. The children learn to make complete statements and to describe details of the world around them. The programs stress instruction and practice in language comprehension and language production. Students are taught logical processes, such as conditionality, causality, multiple attributes, definitions, deductions, synonyms, and opposites. The children also learn to ask questions in order to obtain information. Teachers employ Language III materials to help students expand their logical use of language and basic grammatical rules. Many activities in reading and language also are designed to improve writing and spelling skills.

The major long-term goal of the Direct Instruction Model is to teach low-performing students those basic academic skills that will equip them to compete with their more advantaged peers for higher education and the opportunities available in our society. The immediate goal for students enrolled in the model is to help them achieve, on the average, performance at grade level (fiftieth percentile) on major school achievement test batteries by the end of third grade. These goals are defined more specifically in written statements of program objectives.

Although the primary interest is in promoting children's growth in cognitive academic areas, designers of the model also have strong interests in promoting children's development in social and affective areas. The developers of the model want children to learn arts, crafts, social skills, and values, and students receive instruction in these areas in ways that are suited to local conditions. In most communities, 3 hr of a 5-hr day are devoted to teaching academic skills, and 2 hr to other activities. In communities in which Spanish is spoken, members of the sponsor's staff have developed procedures for teaching Spanish that minimize interference with instruction in English.

The instructional methods employed in Direct Instruction classrooms will produce positive self-concepts among the children. The reasoning is that children who become competent in academic and other skills will consequently feel good about themselves, and that other persons will communicate positive attitudes toward them. From this perspective, a positive self-concept occurs as a by-product of good teaching. The interpretation of the data from the national evaluation of Follow Through, presented later in the section on evaluation, appears to support this position.

ADDITIONAL "TEACHERS" IN CLASSROOMS

Classroom aides, who are usually students' parents, are trained to perform teaching activities. Two aides are added to assist in classroom instruction in kindergarten and the first two grades; one aide is added to third grade classrooms. The aides make it possible to teach two or three groups simultaneously. More than 50 aides have completed the requirements to become certified teachers by accumulating course credits through participation in the training supplied as part of the model and through related supplementary training programs.

STRUCTURED USE OF TIME

The presence of more teaching personnel in classrooms does not necessarily ensure that the quality of teaching actually improves. In addition, a well-organized school day, a good instructional program, and effective training procedures are needed in order to utilize the additional personnel to produce desired outcomes. The organization of the classrooms permits each teacher and aide to teach groups of four to seven students for at least 2 hr per day. The class is usually divided into four groups, but at times more groups are necessary. The teachers and aides become specialists in one of the three basic DISTAR curriculum areas: reading, arithmetic, or language. Students in groups are rotated through subject areas and seat work activities, according to schedules that are compatible with each school's timetable. Small-group instruction lasts approximately 30 min in each subject area at Levels I and II. At Level III in the DISTAR programs, each 15 min of group instruction is followed by 30 min of self-directed practice in workbooks. As noted earlier, the students often proceed almost entirely on their own initiative in reading after Lesson 60. Teachers also plan the students' daily activities to include instruction in large groups.

SCRIPTED PRESENTATION OF LESSONS

The printed instructions in each DISTAR program indicate exactly what the teacher will say and do during classroom instruction. This approach is called a "scripted presentation" and it is recommended for a number of reasons. The scripts provide teachers with directions, sequences of examples, and sequences of subskills and wordings that already have been tested for effectiveness. Teachers can use scripts to improve the quality of their instruction. They can learn effective verbal presentation strategies by repeated practice with scripted lessons. Scripted programs also make the teacher trainer's job more explicit. A trainer easily can help teachers learn more effective teaching skills, because the required skills are standardized and made explicit by the scripted program. Finally, there is a significant saving in the amount of time required for supervising and training teachers because they all employ the same set of programs. The trainer–supervisor knows the performance criteria, pinpoints deficiencies quickly, and provides appropriate remedies.

EFFICIENT TEACHING METHODS

Behavioral principles and a logic for resource utilization have been used to develop a number of methods for teaching children that greatly increase teaching efficiency and student-engaged learning time. The methods described here include the following: small-group instruction, signals, reinforcement, corrections, and procedures to teach every child by giving added attention to the lower performers.

Small-Group Instruction

The use of small-group instruction is a central feature of the model. The first advantage of this approach is that it provides good models of effective student behaviors, and most students learn readily from such models. A second advantage is that teachers can encourage students to develop positive attitudes toward repetition of lessons. Teachers can transform a routine drill exercise into an activity that is fun. A third advantage is that timid students tend to respond more readily in a group than they do in an individual situation. A fourth advantage is that teaching in small groups is both more efficient than one-to-one instruction and retains many of the advantages of individualized instruction (Fink & Carnine, Note 4). Teachers who employ the model do not individualize the sequence of what is taught, but they do individualize entry level, motivational procedures, techniques for making corrections, and the number of practice trials to mastery.

Signals

Another important teaching procedure is the use of hand signals that cue the group to respond together. The scripts indicate when teachers should signal the group to respond. Teachers use signals to prevent children from cuing on the earlier responses of other children and simply imitating those responses, rather than responding to the task stimulus presented by the teacher. Signals also increase students' attending and responding (Cowart, Carnine, & Becker, Note 5).

Reinforcement

The training procedures for the Direct Instruction Model include specifications for the systematic use of positive consequences to strengthen children's motivation for learning. Knowledge of results, behavior-specific praise, enjoyable games, and point systems leading to special consequences are a few of the recommended techniques. An important rule for applying reinforcers is: *Never use a stronger reinforcement system than is necessary to get the job done.* The principles and procedures employed in the approach to training teachers in the use of positive consequences are published in Becker *et al.* (1971, 1975a).

Corrections

When teachers implement traditional instructional programs in group situations, they frequently have to choose among the following awkward alternatives: (*a*) spending much of the period working with one student's problems that are of little concern to other members of the group; (*b*) ignoring many mistakes and "pretending" that they do not occur; and/or (*c*) keying on several students in the group, usually the highest performers, and attending only to their responses. These problems can be avoided or quickly solved when the program is carefully designed to prevent the occurrence of highly probable mistakes.

Procedures to Teach Every Student

When teachers work with children in one-to-one situations, they can maintain students' attention more easily by reinforcing their responses consistently. To achieve that same level of attention among students in small-group teaching, teachers often sit in a location from which they can reach out and touch every child. Teaching is often directed specifically to the lowest performers in the group. The reason for this is that when the lowest performers have mastered a task, all students in the group probably will have mastered it. The lowest performers are seated directly in front of the teacher to be sure that they are taught, and these students are tested more frequently than the high performers. While this procedure might appear to hold back the more capable students, the provision for four or more groups and careful monitoring of student progress safeguards against this possibility.

CAREFUL TRAINING AND SUPERVISION

One important goal of training in the Direct Instruction Model is to provide teachers and aides with the skills they must have to teach small groups of children. Teachers learn how to select members of each group to produce the best results for each child, how to use signals to coordinate group responding, how to present the DISTAR tasks, how to reinforce accurate responses, and how to correct mistakes. This training is necessary in order to properly implement the model (Carnine & Fink, 1978; Siegel, 1977) and is usually accomplished through a 1- or 2-wk preservice workshop, continuing in-service sessions of about 2 hr per week, and classroom supervision. Members of the sponsor's staff have prepared manuals that trainers use to instruct participants in the model (Oregon Follow Through Project, Note 6).

The structured approach to teaching makes it posible to specify the important skills that teachers and aides must have in order to perform well in classrooms. The training sessions include modeling and actual practice teaching in which teachers take turns playing the roles of student and teacher. During this training, teachers and aides are encouraged to perform under supervision and to carefully evaluate their own performance. Teachers view videotaped illustrations of correct procedures for teaching key tasks in the program. In-service training also includes courses about the basic principles of reinforcement and programming that underly the model (Becker et al., 1975a, 1975b). Follow Through teachers and aides have obtained college credit for the completion of many in-service training activities.

Consultants, supervisors, and managers are trained to provide supervision for classroom teachers and aides. Many of the consultants are former teachers from the local schools. Every trainer is required to demonstrate with children every teaching skill required in the model. Supervisors are expected to spend 75% of their working time in classrooms. Managers must be experienced teachers and supervisors who know the classroom procedures well and are able to assume responsibility for all phases of the instructional process. They adapt schedules to local needs, monitor all phases of the program, identify priorities, and continually work to improve implementation. Managers spend most of their time in classrooms working with members of the teaching staff.

MONITORING OF PROGRESS

The work of managers and supervisors provides the first line of quality control for teacher performance in classrooms. The second line consists of biweekly reports of teaching activities and results from tests of student progress. Paraprofessionals monitor student progress by administering criterion-referenced tests in each subject area at 2-wk intervals. The results are recorded on a four-copy IBM form on which names of students and their ID numbers are preprinted. These biweekly reports also include information about the frequency of absences and the current lesson progress of each group in reading, arithmetic, and language. Copies of the report are sent to the teacher, supervisor, local Follow Through director, and to a data analysis center. The reports are used by the teachers and supervisors to regroup children (including skipping them ahead), to provide tutoring, and/or to guide in-service training. The reports also serve to inform staff members about whether each student is achieving an acceptable rate of progress and about the quality of that progress. Managers prepare projections of expected yearly progress for each group. In general, the top ability group is expected to average 1.5 lessons per day and the lowest ability groups, .7 lessons per day. These expectations are adjusted by the managers using specific knowledge of the local groups. The projections are compared with the actual progress of the groups to determine when program adjustments are needed.

ACTIVE PARENT INVOLVEMENT

Parents are actively involved in the program in a variety of ways. A large number of parents work in the program as teacher aides, continuous progress testers, and parent workers. Parents use home practice books to help their children complete learning activities that support their classroom instruction in the DISTAR I and II programs (Schrader, Note 7). Parent workers teach other parents to use the language training materials in these books and to reinforce other school tasks represented by the *Take Homes* that accompany the DISTAR programs. The *Take Homes* consist of tasks presented in a workbook format that contain additional materials and exercises for parents to use to reinforce skills that students have recently mastered in classrooms. Parents are taught to review these tasks with their children and to express pleasure about their children's new learning. Parent workers also use the programmed text, *Parents Are Teachers* (Becker, 1971), to provide training for parents in the area of positive child management skills.

Members of the sponsor's staff work closely with program directors, PAC chairpersons, and parent workers to obtain and provide suggestions for effective parent involvement programs. Members of the sponsor's staff also have developed a manual of procedures that these persons can follow to establish active parent participation programs. A copy of that manual is available at cost to interested persons who address their requests to the sponsor (Oregon Follow Through Model, Note 6).

Many parents whose children are enrolled in the model have participated in the political action often necessary to ensure that desired programs are actually implemented. In addition, they have strongly supported needed changes in school policies and procedures. Parents have walked picket lines, talked to members of school boards and superintendents, and informed the press in their attempts to improve situations that interfered with program implementation. These parents also have played an active role in keeping the national Follow Through Project funded and vigorously have opposed the threats of phase-down since 1972.

None of the statements about parent participation is intended to convey the impression that parent involvement was uniformly strong and effective. There certainly was variability across communities in the degree of involvement, and the number of active participants at any given time rarely exceeded 30–40% of parents. Nevertheless, parent involvement is probably generally higher in Follow Through than in any other project of its kind.

Thus far, the description of the Direct Instruction Model has included information on its origins, rationale, and implementation. The focus of the remainder of this chapter is on the evaluation of the model and the lessons that have been learned about ways to improve the effectiveness of educational programs in schools.

Evaluation

This section consists of three parts. The sponsor's orientation to evaluating the Direct Instruction Model is discussed in the first part. The second part contains data from the sponsor's own evaluation of the model. Data from the national longitudinal evaluation of Follow Through are presented in the third part. Interpretations of the results of evaluation research and statements on their implications for making education more effective are included in the second and third parts of this section.

ORIENTATION TO EVALUATION

Evaluation of the Direct Instruction Model occurs at three levels. The first level consists of systematically pretesting each component of the DISTAR programs among a sample of low-performing children to determine the effectiveness of the lesson formats, instructions for pacing, sequencing of materials, and so forth. The program designers use information about error rates on new tasks and the results of cumulative progress tests to make necessary modifications of the materials before they are printed in large volume for delivery to local schools. In the second level of evaluation, the information from supervisors' observations and teachers' biweekly reports of students' progress tests is used to evaluate the quality of instruction as it occurs in classrooms. The instructional process is judged to be effective if the children make satisfactory progress in completing the DISTAR programs. The focus in this section is on the third level of evaluation, which is the evaluation of the model's impact on children's progress in basic academic skills. Most of the frequently used norm-referenced tests may be employed to assess the overall success of the model and of instructional programs in most schools. The discussion of representative findings from the third level of evaluation is presented below in two major parts, sponsor's evaluation and national longitudinal evaluation.

SPONSOR'S EVALUATION

Members of the sponsor's Follow Through staff supervised the collection of data to evaluate the model. Technical Report No. 76-1 (Becker & Engelmann, Note 8) contains a detailed presentation of the results of the analyses of that data. A summary of that report is presented in the following three sections: (*a*) method, (*b*) results, and (*c*) discussion.

Method
The instruments, data collection and reduction procedures, and the sample of children employed in the sponsor's evaluation of the Direct Instruction Model are described next.

Instruments From 1969 to 1973, the intent was to administer selected tests to all children enrolled in the Direct Instruction Model when they entered the programs and at the end of each school year. The testing of second grade students was omitted during one year, due to a reduction in funding. From 1969 to 1971, both the Wide Range Achievement Test (WRAT) (Jastak, Bijou, & Jastak, 1965) and the Slosson Intelligence Test (SIT) (Slosson, 1971) were administered to thousands of children. The WRAT yields subscores in reading, arithmetic, and spelling. The reading test is a reliable (.91–.92) measure of decoding skills, or word recognition. The arithmetic test has lower reliability (.70–.80), but provides an acceptable measure of computational skills. The spelling test has an acceptable level of reliability (.83). The SIT, which was used primarily to measure children's overall competence in verbal skills, is a brief, individually administered test. It has a high reliability of .92, and there is a correlation of .93 between the total IQ score derived from the SIT and the total IQ score derived from the Stanford–Binet.

Beginning in 1972, the Metropolitan Achievement Test (MAT, 1970) was also administered near the close of the school year to students in grades 1, 2, and 3. Three levels of the MAT (Form F) were used. The Primary I battery was administered to first-grade students and was used to assess word knowledge, word analysis, reading (comprehension), total reading, and total math. The Primary II battery was administered to second grade students and was used to measure word knowledge, word analysis, reading, total reading, spelling, language, math computation, math concepts, math problem solving, and total math. The Elementary battery was administered to third grade students and was used to measure the same areas as the Primary II battery, except that the word analysis subtest was omitted. Internal consistency reliabilities for the MAT subtests, which are presented in the test manuals, range from .85 to .96.

Data collection and reduction procedures The tests were carefully administered by local teachers and aides, who were trained and supervised by members of the sponsor's field staff. The testers followed procedures that were similar to those used by the staff of the Stanford Research Institute for the collection of data in the national longitudinal evaluation of Follow Through. Data clerks checked carefully to insure the accuracy of computations and the consistency of scoring procedures. Computer routines were employed to score protocols, and convert raw scores to norm scores in order to eliminate errors that might reduce the accuracy of data analyses.

Sample of children The children enrolled in the model were from low-income homes in 20 communities located in 14 states. These communities are listed in Appendix B. The communities include a cross-section of "poor" America: rural and inner-city blacks, rural whites, Mexican-

Americans in Texas, Spanish-Americans in New Mexico, Native Americans in South Dakota and North Carolina, and some communities in which the population was ethnically mixed. Approximately 9000 students were enrolled in Direct Instruction classrooms in any given year.

In some communities, children were enrolled initially at the kindergarten level; in other communities children were enrolled initially in first grade classrooms because kindergarten programs did not exist. The main analyses were performed on data obtained from a total of 5922 children, who entered at the kindergarten level (K - entering), and on other data obtained from 5565 children who entered at the first-grade level (first - entering). Data obtained from students were included in these analyses only if (a) their families' reported income was below the poverty level established by the OEO; (b) they enrolled in the program at its earliest grade level; and (c) their progress was formally evaluated on two or more occasions. The data include responses from those students who discontinued attendance in Follow Through classrooms before they completed the third grade.[2]

Results

The information presented in this section was selected from a larger body of data to provide answers for important questions about the effects of the Direct Instruction Model. Those questions, data pertaining to them, and interpretations of the data are presented as follows:

Do children who participate in the Direct Instruction Model reach national norms for academic achievement? One of the major goals was to raise the academic performance of students from low-income homes to national norm levels by the completion of third grade. The results presented in Figure 4.2 indicate that this goal has been achieved for those students who enrolled in the model in kindergarten.[3]

Students who attended Direct Instruction classrooms for 4 years, beginning in kindergarten, made substantial gains compared to the national norms for WRAT tests in reading, arithmetic, and spelling. These gains are

---

[2]This data base provided a maximum sample size for measurement of the model's impact. To check for biases in outcomes due to changes in students over grades (attrition), analyses also were performed on year-to-year gains on the *same* students and on full-term pre-to-post gains (K–3 or 1–3) on the *same* students. The results of these analyses did not materially change any conclusions except to make the actual gains about .2 of a grade level higher than those reported here. When students other than those in the low-income group (20% of the children) were included in the analysis, there was another slight increment in the level of performance. As expected, children who entered the model late performed a year lower on the average as compared to those who entered at the beginning of their school experience.

[3]For the data in Figure 4.1, statistics were computed with standard scores from tables provided by the test publishers. The mean standard scores were then converted to percentiles using the publishers' tables.

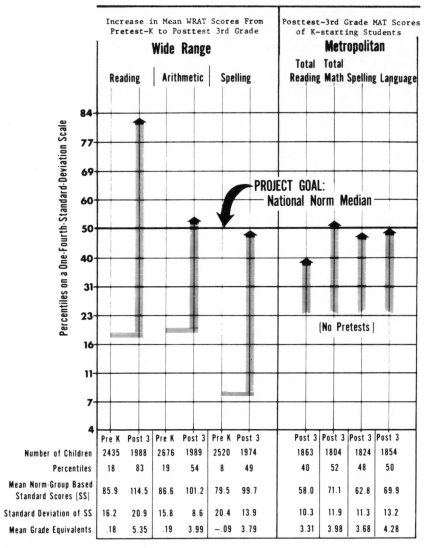

FIGURE 4.2. *Norm-referenced gains on the Wide Range Achievement Test (Pre-K to Post-3) and Post-3 performance on the Metropolitan Achievement Test for K-starting, low income, Direct Instruction Model Follow Through students.*

represented in Figure 4.2 as percentiles on a standard-score scale. The performance of Follow Through students on the WRAT reading (decoding) subtest advanced from the eighteenth percentile to the eighty-third percentile over a period of 4 years. They also achieved large gains on WRAT tests of arithmetic and spelling, and they were functioning at the national norm median (fiftieth percentile) in both areas by the completion of third grade.

No pretest data were available for the Metropolitan Achievement Test; however, it was estimated from the WRAT scores achieved by prekindergarten children who later enrolled in the model that their median performance on the MAT would not have exceeded the twenty-fifth percentile. Therefore, the twenty-fifth percentile was chosen as the best estimate of the students' entry performance level (See Figure 4.2.) The performance of post-third grade students in Direct Instruction classrooms was at or near the national norm for each of the four MAT subtests. Since these MAT scores for students who enrolled in the model in three different years (1969, 1970, 1971) in 12 communities are nearly identical to those reported in the Abt IV Report, which contains results from a more limited sample (see the section entitled "National Longitudinal Evaluation"), they provide additional evidence of the effectiveness of the model.

Is there a cumulative improvement over years of model implementation? In communities where students were enrolled initially in kindergarten, the median WRAT scores among those children who entered the model from 1969 to 1974 improved steadily year by year in reading and arithmetic and to a lesser degree in spelling. The average magnitude of improvement is approximately one-half standard deviation per year. The gains occurred primarily during the kindergarten year and were maintained through later grades.

Do students who spend more time in the model make the greatest gains? The data from communities where students enrolled in the model at the first-grade level indicate that they made substantial progress toward reaching the national norms. But since they had one less year of instruction, the effects across the first-entering groups are about one-quarter standard deviation below those of the K-entering groups. Thus, it was concluded that students make substantially more progress when they enroll in the model at the kindergarten level.

In six communities, some children were enrolled in the model in kindergarten classrooms and others in first-grade classrooms. On nearly every comparison, those students who began their participation at the kindergarten level performed significantly higher on achievement tests at the end of third grade. The average magnitude of their higher performance was one-half standard deviation, or .6 to .8 grade levels at the end of third grade. These findings are consistent with the results of the comparison between K-entering and first-entering students reported in the preceding paragraph, but the within-community comparisons show an effect twice as large. Because there were regional variations in populations and school procedures between K-entering communities and first-entering communities, these within-community comparisons probably more truly reflect the actual gains produced by academic instruction during kindergarten.

In 1970, implementation of the model began in a school sponsored by the Bureau of Indian Affairs (BIA) in Cherokee, North Carolina. The school was the only one in that community, and most of the students and teachers remained in the program throughout the evaluation period. At the beginning of the 1970 school year, some students were enrolled in kindergarten, others in first grade, and others in second grade. This situation provided a unique opportunity to examine the impact of the model by comparing the performance of children who had 2, 3, or 4 years of attendance in the Direct Instruction classrooms.

Table 4.1 contains the results of analyses of data obtained from students who completed the third grade in the Cherokee project. Generally, there is a pattern of gradual improvement in performance on each measure, and that pattern occurs in proportion to the amount of time that children attended Direct Instruction Model classrooms. The magnitude of improvement for each additional year of attendance in the model was generally more than one-half standard deviation per year.

Do students maintain or lose the gains they make through attendance in the Direct Instruction Model after they leave the program? To obtain an answer to this question, two studies were conducted among fifth and sixth grade students in which the WRAT, levels 1 and 2, and the MAT, intermediate level, were administered to approximately 2600 students. In 1975, achievement tests were administered to approximately 700 students who attended the Follow Through classrooms and to a similar number who

TABLE 4.1

Effects of Time Enrolled in Direct Instruction Model on WRAT and MAT Achievement Grade Percentiles among Four Cherokee Groups[a]

	2 years	3 years	4 years	4 years
WRAT N	99	114	103	85
Reading	45	79	79	84
Arithmetic	34	45	55	58
MAT N	—	109	102	83
Total Reading	—	36	47	52
Total Math	—	47	65	68
Language	—	40	67	67
Spelling	—	36	42	49

[a] Data for each group were collected near the completion of third grade. All comparisons of mean standard scores (2- versus 4-year groups and 3- versus 4-year groups) were significant beyond the .05 level, except the comparison for the 3- versus 4-year groups for WRAT Reading. The two 4-year groups represent successive cohorts.

had attended regular classrooms. These data were obtained in a total of seven communities. In 1976, a study of the same design was performed to compare the achievement test scores of approximately 600 students who had attended Follow Through classrooms and a similar number who had not. These data were obtained in a total of six communities. All students were selected from schools having populations of students with roughly similar backgrounds. In addition, covariance analyses were used to adjust mean differences on outcome measures for differences in student background characteristics.

The statements that follow summarize the data analyses for performance on WRAT reading, Level 1; WRAT reading, Level 2; MAT total reading; MAT total math; and MAT science.

1. Among 53 group comparisons of mean scores derived from the data obtained in 1975, a total of 24 mean differences were significantly higher for students who had attended Direct Instruction classrooms (.05 level, one-tailed tests). No mean differences were significantly higher for the non-Follow-Through students.

2. Among 55 comparisons of mean scores derived from the data obtained in 1976, a total of 26 mean differences were significantly higher for students who had attended Follow Through classrooms, and none were significantly higher for the non-Follow-Through students.

3. The greatest number of significant mean differences were found on the two WRAT reading measures. This might have been expected, due to the comparative superiority of the Follow Through students' scores on these tests among the post-third-grade populations, as shown previously in Table 4.1. Approximately one-third of the comparisons of group mean scores for MAT total reading, MAT total math, and MAT science yielded significant mean differences in favor of the Follow Through students. The comparatively higher mean scores for Follow Through students in MAT science may be attributed to the science content contained in the DISTAR Reading III program. For all but five groups, the results are based on first-entering students.

Generally, the *levels* of former students' performance in the years after they leave Follow Through classrooms are disappointing. As they progress from third to fifth and sixth grade, their losses against national norms are sizeable in many cases. Those losses were especially great on MAT total math and MAT total reading (comprehension). In math, they lost about three-fourths of a standard deviation against national norms and dropped from the fiftieth to the twenty-third percentile. Similarly, in reading comprehension, they lost about one-fourth standard deviation and dropped from the thirty-fifth to the twenty-fifth percentile. Decoding skills in reading were maintained. There is a clear implication that the gains that students make in compensatory educational programs cannot be maintained after they leave such programs, unless all schools provide effective teaching for every child in every grade. This is certainly not the case today.[4]

How do low-performing students perform in the Direct Instruction Model? One of the primary goals has been to develop effective procedures for teaching low-performing students. To determine whether the Direct Instruction approach had succeeded in teaching basic skills to those children, the performance of two groups was compared: a large group of low-IQ children who had pretested SIT IQ scores below 80 and *all* children enrolled in Direct Instruction classrooms. The performance of these two groups was compared on the following three dimensions: gains in reading and arithmetic, number of lessons completed, and gains in IQ scores. Data pertaining to the comparisons on each of the three dimensions is presented next.

1. Gains in reading and arithmetic. Figure 4.3 contains comparisons of the gains on WRAT reading tests made by low-IQ children and by all children enrolled at the stated grade levels in the Direct Instruction Model. Inspection of Figure 4.3 reveals that children in the low-IQ group, who had a mean SIT IQ score of 73, gained more than a year on the WRAT reading test for each year of instruction they received in the model, and they achieved similar gains on the WRAT arithmetic tests. The average gain in arithmetic for K-starting, low-IQ students was .95 grade equivalents; the average gain for the all-group was 1.00 grade equivalent. The average gain in arithmetic for the first-starting, low-IQ group was 1.04 grade equivalents and 1.07 grade equivalents for the all-group.[5] Generally, the data indicate

[4]Some individuals might interpret this loss as a serious weakness in the Direct Instruction Model, but that conclusion is opposed by the following facts: (*a*) Students enrolled in the model significantly outperformed those in comparison groups 2 and 3 years after they had completed the third grade; (*b*) these effects were demonstrated primarily in communities where children were enrolled in the model only 3 years, (*c*) no other approach has demonstrated better results; and (*d*) it is unreasonable to expect that gains will be sustained in the absence of effective school programs. Such programs rarely exist in grades 4, 5, and 6 in schools that have high concentrations of low-income children. The results of more complete analysis of these effects is presented in Becker (1977) and is summarized later in this chapter.

[5]Examination of the gains in standard score units does not change the implications of the data. For several reasons, it is clear that these gains are not due to statistical regression effects. First, the low-IQ group was selected on the basis of SIT IQ, not WRAT performance. The regression effect on the IQ scores directly (see Footnote 8) would amount only to two IQ points (from 73 to 75). The effect on WRAT scores, which correlate only .45 to .50 with SIT IQ at entry, would be less. The magnitude of the *gains* in standard score units (SD equals 15 for the WRAT) range from one to two standard deviations in magnitude. This is at least 15 times any possible regression effect.

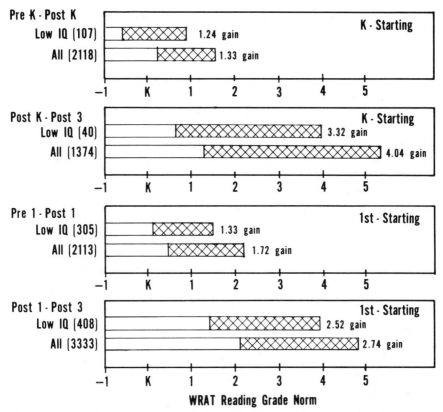

FIGURE 4.3. *Reading gains of low-IQ children from low-income backgrounds. Shaded area indicates gain for the time period shown to the left of each chart. Low IQ = IQ of 80 or less in Direct Instruction Follow Through model. All = All children enrolled in Direct Instruction Follow Through model.*

that low-IQ children can be taught much more than is usually assumed.

2. Number of lessons completed. A comparison of the number of lessons taught each year to children in the low-IQ group and those in the all-group revealed that low-IQ children were taught 30 fewer DISTAR lessons (160 is average) in kindergarten and 25 fewer in first grade. In grades 2 and 3, the difference decreased to less than 15. Thus, by second grade, low-IQ children were progressing at 90% of the average rate.

3. Gains in IQ scores. Children in both the all-group and the low-IQ group made gains in IQ. Those in the all-group had an average IQ score gain at the end of third grade of about 8 points for both K-starting and first-starting groups. The low-IQ groups were estimated to have made an

average gain of between 8 and 14 points, discounting statistical regression effects.[6]

Discussion

The evidence cited above supports the general conclusion that the designers of the Direct Instruction Model have succeeded in teaching basic skills and intellectual competencies to a variety of children from low-income backgrounds. At the end of third grade, the students in the model performed at or near national norms on all indices used for evaluation. The evidence also supports the following summary statements: (*a*) The educationally significant gains that students in the model display at the end of third grade are weaker, but can still be detected, among those students when they reach fifth and sixth grade levels; (*b*) the teaching efforts to help low-performing children "catch up" with their more advantaged peers are more effective when they begin at the kindergarten level; and (*c*) the Direct Instruction DISTAR programs are effective for lower-IQ students. When these findings are combined with other evidence that advantaged children gain 3 years in academic achievement during 2 years of attendance in Direct Instruction classrooms (Engelmann & Carnine, Note 9), it seems reasonable to conclude that the model can be employed to teach basic academic skills to all children.

Rosenshine (1976) summarized the literature on relationships between methods of teaching and learning outcomes for the National Society for the Study of Education (NSSE) yearbook. He concluded, "As one looks at the findings on time, content covered, work groupings, teacher questions, student responses, and adult feedback, one sees a general pattern of results that might be labelled the direct instruction model (sometimes called the structured approach) [p. 364]." Rosenshine also cites similar findings by Stallings and Kaskowitz (Note 10), Soar (Note 11), and Brophy and Evertson (Note 12) in reaching his conclusions. Rosenshine's conclusion that structured approaches to classroom instruction produce the greatest educational gains among students is consistent with and strongly supports the results of evaluation research on the effects of the Direct Instruction Model.

NATIONAL LONGITUDINAL EVALUATION

The Direct Instruction Model was one of the models included in the national longitudinal evaluation of Follow Through. The major report of the results, the Abt Report, was prepared by Abt Associates of Cambridge,

---

[6] The true mean score on pretest was estimated by using this formula: $\overline{X}_T = \overline{X}_K \cdot r_{xx'}$ where $\overline{X}_K$ is the mean of low-IQ group in deviation units, and r_{xx} is the reliability coefficent (.92).

Massachusetts (Stebbins, St. Pierre, Proper, Anderson, & Cerva, 1977, Note 13). Inspection of the Abt IV Report reveals that the Direct Instruction Model ranked at or near the top on most of the measures used in the national evaluation. A summary of the contents of that report is presented in the following six sections: (a) method; (b) results for the Direct Instruction Model; (c) relative comparisons of effectiveness among Follow Through models; (d) absolute comparisons of effectiveness among Follow Through models; (e) variability of effects across sites; and (f) discussion.

Method

The instruments employed in the national longitudinal evaluation and the design of the evaluation research are described in the following.

Instruments The instruments employed in the national evaluation included measures of basic academic skills, cognitive–conceptual skills, self-esteem, and locus of control. The Metropolitan Achievement Test (MAT, Elementary Level, Form F) was employed to assess children's performance in the following four areas of basic skills: word knowledge, spelling, language (usage), and math computation. The MAT also contains subtests that measure the following cognitive–conceptual skills: reading, math concepts, and math problem solving. Raven's coloured Progressive Matrices (Raven, 1956) was also used to measure cognitive–conceptual skills. The Self-Esteem Inventory (Coopersmith, 1967) and the Intellectual Achievement Responsibility Scale (IARS) (Crandall, Katkowsky, & Crandall, 1965) were used to assess self-esteem and locus of control, respectively. Coopersmith's Self-Esteem Inventory contains items that pertain to children's feelings about themselves, the way they think other people feel about them, and their feelings about school. Crandall's IARS instrument measures the extent to which children believe that the consequences of their behavior are under either their personal control or under the control of strong, overwhelming persons, authority figures, or impersonal forces (fate control). The IARS measures the extent to which children attribute their success (+) or failure (−) to their own behavior or to other forces.

The reliabilities (internal consistency) of the MAT scores were discussed previously. Internal consistency coefficients for the other instruments, as reported by Abt Associates (Note 14), are .78 for the Self-Esteem Inventory, .85 for Raven's Coloured Progressive Matrices, and .55 for the IARS (+) scale and .56 for the IARS (−) scale. The reliabilities for the two IARS scales are too low to be useful for making judgments about individuals, but the scales may be useful for making comparisons among groups. All data were collected under the auspices of the Stanford Research Institute, Menlo Park, California.

Design The design of the national evaluation included students from both Follow Through and non-Follow-Through classrooms and has often been referred to as a "comparison group design." For each of the nine major models included in the national evaluation, data were collected in from four to eight communities in which Follow Through classrooms were implemented at the kindergarten level. In most of the communities selected, data were obtained from K-entering children in 1970, who were labeled Cohort II, and from K-entering children in 1971, who were labeled Cohort III. This approach to collecting data permitted the evaluators to compare the results of tests administered in two successive years. In addition, the plan for data collection included a number of communities where students were enrolled initially in first-grade classrooms, because there were no kindergarten classrooms. Data were collected from the children near the beginning of the entry grade and at the end of each school year until they completed third grade. The Cohort II study included a total of 13 model sponsors, 52 communities where children were enrolled initially in kindergarten classrooms, 10 communities where children were initially in first-grade classrooms, 4205 children enrolled in Follow Through classrooms, and 2901 children enrolled in comparison classrooms. The Cohort III study included a total of 16 model sponsors, 63 communities where children were enrolled initially in kindergarten classrooms, 14 communities where children were enrolled initially in first-grade classrooms, 5050 children enrolled in Follow Through classrooms, and 3584 children enrolled in comparison classrooms.

The use of comparison groups presented a number of problems in some communities. Frequently the students in the comparison groups were more advantaged on socioeconomic indicators than those in the Follow Through groups, and often they were the children who remained after the most disadvantaged had been selected for placement in the Follow Through classrooms. Because there were a number of difficulties in equating the students enrolled in Follow Through and comparison classrooms, covariates were used to adjust outcomes for initial differences in the characteristics of the students. The analyses of data also presented a number of other problems for the researchers at Abt Associates, but they handled them with sufficient sophistication to justify placing some confidence in the results. Haney (Note 15) provides a very thoughtful critique of the progress of the national evaluation of Follow Through from its inception, and in particular he addresses the complex issues involved in the use of covariance adjustments.

An extreme example of the difficulties encountered in collecting evaluation data occurred in Grand Rapids, Michigan, one of the communities in which evaluation data were collected to assess the effects of the Direct Instruct Model. However, the Direct Instruction Model was not implemented by teachers in that community during at least 2 years of the data collection period, and the sponsor withdrew formally. The performance levels of Follow Through children in Grand Rapids, in both Cohort II and Cohort III, are the lowest among all the K-starting communities where children were enrolled in Direct Instruction classrooms. More will be stated below in the subsection entitled "Variability of Effects across Sites" about the problems encountered in attempts to implement the model in Grand Rapids.

It would also be possible to state a number of other important qualifications that should be considered by those persons who seek to interpret the data from the national longitudinal evaluation of Follow Through (for example, see Becker, Note 16). But the primary point of emphasis here is that the results of the national evaluation probably underestimate the actual accomplishments of many sponsors' models. Indeed, as much as 25–30% of the impact of sponsors' models may have been "washed out" by various problems that detracted from accurate measurement of the effectiveness of the different models. However, even though the national evaluation effort is open to criticism on a number of specific points, it represents a landmark of progress in the application of empirical procedures to social problems and is one of the most trustworthy field studies yet conducted in education.

Results for the Direct Instruction Model

The major findings of the Abt Report (Note 13) are presented in a series of tables, one for each sponsor. Figure 4.4 contains the summary of evaluation results for the Direct Instruction Model. The scores on each outcome measure were adjusted by covariance techniques that permitted researchers to (a) compare the performance of children in Follow Through and comparison classrooms in *local* communities; and (b) compare the performance of children in a particular Follow Through community with the performance of all non-Follow-Through comparison children in that cohort and entering-grade group. This latter comparison is called the *pooled* comparison in contrast to the *local* comparison.

The plus (+) and minus (−) signs that appear in Figure 4.4 indicate the directionality of differences in performance between children enrolled in Follow Through and comparison classrooms. When the performance of the children in the Follow Through classrooms exceeds the performance of those in the non-Follow-Through comparison classrooms by at least one-fourth standard deviation on a given outcome measure and when the difference is statistically significant, the result is considered to be a positive, educationally significant outcome and a plus sign (+) is placed in the table. When non-Follow-Through exceeds Follow Through by the same criteria,

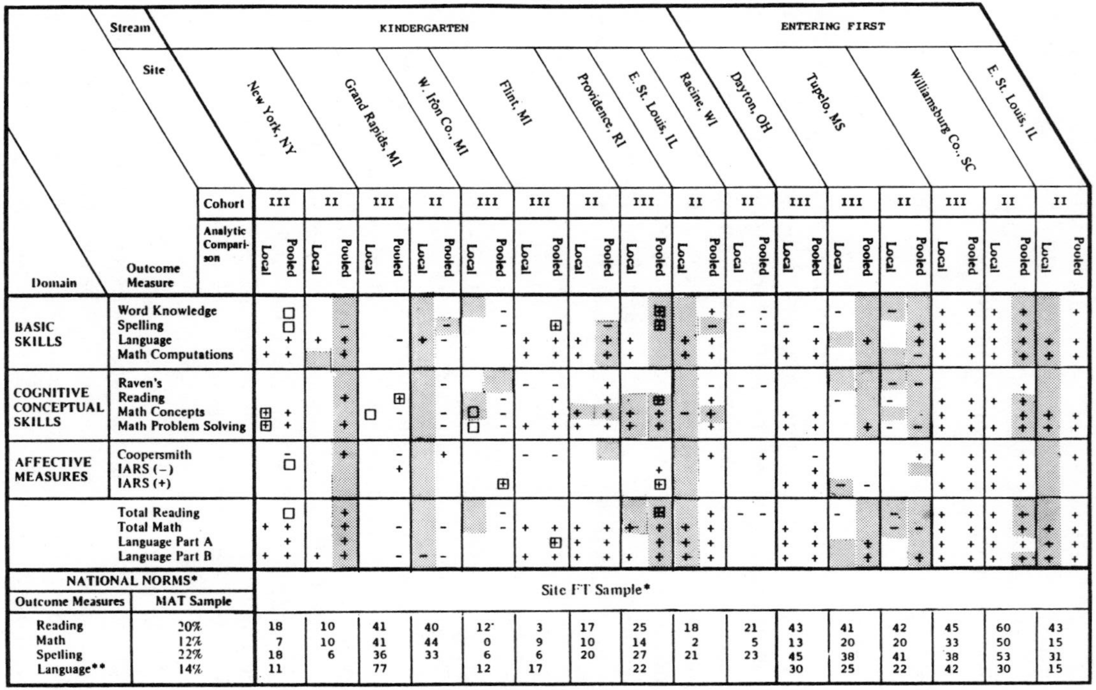

Notes:

* In terms of percentage of children performing one or more years below grade level.

** No national norms comparisons were made for Cohort II-K children on the Language subtest.

\+ FT-favoring effect
\- NFT-favoring effect
blank Null effect

☐ Preschool Adjustment changes effect
▒ Untrustworthy effect

FIGURE 4.4 *Summary of effects for Direct Instruction sites. Figure from Stebbins* et al. *(Note 13, Vol. IVB, page 72).*

the result is considered to be a negative, educationally significant outcome and a minus sign ($-$) is placed in the table. When the results are between these limits, the difference is considered null, and not educationally significant. At the third grade level, the one-fourth standard deviation criterion corresponds to about 2 months' difference in grade norm levels.[7]

Figure 4.4 contains evaluation results for each of the Direct Instruction programs included in the national evaluation. Note that the results for K-entering groups are presented first, followed by the results for the first-entering groups. The students in Cohort III enrolled in Follow Through in 1971 and completed third grade in 1974 or 1975. The members of Cohort II enrolled in Follow Through in 1970 and completed third grade in 1973 or 1974. The four lines of numbers at the bottom of Figure 4.4 contain the percent of children who are 1 year or more below grade level on key MAT measures. An earlier version of the tables represented by Figure 4.4 contained median grade equivalents for each community. This information is included below in the subsection on "Absolute Comparisons of Effectiveness among Follow Through Models."

The grayed outcomes in Figure 4.4 are those that are labeled in the Abt Report as "untrustworthy effects," and they are given no consideration in the final summary report. In effect, this decision eliminated approximately one-third of the total data for most Follow Through models. Effects are grayed out for the follow reasons: (a) The whole column of effects is grayed out if the difference between Follow Through and non-Follow-Through classrooms in the percentage of children attending preschool exceeds 50; and (b) a particular effect is grayed out when the covariance adjustment changes the mean score for a community by more than one-half standard deviation. It may be argued that these rules for applying grayout are inappropriate. Why should significantly positive effects be labeled "untrustworthy" when they occur under conditions in which the adjustments of mean differences make the detection of differences in favor of the Follow Through model less likely?

Consider the grayouts due to differences between Follow Through and non-Follow-Through classrooms in preschool attendance in the following communities: New York II pooled, Grand Rapids II local, E. St. Louis II local K, and E. St. Louis local first. Children enrolled in Follow Through classrooms are more likely to attend preschool than children enrolled in non-Follow-Through classrooms because attendance in Head Start by 50%

---

[7] In the K-entering streams, 25% of the differences designated null were educationally significant but not statistically significant, probably because of attrition effects on sample size. Only 5% were statistically significant but not educationally significant. This outcome again suggests that the results of the analysis may be an underestimate of substantial effects in favor of Follow Through.

or more of the children is a requirement for maintaining a Follow Through classroom. In fact, this is the case in each of the Direct Instruction programs.

Inspection of the data for the students in Cohort III (Note 13, pp. 184–185) reveals that, among children enrolled in Follow Through classrooms, attendance in preschool for the most part (up to $-.09$) correlates negatively with outcome measures. Among non-Follow-Through students, the correlations between attendance in preschool and outcomes tend to be positive (up to $+.05$). Due to the low magnitude of these effects, as compared to other entry differences already included in the covariance adjustment, one could easily argue that there is no reason to even consider such effects, much less eliminate data because of them. Furthermore, due to the direction of the effects noted above, *any such effects would certainly make the detection of differences in favor of students in Follow Through classrooms less likely.* Consequently, it may be argued that postive effects that occur in spite of such negative biases should be retained and reported as conservative estimates, not untrustworthy effects.

Next, consider the grayout of covarience-adjusted effects larger than one-half standard deviation in outcome measure units. The authors of the Abt IV Report (and Campbell & Erlebacher, 1970) note that the effect of a covariance adjustment is to underestimate the true adjustment for the group that is initially lower on the covariates (*lower* means more disadvantaged on SES measures and entry test scores). Examination of the directions of adjustments for the Direct Instruction communities, as presented in the appendices to Abt IV-A, Tables A4-8 to A4-17, reveals that among 78 cases, in only 5 did the adjustment decrease the mean score for the Follow Through groups. The clear implication is that the effect of the adjustment is to create an underestimate of the actual impact of the Direct Instruction Model. Among the 78 grayed-out comparisons, 36 have a positive ($+$) outcome in favor of the Direct Instruction Model, 13 have a negative ($-$) outcome in favor of the non-Follow-Through comparison groups, and 29 show no difference (blank). Since the ratio of positive outcomes to negative outcomes is approximately three to one in spite of the undercorrections, these outcomes should be interpreted as conservative rather than suspect.

Due to the considerations stated above, it seemed necessary to present the sponsor's summary of the Abt findings, which includes all the data presented in Figure 4.4, for purposes of discussing the effects of the Direct Instruction Model. Actually, the results of this procedure for making relative and absolute comparisons of the effects of various Follow Through models do not lead to conclusions that differ significantly from those stated by the authors of the Abt Report, but they do increase substantially the data base from which the conclusions are drawn.

Relative Comparisons of Effectiveness
among Follow Through Models

The authors of the Abt Report and the sponsor developed similar procedures for utilizing the information contained in the tables that summarize evaluation results in order to make relative comparisons among nine Follow Through models. As stated previously, Figure 4.4 is one of a series of tables, one for each sponsor, contained in the Abt Report. Those tables contain pluses and minuses to indicate the outcome of comparisons between the performance of children enrolled in Follow Through and non-Follow-Through classrooms. The authors of the Abt Report developed an index of "significant" outcomes by subtracting the number of minuses from the number of pluses in each area of measurement, such as basic skills, and dividing the result by the total number of comparisons (see Figure 4.4). Thus, the value of each index calculated for each sponsor could vary in the range from plus one to minus one.

Members of the sponsor's staff developed a similar index called an Index of Significant Outcomes (ISO). The ISOs differ from Abt's index in two ways: (*a*) Decimal points are eliminated by multiplying the index by 1000, permitting the index to vary in the range from -1000 to $+1000$; and (*b*) the index was based on a different counting rule. For example, if either the local or the pooled comparison, or both, was plus ($+$) for a given comparison, the effect was designated as a plus; if either, or both, was a minus ($-$), the effect was designated as a minus. Thus, if a sponsor has more positive outcomes than negative outcomes in a given group of effects, the ISO is positive; if a majority of the effects are negative, the ISO is negative. The ISOs can be used to make relative comparisons among models and among areas within models.[8] Some of the most important comparisons are presented in the following sections. (At this point, the reader may wish to review the description of evaluation instruments presented earlier in this section.)

Comparisons on Measures of Basic Skills Table 4.2 contains the following information for each of nine Follow Through models: (*a*) basic skills ISOs for word knowledge, spelling, language, and math computation; (*b*) average ISOs for the four areas of basic skills; and (*c*) a ranking of each model's effectiveness in teaching basic skills. Figure 4.5 contains in graph form the information presented in Column 5 (Average for basic skills) of Table 4.2. The authors in this volume have agreed to refrain from discuss-

---

[8]Subsequent to this report, Becker (1978) presented the Abt significance of outcome data in three ways: (*a*) using all data, but without the either/or rule used in the present analyses; (*b*) selectively keeping grayed-out data where it is significant and operating against a built-in bias; and (*c*) using the Abt IV analysis rules. All three analyses lead to the same conclusions stated here.

TABLE 4.2
Indices of Significant Outcomes (ISOs) for Basic Skills

Model	Word knowledge	Spelling	Language	Math computation	Average for basic skills	Ranking on basic skills
DI	+062	−125	+668	+562	+297	1
B	+250	000	−250	+083	+021	2
C	000	−385	−154	+615	+019	3
A	−500	+125	+375	000	000	4
D	−250	−750	+083	−083	−250	5
E	−312	−625	−188	000	−281	6
F	−400	−667	−333	−067	−367	7
G	−444	−333	−556	−222	−389	8
H	−400	−500	−500	−400	−425	9

ing directly the results of each other's models. Therefore, other models are identified by the letters *A* thru *H*, and the same letter is used consistently for each model in other comparisons presented in this chapter. Readers who wish to obtain additional detailed information about the results of comparisons among Follow Through models are referred to the Abt Reports (Cline, 1976; Note 13 and 14) and to Becker (Note 17). (DI = Direct Instruction in Tables 4.2–4.5 and in Figures 4.5–4.11.)

Inspection of Table 4.2 and Figure 4.5 reveals that on measures of basic skills, the Direct Instruction Model ranks first in language, second in word knowledge and math computation, and third in spelling. The Direct Instruction Model has the highest average ISO for basic skills. Only three sponsors achieved a positive ISO. The average ISO score achieved by students in the Direct Instruction Model is more than 500 points higher than the average score achieved by five of the eight other models.

Comparisons on Measures of Cognitive–Conceptual Skills Table 4.3 contains the following information for each of nine Follow Through models: (*a*) cognitive–conceptual skills ISOs for reading comprehension, math concepts, and math problem solving; (*b*) average ISOs for the three areas of cognitive–conceptual skills; and (*c*) a ranking of each model's effectiveness in teaching cognitive–conceptual skills and basic skills. Figure 4.6 contains in graph form the information presented in Column 4 (Average for cognitive–conceptual skills) of Table 4.3. Many persons expected that children enrolled in the Direct Instruction Model would perform well on tests of basic skills but that they would perform poorly on tests of cognitive–conceptual skills. The data clearly indicate otherwise, since the ISO scores for the Direct Instruction Model rank first on measures of

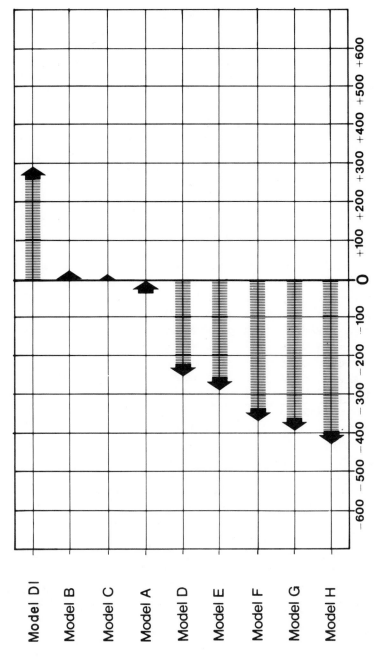

FIGURE 4.5. *Average Index of Significant Outcomes (ISO) for basic skills (word knowledge, spelling, language, and math computation) for nine Follow Through models.*

133

TABLE 4.3
Indices of Significant Outcomes (ISOs) for Cognitive–Conceptual Skills

Model	Reading comprehension	Math concepts	Math problem solving	Average for cognitive–conceptual skills	Ranking on cognitive–conceptual skills	Ranking on basic skills
DI	+312	+250	+500	+354	1	1
A	000	+375	+125	+167	2	4
B	+083	−083	000	000	3	2
D	000	−333	−167	−167	4	5
E	−125	−250	−188	−188	5	6
C	−231	−231	−154	−205	6	3
F	−333	−400	−267	−333	7.5	7
G	−222	−444	−333	−333	7.5	8
H	−500	−400	−400	−433	9	9

reading comprehension and math probelm solving and second on a measure of math concepts. It is also the only model that has positive ISOs in all three areas. Only two models have positive average ISOs for cognitive–conceptual skills. The reader will note that the rankings for each of the nine models are virtually the same for both basic skills and cognitive–conceptual skills. This consistency in the two areas indicates that (a) the skills that comprise the two general areas are closely related; (b) models that are effective in one area are also effective in the other; and (c) models that produce weak effects in basic skills also produce weak effects in cognitive–conceptual skills.

The ISOs for the Raven's Coloured Progressive Matrices are presented in Table 4.4. This instrument was viewed as a measure of problem solving ability and was included in the national evaluation at the urgent request of those sponsors who emphasized the need to assess student's performance in nonverbal, visual–motor areas. The test consists of colored matrix patterns that have a part missing. The task is to choose the correct missing part from six options. Children enrolled in the Direct Instruction Model achieved a negative ISO, and they were not among the top performers on this test. One interpretation of these results is that they demonstrate an important advantage for other models. But a more accurate conclusion is that children's performance on the Raven's is not significantly influenced by programmatic efforts of Follow Through sponsors. This conclusion is supported by both the low values of the two ISOs that were positive (083 and 067), and by the finding that only 3 among the total of 27 comparisons were positive, a result that could have occurred by chance.

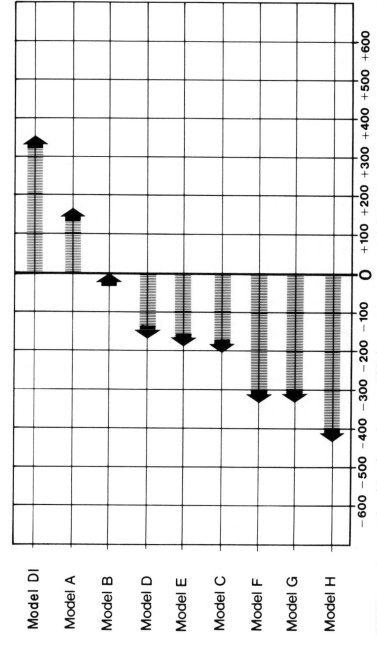

FIGURE 4.6. *Average Index of Significant Outcomes (ISO) for cognitive–conceptual skills (reading comprehension, math concepts, and math problem solving) for nine Follow Through models.*

135

TABLE 4.4
Indices of Significant Outcomes (ISOs) for
Raven's Coloured Progressive Matrices

Model	ISO	Rank
B	+083	1
F	+067	2
D	000	3
H	−100	4
E	−125	5.5
A	−125	5.5
DI	−188	7
G	−333	8
C	−538	9

Comparisons on Measures of Affective Characteristics Table 4.5 contains
the following information for each of nine Follow Through models: (a) affective characteristics ISOs for the Coopersmith Self-Esteem instrument
and the Intellectual Achievement Responsibility Scale (IARS− and IARS+
subscales); (b) average ISOs for the affective characertistics; and (c) rankings of each model's effectiveness in teaching affective characteristics,
cognitive–conceptual skills, and basic skills. Figure 4.7 contains in graph
form the information presented in Column 4 (Average on affective
characteristics) of Table 4.5. In their review of the data obtained from the

TABLE 4.5
Indices of Significant Outcomes (ISOs)
for Affective Characteristics

Model	Coopersmith self-esteem inventory	Intellectual achievement responsibility scale		Average on affective character- istics	Ranking on affective character- istics	Ranking on cognitive– conceptual skills	Ranking on basic skills
		IARS−	IARS+				
DI	+250	+312	+250	+270	1	1	1
C	+538	+308	−154	+231	2	6	3
B	+083	+167	+167	+139	3	3	2
A	+375	000	000	+125	4	2	4
D	+166	−166	−166	−056	5	4	5
G	−111	−111	000	−074	6	7.5	8
E	−062	−250	−125	−146	7	5	6
H	−100	−300	−300	−233	8	9	9
F	−200	−467	−400	−356	9	7.5	7

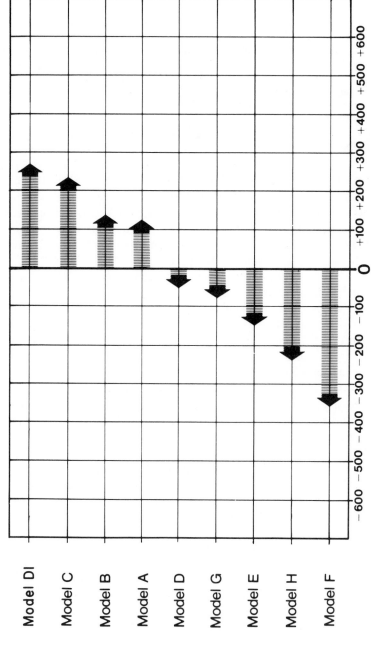

FIGURE 4.7. *Average Index of Significant Outcomes (ISO) for affective characteristics (Coopersmith Self-Esteem Inventory and Intellectual Achievement Responsibility Scale) for nine Follow Through models.*

measures of affective characteristics, the authors of the Abt IV Report stated:

> To some observers, the performance of FT children in Direct Instruction sites on the affective measures was an unexpected result. The Direct Instruction Model does not explicitly emphasize affective outcomes of instruction, but the sponsor has asserted that they will be the consequence of effective teaching. Critics of the model have predicted that the emphasis in the model on tightly controlled instruction might discourage children from freely expressing themselves and thus inhibit the development of self-esteem and other affective skills. In fact, this is not the case [Note 13, p. 73].

Indeed, the children enrolled in the Direct Instruction Model rank first on the average ISO index for the affective measures presented in Table 4.5. The reader will note that there is a remarkable correlation between the rank scores achieved by Follow Through models in the three areas: affective characteristics, cognitive–conceptual skills, and basic skills. The sponsors whose models produced positive average ISO scores on affective measures are generally those who achieve the most impressive academic outcomes. *Competence leads to confidence.* (See Becker *et al.*, 1971, Unit 14. This unit is devoted to the topic of self-esteem and was written in 1968, the same year in which Follow Through began.)

In summary, the results of relative comparisons among the nine Follow Through models support the conclusion that the Direct Instruction Model is more effective than either traditional educational programs, which are represented by the comparison classrooms in local communities, or other Follow Through model approaches that had the same level of resources available to them. The consistency of these findings cannot reasonably be attributed to chance; in fact, the conclusions stated above are also strongly supported by the results of comparisons of absolute levels of performance among the nine models, which are presented next.

Absolute Comparisons of Effectiveness among Follow Through Models

The Abt IV preliminary summary tables for sponsors contained grade-equivalent medians by site and by sponsor for four MAT measures: total reading, total math, spelling, and language.[9] The horizontal "fiftieth per-

---

[9] Medians are less biased by a few extremely high scores, as occur on reading tests. Missing language scores for Cohort II–K were replaced by site means. The preliminary tables used in this analysis were released to the author by Gene Tucker of the USOE-Follow Through evaluation staff. These data may also be recovered from several tables in the Abt III and IV reports (Notes 13 and 14) that contain standardized scores by site and sponsor.

centile line" in each table represents the national median performance level in each subject for *all* children who have completed the third grade. These data were averaged across sites, giving equal weight to each site, and converted to percentiles. Figures 4.8, 4.9, 4.10, and 4.11 display the percentiles on a one-fourth standard deviation scale, and differences among sponsors of one-fourth standard deviation are easily detected in these tables. The twentieth percentile represents the typical performance level of *low-income* children in regular grade classrooms, and serves as a reference baseline in Figures 4.8, 4.9, 4.10, and 4.11.

Figures 4.8, 4.9, 4.10, and 4.11 contain the percentile scores achieved by the children enrolled in the nine Follow Through models. The Direct Instruction Model is clearly the highest in absolute performance and approaches national norms on all four MAT instruments. The reading programs of four sponsors are more than one-fourth standard deviation above the Title I average on total reading by the end of third grade, but the best

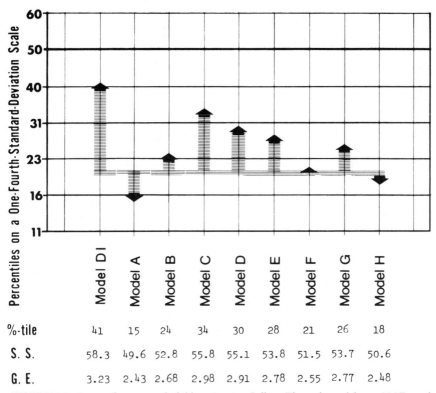

%-tile	41	15	24	34	30	28	21	26	18
S. S.	58.3	49.6	52.8	55.8	55.1	53.8	51.5	53.7	50.6
G. E.	3.23	2.43	2.68	2.98	2.91	2.78	2.55	2.77	2.48

FIGURE 4.8. *Percentile scores of children in nine Follow Through models on MAT total reading measure. The grade equivalent for the fiftieth percentile is 3.5.*

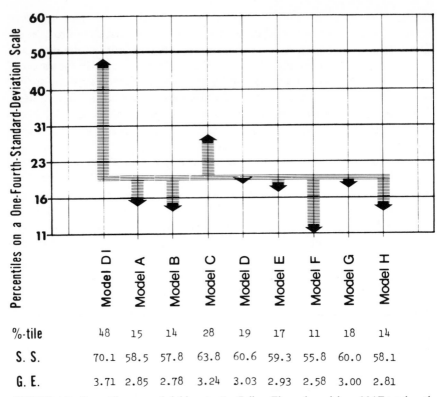

%-tile	48	15	14	28	19	17	11	18	14
S. S.	70.1	58.5	57.8	63.8	60.6	59.3	55.8	60.0	58.1
G. E.	3.71	2.85	2.78	3.24	3.03	2.93	2.58	3.00	2.81

FIGURE 4.9. *Percentile scores of children in nine Follow Through models on MAT total math measure. The grade equivalent for the fiftieth percentile is 3.75.*

results were achieved by students in Direct Instruction classrooms (see Figure 4.8). On total math, children enrolled in the Direct Instruction Model performed at least one-half standard deviation above children enrolled in all other models (see Figure 4.9). On spelling, students in Direct Instruction classrooms were at the national median, as shown in Figure 4.10. On language (usage, punctuation, and sentence type), the children enrolled in the Direct Instruction Model performed at a level that is three-fourths of a standard deviation above all the others (see Figure 4.11).

Taken together, the results of both relative and absolute comparisons among nine Follow Through models clearly reveal the superior performance of children enrolled in the Direct Instruction Model. The results of the absolute comparisons among Follow Through models confirm and strengthen the conclusions derived previously from the results of the relative comparisons among these models. The Direct Instruction Model

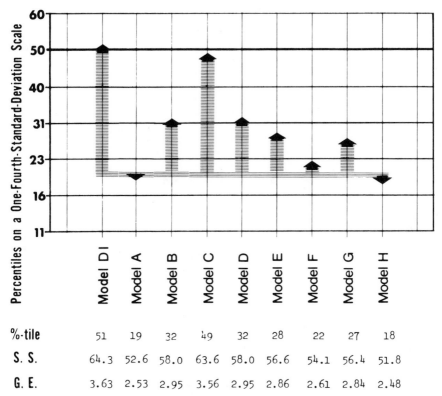

FIGURE 4.10. *Percentile scores of children in nine Follow Through models on MAT spelling measure. The grade equivalent for the fiftieth percentile is 3.6.*

appears to contain instructional methods and materials that teachers can use to produce superior outcomes in nearly every area of instruction.

Variability of Effects across Sites

A major conclusion stated by the authors of the Abt IV Report is that the level of effectiveness of each Follow Through model varies from one community to another. They state, "The main lesson of site variability is that the models are not powerful enough to countervail unmeasured, site-specific determinants of outcomes. Any model can 'fail' by having a group perform lower on a test than it would have without Follow Through. [Note 13, p. 140.]" But this conclusion cannot be accurately applied to the outcomes of the Direct Instruction Model.

One reason for opposing the application of Abt's general conclusion about site variability to the Direct Instruction Model is that the authors of

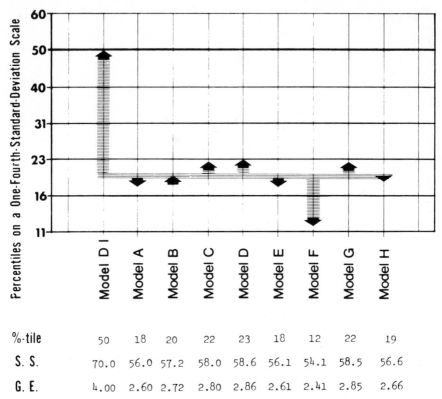

%-tile	50	18	20	22	23	18	12	22	19
S. S.	70.0	56.0	57.2	58.0	58.6	56.1	54.1	58.5	56.6
G. E.	4.00	2.60	2.72	2.80	2.86	2.61	2.41	2.85	2.66

FIGURE 4.11. *Percentile scores of children in nine Follow Through models on MAT language measure. The grade equivalent for the fiftieth percentile is 4.0.*

the Abt Report failed to acknowledge the unusual events that occurred at many Follow Through sites. For example, one of the most obvious set of circumstances that tends to weaken Abt's general conclusion about site variability occurred in Grand Rapids, Michigan. Because the representatives of Grand Rapids would not sign an agreement to implement the Direct Instruction Model according to the specifications, the sponsor withdrew all services. In fact, the sponsor did not implement Direct Instruction classrooms in that community for nearly 2 years for children in Cohort II of the national longitudinal evaluation and for 3 years for children in Cohort III.

Even though the evaluators were made aware of the situation in Grand Rapids, they continued to collect data in that community and they included those data in the general evaluation of the effects of the Direct Instruction Model. Clearly, this was an improper approach to evaluation, and including these results obviously and unfairly contributed to an under-estimate of the true effects of the model. In addition, inclusion of these data exaggerate the appearance of variability of effects across different communities. If other sponsors comment on this problem, they will doubtless report similar incidents.

The substantially lower performance of children enrolled in classrooms at the Grand Rapids site is clearly apparent when one examines the median grade equivalents achieved on the four MAT tests at the end of third grade by children in each of the K-starting sites; these data are presented below (data from Abt III and Abt IV reports, Notes 13 and 14).

	Total reading	Total math	Spelling	Language
	3.7	4.2	4.3	4.8
Norm (3.5)→	3.5	4.0	4.3	4.8[a]
	3.4	4.0	3.9	4.7[a]
	3.4	3.9	3.9	4.6[a]
	3.3	3.9	3.7	4.5
	3.2	3.8	Norm (3.6)→ 3.4	4.2[a]
	3.1	3.8	3.4	4.1
	3.1	Norm (3.75)→ 3.7	3.4	Norm (4.0)→ 4.0
	(2.8)	(3.0)	(3.0)	(2.8)[a]
	(2.8)	(2.8)	(3.0)	(2.6)
( ) Grand Rapids		Norm = 50th percentile		

[a] Means are substituted for missing medians.

If the data from classrooms in Grand Rapids were deleted from the evaluation of the Direct Instruction Model, most of the variability in the norm data for math, spelling, and language would be *above the grade norm*. In reading, this would not be the case, but the range below the grade norm would be only four-tenths (.4) of a grade level. However, as has been argued elsewhere (Becker, 1977) and is discussed later in this chapter, the scores on the MAT reading test (Elementary level) are to a large degree determined by the quality and variety of parental supports for language development in the home, rather than by what the children are taught in schools. Furthermore, this position is strongly supported by the results of recent reseach reported by Elardo, Bradley, & Caldwell (1977).

A second major reason for challenging Abt Report conclusions about program variability is that they are based on control group comparisons among Follow Through and non-Follow-Through clasrooms, not student performance levels. In some communities, children enrolled in Direct Instruction classrooms performed at or near grade level for specific measures of academic achievement. Nevertheless, a minus (−) was recorded in the summary table (Figure 4.4). It is well known that special programs of instruction, some funded by federal sources and others by local sources, were implemented in many comparison classrooms. In such circumstances the observed variability in the comparative performance of Follow Through children at different sites should not be attributed to the weak effects of a Follow Through model. It should be remembered that Follow Through was created because the achievement levels of children from low-income backgrounds were known to be substantially below grade level. If they had been performing at grade level, there would have been no need for Follow Through. Thus, the issue of implementation variability might have been explored more appropriately through the use of norm-referenced measures of "absolute performance" rather than by relying on evidence of statistically significant mean differences between the test scores of children enrolled in Follow Through and non-Follow-Through comparison classrooms.

Discussion

The additional analyses of the performance data on Follow Through models reported in this chapter indicate that it is now possible to answer some important and persisting questions about the effectiveness of different approaches to educating children from low-SES backgrounds. Some of those questions, and responses to them, are presented in the following.

Is extra money sufficient to make the difference? Special programs are often attacked by critics who argue, "Any program that had that much money and that many extra people could do the job." Evaluations of Head Start and Title I programs have shown that this is simply not true (McLaughlin, 1975). The Abt IV Report also provides convincing evidence that good will, people, material, the Hawthorne effect, health programs, dental programs, and hot lunch programs *do not* cause gains in achievement. All Follow Through sponsored programs had these components, but all models did not achieve similar levels of success in basic instruction.

Do cognitively oriented programs really teach cognitive skills more effectively? The data fail to support two expectancies that were stated often during the history of Follow Through: (*a*) Cognitively oriented programs would be more successful than other approaches in teaching cognitive skills to children; and (*b*) the success of behaviorally oriented models would be limited to improvements in the area of rote learning. The data clearly indicate that cognitive skills can be taught most successfully by analyzing component skills and building those skills through systematic instruction, and that is what occurs in the Direct Instruction Model.

Is self-directed learning best? The contention that cognitive skills are taught best through child-directed learning activities has not been supported by the evaluation data from Follow Through. Many educators have adopted the "self-directed-is-the-best" assumption, probably due in large part to Piaget's emphasis on the importance of children's interactions with the physical environment. Supposedly, children will learn by experiencing the consequences of their encounters with the environment. From that viewpoint, if the hand reaches for what the eye sees and gets it to the mouth, some form of reinforcement (or punishment) may occur. Indeed, most movement of persons through space is clearly consequated. Nevertheless, children are unlikely to learn the arbitrary conventions of a language system (symbolic operations) unless some person in their environment provides direct and systematic teaching. For example, children in Russia do not "develop" English as their primary spoken language, and children in England do not "develop" Russian. However, children in both countries learn to walk in similar ways. Concepts will be taught more effectively when a programmer selects and sequences critical examples in advance than when children direct their own learning. The greater potential power of learning experiences designed and directed by adults should be obvious. Nevertheless, many educators continue to advocate misconceptions about children's learning processes. Clearly, reexamination of the premises that underlie educational practice is long overdue.

Does individualization require many different approaches to teaching children? Low levels of success in teaching academic skills occurred most frequently among Follow Through models in which teachers sought to individualize instruction by teaching different students in different ways. The evaluation data presented above indicate that children can be taught effectively when they experience *the same sequence of skill development*, as provided by the DISTAR curriculum, even though they may begin instruction at different levels within the curriculum. Correction procedures are individualized in the sense that they are used as needed by individual children; however, the correction procedures, as described earlier, are the same for each child. What is actually individualized is *when* a correction procedure is used with a particular child, not *how* it is made. The same reasoning applies to the use of reinforcement procedures, the number of practice trials to mastery, and so forth. This approach to individualization, built around a common skill sequence, makes teacher training more efficient and leads to more productive use of teaching time.

Are positive affective outcomes produced by good intentions? The Follow Through sponsors who were most vocal about the importance of affective outcomes in education did not produce the best results in that area. The evaluation data suggest that positive affective outcomes are a consequence of effective teaching procedures. When children acquire skills that they can use to solve problems, positive comments from others are likely to be generated. Self-esteem arises from such comments and demonstrations of competence to oneself.

Lessons Learned: Implications for School Systems and Programs

Becker (1977) described many lessons that he and his associates had learned from their decade of experiences in Follow Through. The purpose of this concluding section is to extend that previous statement and to state two specific objectives for the improvement of the education of children from low-income backgrounds. Schools should be redesigned to (a) improve the teaching of vocabulary; and (b) improve all instructional programs.

IMPROVE THE TEACHING OF VOCABULARY

Perhaps the most important general conclusion that emerged from the sponsor's experiences in Follow Through is that an initial assumption about schools was correct. Many existing schools *are* designed primarily for teaching white, English-speaking, middle-class children, and they *should* be redesigned to respond to the entry skills and instructional needs of children from low-income homes. But the recognition of an important corollary of that assumption was missed. Initially, it was not perceived that schools fail to teach in a systematic manner the most important building blocks for intelligent functioning—*a knowledge of words and what they refer to.* Many children from low-income homes are more likely to fail to acquire a systematic knowledge of basic skills in oral language comprehension, which is the basis for reading comprehension.

The sponsor arrived at this conclusion about deficiencies in oral language through efforts to understand the reasons for the varying levels of success in different areas of instruction. When instruction in some areas of a curriculum is more effective than in others, one can draw conclusions about why some procedures work and others are less productive. Consider the pattern of findings in the evaluation data on the effects of the Direct Instruction Model. On WRAT Reading, children in the model scored at the eighty-third percentile, a full standard deviation above the norm. But on MAT Total Reading, they scored at the forty-first percentile, or one-fourth of a standard deviation below the .norm. In arithmetic, spelling, and language their mean scores approximated the norm.

How does one explain the differential pattern of findings described in the preceding paragraph? The answer to that question may be pursued by looking more closely at the nature of the achievement tests themselves. For example, the WRAT Reading instrument is primarily a measure of decoding skills. In the DISTAR approach to instruction, children are taught decoding skills by teaching them 40 sounds, how to blend those sounds together, and how to say them fast. In this manner, the children learn a general case that they can use to pronounce any regular-sound English word. The DISTAR method of teaching a relatively small set of building blocks that children can organize into a large set of applications accomplishes great efficiency in teaching decoding skills, especially as compared to the results obtained through the use of sight–word methods.

The DISTAR curriculum materials also were used to help children in the model reach national norms in spelling, arithmetic, and language. Their success in spelling is probably a "spin-off" from the success in teaching them reading-by-sounds. The related process, spell-by-sound, is an effective procedure for teaching children to spell regular-sound words and assists them to spell irregular words. In contrast to decoding in reading, the general cases taught in arithmetic have a more limited range of applications and thus yield less "net gain" than the decoding skills. Also, the language skills, which pertain to grammatical rules and classifications, have a level of potency similar to that of arithmetic.

Now consider again the performance of the students on MAT total reading. At the elementary level, this instrument is comprised of two parts, word knowledge and reading. The first part assesses vocabulary ability, and the latter part is a test of reading comprehension. Most analyses of reading comprehension skills indicate that the vocabulary–concept load is the largest factor in comprehension (Carroll, 1971; Chall, 1958; Davis, 1968). If children lack knowledge of what words mean, they are not likely to perform well in reading comprehension. The vocabulary–concept load of the MAT reading test probably is beyond the experience of most disadvantaged third graders. For example, most of them probably do not comprehend terms, such as *country* (used to mean *nation*), *Amazon ant*, *probably*, *exterminator*, *penicillin*, *disease-causing germs*, *Egyptians of old*, or *a seated cat*. The test also requires that children make certain logical inferences and deductions that may be beyond their comprehension. But the big obstacle to children's performance on the test is doubtless, the vocabulary load.

When children acquire skills in decoding, arithmetic, grammar, and spelling-by-sounds, they learn general cases. After they have been taught some members of the set, the students can identify any member. But vocabulary is a linear–additive set (Becker & Engelmann, 1976), and the mastery of one member is of little assistance in learning new members. To be sure, there are families of words that have common root meanings, and there are common meanings of affixes that permit some limited general cases. But when children learn most proper names, synonyms for concepts already known by another name, and new concepts, each one must be taught. Basically, children must have an effective comprehension of vocabulary if they are to function intelligently (Miner, 1957).

Teaching the comprehension of language is a task of the first magnitude, but with better analysis and sequencing of the component tasks, a better job can be done. Some critical questions are, "How big is the task?" and "How can it be simplified?" Basal texts generally limit the teaching of vocabulary during the first three years of children's school experience. Chall (1967) indicates that about 1500 words are taught during this time. Then, the vocabulary level of most textbooks used in instruction jump to a comparatively unlimited, adult level of vocabulary. Thorndike and Lorge (1944) estimate that the average high school senior, or adult, knows about 15,000 words (including proper nouns and derivatives, but not inflections). Dupuy (1974) estimates that the number of basic words known by the average high school senior is about 7800 (basic words do not include proper nouns, derivatives, inflections, and compounds). On the average, students learn about 5800 of these basic words after they complete third grade. Since schools do not attempt to systematically build the knowledge of these words, children who enter school with weak language skills are likely to experience serious difficulties by the time they enroll in fourth grade, if not before.

If schools do not attempt to systematically build children's knowledge of basic words, where do most children acquire that knowledge? Most likely from the home (Coleman, 1975; Elardo et al., 1975, 1977; Freeberg & Payne, 1967; Glass, 1973). But often the learning environments of many low-income homes do not support and encourage language development among children. In a review of research on socioeconomic factors in intelligence, Terhune (1974) states that the development of effective language comprehension is less likely to occur when the following conditions prevail:

1. There is a single parent in the home.
2. Per capita income is significantly below average.
3. Education of caretakers is low.
4. Birth order of children is higher.
5. Number of children is greater.

If "parent's primary language is not English" is added to this list, the conditions that frequently characterize many low-income families in the United States are identified.

Unless educators develop procedures for systematically building the knowledge base that makes language comprehension (words and their referents) possible, children from language-limited backgrounds certainly will not be successful in school and the poverty cycle will continue. Even the positive effects of a "successful" Follow Through model for children in kindergarten and the primary grades will tend to disappear in the years after they leave the program. The data reported earlier on the performance of former students when they reached fifth- and sixth-grade levels are predictable from this analyses. Also, various relations between IQ and differential performance in the data are consistent with this analysis.

The solution to the vocabulary–concept-learning problem will not come easily. The first approach might be to organize the presentation of vocabulary in such a way that words may be taught more easily. One might begin with a reduced set of words, such as basic words (Dupuy, 1974) or Basic English (Ogden, 1932), and analyze this set for groupings of concepts having shared attributes or operators. A knowledge of structure could simplify the teaching of concepts. Miller and Johnson-Laird (1976) have made some suggestions in this direction. Engelmann's logical analyses, which underly the development of the DISTAR curriculum materials, also began with a similar assumption. An economy in the expansion of learning in the area of vocabulary–concept also could be accomplished by focusing on root meanings and affix meanings in generating derivatives from basic words. Eventually, it would be possible to identify a basic vocabulary that all students should master by the time they complete their senior year of high school, as well as the minimum increments that students should master as they progress through the grade levels. Also, a computer program could be built to analyze the content of any textbook before it is printed (most texts are type set by computer now) to serve as a guide for controlling the vocabulary level. If words used in the text were not included in "free use" lists for a given grade level, they would have to be *changed, taught* in the text, or at a minimum *listed* so that the teacher could preteach them before making an assignment in the text. The goal would be to move toward the teaching of a systematic and cumulative basic vocabulary for all students.

IMPROVE ALL INSTRUCTIONAL PROGRAMS

Contrary to much prior research and opinion (McLaughlin, 1975), the results from Follow Through reported in this chapter demonstrate that schools can improve education for children from low-income homes. The results of the analyses of both the data and the problem indicate that changing school systems to make them effective for all children will not be a simple task. What is required is a massive reengineering of the total educational system. There is no little bit of magic or tinkering that can be performed at some critical stage of children's development to bring about significant improvement. The learning of language is a task of the first magnitude that does not end at third grade. Reaching this goal will require a redesigning of all instructional programs. In addition, schools should be improved in the following areas:

1. Develop management systems in which the focus is on the quality of instruction delivered to students, not on "keeping the staff placated." This will require teaching-skill-oriented training and supervision, clear statements of objectives, and careful monitoring of progress toward those objectives.

2. Develop schedules for using classroom time to ensure that more teaching occurs. We cannot be satisfied if only 65 min of the school day is actually devoted to teaching children. The minimal objective should be to present 180 min of effective teaching time per student per day.

3. Design programs to teach the general case and in fact do it. It is not enough to rely on programs that might work for some children if we are lucky. We must insist that instructional programs have demonstrated effectiveness for all the children for whom they are intended.

The results presented in this chapter and elsewhere have shown that essential instructional objectives can be accomplished for preschool children, for children in kindergarten and the primary grades, and for older children in the remedial programs. Why not do it for all?

Reference Notes

1. Bereiter, C. *Acceleration of intellectual development in early childhood.* Final Report, Project No. 2129. Contract No. OE 4-10-008. Urbana, Ill.: College of Education, University of Illinois, June 1967.
2. Engelmann, S., & Carnine, D. *Theory of instruction,* Book in preparation, 1980.
3. Carnine, D. *Three procedures for sequencing instances in discrimination learning tasks.* Journal of Educational Psychology, 1980, 72, 452–456.
4. Fink, W. T., & Carnine, D. W. *Comparisons of group and individual instruction and individual and unison responding.* Unpublished manuscript (mimeo), University of Oregon, 1977.
5. Cowart, J., Carnine, D. W., & Becker, W. C. *The effects of signals on attending, responding, and following in direct instruction.* Unpublished manuscript (mimeo), University of Oregon, 1978.

6. Oregon Follow Through Model. *Direct Instruction Model Implementation Manual.* 1. *Guidebook for Teachers.* 2. *Guidebook for Supervisors.* 3. *Guidebook for Administrators.* 4. *Guidebook for Directors, Parent Workers, and PACs.* Eugene, Oreg.: Follow Through Model, College of Education, University of Oregon, 1977.
7. Schrader, M. (Ed.). *Parent and child home practice guide.* Eugene, Oreg.: University of Oregon Follow Through Model, 1975.
8. Becker, W. C., & Engelmann, S. *Analysis of achievement data on six cohorts of low income children from 20 school districts in the University of Oregon Direct Instruction Follow Through Model* (Technical Report No. 78–1, prepared for Office of Education). Eugene: University of Oregon, Follow Through Model, 1976.
9. Engelmann, S., & Carnine, D. W. *A structured program's effect on the attitudes and achievement of average and above average second graders.* Unpublished manuscript (mimeo), University of Oregon, 1975.
10. Stallings, J. A., & Kaskowitz, D. H. *Follow Through classroom observation evaluation (1972–1973).* Menlo Park, Calif.: Stanford Research Institute, 1974.
11. Soar, R. S. *Follow Through classroom process measurement and pupil growth (1970–1971). Final report.* Gainesville, Fla: College of Education, University of Florida, 1973.
12. Brophy, J. E., & Evertson, C. N. *Process–product correlations in the Texas teacher effectiveness study. Final report.* Austin: University of Texas, 1974.
13. Stebbins, L. B., St. Pierre, R. G., Proper, E. C., Anderson, R. B., & Cerva, T. R. *Education as experimentation: A planned variation model* (Vol. IV). Cambridge, Mass.: Abt Associates, 1977. (Also issued by the U.S. Office of Education as *National Evaluation: Patterns of effects,* Vol. II-A of the *Follow Through planned variation experimentation series.).*
14. Cline, M. G. *Education as experimentation: A planned variation model* (Vol. III). Cambridge, Mass.: Abt Associates, 1976.
15. Haney, W. *Analysis of previous Follow Through national evaluation reports.* Cambridge, Mass.: The Huron Institute, 1976.
16. Becker, W. C. *Symposium on direct instruction: The Follow through data show that some programs work better than others.* Paper presented at the annual meeting of the American Educational Research Association, Toronto, Canada, March 1978.
17. Becker, W. C. (Ed.). *Review of research on direct instruction.* Book in preparation, 1981.

Acknowledgments

The authors are indebted to all the project managers, project directors, supervisors, teachers, aides, parents, and children who made possible the work reported in this chapter. They also are indebted to Maude May and Jacque Beymer for their clerical efforts in preparing this manuscript.

References

Becker, W. C. Application of behavior principles in typical classrooms. In C. Thorenson (Ed.), *Behavior modification in education* (NSSE Yearbook). Chicago: University of Chicago Press, 1973. Pp. 77–106.

Becker, W. C. *Parents are teachers*. Champaign, Ill.: Research Press, 1971.

Becker, W. C. Teaching reading and language to the disadvantaged—What we have learned from field research. *Harvard Educational Review*, 1977, *47*, 518-543.

Becker, W. C. The national evaluation of Follow Through: Behavior-theory based programs come out on top. *Education and Urban Society*, 1978, *10*, 431-458.

Becker, W. C., Carlson, C., Arnold, C. R., & Madsen, C. H., Jr. The elimination of tantrum behavior of a child in an elementary classroom. *Behavior Research and Therapy*, 1968, *6*, 117-119.

Becker, W. C., & Engelmann, S. *Teaching 3: Evaluation of instruction*. Chicago: Science Research Associates, 1976.

Becker, W. C., Engelmann, S., & Thomas, D. R. *Teaching: A course in applied psychology*. Chicago: Science Research Associates, 1971.

Becker, W. C., Engelmann, S., & Thomas, D. R. *Teaching 1: Classroom management*. Chicago: Science Research Associates, 1975. (a)

Becker, W. C., Engelmann, S., & Thomas, D. R. *Teaching 2: Cognitive learning and instruction*. Chicago: Science Research Associates, 1975. (b)

Becker, W. C., Madsen, C. H., Jr., Arnold, C. R., & Thomas, D. R. The contingent use of teacher attention and praise in reducing classroom behavior problems. *Journal of Special Education*, 1967, *1*, 287-307.

Becker, W. C., Zipse, D., & Madsen, C. H. Effects of exposure to an aggressive model and "frustration" on children's aggressive behavior. *Child Development*, 1967, *38*, 739-745.

Bereiter, C., & Engelmann, S. *Teaching disadvantaged children in the preschool*. Englewood Cliffs, N.J.: Prentice-Hall, 1966.

Campbell, D. T., & Erlebacher, A. How regression artifacts in quasi-experimental evaluations in compensatory education tend to underestimate effects. In J. Hellmuth (Ed.), *Disadvantaged child. Compensatory education: A national debate (Vol. 3)*. New York: Brunner/Mazel, 1970, 185-225.

Carnine, D. W. Similar sound separation and cumulative introduction of learning letter-sound correspondences. *Journal of Educational Research*, 1976, *69*, 368-372.

Carnine, D. W., & Fink, W. T. Increasing rate of presentation and use of signals in elementary classroom teachers. *Journal of Applied Behavioral Analysis*, 1978, *11*, 35-46.

Carnine, L., & Carnine, D. W. Determining the relative decoding difficulty of three types of simple regular words. *Journal of Reading Behavior*, 1978, *10*, (4), 440-441.

Carroll, J. B. *Learning from verbal discourse in educational media: A review of the literature* (Research Bulletin 71-61), Princeton, N.J.: Educational Testing Service, October, 1971.

Chall, J. S. Readability: An appraisal of research and application. *Bureau of Educational Research Monographs*, 1958, No. 34, Columbus, Ohio: Ohio State University.

Chall, J. S. *Learning to read—The great debate*. New York: McGraw-Hill, 1967.

Coleman, J. S. Methods and results in the IEA studies of effects of schools on learning. *Review of Educational Research*, 1975, *45*, 335-386.

Coopersmith, S. *The antecedents of self-esteem*. San Francisco: W. H. Freeman, 1967.

Crandall, V. C., Katkowsky, W., & Crandall, V. J. Children's beliefs in their own control of reinforcements in intellectual–academic achievement situations. *Child Development*, 1965, *36*, 91-109.

Davis, F. B. Research in comprehension in reading. *Reading Research Quarterly*, 1968, *3*, 499-545.

Dupuy, H. J. *The rationale, development, and standardization of a basic word vocabulary test*. DHEW Publication No. (HRA) 74-1334, Washington, D.C.: U.S. Government Printing Office, 1974.

Elardo, R., Bradley, R. H., & Caldwell, B. M. The relation of infants' home environments to mental test performance from 6 to 36 months: A longitudinal analysis. *Child Development*, 1975, *46*, 71-76.

Elardo, R., Bradley, R. H., & Caldwell, B. M. A longitudinal study of the relation of infants' home environments to language development at age three. *Child Development*, 1977, *48*, 595–603.

Engelmann, S. The effectiveness of direct verbal instruction on IQ performance and achievement in reading and arithmetic. In J. Hellmuth (Ed.), *Disadvantaged child* (Vol. 3). New York: Brunner/Mazel, 1968. Pp. 339–361.

Feldman, S. M., & Underwood, B. J. Stimulus recall following paired-associate verbal learning. *Journal of Experimental Psychology*, 1957, *53*, 11–15.

Ferster, C. B., & Perrott, M. C. *Behavior principles.* New York: Appleton-Century-Crofts, 1968.

Freeberg, N. E., & Payne, E. Parental influence on cognitive development in early childhood: A review. *Child Development.* 1967, *38*, 65–87.

Glass, G. V. Statistical and measurement problems in implementing the Stull Act. In N. L. Gage (Ed.), *Mandated evaluation of education: A conference on California's Stull Act.* Stanford, Calif.: Stanford Center for Research and Development in Teaching, 1973. Distributed by Educational Resources Division, Capital Publications, Washington, D.C., 1974.

Granzin, A. C., & Carnine, D. W. Child performance on discrimination tasks: Effects of amount of stimulus variation. *Journal of Experimental Child Psychology*, 1977, *24*, 332–342.

Higa, M. Interference effects of intralist word relatedness in verbal learning. *Journal of Verbal Learning and Verbal Behavior*, 1963, *2*, 170–175.

Honig, W. K. (Ed.) *Operant behavior: Areas of research and application.* New York: Appleton-Century-Crofts, 1966.

Jastak, J. F., Bijou, S. W., & Jastak, S. R. *Wide Range Achievement Test.* Wilmington, Del.: Guidance Associates, 1965.

Madsen, C. H., Jr., Becker, W. C., & Thomas, D. R. Rules, praise, and ignoring: Elements of elementary calssroom control. *Journal of Applied Behavior Analysis*, 1968, *1*, 139–159.

McLaughlin, M. W. *Evaluation and reform.* Cambridge, Mass.: Ballinger Publishing, 1975.

Metropolitan Achievement Tests. New York: Harcourt, Brace & Jovanovich, 1970.

Millenson, J. R. *Principles of behavioral analysis.* New York: Macmillan, 1967.

Miller, G. A., & Johnson-Laird, P. N. *Language and perception.* Cambridge, Mass.: The Belnap Press of Harvard University Press, 1976.

Miner, J. B. *Intelligence in the United States.* New York: Springer, 1957.

Ogden, C. K. *The basic words: A detailed account of uses.* London: Kegan Paul, 1932.

O'Leary, K. D., & Becker, W. C. Behavior modification of an adjustment class: A token reinforcement program. *Exceptional Children*, 1967, *1*, 287–307.

O'Leary, K. D., O'Leary, S. G., & Becker, W. C. Modification of a deviant sibling interaction pattern in the home. *Behavior Research and Therapy*, 1967, *5*, 113–120.

Raven, J. C. *Coloured progressive matrices.* Sets A, A^B, B. Dumfries, England: The Crichton Royal, 1956.

Reynolds, G. S. *A primer of operant conditioning.* Glenview, Ill.: Scott, Foresman, 1968.

Rosenshine, B. Classroom instruction. In N. L. Gage (Ed.), *The psychology of teaching methods* (Seventy-fifth NSSE Yearbook). Chicago: University of Chicago Press, 1976. Pp. 335–371.

Salzinger, K. *Psychology: The science of behavior.* New York: Springer Publishing, 1969.

Siegel, M. A. Teacher behaviors and curriculum packages: Implications for research and teacher education. In L. J. Rubin (Ed.), *The handbook of curriculum.* Boston: Allyn & Bacon, 1977.

Skinner, B. F. *The behavior of organisms.* New York: Appleton-Century-Crofts, 1938.

Skinner, B. F. *Science and human behavior.* New York: Macmillan, 1953.

Skinner, B. F. *The technology of teaching.* New York: Appleton-Century-Crofts, 1968.

Slosson, R. L. *Slosson Intelligence Test.* E. Aurora, N.Y.: Slosson Educational Publications, 1971.

Terhune, K. W. A review of the actual and expected consequences of family size (Colspan Report No. DP-5333-G-1, Publication No. (NIH) 75-779). Washington, D.C.: U.S. Government Printing Office, 1974.

Thomas, D. R., Becker, W. C., & Armstrong, M. Production and elimination of disruptive classroom behavior by systematically varying teacher's behavior. *Journal of Applied Behavioral Analysis,* 1968, *1,* 35-45.

Thorndike, E. L., & Lorge, I. *The teacher's word book of 30,000 words.* New York: Bureau of Publications, Teachers College, Columbia University, 1944.

Underwood, B. J., Runquist, W. N., & Schultz, R. W. Response learning in paired-associate lists as a function of intralist similarity. *Journal of Experimental Psychology,* 1959, *58,* 70-78.

Wittgenstein, L. *Philosophical investigations* (2nd ed.). New York: Macmillan, 1958.

EUGENE A. RAMP
W. RAY RHINE

5

Behavior Analysis Model[1]

[1] Preparation of this chapter was supported by USOE Grant G-007507226 and Contract 200-78-0457, but no endorsement of its contents by the federal government should be inferred.

Overview

The Behavior Analysis Model was developed by Don Bushell, Jr., Eugene A. Ramp, and their colleagues at the University of Kansas. The conceptual roots of the model are in applied behavior analysis, a vigorous area of contemporary psychology. The model's operational characteristics include a number of systems for motivating students, such as contingent teacher attention and praise for desirable student behavior, token reinforcement systems, and behavioral contracts between teachers and students; individualized curriculum materials; team teaching; small-group and individualized instruction; participation by parents in classroom instruction; close monitoring of students' academic performance; and careful planning of instruction (Bushell & Ramp, 1974). The major goals of the model are to help students attain competence in basic academic subjects, to create a feeling of satisfaction among the children and adults who are the primary consumers of program services, and to promote participation by parents whose children are enrolled in Behavior Analysis classrooms.

The description of the Behavior Analysis Model in this chapter begins with a listing of formative events that occurred during the period from 1964 to 1968. The section on rationale consists of a review of research in the area of applied behavior analysis, particularly the application of behavioral techniques in school settings. The focus in the section on implementation is on the characteristics of the instructional program, delivery system, and support system. The next section contains a summary of results from the sponsor's evaluation and an examination of selected parts of the national longitudinal evaluation. The chapter concludes with a discussion of the role of sponsorship in Follow Through and the need for intensive studies of implementation processes in educational programs.

Origins

A number of important events occurred in 1964, and their effects later converged to support the development of the Behavior Analysis Follow Through Model. For example, in 1964 the Congress passed the Civil Rights Act and the Economic Opportunity Act, legislation that signalled a national commitment to equal educational opportunity for all citizens and prepared the foundations for Project Head Start. In that same year at the University of Washington in Seattle, Donald M. Baer, Sidney W. Bijou, Montrose M. Wolf, and other behavioral psychologists began to publish their findings concerning functional relationships between human behavior and contingencies of reinforcement. Concurrently, at the University of Kansas in Lawrence, Frances Degen Horowitz began to organize the

Department of Human Development. Baer, Wolf, and others soon accepted faculty appointments in this new academic department. During the past 15 years, the members of the Department of Human Development have applied behavioral research methods to analyze and improve human performance in many settings, including school environments.

Other events that contributed to the eventual development of the Behavior Analysis Model occurred in St. Louis, Missouri. In 1964, Bushell established a preschool in which behavioral techniques were applied to instruct preschool children in reading, arithmetic, and handwriting— academic skills that were usually not taught to children until they enrolled in the primary grades. His preschool program proved successful with predominately white, middle-class children in St. Louis County, and in 1966 he implemented the approach in a Head Start program serving black children who lived in St. Louis' Pruitt-Igoe public housing project.

In 1967, Bushell accepted an appointment in the Department of Human Development at the University of Kansas. Here he implemented his academic preschool approach in the Parent Cooperative Preschool, a Head Start demonstration center at the Juniper Gardens Children's program located in the Public Housing Project of Kansas City, Kansas. The parents of the children enrolled in this program served as teachers, and they learned to employ behavioral techniques for teaching academic skills to preschool children.

In 1967, Congress amended the Economic Opportunity Act to authorize Project Follow Through. Planners in the USOE convened a panel of experts on child development to obtain their recommendations for structuring the new project. Baer, who had gained national recognition for his research with young children, was selected as a member of that panel. When he was invited later to participate as a model sponsor in Follow Through, Baer declined but suggested that his colleague Bushell might be willing to apply his preschool educational approach to older children in kindergarten and the primary grades. Bushell agreed to participate in Follow Through, organized his staff during the spring of 1968, and began to implement the Behavior Analysis Model in the fall of that year.

Ramp began his participation in the Behavior Analysis Model soon after he received his master's degree in psychology from Western Michigan University in 1968. Bushell invited Ramp, who had strong interests in the application of behavioral approaches to classroom settings, to help develop the new Follow Through model at the University of Kansas, and, at the same time, complete his doctoral studies in developmental and child psychology in the Department of Human Development. During his participation in Follow Through, Ramp has worked in all areas of program development. Bushell served as director of the Behavior Analysis Model until 1974. Ramp has directed the model since that time.

Rationale

The Behavior Analysis Model is derived from methods, findings, and techniques of applied behavior analysis (Baer, Wolf, & Risley, 1968). Most behavior analysts base their work on the results of laboratory research performed by operant psychologists and on the results of applied behavioral research conducted in schools, clinics, hospitals, and other settings since the early 1960s. The general principles and empirical foundations of behavior analysis are stated in the writings of a number of authors, including Skinner (1938, 1953), Holland and Skinner (1961), and Honig (1966). Krasner and Ullmann (1965) and Ulrich, Stachnik, and Mabry (1966) edited volumes that contain descriptions of the successful application of behavior analysis to many areas of human performance. *The Journal of Applied Behavioral Analysis*, first published in the spring of 1968, contains much of the recent literature on applied behavior analysis.

Behavior analysts have conducted many studies in school settings, and the results of those investigations may be employed to help teachers better understand and manage classroom contingencies in order to improve the performance of students. This research has been reviewed and critiqued by Becker (1971), Ramp and Hopkins (1971), O'Leary and O'Leary (1972), Sulzer and Mayer (1972), Ramp and Semb (1975), and Sulzer-Azaroff and Mayer (1977). The results of research on the effects of (a) contingent teacher attention and praise; (b) token reinforcement systems; and (c) other behavioral procedures (including time-out from positive reinforcement, behavioral contracts, and group consequences) were especially useful to the individuals who designed the Behavior Analysis Follow Through Model during the late 1960s and early 1970s. Some representative studies in each of these areas are described below.

CONTINGENT TEACHER ATTENTION AND PRAISE

During the early 1960s, researchers at the University of Washington in Seattle employed contingent adult attention, praise, smiles, eye contact, and physical proximity to modify and improve the social behavior of preschool children (Allen, Hart, Buell, Harris, & Wolf, 1964; Bijou & Baer, 1963; Harris, Wolf, & Baer, 1964). The results of these early studies revealed that the behaviors of children enrolled in nursery school were controlled by their consequences. Furthermore, the investigators found that these behaviors could be modified by carefully analyzing and planning the "contingencies of reinforcement."

Other researchers extended the work at the preschool level by investigating the effects of reinforcement contingencies among children enrolled in elementary grade classrooms. For example, Becker, Madsen, Arnold, and Thomas (1967) identified a total of 10 children who frequently engaged in disruptive behavior. During a 5-week baseline period, trained observers systematically observed the targeted 10 students and their teachers to establish the frequency of disruptive behavior among the students and the frequency of positive and negative teaching behavior among their teachers. In the experimental phase of the study, teachers were requested to (a) make rules for classroom behavior explicit and repeat them frequently; (b) give praise and attention for appropriate student behavior and for behavior that was incompatible with the disruptive behavior; and (c) ignore behavior that interfered with learning or teaching, unless one child was hurting another, and attempt to limit punishment to the withdrawal of positive reinforcement. During the 9-wk experimental phase, the average percent of intervals during which the 10 students engaged in disruptive behavior declined to 29%, as compared to 63% during the 5-wk baseline period.

A replication and refinement of the study described in the preceding paragraph was performed by Madsen, Becker, and Thomas (1968). These authors compared the separate effects of teachers' statement of rules, praising positive student behavior, and ignoring disruptive behavior. The results indicated that the statement of rules alone did not decrease the frequency of disruptive behavior. Ignoring inappropriate behavior was somewhat more effective, but the greatest reductions in disruptive behavior occurred when teachers combined ignoring disruptive behavior with praising positive behavior.

In a study conducted by Hall, Lund, and Jackson (1968), teachers used behavioral methods to modify children's study behavior and nonstudy behavior. After a baseline period, teachers gave attention and praise only for study behavior and ignored nonstudy behavior. The result was that study behavior increased among the students and nonstudy behavior decreased. In a reversal procedure, the teachers directed their attention only to nonstudy behavior, and the result was that nonstudy behavior greatly increased and study behavior decreased. When they resumed the use of behavioral procedures, study behavior increased and nonstudy behavior decreased. Thus, contingent teacher attention appeared to serve as a positive reinforcer for whatever student behavior it followed.

Two general conclusions can be drawn from research of the sort cited above. First, contingent teacher attention and praise strengthened desirable behavior among children when they followed this behavior immediately in time, and children's undesirable behavior was eliminated by systematically withholding teacher attention when the undesirable behavior occurred. Second, when teachers understood the basic relationships between their own behavior and the responses of students, they were usually able to apply this knowledge consistently and were more effective in classrooms.

TOKEN REINFORCEMENT SYSTEMS

Contingent teacher attention and praise are powerful motivators for modifying and improving the behavior of children in classrooms. But much evidence suggests that there are additional advantages to the use of token reinforcement systems (sometimes called token economies). Tokens are tangible items that children can accumulate and later exchange for "back-up" reinforcers, which may be articles and/or activities of their choice. Tokens may be selected from among things that are small and that have little or no value in and of themselves, such as poker chips, check marks, plastic discs, popsicle sticks, and so forth. Even though the tokens have little or no motivating power, they may be paired with many different reinforcers and thus become "generalized reinforcers" (Skinner, 1953).

A number of researchers have conducted studies that provide an empirical basis for the use of token systems in classrooms. In one of the early studies (Birnbrauer, Wolf, Kidder, & Tague, 1965), teachers used tokens to improve the classroom behavior of retarded pupils. The tokens were check marks that the children acquired for appropriate behavior. At the close of the school day, they exchanged check marks for candy, toys, and school supplies. Teachers compiled daily records of completed academic work, percentage of errors, and frequency of disruptive behavior for each student during both the establishment of the token economy and its withdrawal. The students were more task-oriented, accurate, and less disruptive during the periods when tokens were dispensed.

O'Leary and Becker (1967) employed a token economy in order to decrease the disruptive behavior among 9-year-olds in an "adjustment class." After the baseline frequency of disruptive behavior was established, the children were told that each day they would receive five ratings on a 10–point rating scale, that their ratings would depend on how well they performed in class, and that they could exchange the points they accumulated for back-up prizes such as candy, kites, comics, and so forth. The authors stated that at the close of the school year, the frequency of disruptive behavior was greatly reduced, as compared to the baseline rate, and that task-oriented behaviors greatly increased. In some instances, children who had not completed any assigned work for 2 years and who were diagnosed as "minimally brain-damaged" repeatedly achieved perfect scores on their academic work.

A replication and extension of this study was performed by O'Leary, Becker, Evans, and Saudargas (1969). These authors concluded that token programs were most effective when they were combined with classroom rules, educational structure, teacher praise of appropriate behavior, and teacher inattention to (ignoring) disruptive behavior. Furthermore, the token economies continued to be effective, even when back-up reinforcers were changed from tangible items to intangibles, such as teacher praise, and reduced in frequency.

Some researchers employed token reinforcement systems that included only reinforcers that were readily available in classrooms and which therefore required no additional costs. In one such study Bushell, Wrobel, and Michaelis (1968) reported that preschool children increased their amount of study behavior in order to obtain tokens that they could use to purchase participation in special events available at school, such as listening to a story, engaging in gym class, or viewing a short movie. In another study, McKenzie, Clark, Wolf, Kothera, and Benson (1968) found that students engaged in more academic behavior when both their classroom grades and home allowances were contingent upon that behavior than when grades alone were used. Osborne (1969) employed free time from school as an effective back-up reinforcer.

In their review of research on the use of token reinforcement systems, Bushell and Brigham (1971) concluded that educators may use tokens to improve students' motivation, productivity, and quality of work, as well as to influence teachers toward more positive behaviors in the classroom. They also stated, "token systems represent a well-developed and expanding educational technology. . . rooted in experimentally established principles of behavior. . . . there is mounting evidence that the application of this technology is allowing children to learn more with greater enjoyment and confidence than has been possible in the past [p. 17]."

OTHER BEHAVIORAL PROCEDURES

During the 1960s, many applied behavioral researchers examined the effects of contingent praise and attention and token economies. However, some investigators explored a number of other procedures that also influenced the development of the Behavior Analysis Model, including time-out from positive reinforcement, behavioral contracts, and group consequences.

Time-Out from Positive Reinforcement
In this procedure, a student is usually required to cease ongoing activities and to move from a setting that is presumed to be reinforcing to one that is not. The time-out procedure includes a brief period of social isolation that might consist of separation from a study group or removal from the room. The consequence is that for a period of time the individual does not have

an opportunity to gain reinforcement. Following a brief period of appropriate behavior, the time-out period is terminated and the individual usually is permitted to return to the setting where reinforcers are available.

There have been a number of studies on the effects of using time-out procedures in a variety of circumstances. For example, Wolf, Risley, and Mees (1964) reported that tantrums and self-destructive behavior of an autistic child were reduced when he consistently was placed alone in a room immediately after he engaged in the undesirable behavior. In another study, Bostow and Bailey (1969) combined a brief (2-min) time-out period with systematic reinforcement for acceptable behavior to reduce severe aggressive and disruptive behavior of two retarded patients in a state hospital. Wahler (1969) reported that parents successfully used time-out and attention for appropriate behavior to reduce the frequency of behavior problems exhibited by two children. Wasik, Senn, Welch, and Cooper (1969) examined teachers' use of time-out, attention to appropriate behavior, and ignoring inappropriate behavior in an elementary classroom to reduce aggressive, disruptive behaviors. Ramp, Ulrich, and Dulaney (1971) employed a slight modification of the time-out technique in a classroom setting. Rather than removing a student from the classroom immediately following disruptive behavior, a delayed time-out procedure was employed in which a signalling device located on the student's desk was activated to indicate when the student violated the rules of the classroom. The student who violated the rules was required to spend 5 min of gym time or recess in social isolation. This method was effective in eliminating high rates of inappropriate and disruptive classroom behavior.

Behavioral Contracts

Teachers may use behavioral contracts to permit students to engage in desired activities after they complete an assigned task. The approach is based on Premack's principle: Behaviors that have a high probability of occurring can be used to support or strengthen behaviors that have a low probability of occurring. For example, reading (a low probability behavior) is more likely to occur when it is a precondition for playing at recess (a high probability behavior).

Information about behavioral contracts is contained in a number of sources. Cantrell, Cantrell, Huddleston, and Wooldridge (1969) employed contingency contracting to manage behavior problems among school-age children. The contracts used in this study were not between teachers and students, but between researchers and the parents and teachers of students.

The number of behavior problems in classrooms markedly decreased when parents and teachers agreed in writing to consistently provide contingencies of reinforcement for students. Homme, Csanyi, Gonzales, and Rechs (1970) describe contingency contracting and its application in classrooms in their book entitled *How to Use Contingency Contracting in the Classroom*. They describe how to prepare contracts, how to organize classrooms in order to make contracts effective, and how to manage the use of contracts in educational settings. Additional information about the use of behavioral contracts is contained in a number of other publications, including Hankins (1973) and Sulzer-Azaroff and Mayer (1977).

Group Consequences

Bushell *et al.* (1968) were among the first researchers to use the term *group consequences* (contingencies). They stated uniform criteria for using a token system to reinforce study behavior among 12 preschool children. In their "good behavior game," Barrish, Saunders, and Wolf (1969) made group consequences contingent on the behavior of individuals in an attempt to reduce disruptive classroom behavior. Although the study involved all members of a fourth grade classroom, it was designed to reduce outbursts by a few "problem children." These investigators divided the members of the classroom into two teams. Each inappropriate response by a member of the team was recorded by placing a mark on the chalk board. When the total marks for a team exceeded a specific number, the result was a loss of privileges by all members of the team. Use of the good behavior game produced a significant reduction in the frequency of disruptive classroom behavior.

Schmidt and Ulrich (1969) reported that group consequences were effective in reducing noise levels in a classroom. Their procedure also was conducted in a fourth grade classroom and consisted of a 2–min addition to the class gym period and a 2–min break as rewards for each 10–min period of uninterrupted quiet in the classroom, as monitored by a sound meter. When the sound level reached a predeterminded level, the sound meter timer was reset for the full 10-min interval. In this situation, misbehavior by any student could cause all members of the class to lose free time in the gym or classroom. The results of the study indicated that noise levels in the classroom were reduced greatly.

In summary, the investigations that applied behavior analysts conducted during the late 1960s and early 1970s were important because they represented the emergence of a new educational technology for producing higher levels of teacher and student effectiveness. However, the new educational technology had been developed primarily in studies that included only small numbers of individuals, and its components usually had been tested in well-controlled environments. Consequently, the number of studies that had been conducted with students in regular grade classrooms was not large. But these studies were characterized by an emphasis upon precise observation and measurement of behavior in classrooms, and this emphasis also became a characteristic of the Behavior Analysis Model. The next section of this chapter contains a description of the characteristics that may be observed in well-implemented Behavior Analysis Follow Through classrooms.

The Well-Implemented Model

The Behavior Analysis Model will be described in three parts: (a) the instructional program, consisting of seven components; (b) the delivery system, including training and quality control functions; and (c) the support system, composed of individuals who provide essential services to maintain and improve the program after it is installed in a school district.

INSTRUCTIONAL PROGRAM

In all Behavior Analysis classrooms, teachers employ a number of techniques and procedures, including the following: (a) motivational systems; (b) individualized curriculum materials; (c) team teaching; (d) small group and individualized instruction; (e) parent participation; (f) close monitoring of the academic performance of students; and (g) careful planning of activities in classrooms.

Motivational Systems

All Behavior Analysis teachers receive systematic training in the principles and procedures of positive reinforcement, and they are expected to apply this knowledge to the management of behavior in classrooms. Following the results of the research reported in the "Rationale" section, teachers reward students for appropriate academic and social behavior in order to increase it, and they usually ignore inappropriate behavior in order to diminish or eliminate it. They also employ token economies and behavioral contracts between teachers and students. The use of corporal punishment to manage children's behavior is not permitted.

If a student's behavior is destructive to materials and/or potentially dangerous, it will be dealt with by an effective procedure, such as time-out.

For example, the teacher calmly will remove the child who exhibits such behavior from the group to an area of relative isolation for a period of time. During the time-out period, the child has no opportunity to earn rewards, such as teacher praise and attention or tokens. After the child displays a short interval of appropriate behavior, he or she is invited to rejoin the group.

In Behavior Analysis classrooms, teachers dispense tokens to students in a prescribed manner during instruction, and the children exchange the tokens for back-up items and activities after the completion of an instructional period. An adult in each instructional group presents a list of items and activities that children later may purchase with tokens after an instructional period ends. Information about the number of tokens required to purchase each item or activity is presented to the children only at the close of an instructional period.

Token economies are more likely to be effective when they are employed with students enrolled in kindergarten, first grade, and possibly second grade. In the Behavior Analysis Model, teachers who use tokens in second and third grade distribute them less frequently than do teachers in kindergarten and first grade. The reason is that older children acquire more independent study habits as they increase their mastery of academic subjects. In addition, students are not enrolled in the program after they complete third grade. Consequently, it is important to help them begin to make the transition to regular grade classrooms.

Two examples will illustrate how teachers may use the principles and procedures stated thus far to manage the behavior of children in classrooms. In the first example, a child in the math group may decide to rise from her chair and walk about the room during instruction. Rather than scolding the child, the teacher praises the other children and may administer a few tokens to each of them for continuing to engage in the desirable (and incompatible) behavior of attending to the completion of their lessons. Usually, the child who is wandering will observe that the behavior of the other children is rewarded, but that her behavior is not. She then decides to resume her participation in math instruction, and the teacher quickly acknowledges the child's return to appropriate behavior by praising her and awarding a token for resuming her work.

In the second example, another child in the handwriting group may decide to use his pencil as a missile, firing it across the table at another child. The teacher responds quickly but calmly to this dangerous act, takes the child by the hand, and seats him in a chair at the side of the room. In the unlikely event that the child is not already aware of the possible serious consequences of his behavior, the teacher reminds him and states that he must remain seated, apart from the group, for a 5-min time-out period. After the time-out period has elapsed, the child returns to the group and resumes his participation in instructional activities.

Individualized Curriculum Materials

Most of the curriculum materials used in Behavior Analysis classrooms are available from commercial publishers. Teachers are not required to use a specific curriculum, but they are required to select materials that meet certain stated criteria. For example, the materials must be individualized (or "individualizable"), they must provide for the periodic assessment of student progress, and they must provide frequent opportunities for students to respond. The purpose of these criteria is to ensure that the curriculum materials selected by local schools will lend themselves to the Behavior Analysis classroom quality control procedures described later in this section.

Team Teaching

Three or four adults, depending on the grade level of the children, teach in a classroom. In kindergarten and first grade classrooms, the teaching teams usually consist of four individuals; a lead teacher, a paraprofessional, and two parents. In second and third grade classrooms, the teaching teams usually are composed of three persons: a lead teacher, a paraprofessional, and a parent. The paraprofessionals may or may not be parents.

Small Group and Individualized Instruction

The team teaching approach creates a relatively small student–teacher ratio and makes it possible to provide students with small-group and individual instruction. The lead teacher usually is responsible for instruction in reading, the paraprofessional for math instruction, and the parents teach handwriting and spelling. However, this arrangement may be changed in order to capitalize on the special interests and/or training of the adults who comprise the teaching team.

Instructional periods may vary in length, depending on the grade level of the students or the time of year. Among kindergarten children, instructional periods may be 15–40 min in length, but third grade children may engage in academic instruction for 2 hr or more in one instructional period. At the beginning of the school year, kindergarten children are likely to have short instructional periods of 15 to 20 min, followed by relatively long back-up periods of 20 to 40 min. By the end of the school year, the instructional periods should be longer than the back-up periods.

During a typical day in a Behavior Analysis classroom, children complete several cycles of instruction. Each cycle consists of an instructional period and a back-up period. Instruction in small groups occurs concurrently in reading, math, spelling, and handwriting. After children complete one cycle, they enter a different instructional group in the next cycle. By rotating through the instructional groups, each student receives instruction in all academic areas during the school day.

Parent Participation

Participation by parents is essential for the success of the Behavior Analysis Model. Parents are expected to exercise influence in decisions about educational goals, instructional methods, and the general direction of the program. Through the use of a rotating system for assigning parents to classrooms, each parent employed in the program works for 6–8 weeks. Thus, they rapidly acquire knowledge about the program, and they often are able to use this knowledge in teaching their own children at home. After this brief experience, many parents are employed for a full semester or an entire year. Some have worked in the program since it began 10 years ago. In addition, parents employed in the program are encouraged to complete the educational requirements for becoming fully certified teachers.

Close Monitoring of the Academic Performance of Students

Teachers in the Behavior Analysis Model closely monitor both the academic achievement of individual students and the amount of instructional time they receive in each academic area. The weekly academic performance of each student in reading, math, spelling, and handwriting is recorded on Weekly Individual Progress Records (WIPR), and these forms are displayed in classrooms to reveal the level and range of academic performance for each class.

An example of a reading WIPR completed for a first grade class is presented in Figure 5.1. Book and page number intervals of the *Phonics Primer* are listed along the left side of the WIPR. The *Primer* is used to prepare first graders to comprehend commercial curriculum materials in reading. During their completion of pages 81–105 of the *Primer*, children also begin working on pages 1–6 in Book 1A of the commercial curriculum. Books 1–4 of this curriculum series are divided into quarterly units, and books 5–23 are divided into half units. The numbers along the bottom and right side of the WIPR designate the weeks of the school year and progress steps in the curriculum series, respectively.

The numbers within the cells of the grid indicate the number of students who performed at each step or interval of the curriculum during each week of the school year. For example, during the third week, nine children were reading at Step 4 and two children were reading at Step 19, which refers to pages 73–108 of Book 3. During the thirty-fifth week, the lowest student in

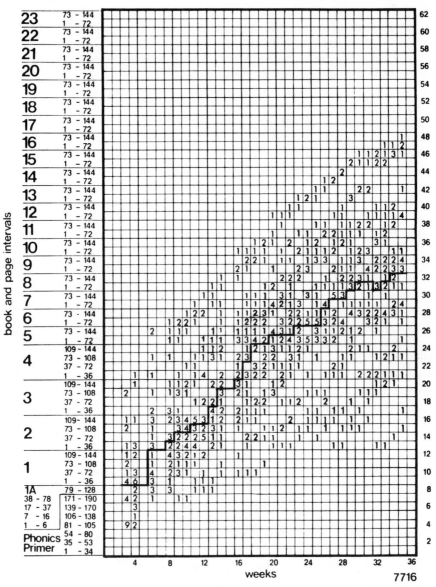

FIGURE 5.1 *Example of a Completed Weekly Individual Progress Record (WIPR).*

the class was reading at Step 15 and the highest student was reading at Step
48. The heavy dark line under the cell in the middle of each column
represents the median placement of students each week. For example, the
median performance level was at Step 9 during the third week and at Step
33 during the thirty-fifth week.

Careful Planning of Activities in Classrooms

The final procedure that is used in Behavior Analysis Follow Through classrooms is careful planning of activities. For a period of 15–20 min at the beginning of each day, the members of the classroom teaching team discuss the events of the previous day and plan carefully the activities for the next 6 hr. The planning and scheduling of classroom activities often may be complex, and decisions made spontaneously can create numerous problems. When each member of the teaching team is involved in educational planning, the day's activities are more rewarding for the adults and more beneficial to students.

DELIVERY SYSTEM

Many components of the Behavior Analysis Follow Through Model were direct applications or logical extensions of behavioral techniques developed during the 1960s. But there were no guidelines for delivering and implementing an instructional program over a long period of time in many schools and classrooms scattered throughout the country. Therefore, the sponsor had to generate these capabilities.

The system for delivering instructional services evolved through several phases before the current methods were established. The *first phase* began during the summer of 1968, when staff members from local school districts attended a seminar on applied behavior analysis presented at the University of Kansas. Those individuals who planned the seminar assumed that when teachers acquired descriptive information and pertinent research findings about the model, they would be able to implement an appropriate instructional program in their classrooms. But soon after the school year began, it was evident that even though the teachers possessed a good textbook knowledge of the model, they were unable to effectively apply their knowledge to teaching in classrooms.

The *second phase* of the delivery system commenced in the summer of 1969, when key staff members from local communities participated in training sessions conducted in a series of regional workshops, followed by field training procedures. The participants reviewed the rationale for the Behavior Analysis Model, observed demonstrations of appropriate classroom procedures, and attended small group instructional sessions. Finally, their teaching practices were videotaped, critiqued, and compared with the required instructional practices. Soon after the school year began, members of the university-based staff conducted follow-up field training sessions for all staff members in local school districts. These procedures markedly improved the fidelity of program implementation, but the large amount of time required in traveling and completing the training sessions exhausted the University of Kansas staff members who supervised the work.

In the summer of 1970, the *third phase* of the delivery system began with the establishment of two regional training centers, one located in Philadelphia and the other in Lawrence, Kansas. Teachers, paraprofessionals, and parents completed 1 week of training at either center. This approach produced a high quality of model implementation in classrooms, but it proved to be extremely costly.

In the summer of 1972, most of the elements included in the *current phase* of the delivery system were established. These elements are appropriate for a program that has been implemented for a period of 4–5 years, but they would not necessarily be appropriate for use in initiating a new program. The elements of the current delivery system comprise two major functions, training and quality control.

Training

In each community, training is supervised by a district advisor, who is a representative of the sponsor, and by a staff trainer, who resides in the local community. Nelson, Saudargas, and Jackson (1974) state that the ultimate goal of the training sequence is to prepare effective teachers to qualify for certification as Behavior Analysis Teachers. They may qualify for that certification by attaining competence in (a) exhibiting specific teaching behaviors that are prescribed in the Behavior Analyis Model; (b) maintaining student academic progress at predetermined target levels and monitoring their academic performance; and (c) performing other noninstructional classroom activities. Ramp, Jackson, Green, Weis, and Bushell (1976) reported that students in classrooms served by certified Behavior Analysis Teachers had higher achievement test scores than students in classrooms served by Behavior Analysis teachers who were not certified.

To assist the district advisor and staff trainer, one classroom at each grade level (kindergarten through third grade) was designated in each community for purposes of training and demonstration. These classrooms are staffed by teachers who have achieved excellence in all areas of classroom teaching. In addition, members of the sponsor's staff have developed a series of training manuals that describe the procedures for implementing and maintaining the Behavior Analysis Model. The district advisor, staff trainer, and staff members in the training and demonstration classrooms use these manuals in their activities.

Quality Control

The other major element of the delivery system is quality control, consisting of four components. First, *Continuous Progress Assessment* is a computerized curriculum feedback system, which was derived from a previous monitoring system called Behavior Analysis National Communication System (BANCS) that was described by Jenkins and Jackson

(1974). Teachers use the results to analyze each student's progress toward meeting weekly and year-end achievement goals. These year-end goals are established at the beginning of each school year in meetings that include the teacher, members of the sponsor's staff, the staff trainer, and parents. *Annual Achievement Testing*, the second component of the quality control system, is conducted in the spring of each school year. The third component, an *Annual Consumer Evaluation*, is a questionnaire that is administered each spring to parents, teachers, paraprofessionals, staff trainers, program directors, school administrators, and the children enrolled in the program. Finally, an external consultant conducts an *Educational Audit* at least once per year in each local program to assess five areas of model implementation: student academic progress, staff training, consumer satisfaction ratings, parent involvement, and the sponsor's performance in delivering services. Each of these quality control procedures provides valuable information that members of the sponsor's staff may use to identify areas of strength and weakness in each local program. Thus, they may take corrective action before problems reach crisis proportions.

SUPPORT SYSTEM

After the Behavior Analysis instructional program has been delivered and implemented in classrooms, it requires support and protection in order to reach maturity. The pattern of support that evolves differs somewhat from one community to another, but the key participants in a support system are the same in each community—school district administrators (including superintendents, principals, and coordinators), teachers, members of the parents' Policy Advisory Committee (PAC), members of the program management team, members of the sponsor's staff, and USOE officials.

Active support from school administrators at all levels is essential to the survival of local Follow Through programs. When they understand the program and recognize the positive contributions it makes to their school system and community, school administrators often help to create an environment that facilitates the implementation of the program and makes its success much more likely. To ensure that administrators are informed and involved, the sponsor provides annual meetings or workshops for them.

As anyone who has worked in school systems knows, teacher support is necessary for the survival of a program at the classroom level. Consequently, the Behavior Analysis sponsor makes a major effort to ensure that teachers are informed and well trained. In fact, more time usually is devoted to inservice training of teachers and other members of the classroom staff than to any other element of the support system.

A well-organized parent PAC may contribute to effective relationships between Follow Through personnel and school administrators. When parents are enthusiastic about the program and have some knowledge of the school system, they are more likely to encourage school personnel to support the program. Because many parents teach in Behavior Analysis classrooms, they know a great deal about the program and the benefits it delivers to their children. They also receive much of the inservice training that is provided for teachers. These circumstances often contribute to the development of strong alliances between parents, program personnel, and school administrators.

Program management teams have been developed to facilitate the flow of information in large school systems, since communication within such programs and among their various support elements may be difficult. Typically, these teams are composed of an assistant superintendent, the program director, the chairperson of the PAC, principals, staff trainers, and representatives of the sponsor. The program management team usually meets once per month to discuss and make decisions on a wide range of issues.

Members of the sponsor's staff must also be involved in school district activities in order to facilitate program operations at the local level. For example, the district advisor has close ties with the Behavior Analysis Model, and may be an effective troubleshooter and problem solver for the local program. At the beginning of each school year, representatives of the sponsor and the school district prepare a written memorandum of agreement in order to describe the terms of their working relationship. The agreement specifies the objectives that the sponsor and the district agree to accomplish during the next 12-month period.

Finally, a program officer is assigned by the USOE and may contribute in a number of ways by helping to resolve problems in local communities. Since the program officer represents "official" support from the federal granting agency, that individual often may be able to accomplish things that others in the support system cannot.

Evaluation

Evaluation of the Behavior Analysis Model is described in three parts: Orientation to Evaluation, the Sponsor's Evaluation, and the National Longitudinal Evaluation. Members of the sponsor's staff planned and conducted their own evaluation. The national longitudinal evaluation was the responsibility of researchers employed at Stanford Research Institute and Abt Associates, Inc.

ORIENTATION TO EVALUATION

One of the major challenges in developing an instructional program is learning how to collect, organize, and utilize information about the implementation process. In 1968, many sponsors of Follow Through models expected to employ information from the national longitudinal evaluation to guide their program development activities. For several reasons, it soon became apparent that data from the national evaluation could not be used for making timely changes in program operations. Consequently, the sponsor developed a number of internal procedures for obtaining the information required to conduct a formative approach to program development. These procedures, described previously in the subsection entitled "Delivery System," include Continuous Progress Assessment, the Educational Audit, observational procedures completed as part of the teacher certification requirements, Annual Achievement Testing, and the Annual Consumer Evaluation. In addition, Annual Achievement Testing and the Annual Consumer Evaluation yield information that is useful for purposes of summative evaluation of program outcomes.

The sponsor's approach to evaluation had to meet a number of criteria. For example, the procedures had to be easily administered and not costly, since most of the funds for evaluating Follow Through models already had been allocated for use in the national longitudinal evaluation. They also had to provide data that could be used to compare the academic performance of students in Behavior Analysis Follow Through classrooms with (a) the normative performance of middle-class students; and (b) the performance of comparable low-income students who were not enrolled in Follow Through classrooms. Finally, the procedures had to yield data that could be interpreted easily by other researchers, school administrators, teachers, and parents, as well as data that could be compared with the outcome data collected in the national longitudinal evaluation.

SPONSOR'S EVALUATION

The sponsor's evaluation was conducted in order to assess whether important goals of the model were met. The three primary goals that were stated at the beginning of this chapter are (a) to help students attain competence in basic subjects; (b) to create a feeling of satisfaction among the children and adults who are the primary consumers of program services; and (c) to promote participation by parents whose children are enrolled in Behavior Analysis classrooms. Improving levels of academic achievement among children from low-income families was a priority goal of Project Follow Through. Accordingly, the primary focus of the sponsor's evaluation was on assessing the academic achievement levels of students enrolled in Behavior Analysis classrooms. Consequently, the evaluation of levels of consumer satisfaction and parent participation thus far have been comparatively less intensive. In addition, it could be argued that high levels of academic achievement among students would be more likely to occur when consumers were satisfied with the program and parents were actively involved. The method employed in the sponsor's evaluation of outcomes and some representative results are discussed next.

Method

The scope and size of the model, the characteristics of Behavior Analysis students and their families, the identification of non-Follow-Through comparison groups of students in local communities, the instruments employed in the sponsor's evaluation of outcomes, and the data collection procedures are described below.

Scope and Size of the Behavior Analysis Model Table 5.1 contains information about the number of programs, schools, classes, and children enrolled during the period from 1968 to 1977. When the 1968–1969 school year began, operations in five programs, 16 schools, and 29 classrooms served a total of 749 children. Model enrollment peaked at 7058 students during the 1972–1973 school year and declined slowly in subsequent years.

Table 5.2 contains a list of the 12 communities in which the Behavior Analysis Model was implemented during the 1976–1977 school year, along with the number of schools, classes, and children enrolled in each community. There were as many as eight schools in one community (Trenton, New Jersey), and as few as one school in some communities. The largest number of Behavior Analysis classrooms was in three programs in Philadelphia. The largest single program was in Trenton and the smallest was in Pittsfield, Massachusetts. The model was disseminated throughout the country in many diverse environments, including inner-city ghettos and urban communities, small towns in rural areas, and on Indian reservations.

Characteristics of Behavior Analysis Students and Their Families Information about the characteristics of students and families served by the

TABLE 5.1
Growth of the Behavior Analysis Model
(1968–1977)

School year	Programs	Schools	Classes	Children
1968–1969	5	16	29	749
1969–1970	12	33	116	2800
1970–1971	12	40	193	5008
1971–1972	12	41	268	6615
1972–1973	12	39	284	7058
1973–1974	12	39	279	6954
1974–1975	12	38	271	6965
1975–1976	12	41	269	6716
1976–1977	12	35	240	6316

TABLE 5.2
Behavior Analysis Programs
(1976–1977)

Location	Schools	Classes	Children
Bronx, New York	2	19	596
Hopi Reservation, Arizona	2	21	300
Indianapolis, Indiana	3	13	300
Kansas City, Missouri	3	24	608
Louisville, Kentucky	5	20	600
Meridian, Illinois	1	13	364
Northern Cheyenne, Montana	2	12	350
Philadelphia, Pennsylvania	3	38	1165
Pittsfield, Massachusetts	2	8	187
Portageville, Missouri	1	16	385
Trenton, New Jersey	8	36	892
Waukegan, Illinois	1	20	569
Totals	35	240	6316

model was obtained in a number of studies. For example, Stebbins, St. Pierre, Proper, Anderson, and Cerva (1977) reported that the results of their analyses of data collected by the Stanford Research Institute from a sample of several hundred children located in six Behavior Analysis communities supported the following conclusions: (a) The median family income of children enrolled in the model was $3890, as compared with $9590 for the national average; (b) 27% of the children enrolled in the model came from homes in which a female served as head of the household, as compared with 9% for the national average; and (c) 40% of the mothers of these children had completed high school, as compared with 50% for the national average. Studies of the childrens' characteristics indicate that 80% were black, as compared to the national average of 11%; 4% were of other ethnic origins, as compared to 2% for the national average. Bock, Stebbins, and Proper (1977) stated that among Behavior Analysis sites included in their sample, all but one had large concentrations of ethnic–linguistic minorities. Among the students enrolled in Behavior Analysis classrooms were a large number of Spanish-speaking children in inner-city programs and two groups of American Indian children who lived on reservations located in western states.

Identification of Non-Follow-Through Comparison Groups of Students in Local Communities The sponsor's evaluation plan included testing a large group of non-Follow-Through comparison children in each community in which the model was implemented. But numerous obstacles arose during the attempt to identify groups of children whose characteristics matched those of children enrolled in Behavior Analysis classrooms. For example, the enabling legislation for Follow Through required that programs in local communities must serve the most needy children. Administrators in many school districts were eager to comply because it provided an opportunity to transfer large numbers of "high risk" students from regular classrooms to Follow Through classrooms. In such circumstances, the dilemma was whether to test non-Follow-Through children whose characteristics might not be exactly comparable to those of children in Behavior Analysis classrooms or to abandon the attempt to identify local comparison groups. The model sponsor decided to maintain the original plan and evaluate the performance of non-Follow-Through children in each community, attempting to select those children whose characteristics were most similar to those in Follow Through classrooms. Since the sponsor's testing program already was being conducted in all Behavior Analysis communities, little additional effort or cost was required to obtain data from representative groups of non-Follow-Through comparison children in each community.

Most of the children included in local comparison groups were enrolled in regular classrooms located either in schools that contained Behavior Analysis classrooms or in schools that served a similar population. When school records were available, it was possible to match the characteristics of comparison and Follow Through children more accurately. But often the amount of descriptive information about children included in the comparison groups was limited, and identification of these children had to occur within the particular circumstances encountered in each community.

Instruments Employed in the Sponsor's Evaluation of Outcomes The Wide Range Achievement Test (WRAT) (Jastak, Bijou, & Jastak, 1965) was selected as the instrument for evaluating academic performance of students for two reasons. First, the WRAT met the criteria stated previously in the subsection entitled "The Sponsor's Evaluation," and second, the same form of the WRAT could be administered to students enrolled in kindergarten and the first three grades. Also, some items from the instrument were included in the national longitudinal evaluation pretest of Follow Through children. Reliabilities reported for the WRAT reading and arithmetic subtests are .91 to .92 and .70 to .80, respectively. In addition, the Annual Consumer Evaluation questionnaire was administered to assess the attitudes and opinions of school administrators, teachers, parents, and children toward the entire range of services provided through the model. This Likert-type scale appeared to have face validity, inasmuch as it had been shown to reflect changes in attitudes that were highly consistent with desired changes in local programs. In his discussion of social validity, Wolf (1978) emphasized the importance of such measures.

Data Collection Procedures in the Sponsor's Evaluation of Outcomes In order to ensure reliable and consistent administration of the WRAT, testers participated in a 3-day training session. They studied specially prepared administration manuals, viewed videotapes, and were required to achieve 100% accuracy on quizzes on these materials. Each tester was also required to administer the WRAT correctly during the training session, and periodic follow-up observations were made to ensure that accurate test procedures were maintained. The WRAT was administered near the close of the school year to large numbers of students in an attempt to offset the possible effects of attrition over the years. Tests were scored independently by at least two persons, thus increasing the likelihood that errors in administration and scoring would be detected. Test protocols were removed from the sample if they had been administered incorrectly.

The Annual Consumer Evaluation questionnaires were distributed to parents, teachers, and administrators. All questionnaires were answered anonymously and mailed to the offices of the model sponsor for scoring and analysis. In order to evaluate levels of satisfaction among students, testers who administered the WRAT also obtained information about children's perceptions and feelings toward school. The testers carefully avoided influencing the children's answers.

Representative Results from the Sponsor's
Evaluation of Outcomes

Data were analyzed to evaluate the impact of the Behavior Analysis Model in three major areas: academic performance among students, consumer satisfaction, and parent involvement. A number of specific questions about outcomes and the results of analyses of data pertaining to these questions are presented here.

Did students enrolled in Behavior Analysis classrooms attain competence in basic academic subjects? Those children who had continuous enrollment in Behavior Analysis classrooms from the beginning of kindergarten through the completion of third grade comprised a *cohort* of Follow Through students at each grade level. The mean WRAT reading and arithmetic scores achieved by all cohort students at each grade level during successive years from 1968 through 1978 are presented in Figures 5.2 and 5.3, respectively. The average raw score was calculated for each cohort at each grade level and then converted to the appropriate grade equivalent. The achievement levels expected from Behavior Analysis students, when they were tested near the end of each school year, are indicated on the left side of the tables. For example, kindergarten children were expected to

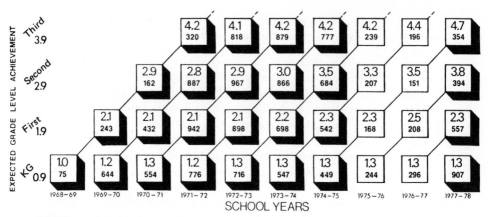

FIGURE 5.2 *Mean WRAT reading scores for Behavior Analysis cohort students (1969-1978).*

achieve a mean grade level score of 0.9, first grade children were expected to achieve a mean grade level score of 1.9, and so forth. The large numbers in the boxes represent the actual mean grade level scores achieved by the children.

In Figures 5.2 and 5.3 each set of boxes connected by a solid line represents a cohort of children. All cohort children leave the Behavior Analysis Follow Through Model after they complete third grade. The smaller numbers at the bottom of each box represent the number of children tested in each cohort. For example, the testing program was not vigorous during the 1968-1969 school year, as evidenced by the small number of children (N = 75) who were tested in Cohort I. During the 1969-1970 school year, tests were administered to 243 children from

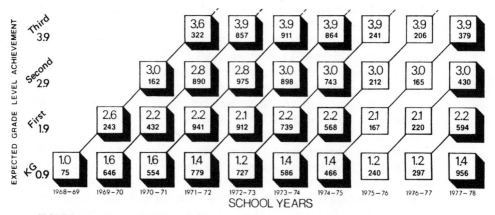

FIGURE 5.3 *Mean WRAT arithmetic scores for Behavior Analysis cohort students (1969-1978).*

Cohort I and to a much larger number (N = 644 and N = 646 for reading and arithmetic, respectively) from Cohort II. The discrepancy in the number of reading and arithmetic scores resulted from the misadministration of two reading tests.

Annual Achievement Testing was discontinued after the 1974–1975 school year for a number of reasons. For example, the model's effectiveness had been established, the national longitudinal evaluation was completed, and funds for testing were scarce. However, school personnel in some Behavior Analysis sites continued to administer the sponsor's achievement tests during the following two school years. The data for this period (1975–1976 and 1976–1977) can be seen in the unshaded boxes in Figures 5.2 and 5.3. In the spring of the 1977–1978 school year, the sponsor's evaluation group resumed the Annual Achievement Testing.

The results presented in Figures 5.2 and 5.3 indicate that children enrolled in Behavior Analysis classrooms achieved at or above grade level each year, with few exceptions. For example, the only instance of performance below the expected grade level in reading occurred during the 1971–1972 school year when second-grade children in Cohort II were 1 mo below the expected grade level. There were three instances of performance below the expected grade level in arithmetic (third-grade children in Cohort I during the 1971–1972 school year, and second-grade children in Cohorts II and III during the 1971–1972 and 1972–1973 school years, respectively).

It also should be noted that in most cases, in the tenth year of implementation, students enrolled in Behavior Analysis classrooms were achieving at levels equal to or higher than those attained at any time during the model's history. During the 1977–1978 school year, the reading scores of kindergarten and first grade children compared favorably with those attained during any previous year of the sponsor's testing. Among second and third graders, average reading achievement was 3 and 5 months higher, respectively, as compared to previous years. Arithmetic achievement during the 1977–1978 school year was comparable to previous years among second- and third-grade students, but slightly below previous high levels attained among kindergarten and first-grade students.

What were comparative levels of academic achievement among Behavior Analysis and non-Behavior-Analysis students? Figures 5.4 and 5.5 contain mean reading and arithmetic achievement test scores for Follow Through and non-Follow-Through comparison children at each grade level. These data were collected each spring from 1969 through 1975. Although the sponsor's evaluation includes data on Behavior Analysis children through 1978, no data were available on comparison children after 1975. Consequently, the data in Figures 5.4 and 5.5 pertain only to the period from 1969 to 1975.

For students at each grade level, the average raw score was calculated

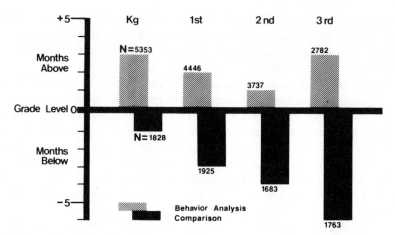

FIGURE 5.4 *Mean WRAT reading scores for Behavior Analysis cohort students and comparison students (1969–1975).*

and converted to a grade equivalent. Next, the number of months above or below the national norm was computed for the average child at each grade level. As shown in Figures 5.4 and 5.5, Behavior Analysis children scored at or above the national norm at each grade level. On the other hand, non-Follow-Through comparison children fell further below the national norm

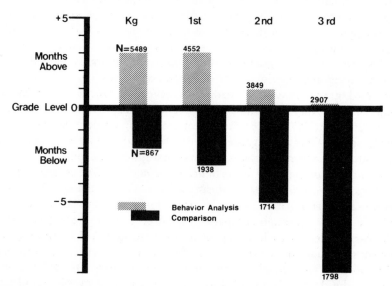

FIGURE 5.5 *Mean WRAT arithmetic scores for Behavior Analysis cohort students and comparison students (1969–1975).*

during successive years of school attendance. In fact, the comparative average reading and arithmetic scores at the end of third grade were 9 months higher for students in Behavior Analysis classrooms.[2]

Do children who attend Behavior Analysis classrooms for relatively longer periods of time have higher levels of academic achievement? The WRAT was administered to many children in Behavior Analysis classrooms who did not qualify as a member of any cohort group. Some of these children enrolled in Follow Through kindergarten classrooms but discontinued attendance in the model before they completed third grade; others had a record of intermittent attendance. Consequently, one approach to assessing the effects of the model was to compare the WRAT reading achievement test scores among groups of children whose length of attendance in Behavior Analysis classrooms ranged from 0 to 4 years. (The results for arithmetic are not presented, but the pattern of comparisons is similar to those obtained in reading.)

Inspection of Figure 5.6 reveals that children who had longer periods of attendance in Behavior Analysis classrooms also had higher mean scores in reading. At the kindergarten level, Behavior Analysis cohort children clearly performed better than those in local non-Follow-Through comparison groups and the middle-income norm, which is represented by the thin horizontal line that indicates the expected grade-level achievement of 0.9. Among first graders, Behavior Analysis students who were not members of a cohort group achieved at a level that was 3 months below the mean score of cohort children, but 2 months above the non-Follow-Through comparison group. Among second and third graders, similar patterns of differences occurred. Children who attended Behavior Analysis classrooms for the entire period of 4 years performed better than children who had only 3 years of program experience; those who had 3 years of attendance had higher scores than others who had only 2 years; students with

[2]Due to limited space, additional achievement test data that were collected at the end of fourth and fifth grades could not be presented and discussed at length in this chapter. Briefly, the mean WRAT Reading and Arithmetic scores for approximately 650 graduates of the Behavior Analysis Follow Through Model at the end of fifth grade were 5.5 and 4.7, respectively, as compared to mean scores of 4.8 and 4.5, respectively, for a comparable group of approximately 3200 non-Follow-Through fifth graders. The expected grade-level achievement score for students at the end of fifth grade is 5.9. Thus, even though the former Behavior Analysis cohort students were performing at or above the expected grade level in reading and arithmetic in Follow Through classrooms at the end of third grade, their mean scores had fallen below the expected grade level 4 months in reading and 12 months in arithmetic after they had attended regular fourth- and fifth-grade classrooms. These findings strongly support the conclusion that Follow Through Project services should be extended at least through the completion of sixth grade in order to support and maintain the positive gains in academic achievement that occur when students are enrolled in Behavior Analysis Follow Through classrooms.

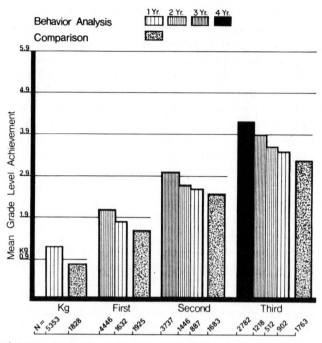

FIGURE 5.6 *Effects of length of attendance in Behavior Analysis classrooms on WRAT reading scores.*

2 years of experience performed better than those who had only 1 year of attendance; and children who had only 1 year of experience in Behavior Analysis classrooms performed better than children who had none.

Are consumers satisfied with the services provided through the Behavior Analysis Model? Each year, beginning in 1974, consumers of Behavior Analysis services were asked a variety of questions about the model and its effects. The questions focused on a number of program areas, and the consumers included parents, teachers, project directors, staff trainers, and students. One question was asked to assess whether adults were satisfied with the education that the children received in the Behavior Analysis Model. The most recent responses of 1798 parents, 429 teachers, and 60 program directors and staff trainers are summarized in Figures 5.7, 5.8, and 5.9. Approximately 90% of the adults in each of the three groups were "satisfied" or "completely satisfied" with the children's education. The children were asked how much they liked reading, math, and school. Their response options were "a lot," "some," or "not at all". The percent of Behavior Analysis and comparison children who responded "a lot" for reading (73% versus 66%), math (62% versus 57%), and school (71% versus 62%) is presented in Figure 5.10.

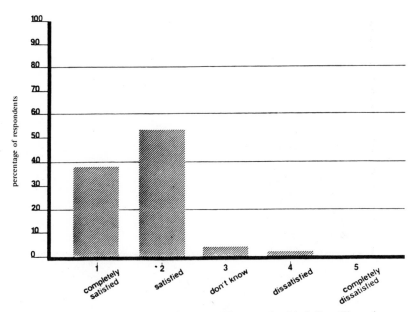

FIGURE 5.7 *Levels of satisfaction of parents (N = 1798) with Follow Through program. Parents were asked "How satisfied are you with the education your child has received in the Follow Through program?"*

Are parents involved in the education of their children? It was assumed that because many parents were employed as classroom teachers in the model, relatively high levels of parent involvement would be assured. But this goal was reached more completely in some communities than in others. Generally, it appears that levels of parent involvement in Behavior Analysis communities have been very high, as compared to levels of parent involvement in most communities throughout the nation. Members of the sponsor's staff recently designed new procedures that will be used during the 1979–1980 school year to obtain objective data on parent involvement in all Behavior Analysis communities.

The increased parent participation that occurred generally in the Behavior Analysis Model is illustrated by data collected in the Northern Cheyenne Indian Behavior Analysis program in Montana. As seen in Figure 5.11, Indians represented only 21% of the classroom teachers before the Behavior Analysis Follow Through Model was adopted. Five years later, Indians represented 70% of the teaching staff. Figure 5.12 shows the results of the application of decision-making powers by parents who were members of the local PAC during a 7-year period. When the Northern Cheyenne program began in 1969, the PAC had few responsibilities and made very few decisions involving the education of children. During the

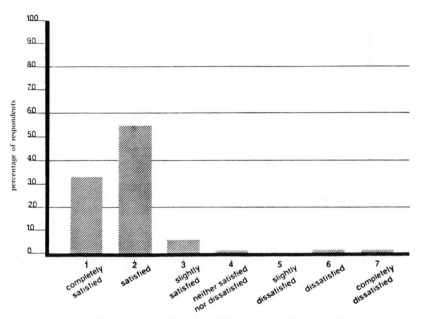

FIGURE 5.8 *Levels of satisfaction of teachers (N = 429) with Follow Through program.*
Teachers were asked "How satisfied are you with the education the children have received in
the Follow Through program?"

1976–1977 school year, the PAC discussed a total of 235 topics and took
action on 187. In addition, Indian representation on the Northern
Cheyenne school board has increased from 60% to 100% since the
Behavior Analysis program began. This increase of parent participation in
education among the Northern Cheyenne Indians is representative of increases in parent participation in many communities served by the model.

Are there other indicators of Behavior Analysis Model effectiveness? According to Baer (1978, p. 10), the ultimate criterion of effectiveness is social
adoption, and a prerequisite for social adoption is to be notable, or pub-
licly recognizable. Recent events have increased public recognition of the
Behavior Analysis Model. For example, the USOE has established seven
national resource centers for disseminating and replicating the Behavior
Analysis Model.

In 1977, many Behavior Analysis programs were certified as "effective
and exemplary" by the Joint Dissemination Review Panel (JDRP). The
JDRP was established by the education division of the Department of
Health, Education, and Welfare in 1972. This panel consists of 22
members, 11 from the National Institute of Education (NIE) and 11 from
the USOE. Panel members are appointed by the USOE commissioner and
the director of NIE. According to Tallmadge (1977), "The members are
chosen for their experience in education and their ability to analyze

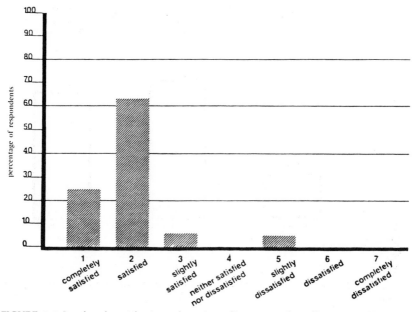

FIGURE 5.9 *Levels of satisfaction of project directors and staff trainers (N = 60). Respondents were asked "How satisfied are you with the education the children have received in the Follow Through program?"*

evaluative evidence on the effectiveness of educational products and practices [p. 1]."

Eight of the 12 Behavior Analysis programs were reviewed by members of the JDRP, and all were approved as "exemplary and effective." Six programs were approved unanimously. If the remaining four programs are

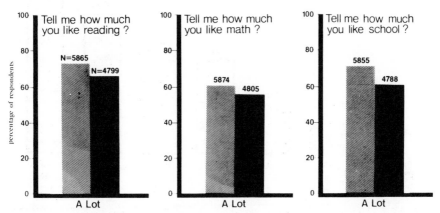

FIGURE 5.10 *Comparison of the attitudes towards reading, math, and school of Behavior Analysis students and comparison children.*

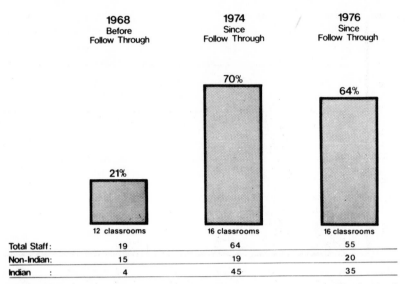

	1968 Before Follow Through	1974 Since Follow Through	1976 Since Follow Through
	21%	70%	64%
	12 classrooms	16 classrooms	16 classrooms
Total Staff:	19	64	55
Non-Indian:	15	19	20
Indian :	4	45	35

FIGURE 5.11 *Increase in percent of Indian representation on teaching staff in the Northern Cheyenne program.*

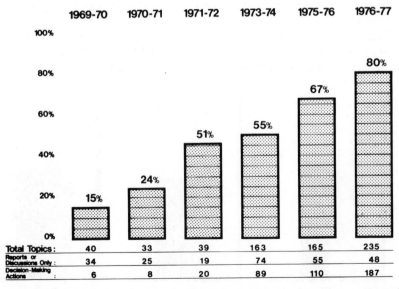

	1969-70	1970-71	1971-72	1973-74	1975-76	1976-77
	15%	24%	51%	55%	67%	80%
Total Topics:	40	33	39	163	165	235
Reports or Discussions Only :	34	25	19	74	55	48
Decision-Making Actions :	6	8	20	89	110	187

FIGURE 5.12 *Increase in PAC decision-making activities in the Northern Cheyenne Program.*

reviewed by the JDRP, it is likely that they also will be approved. The members of the JDRP base their decisions on the quality of data and magnitude of effects, and the outcome data on the four programs are equal to or more impressive than the outcome data for some of the eight programs already approved.

Of the eight programs approved by the JDRP, seven were awarded more than $1 million annually to operate resource centers. These centers are located in seven states, and the activities generated in them are contributing to national recognition (notable) for the Behavior Analysis Model. These efforts have not yet led to "social adoption" of the model on a large scale, but the possibility that this may happen is now greatly increased.

NATIONAL LONGITUDINAL EVALUATION

The outcomes of this evaluation appear to vary according to the variables included in the analyses of data. For example, the performance of the Behavior Analysis Model has been ranked by three different teams of researchers as better than other Follow Through models (Stebbins *et al.*, 1977), second in the overall standings (Bereiter & Kurland, 1978), and relatively mediocre (House, Glass, McLean, & Walker, 1978). Those individuals who wish more detailed comparisons of the various analyses performed on the data collected in the national evaluation should consult the original sources cited in this paragraph and elsewhere in this volume.

One of the prominent characteristics of the national evaluation is that it has produced much conflict (Haney, 1977; Kennedy, 1978). Nevertheless, it represents a milestone in the history of educational research and the conflict should not be permitted to obscure the useful knowledge that has been accumulated about educational practices and research methodologies. Thus, this discussion will focus on what has been learned about conducting large-scale intervention research in education. The topics discussed below include (*a*) the need for preliminary agreements; (*b*) expanding the scope of research; and (*c*) a quasi-experimental design for evaluation research.

The Need for Preliminary Agreements

The history of the Follow Through experiments indicates clearly that large-scale efforts in social intervention research should begin with at least a working consensus among representatives of major stakeholder groups. The process of reaching a consensus should include the definition of dependent and independent variables for each model; a statement of appropriate evaluation procedures; and projections on the length of the study, the number of cohorts involved, and the facilitating modes that model sponsors will pursue in developing local program operations. Participants at local levels should be helped to understand why experimentation in education is important and that essential conditions must be maintained in order to complete it.

Expanding the Scope of Research

Promising areas of research in Follow Through and in other similar projects include the relationships between educational processes and products, the role of sponsors as social change agents, and the implementation process. Studies of educational processes and products could be directed toward identifying the operations and results associated with educational models derived from various conceptual approaches. Information on the classroom management and instructional techniques that produce high levels of academic achievement and positive attitudes toward school probably would be applicable to educational programs for the handicapped, gifted, and other special populations of students.

Investigations of sponsorship could be designed to reveal the characteristics of effective delivery systems for educational and other services, the conditions required for an innovative program "to take" in a social system (school and/or community), the levels of implementation in which problems are most likely to occur, and ways to anticipate and perhaps avoid these problems. Research on sponsorship could help establish coherent linkages between educational theory, research, and practice in schools, thus contributing to more constructive relationships among communities, schools, and universities or research centers. A definition of effective sponsorship could be valuable for conducting innovative research and service programs in other community institutions, such as hospitals and mental health centers.

Studies of implementation were not included in the national longitudinal evaluation of Follow Through. This lack of attention to studying implementation and the relationships between implementation and consumer feelings of satisfaction necessarily limited the value of the study. Because research on program implementation deserves a high priority in planning the evaluation of social intervention studies, this topic is also discussed below in the section on "Lessons Learned."

A Quasi-Experimental Design for Evaluation Research

It is often impractical to employ classical, experimental designs in social intervention research. Stufflebeam, Foley, Gephart, Guba, Hammond, Merriman, and Provus (1971) noted that implementing such designs imposes the following restrictions: (a) Program operations must remain unchanged, thus preventing reasonable efforts to improve them; (b) the results are useful for making decisions only after a program has run full cycle and not during its planning and implementation; and (c) rigorous control must be exerted over many variables, thus creating program conditions that are often unrealistic and therefore not generalizable to real-world situations. An appropriate design for a project such as Follow Through must be able to detect causal relationships between treatment and outcome variables. But past experience in Follow Through indicates that political and practical considerations nearly always prohibit the selection of appropriate comparison groups. In addition, the use of analysis of covariance techniques has not been able to correct for the noncomparability between groups (Haney, 1977).

An alternative approach to detecting causation in dynamic projects such as Follow Through would be to use a quasi-experimental research design (Campbell & Stanley, 1966). For example, evaluation researchers should consider the use of a multiple baseline design (Baer et al., 1968) in which students in each school would serve as their own comparison group, thus eliminating the problem of noncomparable comparison groups. Figure 5.13 contains an example of a schedule for enacting the multiple baseline design for grade levels K through 6. This design would require extensive pretesting before implementation began and sponsors would have to implement their models later in some schools than others.

Enacting the plan indicated in Figure 5.13 would require that sponsors be "matched" with a community 1 year before program implementation began in order to establish relationships and prepare the groundwork for their programs. The appropriate test batteries would be administered as a pretest

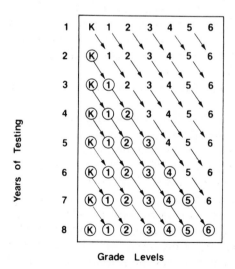

Grade Levels

FIGURE 5.13 *Suggested schedule for implementing a multiple baseline design for evaluation. A circle indicates that the model program is fully implemented at that grade level.*

in classrooms across all grades in which the programs would eventually be implemented, whether K through 3 or K through 6. This testing must occur at the beginning of the school year. The batteries also would be administered during the last month of the school year in the same classrooms and grade levels. The following year, the evaluation batteries would be administered to entering kindergarten students, and end-of-year posttests would be administered to students at all other grade levels. The model program would be implemented in successive grade levels each year until it had been implemented at all grade levels. Testing would occur as indicated in Figure 5.13 during the second year (A circle indicates that the model program is fully implemented at the grade level).

The design for evaluation that is illustrated in Figure 5.13 would provide one baseline point at kindergarten, two at first grade, three at second grade, four at third grade, and so forth. If each sponsor could stagger program implementation in 10 communities, more baseline points could be obtained. This would strengthen the overall evaluation plan. For example, sponsors could implement their model after the first year in 3 communities, after the second year in 3 more communities, and after the third year in 4 more communities. Thus, in the last 4 communities to implement there would be three kindergarten baseline points.

The multiple baseline technique could be used to implement grades 4–6 in existing programs and to implement K–3 in new model communities. This not only would provide more data, but also would ensure that all models had well-developed programs in grades 4–6 before implementation began in new communities. This design could be used to assess the overall effects of a project such as Follow Through by combining and comparing the baseline data with the experimental data for all model sponsors on each outcome variable selected for inclusion in the national evaluation. Data should be analyzed only when programs meet minimal implementation criteria.

The data collected in a multiple baseline study also could be used to compare the effects of baseline differences on outcomes both within and among models. Data on levels of implementation and on characteristics of communities would provide frameworks to guide such comparisons. For example, well-implemented programs in model A could be compared with well-implemented programs in model B, and the poorly implemented programs in both models could be compared separately. Similarly, separate comparisons could be performed for rural, urban, bilingual, Native American, or other distinctive classes of programs. Model comparisons also could be performed in similar communities, in order to identify models that might require longer periods of time to produce positive effects.

The multiple baseline design also could be used by sponsors to assess their effectiveness in achieving model-specific objectives. Many sponsors would probably want to include each year both their own model-specific evaluation instruments and a common core of outcome measures that were applicable to all models. Furthermore, specific studies conducted by each sponsor should supplement knowledge gained from the overall study. For example, some sponsors might want to conduct component analyses of classroom processes, of parent involvement, or of model delivery systems. When there were a number of common components in these areas in many models, cooperative analyses of pooled data could be used to identify relationships among clusters of components and outcome measures.

Lessons Learned

The three primary goals of the Behavior Analysis Model are to help students become competent in academic subjects, to satisfy the consumers of program services, and to promote parent participation in the education of their children. These goals have been pursued by utilizing the methods, findings, and techniques of applied behavior analysis in school settings. The evaluation results cited previously are positive and encouraging. The lessons learned from participation in Follow Through are numerous, complex, and could doubtless fill many volumes. Consequently, the comments in this section are selective in order to highlight (a) the challenge and promise of sponsorship; and (b) the need for studies on implementation.

THE CHALLENGE AND PROMISE OF SPONSORSHIP

The model sponsors may have learned more than any other group of participants in Follow Through. Armed with educational theories, empirical methods, and curriculum materials, the sponsors were expected to be leaders. But when they began their participation in Follow Through more than a decade ago, none of them anticipated the range of challenges that lay ahead. In the beginning, the most formidable task for all sponsors appeared to be the design of effective educational programs in a number of communities. Here was an opportunity for sponsors to prove that their particular approach was meritorious. However, in retrospect it appears that designing educational programs may have been one of the least difficult responsibilities of sponsorship.

Perhaps the most important lesson that sponsors have learned is that people (thousands of people in Follow Through) are the most important elements in building and maintaining successful educational programs. The effects of things people do, the decisions they make, and the changes in their perspectives constantly impact on program development activities.

Experiences with people in communities, people in local educational agencies, and people at state and federal levels of government taught all sponsors that even the most well-implemented programs may be fragile and vulnerable when unexpected events occur.

At local levels, the decisions that school administrators made to change curriculum or to reassign teachers, principals, and other school personnel often created serious problems in Behavior Analysis classrooms. Local financial crises led to mass firings of teachers and reductions in numbers of classrooms. In turn, these conditions often led to increased student–teacher ratios, the loss of key personnel, and the transfer of students at midyear. Inevitably, teacher strikes seemed to occur at either the beginning of the school year when essential training programs were being conducted or at the end of the year during the collection of evaluation data. Voluntary and government-mandated desegregation plans were implemented, bringing some local programs to an abrupt halt. When this occurred, the sponsor was required to pick up the pieces and begin again, sometimes in completely different schools and with different teachers and students.

People at state levels of government also made many decisions that affected Follow Through programs. Changes in priorities of state legislatures and administrators led to changes in school districts that frequently disrupted local operations. Changes in allocation of state revenues sometimes caused major negative effects on programs. Changes in tax bases and in plans for financing education made the planning of program operations from year to year extremely difficult.

In addition, people at federal levels of government also exerted important influences on the day-to-day operation of Follow Through programs. Because a variety of federal funds and programs had to coexist at local levels, reduced funding of non-Follow-Through programs often had unanticipated effects on children enrolled in Follow Through programs. Furthermore, children were sometimes scheduled to participate in activities in other classrooms during the middle of the school day in order to meet the requirements of other federally funded programs. There appeared to be no master plan for coordinating the activities of numerous programs at local levels. Confrontations between the Congress and the administration on whether to terminate or expand Follow Through produced severe morale problems at local levels. There was an escalation of uncertainties and disruptions each time a new president was elected. Finally, long-range planning in Follow Through was difficult, because federal programs are funded on an annual basis. Consequently, key people at local levels often accepted other positions in order to attain a greater degree of job security.

The discussion of sponsorship thus far has focused only on the problems that sponsors had to confront. But sponsors also learned that in communities throughout America there are large numbers of dedicated parents, school personnel, and community leaders who strongly support efforts to improve the quality of educational and life opportunities for children. In fact, sponsors could not possibly have found solutions to the problems stated above without the good will, cooperation, and inspirational support of many people at local, state, and federal levels. For example, groups of well-organized and knowledgeable parents support Follow Through programs, and they are a potent force for overcoming obstacles in many communities. Local programs could not have survived without the participation of dedicated teachers. Nor could programs have been implemented without the support and cooperation of many principals and school administrators.

Many people at local levels had important roles in the development of the Behavior Analysis Model, but it was the district advisors who were most responsible for adapting the model to a variety of community and classroom situations. They had to understand how local school policies affected their programs and how to balance the needs of the local district with those of the model. School administrators sometimes requested changes in programs that threatened the integrity of the model. In such instances, the district advisors used data and common sense to defend the model.

Many officials at state levels were willing and able to help when difficulties arose. State superintendents of public instruction were often knowledgeable and sympathetic in their responses to local concerns. Some of them visited local Follow Through programs and provided encouragement and/or financial support when possible. State directors of Title I programs often provided clarification of federal regulations that allowed better coordination of federal programs at local levels. In one state, legislators passed a law supporting the goals of the Behavior Analysis Follow Through Model and promising financial support for local programs in that state if the federal government failed to provide funds. Finally, state Follow Through technical assistants, who were responsible for coordinating state-related activities of local programs, were often helpful in resolving disputes between local and state education agencies.

A majority of the members of both the House and the Senate have frequently voted authorization and appropriation bills that strongly supported the continuation of Follow Through. Many members of Congress and their staffs have obtained information about Follow Through by actually visiting local programs throughout the nation and requesting regular reports from those involved. Currently, representatives of the Congress, the White House, and the USOE are studying the lessons learned from the Follow Through experience during the past 10 years in order to improve the delivery of research and other educational services through the schools.

The good will, cooperation, and support of many people have been essential to the success of Follow Through, and the model sponsors have had a crucial role in coordinating these contributions. In fact, the cohesive force represented by the sponsors has been a key factor in the success of Follow Through. In 1973, the sponsors formed the Sponsor Communication Advisory Network (SCAN), a national organization that has been instrumental in reaching solutions for many difficult problems. The sponsors have used SCAN to communicate with each other on a regular basis in order to identify and seek solutions for problems that occur in many Follow Through models. The sponsors conduct annual meetings in which they discuss their concerns in depth. By working intensively for an entire week, they often are able to define issues and to agree on proposals that ultimately stimulate constructive actions at local, state, and federal levels.

During the past 2 years, the SCAN organization has been expanded to include representatives from local sites and state technical assistants. Consequently, sponsors have been able to improve the coordination of their own actions with those of other stakeholders in Follow Through. The members of the SCAN network also have served as a resource for policymakers in the federal government. It has indeed been an exhilarating experience for the sponsors to learn that even though they represent varying philosophical and psychological viewpoints, they can communicate, work together, and work with other stakeholders in a national coalition to support quality and equality of education in America.

The Follow Through experience has shown that sponsorship can be a powerful influence for using the methods and findings of the social sciences to improve educational practices in schools. However, if the benefits of new Follow Through experiments are to be fully realized, it will be necessary to study sponsorship as well as educational procedures. Thus, model implementation should be viewed as a product of sponsorship, as well as a process for changing and improving the behaviors of students, teachers, and parents. Hodges, Sheehan, and Carter (1979) stated, "Many sponsors have become successful change agents in relation to their own specific programs. The problem now is to focus carefully on the dynamics of sponsorship and to view the process of implementing Follow Through as a critical outcome of the project [p. 669]."

THE NEED FOR STUDIES ON IMPLEMENTATION

Intervention studies such as Follow Through provide excellent opportunities to examine carefully the implementation of innovative educational models (Stallings, 1975). Such research appears to have the potential for revealing the components of effective model delivery systems, the initial influences that can facilitate or hinder desirable educational change, and the dynamics of change in an interacting system of administrators, trainers, teachers, parents, and children. These studies would require the collection of data on the behavior of participants, as well as descriptive data on program settings, formats, and operations. Sponsors could initiate the study of implementation by defining the characteristics of their models and developing instruments for measuring them. They also could formulate research questions on the linkages between program characteristics and outcome measures of particular importance. In addition, there should be studies on the delivery of services through program implementation.

In recent years, there have been advances in conceptualizing the process of program implementation. For example, Hall, Loucks, Rutherford, and Newlove (1975) proposed a system consisting of eight Levels of Use that appears to be a promising approach to studying implementation. For purposes of this discussion, the description of their system will be limited to the following three levels:

1. Orientation. The users acquire knowledge about the innovative program and explore its strengths and possible weaknesses.
2. Mechanical use. The users comprehend the day-to-day requirements of the program and perform functions satisfactorily by rote.
3. Innovative use. The users grasp the basic principles of the program and adapt its procedures in an innovative way to situations as they arise. New procedures may be tested, but these are always consistent with (or derived from) the basic program principles.

Another attempt to conceptualize the implementation process has been outlined in a preliminary (draft) document prepared by Ramp, Stivers, Williams, and Branden (1979) under the auspices of a federal contract. According to this approach, information about educational systems should be obtained at the following five points:

1. Sponsor's plans and behaviors. Information about the sponsor's description of the model could be obtained through descriptive materials, a structured interview, or other appropriate procedures. Sponsor behaviors (manuals, workshops, or visits) directed toward communicating or implementing the model could be described and documented.
2. Project administrator's plans and behaviors. The plans (or lack of plans) stated by program directors, principals, and staff trainers for the operation of a program during a typical school day and for parent involvement should be identified. Next, the behaviors that will be directed toward implementing these plans should be described and documented.

3. Teacher's plans. Information on teachers' (or parents') plans for a typical school day should be obtained through an interview and/or the examination of written schedules and lesson plans.

4. Classroom settings and formats. Descriptions of actual classroom or home settings and formats could be obtained through direct observation in classrooms. Examples of important classroom variables might include instructional time, opportunities for pupil responses, and pupil participation or occupancy time in highly structured and loosely structured formats.

5. Impact of classroom events on children's behavior. Observation of students and teachers for brief periods of time can indicate whether patterns of behavior in classrooms or homes are consistent with a sponsor's stated goals. Other indices, such as children's rates of verbal responses or their rate of progress in the curriculum may be used to study whether the instructional methods are successful.

The conceptual frameworks proposed above, and possibly others, could be used to formulate a broad approach to the study of implementation processes. Studies of implementation could be used to examine the effects of selected community characteristics on model implementation. The first step might be to study the influence of community characteristics such as size and geographic location on the degree of implementation and on the time required to reach a high level of implementation. A study of implementation is likely to be more successful if adequate descriptive data on the community has been accumulated before program implementation begins. Such baseline data would permit more accurate assessment of the changes that occur at various organizational levels of communities and schools.

One of the potential benefits of implementation research is that it may contribute to the development of procedures for identifying sources of stress before they develop into major problems. Through several months of descriptive work in a community, researchers could identify power structures, sources of intracommunity conflict, and sources of compatibility and incompatibility for the innovative program. The variables that should receive attention include the rigidity or flexibility of school policy and school personnel, history of local bond issues, history of educational decision making, degree of rapport between educational administrators and members of school boards, and attitudes of people in communities toward schools.

Implementation research also could be used to support sponsors' efforts to refine their models. For example, the Behavior Analysis sponsor would like to examine the relationship of academic skills, as they are represented in curriculum materials, to grade-level targets on various standardized achievement tests. Another use of implementation research might be to study the effects of varying the number of adults present in classrooms at different grade levels on outcomes such as student achievement, program costs, and levels of satisfaction among consumers. The results of such research then could be used to refine procedures and to deliver the most cost-effective educational services. In addition, a number of sponsors might wish to pool data on classroom processes such as instructional time, rates of teacher–pupil contacts, pupils' opportunities to respond, and students' opportunities to initiate interactions in order to delineate differences in classrooms representing the various models.

The 1980s promise to be an exciting period in the development of Follow Through. The project may be expanded into other grades in existing Follow Through programs and into new communities as well. Officials in the USOE and the Congress are currently planning events for the next decade. Sponsors, citizens in local communities, and State Technical Assistants have formed a national Forward Planning Task Force to develop a plan in cooperation with planners at federal levels of government. New priorities are being developed, and the range of research and services to be provided through the project are being discussed.

Follow Through has emerged as an important national educational resource. In fact, its current network of more than 150 participating communities and large number of sponsoring organizations comprise a vast educational laboratory. The resources, experience, and expertise in research and services represented in the project probably are unmatched anywhere. Perhaps the chief accomplishment in Follow Through is that researchers have been able to bridge the gap between educational theories and research findings on the one hand and practical educational services to children and their families on the other. The present challenge is to comprehend the full range of knowledge that has been gained from Follow Through during the past decade and to incorporate it in an action plan to shape future events.

Acknowledgments

Ramp is deeply indebted to Don Bushell, Jr., to colleagues in the Behavior Analysis Office, the Department of Human Development, and elsewhere within the University of Kansas, and to other Follow Through model sponsors for their support and encouragement. Sincere thanks and gratitude also are expressed to Behavior Analysis program administrators, teachers, parents, and children. And a very special debt of gratitude is acknowledged to Opal Folks, whose patience and competence contributed so much to the compiling and typing of this chapter. These individuals and many others aided substantially in both the success of the Behavior Analysis Model and the completion of this chapter.

References

Allen, K. E., Hart, B. M., Buell, L. S., Harris, F. R., & Wolf, M. M. Effects of social reinforcement on isolate behavior of a nursery school child. *Child Development*, 1964, *35*, 511–518.

Baer, D. M. Applied behavior analysis: Ten years later. *BA Update*, 1978, *3*, 10.

Baer, D. M., Wolf, M. M., & Risley, T. R. Some current dimensions of applied behavior analysis. *Journal of Applied Behavior Analysis*, 1968, *1*, 91–94.

Barrish, H. H., Saunders, M., & Wolf, M. M. Good behavior game: Effects of individual contingencies for group consequences on disruptive behavior in a classroom. *Journal of Applied Behavior Analysis*, 1969, *2*, 119–124.

Becker, W. C. *An empirical basis for change in education.* Chicago: Science Research Associates, 1971.

Becker, W. C., Madsen, C. H., Arnold, C. R., & Thomas, D. R. The contingent use of teacher attention and praise in reducing classroom behavior problems. *The Journal of Special Education*, 1967, *1*, 287–307.

Bereiter, C. A., & Kurland, M. *Are some Follow Through models more effective than others?* Paper presented to the annual meeting of the American Educational Research Association, Toronto, Ontario, Canada, March 1978.

Bijou, S. W., & Baer, D. M. Some methodological contributions from a functional analysis of child development. In L. P. Lipsitt & C. S. Spiker (Eds.), *Advances in child development and behavior.* New York: Academic Press, 1963. Pp. 197–231.

Birnbrauer, J. S., Wolf, M. M., Kidder, J. D., & Tague, C. Classroom behavior of retarded pupils with token reinforcement. *Journal of Experimental Child Psychology*, 1965, *2*, 219–235.

Bock, G., Stebbins, L. B., & Proper, E. C. *Education as experimentation: A planned variation model, Vol. IV-B, effects of Follow Through models.* Cambridge, Mass.: Abt Associates, Inc., 1977. (Also issued by the U.S. Office of Education as *National evaluation: Detailed effects*, Vol. II-B of the Follow Through Planned Variation Experiment series.)

Bostow, D. E., & Bailey, J. B. Modification of severe disruptive and aggressive behavior using brief time-out and reinforcement procedures. *Journal of Applied Behavior Analysis*, 1969, *2*, 31–37.

Bushell, D., Jr., & Brigham, T. A. Classroom token systems as technology. *Educational Technology*, 1971, *11*, 14–17.

Bushell, D., Jr., & Ramp, E. A. *The behavior analysis classroom.* Lawrence, Kans.: Behavior Analysis Follow Through, University of Kansas, 1974.

Bushell, D., Jr., Wrobel, P. A., & Michaelis, M. L. Applying "group" contingencies to the classroom study behavior of preschool children. *Journal of Applied Behavior Analysis*, 1968, *1*, 55–61.

Campbell, D. T., & Stanley, J. C. *Experimental and quasi-experimental designs for research.* Chicago: Rand-McNally, 1966.

Cantrell, R. P., Cantrell, M. L., Huddleston, C. M., & Wooldridge, R. L. Contingency contracting with school problems. *Journal of Applied Behavior Analysis*, 1969, *2*, 215–220.

Hall, G., Loucks, S., Rutherford, W., & Newlove, B. Levels of use of the innovation: A framework for analyzing innovation adoption. *Journal of Teacher Education*, 1975, *26*, 52–56.

Hall, R. V., Lund, D., & Jackson, D. Effects of teacher attention on study behavior. *Journal of Applied Behavior Analysis*, 1968, *1*, 1–12.

Haney, W. *A technical history of the national Follow Through evaluation.* Cambridge, Mass.: Huron Institute, 1977. (Also issued by the U.S. Office of Education as *The Follow Through evaluation: A technical history*, Vol. V of the *Follow Through planned variation experiment series.)*

Hankins, N. E. *Psychology for contemporary education.* Columbus, Ohio: Charles Merrill, 1973.

Harris, F. R., Wolf, M. M., & Baer, D. M. Effects of adult social reinforcement on child behavior. *Young Children*, 1964, *55*, 35–41.

Hodges, W. L., Sheehan, R., & Carter, H. Educational intervention: The role of Follow Through sponsors. *Phi Delta Kappan*, 1979, *60*, 666–669.

Holland, J. G., & Skinner, B. F. *The analysis of behavior.* New York: McGraw-Hill, 1961.

Homme, L., Csanyi, A. P., Gonzales, M. A., & Rechs, J. R. *How to use contingency contracting in the classroom.* Champaign, Ill.: Research Press, 1970.

Honig, W. K. (Ed.). *Operant behavior: Areas of research and application.* New York: Appleton-Century-Crofts, 1966.

House, E. R., Glass, G. V., McLean, L. D., & Walker, D. F. No simple answer: Critique of the Follow Through evaluation. *Harvard Educational Review*, 1978, *48*, 128–160.

Jastak, J. F., Bijou, S. W., & Jastak, S. R. *Wide Range Achievement Test.* Wilmington, Del.: Guidance Associates, 1965.

Jenkins, J., & Jackson, D. A. *Computer feedback in the behavior analysis classroom: A users guide.* Lawrence, Kans.: Behavior Analysis Follow Through, University of Kansas, 1974.

Kennedy, M. M. Findings from the Follow Through planned variation study. *Educational Researcher*, 1978, *7*, No. 6, 3–11.

Krasner, L., & Ullmann, L. P. (Eds.) *Research in behavior modification.* New York: Holt, Rinehart & Winston, 1965.

Madsen, C. H., Jr., Becker, W. C., & Thomas, D. Rules, praise, and ignoring: Elements of elementary classroom control. *Journal of Applied Behavior Analysis*, 1968, *1*, 139–150.

McKenzie, H. S., Clark, M., Wolf, M. M., Kothera, R., & Benson, C. Behavior modification of children with learning disabilities using grades as tokens and allowances as back-up reinforcers. *Exceptional Children*, 1968, *34*, 745–752.

Nelson, A., Saudargas, R. A., & Jackson, D. A. *Behavior analysis certification: Observation and training. Procedures for the Staff Trainer.* Lawrence, Kans.: Behavior Analysis Follow Through, University of Kansas, 1974.

O'Leary, K. D., & Becker, W. C. Behavior modification of an adjustment class: A token reinforcement program. Exceptional Children, 1967, *33*, 637–642.

O'Leary, K. D., Becker, W. C., Evans, M. B., & Saudargas, R. A. A token reinforcement program in a public school: A replication and systematic analysis. *Journal of Applied Behavior Analysis*, 1969, *2*, 3–13.

O'Leary, K. D., & O'Leary, S. G. (Eds.) *Classroom management.* New York: Pergamon Press, 1972.

Osborne, J. G. Free-time as a reinforcer in the management of classroom behavior. *Journal of Applied Behavior Analysis*, 1969, *2*, 113–118.

Ramp, E. A., & Hopkins, B. L. (Eds.) *A new direction for educators: Behavior analysis 1971.* Lawrence, Kans.: University of Kansas, 1971.

Ramp, E. A., Jackson, D. A., Green, D. S., Weis, L. C., & Bushell, D., Jr. Behavior Analysis Follow Through: State of the art six years after. In T. Brigham, Hawkins, R., Scott, J., & McLaughlin, T. (Eds.), *Behavior analysis in education: Self-control and reading.* Dubuque, Iowa: Kendall/Hunt Publishing Co., 1976. Pp. 312–346.

Ramp, E. A., & Semb, C. *Behavior analysis: Areas of research and application.* Englewood Cliffs, N. J.: Prentice Hall, 1975.

Ramp, E. A., Stivers, M., Williams, R., & Branden, A. *Planning experiments for future Follow Through studies: The Behavior Analysis Model* (Vol. I-A). Lawrence, Kans.: University of Kansas, 1979. (Also issued by the U.S. Office of Education, Office of Evaluation and Dissemination, Washington, D.C.)

Ramp, E. A., Ulrich, R., & Dulaney, S. Delayed time out as a procedure for reducing disruptive classroom behavior: A case study. *Journal of Applied Behavior Analysis*, 1971, *4*, 235-239.

Schmidt, G. W., & Ulrich, R. E. Effects of group contingent events upon classroom noise. *Journal of Applied Behavior Analysis*, 1969, *2*, 171-179.

Skinner, B. F. *Science and human behavior*. New York: Free Press, 1953.

Skinner, B. F. *The behavior of organisms*. New York: Appleton-Century-Crofts, 1938.

Stallings, J. A. Implementation and child effects of teaching practices in Follow Through classrooms. *Monographs of the Society for Research in Child Development*, 1975, *40*, (7-8, Serial No. 163).

Stebbins, L. B., St. Pierre, R. G., Proper, E. C., Anderson, R. B., & Cerva, T. R. *Education as experimentation: A planned variation model. Vol. IV-A: An evaluation of Follow Through*. Cambridge, Mass.: Abt Associates, 1977. (Also issued by the U.S. Office of Education as *National evaluation: Patterns of effects*, Vol. II-A of the *Follow Through planned variation experiment series*).

Stufflebeam, D. L., Foley, W. J., Gephart, W. J., Guba, E. G., Hammond, R. L., Merriman, H. O., & Provus, M. M. *Educational evaluation and decision making*. Itasca, Ill.: F. E. Peacock, 1971.

Sulzer, B., & Mayer, G. R. *Behavior modification procedures for school personnel*. Hinsdale, Ill.: The Dryden Press, 1972.

Sulzer-Azaroff, B., & Mayer, G. R. *Applying behavior analysis procedures with children and youth*. New York: Holt, Rinehart & Winston, 1977.

Tallmadge, G. K. *Ideabook: The Joint Dissemination Review Panel*. Mountain View, Calif.: RMC Research Corporation, 1977.

Ulrich, R., Stachnik, T., & Mabry, J. (Eds.). *Control of human behavior* (2 vols.). Glenview, Ill.: Scott, Foresman, 1966.

Wahler, R. G. Oppositional children: A quest for parental reinforcement control. *Journal of Applied Behavior Analysis*, 1969, *2*, 159-170.

Wasik, B. H., Senn, K., Welch, R. H., & Cooper, B. R. Behavior modification with culturally deprived school children: Two case studies. *Journal of Applied Behavior Analysis*, 1969, *2*, 181-194.

Wolf, M. M. Social validity: The case for subjective measurement. *Journal of Applied Behavior Analysis*, 1978, *11*, 203-214.

Wolf, M., Risley, T., & Mees, H. Application of operant conditioning procedures to the behavior problems of an autistic child. *Behavior Research and Therapy*, 1964, *1*, 305-312.

DAVID P. WEIKART
CHARLES F. HOHMANN
W. RAY RHINE

6

High/Scope Cognitively Oriented Curriculum Model[1]

[1] Preparation of this chapter was supported by USOE Grant G007507225 but no endorsement of its content by the federal government should be inferred.

201

Overview

The High/Scope Cognitively Oriented Curriculum Model is derived primarily from theories and research on children's cognitive development, from information on selected instructional techniques, and from the results of considerable experience in planning and implementing educational programs for young children. Teaching basic academic skills is an important goal of the model, but during the primary years the highest priority is to help children develop a broad range of problem-solving abilities and communication skills in both verbal and written expression. Students plan many of their own active learning experiences, communicate freely with peers and teachers in small groups, and design individual study projects. Parents may participate in local Follow Through programs by serving as paraprofessionals and volunteers in classrooms, by planning home learning activities with school personnel during home visits, and by attending group meetings.

The first section of this chapter contains a review of some major events in the evolution of the High/Scope Follow Through Model. Next, the discussion of rationale includes a comparison of several approaches to educating children and information on the conceptual roots and goals of the model. Characteristics of classrooms, the daily classroom routine, the curriculum, and the staff development and support system are described in the section on implementation. The description of evaluation includes examples of new instruments that were developed to evaluate distinctive objectives of the High/Scope Model and representative outcome data from several approaches to evaluation. The last section contains a summary of the lessons learned about educating young children through participation in Follow Through.

Origins

In 1962, David P. Weikart and his associates initiated the Perry Preschool Project in Ypsilanti, Michigan. The child-centered orientation characterized most preschool education programs at that time, but the members of Weikart's group chose to emphasize planning by teachers and an organized curriculum in their work. By 1964, they were committed to developing a new cognitively oriented approach to educating young children (Hohmann, Banet, & Weikart, 1979), using sources such as the developmental theories stated by Jean Piaget (1962, 1970) and instructional techniques described by Sara Smilansky (1968).

The first contacts between Weikart and representatives of the national Follow Through Project occurred in 1967. The innovative characteristics of Follow Through were impressive and challenging, but the results of research and program activities conducted by Weikart and his colleagues had persuaded them to concentrate their efforts on developing programs for infants, preschoolers, and their parents rather than kindergarten or primary children. That decision was communicated to USOE-Follow Through administrators in January, 1968. However, the representatives of several public school districts soon requested that Weikart sponsor Follow Through programs in their communities. Consequently, a reexamination of the previous decision to work only in preschool educations and further discussions with the planners of Follow Through led to an agreement for participation as a program sponsor.

During 1968, Weikart launched three major new projects: (a) a curriculum development effort, funded by USOE-Follow Through, to implement the Cognitively Oriented Curriculum Model at kindergarten and primary levels in a number of public school classrooms; (b) an intervention study, funded by the Carnegie Corporation, to assess the effectiveness of a home teaching program with parents and their infants starting at 3 months of age; and (c) the Ypsilanti Preschool Curriculum Demonstration Project, funded by USOE under Title III of the Elementary and Secondary Education Act, to study the long-term impact of preschool education and to compare the effects of three differing educational curricula, including the Cognitively Oriented Curriculum.

Prior to 1970, the research and development work was conducted through the Ypsilanti Public Schools, where Weikart served as Director of Research and Development, and Eastern Michigan University, where he was a project director. The increasing complexities that resulted from planning and conducting large-scale projects through two separate institutions and the recognition that this work was increasingly national and international in scope were among the reasons for establishing the High/Scope Educational Research Foundation as an independent agency.

The staff of the Foundation conduct many projects in curriculum development and evaluation research in education. These projects currently include developing a bilingual–bicultural preschool curriculum, conducting a commmunity-based educational program for parents and their infants, integrating children who have special needs into regular classrooms, operating a demonstration preschool and elementary school, offering a summer program for gifted and talented teenagers from overseas and throughout the United States, organizing a graduate program leading to a master's degree in human development and education for those individuals who want to specialize in the cognitively oriented approach to curriculum and instruction, as well as coordinating several training and curriculum projects in Latin America and Australia.

The Staff Training and Curriculum Development Center (TDC) located in Ypsilanti, is the demonstration preschool and elementary school that was established by the Foundation in 1971. Since that time, the TDC has grown in importance as a place where new approaches to curriculum and teaching methods can be pilot tested before they are disseminated for use by teachers in local communities. The TDC also serves as a training facility for instructing field site personnel, graduate students, and the members of the Foundation staff. The children enrolled in the TDC range in age from kindergarteners to sixth graders.

Rationale

The three purposes of this section are (a) to compare the High/Scope Cognitively Oriented Curriculum Model with other approaches to childhood education; (b) to identify the beliefs about education, theories, and research that provide the conceptual base of the model; and (c) to state the goals of the model.

COMPARISONS AMONG APPROACHES TO CHILDHOOD EDUCATION

Figure 6.1 represents the framework developed at the High/Scope Foundation for comparing different approaches to childhood education (Lambie, Bond, & Weikart, 1975; Weikart, 1972, 1974). Two axes represent the roles of teachers and students in classrooms. Observation of events in classrooms reveals that their roles may be described as either *initiating* or *responding*. Generally, the more frequently a teacher initiates, the more often a pupil is required to respond. The approaches represented in Quadrants 1, 2, and 3 (programmed curricula, child-centered curricula, and open-framework curricula, respectively) are discussed below. Custodial care, represented in the fourth quadrant, pertains to the limited, inadequate educational opportunities that may characterize some nursery school or orphanage situations and will not be discussed further in this chapter.

Programmed Curricula

In educational programs represented in the first quadrant of Figure 6.1, teachers plan and initiate learning opportunities and students respond to teachers' behavior. This pattern of teacher–student interaction in classrooms occurs in programmed instruction approaches and generally in

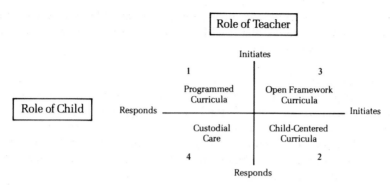

FIGURE 6.1 *Comparison of educational curriculum models on basis of roles of teacher and child.*

educational settings where the primary goal of adults is to indoctrinate learners with highly structured academic knowledge. Behaviorists usually support this approach on the grounds that it may be used to efficiently provide students with information and skills that are required to compete successfully at a later time in the adult society. Those individuals who oppose this approach contend that teaching children answers to questions formulated by adults is not a good method for educating students to become independent problem solvers. The important tasks in this "knowledge transfer" approach to education include defining learning sequences in academic skills areas and designing efficient teaching methods for helping learners acquire this information as rapidly as possible.

Child-Centered Curricula

In the educational programs represented by the second quadrant of Figure 6.1, teachers seek to be responsive to the interests and activities initiated by students. Some examples of child-centered approaches are John Dewey's progressive education, traditional preschool education programs in which children engage often in free play and adults limit their supervision and involvement to supporting children's development in social and affective areas, and some contemporary programs that may be grouped under the rubric of "open education." Advocates of the child-centered approach reject the view that the most important goal of instruction should be to help children acquire sequences of academic skills. They believe that academic skills should be taught primarily within the context of children's interest and their self-initiated activities. The critics of this approach state that some children may develop basic academic skills slowly in such programs, and that teachers who have this orientation do not use current knowledge about sequencing academic concepts for instructional purposes. Educators who wish to implement this approach must help teachers both to understand the dynamics of interaction among children and to construct procedures and materials that enable children to exercise control over their own behavior in classrooms.

Open-Framework Curricula

The open-framework approaches, which are represented in the third quadrant of Figure 6.1, include the High/Scope Cognitively Oriented Curriculum Model. They feature frequent initiation behaviors by both teachers and students in the teaching–learning process. As in the child-centered approach, students construct their own learning experiences from the interests and prior experiences that they bring to classrooms. But the teacher's role is somewhat more directive than in the child-centered approach. Teachers facilitate children's learning by asking questions and providing materials and activities that are appropriate to each child's developmental level. The pattern of teacher–student interaction in which teachers both help students achieve sequenced learning goals and also encourage them to set many of their own learning goals is an important distinction between programs in this quadrant and those in other quadrants. Teachers use a conceptual framework of child development, one that includes many Piagetian concepts, to guide their assessments of each child's developmental level and their formulation of appropriate questions.

Supporters of open-framework instruction claim that this approach stimulates the development of many skills, such as self-management and decision-making, that cannot be measured by standardized aptitude and achievement tests. They also argue that open-framework programs are more effective in meeting the special needs of children whose abilities and/or backgrounds differ from the majority of students. Critics state that teachers in these approaches require too much specialized training, that they are committed to a vague philosophical concept of "developmental pull" that is assumed to be present within each child, and that some children may acquire academic skills at a comparatively slow rate. Educators who wish to implement open-framework educational programs must become well-informed about the growth and development of children, methods for recognizing individual differences in classrooms, and instructional methods and materials that support learners' construction of their own knowledge.

CONCEPTUAL BASIS OF THE
HIGH/SCOPE MODEL

The rationale for the High/Scope Cognitively Oriented Curriculum Model is based in part upon beliefs about what is desirable in the education of children. In addition, the developmental theories and research of Piaget and others have guided the choice of goals and instructional procedures.

Beliefs about Education

The rate of change in our society is increasingly rapid, and educational programs should reflect the new requirements for living successfully in such a society. It is unlikely that students can acquire through their educational experience all the knowledge that they will require in the future. Indeed, children must become competent in academic skills, but they also need personal skills and attitudes that enable them to enter confidently into human relationships and to use knowledge for solving problems in the present as well as unanticipated problems that may occur in the future.

The cognitive and affective goals of education are more likely to be accomplished when educators develop explicit plans for achieving both types of goals. Children learn at different rates and have different interests and backgrounds of experiences. Their unique potentials for growth are more likely to develop when they are encouraged to initiate and plan many of their own learning experiences in lifelike settings in which they can communicate freely with peers and adults. These learning experiences should include frequent opportunities to formulate interesting problems through activities in which they work with concrete materials. Instruction in language and other academic skills often can be accomplished during the time when children are working to solve the problems that they developed themselves. Their "underlying" cognitive abilities develop in stages, and learning activities in schools should support the growth of these abilities.

An important purpose of recent educational reform has been to improve academic learning opportunities for low-income children. Some individuals have developed an apparently simple approach to meeting the needs of these children—a "cure" that consists of teaching basic academic skills through the frequent use of drill and other direct instruction methods. In contrast, parents and teachers who participate in the High/Scope Model seek to develop a broad range of skills in conceptual problem solving and interpersonal communication that are essential to successful living in school and later in adult life. Thus, academic skills are a necessary but limited part of the students' total learning.

The members of the High/Scope staff do not believe that the major purpose of educational programs should be to accelerate the rate at which children acquire fundamental cognitive skills (Kohlberg, 1968). Consequently, the High/Scope Cognitively Oriented Curriculum Model contains no intensive exercises that are designed to "speed up" children's cognitive development. Instead, the intent is to provide children with many opportunities to use, in constructive ways and in a wide variety of settings, the abilities that they already possess.

Contributions from Theories and Research

During the early 1960s, many educators began to examine cognitive developmental theories such as those proposed by Piaget. They hoped to identify principles that could be useful in explaining how environmental stimulation influenced the development of intellectual abilities required for success in school. A number of authors translated Piaget's writings into English, and others presented the results of research based on his theories (Bruner, Oliver, & Greenfield, 1966; Flavell, 1963; Sigel & Hooper, 1968).

Some educators became convinced that Piaget's descriptions of "underlying capacities" could contribute to the construction of instructional programs to help children be more successful in school learning. Indeed, the importance of underlying capacities appeared to be supported by reports that initial cognitive gains in Head Start disappeared early in the primary grades (Cicirelli, Cooper, & Granger, 1969). Weikart and his associates questioned whether children may have lost the gains they attained in preschool programs because programmed and child-centered approaches to instruction failed to develop the cognitive skills that children required for effective school learning. They also suggested that educational programs based on Piagetian principles might be more successful.

High/Scope classrooms do not represent direct or isomorphic enactments of Piaget's developmental theory into practice. The classrooms do represent adaptations of a number of ideas from his writings that have influenced the development of the Cognitively Oriented Curriculum Model. Some ideas that have been especially useful are described here.

Stages of Cognitive Development Piaget portrays children's intellectual development as a discontinuous process. In each stage of development they master some concepts but not others. Apparently, these stages are invariant sequences that are loosely linked to chronological age (Flavell, 1971). From the High/Scope perspective, these age-related cognitive changes establish some limits on the range of tasks that children at any given age level are likely to comprehend.

Information about characteristic abilities that emerge during various stages of development may be used to prescribe instructional materials and activities that are appropriate to students' levels of comprehension. For example, children usually do not possess an understanding of conservation of number before the age of 6 to 7 years. Therefore, it seems reasonable to delay instruction in mathematical computation until late in the first or second grade. Or, since students are unable to comprehend experimental control of variables until early in adolescence, instruction in the experimental method should not be incorporated into the science curricula presented to preadolescents. Educators also may wish to organize kindergarten environments in order to capitalize on the knowledge that preoperational children can solve simple problems that require a knowledge of similarities and differences, cause and effect, and space and time relations.

Scientific and Mathematical Concepts A number of Piagetian concepts such as classes, relations, quantity, conservation, space, time, and causality are useful in teaching science and mathematics. Children employ these concepts to comprehend and organize details of their environment. Teachers in High/Scope Curriculum classrooms seek to support the learning of many concepts described in Piaget's writings by providing a breadth of practical learning experiences that encourage the development of concepts in many areas. Thus, the activities in classrooms include sewing, weaving, woodwork, music, and other forms of expression that provide opportunities for children to use their repertoires of concepts in active reasoning and problem solving.

Attempts to teach a number of Piagetian concepts directly have produced inconclusive results (Braine & Shanks, 1965; Smedslund, 1962). Apparently, most children will acquire these concepts in the "natural" course of their life experience. Even in extremely deprived settings, children appear to develop the cognitive abilities described by Piaget, although the emergence of these abilities may be somewhat delayed by exceptionally adverse environmental conditions (Bruner *et al.*, 1966).

Mechanisms for Learning Piaget also identified a number of mechanisms for learning that have influenced the formulation of the High/Scope Curriculum Model. Three of these mechanisms are described as follows:

1. Representation. Piaget (1970) stated that children acquire knowledge through a "representational" process that leads to the formation of cognitive structures called *schemes*. Furth (1969), Smilanski (1968), and Bruner *et al.* (1966) described the representational process, and they emphasized the important link between children's representation of ideas and objects and their development of "understanding." Members of the High/Scope staff translated information about representation into a "child process" of *plan–work–represent–evaluate*. Students use representation as an active tool for gaining and consolidating understanding.

In the High/Scope Cognitively Oriented Curriculum Model, children accomplish the representation of knowledge through procedures such as the following: (*a*) planning activities to be completed and later describing these activities and their outcomes in verbal or written statements; (*b*) imitating past experiences in play activities and building representations of familiar objects from blocks and wood; (*c*) drawing pictures, maps, diagrams, charts, and graphs to represent interactions with the environment; and (*d*) preparing written materials in order to build communication and expressive skills.

Each of the procedures listed above requires that children develop mental representation of experiences. In addition, they are useful in prompting the "distancing" of students from the events that they represent, thus requiring children to conceptualize their experiences. The representation process is employed in the High/Scope Curriculum Model to encourage the transformation of experience into conceptual content. The use of the plan–work–represent–evaluate process in classroom instruction is described below in the section entitled "The Well-Implemented Model."

2. Experience with material objects. In his experiments, Piaget usually presented problems in which children were required to manipulate concrete materials. He contended that experiences in active problem solving with materials and objects are the chief sources of learning. Accordingly, a central theme in the High/Scope Curriculum Model is the encouragement of children to work with concrete materials. But these experiences alone do not assure that learning occurs, since access to carefully selected materials only makes activities possible. When these activities lead to the formulation of problems and thoughtful efforts to solve them, learning is likely to occur.

3. Developing social and communication skills. The results of research conducted by Piaget (1962), Smilanski (1968), and Bruner et al. (1966) indicate that social interaction experiences may influence the rate of cognitive development. Consequently, facilities in classrooms are arranged to permit students to interact frequently in small groups in order to represent their perceptions and feelings. Activity centers provide many opportunities for child–child and child–adult interactions. Furthermore, the teaching of language arts is based on the beliefs that language is a social skill and that spoken language provides the basis for written language (not vice versa), as stated by Van Allen (1976), Van Allen and Van Allen (1966), and Stauffer (1975). Therefore, students have many opportunities to communicate verbally with peers and adults about their activities and to write daily reports and experience stories about the details of those activities. They improve many of their reading skills by reading directions or recipes and obtaining other information that may be required to complete projects. Many activities in writing and reading also include opportunities for children to exercise social and communication skills.

GOALS OF THE HIGH/SCOPE
CURRICULUM MODEL

The goals of the High/Scope Cognitively Oriented Curriculum Model may be grouped into the following three areas: pursuing interests and ideas, living and working successfully with others, and using a wide range of intellectual and physical abilities.

1. Pursuing interests and ideas
   a. Making decisions about what to do and how to do it.
   b. Define and solve problems.
   c. Exercise self-disipline, identify personal goals, and pursue and complete self-chosen tasks.

    d. Acquire a spirit of inquiry and a personal sense of goals and values.

    e. Develop interests and/or avocations that can be cultivated both during and after the completion of the school experience.

2. Living and working successfully with others.

    a. Engage with other children and adults in group planning, cooperative effort, and shared leadership.

    b. Comprehend others' self-expression through spoken, written, artistic, and graphic representations.

    c. Acquire an openness to the points of view, values, and behaviors of others.

3. Using a wide range of intellectual and physical abilities

    a. Develop abilities to speak, write, dramatize, and graphically represent experiences, feelings, and ideas.

    b. Apply classification, seriation, spatial, temporal, and quantitive reasoning in a variety of life situations.

    c. Develop skills and abilities in the arts, science, and physical movement as vehicles with which to express personal talents and energy.

These general goals also are stated in the form of more specific objectives that are sequenced for kindergarten and the first three grades. The more specific statements of objectives pertain to instruction in the following content areas: planning, work on independent projects, cooperation, writing, reading, language arts (including phonics, punctuation, and grammar), number and measurement, space, time, classification and ordering, art, drama, music, woodworking, sewing, and movement. How students attain objectives in these areas through their participation in the High/Scope Follow Through Model will be discussed in the next section of this chapter.

The Well-Implemented Model

The implementation of the High/Scope Curriculum Model will be presented in three parts: (*a*) description of classrooms and curriculum; (*b*) staff development and support system; and (*c*) parent participation.

DESCRIPTION OF CLASSROOMS AND CURRICULUM

High/Scope Follow Through classrooms contain learning centers for building, language, math, science, and art. The learning centers are stocked with a variety of materials and equipment. For example, children can obtain paper, paints, brushes, scissors, clay, easels, cloth, paste, and sewing materials in the art center. The math center contains puzzles, games, rulers, graphs, scales, weights, caculators, and maps. In each classroom, there are several tables at which adults can meet with small groups of children. In addition, there is a large space where the total group can convene for performances, songs, dances, presentations, and other group meetings.

The Daily Classroom Routine

The daily classroom routine is listed here.

8:30	Large Group Time
8:50	Language Small Group Time
9:15	Planning Time
9:30	Work Time
10:30	Representation Time
11:00	Evaluation Time
11:20	Lunch and Outside
12:00	Large Group Time
12:30	Math Small Group Time
1:00	Work Time
1:45	Representation Time
2:10	Evaluation Time

The focus of daily activities in classrooms is on the enactment of two cycles of planning–working–representing–evaluating. *Planning Time* consists of small group meetings in which adults help children plan projects or activities of interest to them. Plans usually include statements about the materials that will be used, the other people who also may be involved, the sequence of steps in the completion of the project, and the problems that may have to be solved.

During *Work Time*, children go to learning centers where they select materials that they may use to produce products or performances. Adults often initiate dialogues with children concerning their work. These dialogues usually center on the task and the procedures that the child expects to use to complete it. The adult's intent is to help the child extend or elaborate the initial conceptualization of the task in ways that are consistent with the child's interests, general level of comprehension, and past performance.

The purpose of *Representation Time* is to allow children to transform their direct experiences in work into concepts. They do this by sharing their achievements with others in the form of written reports, graphs, charts, drawings, diagrams, dramatizations, or by answering questions. Adults help the children select appropriate formats for their representations. The uses of representation strategies in the High/Scope Model are intended to accomplish what Bruner (1966) described as "turning experiences into notation and order [p. 21]" and what Piaget (1970) referred to as "reflective abstraction [p. 728]."

An adult also may help a child decide how to evaluate the success of a project during *Evaluation Time*. This activity immediately follows Representation Time and is conducted in small groups. The process is usually initiated by a child who wishes to review the plan she has made and then procedes to share the product of her work and the report, diagram, or other representation of it that she has made with other children in the group. The teacher and other children often help the child to compare the original plan with the work produced and to probe the work process by asking questions concerning how the work was accomplished, what remains to be done, and what the child has learned during the completion of the work.

Large Group Time is another component of the daily classroom routine and is used to conduct meetings attended by all members of a class. The activities that occur during Large Group Time include dramatic performances, the presentation of completed classroom projects, dances, games, physical exercises, general meetings, and announcements.

During *Small Group Time*, teachers may conduct carefully sequenced learning activities as they introduce the use of new materials or teach academic concepts and skills in areas such as language arts, mathematics, science, art, drama, and music. These activities are based upon sets of objectives that are sequenced in accordance with developmental criteria. Thus, the objectives that are appropriate for a particular student are those that stimulate and strengthen the abilities that characterize that child's current developmental status. For example, instruction in mathematics at the first grade level begins with counting and recording data in graphs or tallies and experiences with concrete objects, events, or measurements. Students will use these skills when they enroll in second grade classrooms to perform arithmetic operations such as addition and subtraction.

Small Group Time activities are planned by each teacher or the members of each teaching team during daily and weekly planning sessions. The activities for each child are sequenced to correspond with both the appropriate lists of objectives and the teachers' knowledge of the performance and experience of the children. The activities include the use of manipulative and print materials available in the classroom. Teachers present the activities in a manner consistent with developmental learning principles that emphasize the initiation of physical and mental actions, representation of actions, and communication. The planning of Small Group Times and how children achieve sequenced learning objectives are described more completely in *Planning by Teachers*, a curriculum guide prepared by members of the High/Scope staff.

Curriculum

The orientation and content of a number of curriculum areas are briefly described here.

Language Instruction in language encompasses the basic skills of reading and writing (letter names and sounds, phonics, vocabulary, spelling, handwriting, punctuation, usage, and comprehension). It also includes the teaching of *productive language*, or effective skills for verbal and written communication, which emerges from children's direct experiences in using spoken and written language in order to communicate. For example, they may wish to make written reports on a cooking project, write a script for a play, or write lyrics for a song. Instruction in language skills may be integrated with the writing experiences or may occur independently.

The teaching of productive language has a high priority in the Cognitively Oriented Curriculum Model. But the methods for teaching productive language in High/Scope Follow Through classrooms differ from the usual instructional practices in regular grade classrooms. Typically, writing skills are taught in a piecemeal fashion, and children learn an assortment of discrete facts and skills in grammar, spelling, punctuation, capitalization, and calligraphy. But students may master the mechanics and conventions of writing and yet not develop skills in productive language. In the High/Scope Model, students acquire effective writing skills by actually preparing written materials that inform, persuade, instruct, or elicit information. Britton, Burgess, Martin, McLeod, and Rosen (1975) called this kind of writing *transactional writing*, in contrast to *pseudo-transactional* writing, in which students in most classrooms write to demonstrate the mastery of technical skills or to paraphrase statements that were either made by teachers or presented in textbooks.

Teachers in kindergarten and first-grade classrooms devote a significant amount of time to developing productive language skills among their students by encouraging them to initiate and plan independent projects in activity centers. Another technique that teachers use to increase the amount of productive language that students generate in classrooms is to ask divergent questions rather than convergent questions. Convergent questions are those that require one specific answer and therefore tend to restrict the elaboration of children's thought processes and verbal responses. Divergent questions are more likely to provoke thought, extended problem solving activities, and elaborated verbal responses.

Teachers actually allocate more time to developing productive language skills than to drill activities in language and mathematics during the primary grades. This approach is believed to be appropriate for two reasons. First, when children develop and apply language skills through their own initiative, they are more likely to retain and use this knowledge. Second, older children are capable of using more complex, higher-order cognitive processes than younger children. Consequently, older children should be able to assimilate instruction in basic academic skills more rapidly.

Mathematics and Science In mathematics instruction, the goal is not only to teach basic skills in counting and computation, but also to encourage students to use these skills in lifelike problem situations. Children discover that they must have skills in number facts and computations in order to complete their projects and activities. These skills also are taught in separate periods of instruction. Mathematics instruction is adapted to each child's comprehension of Piagetian concepts, such as one-to-one correspondence, conservation of number, and serial ordering. As stated previously, instruction in computational facts is delayed until children acquire conservation of number and related concepts.

During instruction in science, children have frequent opportunities for learning and applying concepts in problem-solving situations. Many scientific concepts may be taught through the completion of tasks such as sewing, wood constructions, block building, weaving, and beading. These tasks require that children manipulate materials, observe cause and effect relationships, perform measurements, and formulate quantitative relationships. Other scientific concepts are required in order to complete activities such as cooking and the feeding and care of animals. Instruction in math and science may be conducted during the projects that children initiate and plan or during separate periods.

Art, Drama, and Music Teachers supervise small groups of students as they study concepts of visual art (color, line, shape, and texture), explore spatial relationships by designing a beaded necklace or a woven potholder, or use a variety of media to represent lifelike objects such as people or landscapes. Their products also may include paintings, greeting cards, dolls, puppets, necklaces, posters, and collages.

The study of drama encourages language production in both spoken and written forms and also stimulates cooperation and interpersonal communication. Drama often occurs spontaneously among young children as they play in homemaking activities, block building, and other activities. Older children may dramatize stories or scripts that depict thoughts, feelings, or the effects of the passage of time.

In the study of music, children examine the relationships among sounds and learn to organize them in a variety of patterns. They also create sounds, learn songs and dances, and may participate in group or individual musical presentations.

Commercially produced materials such as textbooks and student guides also are used in Cognitively Oriented Curriculum Follow Through classrooms. Teachers are encouraged to select materials that embody the learning principles and objectives of the curriculum. The commercially produced materials that are used in the model are primarily supplies, equipment, and furniture used to equip the activity centers and small group tables. These materials and their use are described in the *Teacher's Guide to Room Arrangement and Materials.*

STAFF DEVELOPMENT AND SUPPORT SYSTEMS

Staff development and support systems include training, uses of media, and supervision.

Training

The training sequence for teachers begins with an overview of the curriculum, instructions for arranging and equipping classroms, and the details of the daily classroom routine. Next, the methods for teaching language arts and mathematics are presented, followed by a thorough examination of the rationale for and uses of the representation process. Finally, the training sequence is completed with a description of a number of Piagetian concepts (classification, seriation, space, time, and causality), followed by instruction on the content of curricula in science, art, drama, and music. The preparation of teachers for High/Scope Follow Through classrooms begins with a preservice workshop conducted by a curriculum assistant or another experienced teacher working with a High/Scope field trainer. Subsequent training is conducted on an in-service basis and includes workshops, classroom observations, and demonstration teaching. When conducted on an in-service basis, this training sequence may be completed in approximately 3 school years.

Uses of Media

Many types of media are used for training purposes. A number of 16-mm films have been developed to illustrate important concepts and processes in the model. These are color, sound films which are from 16 to 30 min in length. Each film in the *Cognitive Development Series* portrays a separate thought process–classification, seriation, spatial relations, or temporal relations. Another film describes the daily classroom routine and includes scenes from a typical cognitively oriented classroom. Two films contain explanations of how children may use representation to stimulate and clarify their thought processes in order to develop more detailed and accurate conceptions.

A number of booklets have been prepared to explain important concepts and processes to teachers, instructional specialists, and parents. For example, the *Elementary Education Series* for teachers includes booklets on the Cognitively Oriented Curriculum; the daily classroom routine; room arrangement and materials; planning, representation, and cognitive development; writing and reading; and mathematics. The *Curriculum Content Guides* contain descriptions of how children learn through the study of art, play and drama, construction, sewing and pattern design, and music. Other booklets for instructional specialists are used to provide an overview of training procedures for teachers and implementation checklists. Booklets for parents include information on procedures for teaching children, as well as descriptions of the daily classroom routine and methods for stimulating language development in children. Additional information about films, booklets, and other materials may be obtained by writing to the High/Scope Educational Research Foundation, 600 N. River Street, Ypsilanti, Michigan 48197.

Supervision

Adequate supervision is an essential part of the implementation process. Teachers and administrators require assistance in solving classroom problems, in-service training on the elements of the curriculum, and facilitation in decision making and curriculum planning. Some of this supervision is provided by local curriculum supervisors, called curriculum assistants, who are usually experienced teachers who have learned the curriculum through in-service training and teaching experiences in classrooms. Other supervision is provided by curriculum assistants who review plans the teachers prepare, make observations in classrooms, and arrange for videotaping of key lessons.

PARENT PARTICIPATION

When the Cognitively Oriented Curriculum was initiated in 1962 in the Ypsilanti Perry Preschool Project, teachers made weekly visits to meet with preschool children and parents in their homes. During these visits, teachers drew attention to the general concepts in the curriculum by involving the parents and their children in activities such as sorting buttons, seriating stuffed animal dolls, making paper cutouts, baking cookies, and so forth. Teachers also discussed with parents their child's performance in the preschool, as well as the general goals and methods of the Cognitively Oriented Curriculum. Teachers also modeled a number of instructional

techniques such as using divergent questions to encourage children's learning. During these visits, parents helped teachers understand their children's
family and general social context. The two-way sharing that took place
during home visits was important for both teachers and parents.

When the Cognitively Oriented Preschool Curriculum was implemented
in elementary schools as a Follow Through educational model, home
teachers were included among the staff recruited for local projects. In the
months that followed, home teachers were trained and began to make
home visits to parents of children in Follow Through classrooms. The purpose of these visits was to acquaint parents with the Cognitively Oriented
Curriculum and to increase their use of activities to teach and strengthen in
their homes the concepts that children learned at school. In addition, the
knowledge that members of the project staff gained from these visits helped
them to understand the needs of the children.

In accordance with the guidelines for Follow Through, Policy Advisory
Committees (PACs) comprised of parents of Follow Through children and
other community representatives were formed to make it possible for these
individuals to participate with school and project administrators in making
decisions on local projects. The signature of the authorized PAC chairperson was required on funding proposals for the school to the Office of
Education. Many parents became more active in the decision–making role
during subsequent years as their political awareness increased, and they
vigorously opposed the proposals for reductions in funds that threatened
the existence of many local Follow Through projects during the early- and
mid-1970s.

Parents who became active in PAC groups also generally were active in
supporting the local Follow Through programs. But the particular activities
in which parents participated varied from one community to another,
depending on the acceptance of the role of the home visitors in each community. For example, the parent participation program in the Leflore
County Public Schools in Mississippi included the PAC, home teaching,
family support through a coordinated program of health, nutrition, social
services, and parent activity rooms in each of six elementary schools. In
some communities, parent involvement may include activities such as PAC
participation and parent volunteering, but does not include scheduled
teaching sessions in homes. Efforts in home teaching were discontinued in a
few large, urban communities because the safety of home visitors could not
be assured, and in a few other communities funds for employing home
visitors were not available. In other communities, such as Central Ozarks,
each school employed a parent program coordinator, usually a Follow
Through parent, who facilitated PAC activities and organized parent
volunteers for participation in such activities as making or collecting

Christmas gifts and planning field trips. Even when these activities were not directed toward specific educational goals, they were useful in bringing parents together, providing them with information about the learning experience of their children in school, and giving them an opportunity to participate in decisions about the project.

Evaluation

This section contains an overview of the sponsor's orientation to evaluation and descriptions of a number of traditional and innovative approaches to evaluating the High/Scope Cognitively Oriented Curriculum Model in Follow Through.

ORIENTATION TO EVALUATION

For many years, standardized aptitude and achievement tests have been used as the primary instruments for evaluating educational programs. This approach to evaluation has placed certain limits on the scope of efforts to develop new approaches to curriculum, since it appears to imply that the most important goal of education should be to teach basic academic skills. But most of the problems that individuals encounter as adults appear to result not from inadequate academic skills but from inadequate personal–affective characteristics such as inability to select, plan, and initiate activities; inability to make accurate self-evaluation; low levels of self-confidence; inability to deal effectively with ambiguity; and lack of personal and interpersonal skills that enable them to work successfully alone and cooperatively with peers. Educators at the High/Scope Foundation believe that it is possible to plan appropriate curriculum content in order to attain these broad goals for both cognitive and affective development, and thus to change and improve the status quo in education.

In the early years of Follow Through, traditional aptitude and achievement tests were the primary means for evaluating the High/Scope Model in both the sponsor's evaluation and the national longitudinal evaluation. However, the members of the High/Scope group recognized that these tests did not yield information about many essential goals of the Cognitively Oriented Curriculum Model. At best, they were useful in measuring only a few goals of the model; at worst, they were opposed to the philosophy and educational methods of the model. Consequently, one major thrust in the High/Scope approach to evaluation has been to develop alternative methods for evaluating the impact of an innovative educational model. The intent was to break the connection between the exclusive use of standardized achievement tests for evaluation and the continuing dominance of standard academic curriculum approaches to childhood education. Some representative uses of standardized aptitude and achievement tests to measure outcomes of the model, as well as the uses of new approaches to evaluation, are described in the remainder of this section.

USES OF STANDARDIZED APTITUDE
AND ACHIEVEMENT TESTS

This subsection includes information on the size of the High/Scope Curriculum Model sample, aptitude and achievement instruments, data collection procedures, and representative results of the evaluation.

Size of the High/Scope Model

The largest enrollment of children in High/Scope Follow Through classrooms occurred during the 1972–1973 school year, when a total of 4081 were enrolled. Approximately 50% of the children were Black, 30% were White, and 20% were American Indian and Mexican-American. The 10 participating communities included large cities, small rural towns, and an Indian reservation. These communities are listed in Appendix B. Most of the children enrolled in the Follow Through classrooms were from families whose annual incomes were below the poverty levels established by the Office of Economic Opportunity. In some communities, a number of mentally retarded and physically handicapped children were included in the target population because local school officials stated that these children needed the comprehensive services provided by Follow Through programs. In other communities, the complete population of children in kindergarten and the first three grades in some schools were enrolled in High/Scope Follow Through classrooms.

Instruments and Data Collection Procedures in the Sponsor's Evaluation and in the National Longitudinal Evaluation

During the first few years of model implementation, two instruments were employed by the sponsor to evaluate program outcomes. The Stanford–Binet Intelligence Test was administered to evaluate the impact of the model on children's level of mental ability. It was expected that the Stanford–Binet scores of children enrolled in Follow Through classrooms would increase, since children enrolled in the Perry Preschool Cognitive Curriculum had previously attained significant increases in their Binet scores (Weikart, 1967). The Comprehensive Test of Basic Skills (CTBS) was used to evaluate changes in children's levels of academic achievement. Achievement tests that were used for evaluation purposes in other studies included the California Achievement Tests (CAT), Iowa Tests of Basic Skills (ITBS), the Metropolitan Achievement Tests (MAT), and the Short Form Test of Academic Aptitude (SFTAA).

Local project directors supervised the selection of testers, arranged testing schedules, and maintained quality control over the collection of data near the end of each school year. Students were selected randomly from both Follow Through and comparison classrooms. Test protocols were mailed to the offices of the High/Scope Foundation for coding and data processing.

The Raven's (1958) Coloured Progressive Matrices and the MAT were administered to samples of Follow Through and comparison children in the national longitudinal evaluation of Follow Through. The details of this evaluation are described by Stebbins, St. Pierre, Proper, Anderson, and Cerva (1977) and by other authors of chapters in this volume. The problems encountered in the selection of comparison groups and in the analyses of data have been discussed by a number of authors (House, Glass, McLean, & Walker, 1978; Kennedy, 1978; Stebbins *et al.*, 1977).

Representative Studies and Results

The administration of aptitude and achievement tests to High/Scope and comparison students yielded mixed results. For example, in one study conducted by High/Scope researchers from 1971 to 1974, the CTBS and Binet were administered annually in late spring to Follow Through and comparison third-grade students in seven communities located in seven states. In the majority of comparisons, mean CTBS scores of Follow Through and non-Follow-Through students were not significantly different. However, the mean Binet score (93.2) for the Follow Through sample ($N = 951$) was 4.1 points higher than the mean Binet score (89.1) of the comparison sample ($N = 580$), and the mean difference was statistically significant (p $< .01$). These 4.1 points represent a significant increase in measured intellectual ability by the High/Scope Follow Through students over a 3-year period.

In three of the seven communities, mean differences in Binet scores were in favor of High/Scope Follow Through students, and the magnitude of differences exceeded .25 standard deviation units. In the remaining four communities, the mean differences between Follow Through and comparison groups were not significant. The increase in Binet scores in some communities was not as impressive as the dramatic gains in IQ scores reported previously in the evaluation of the Perry Preschool Project (Weikart, 1967), but the results from Follow Through do appear to support the conclusion that the Cognitively Oriented Curriculum had a positive influence on the scores that children attain on the Binet. A detailed description of this study is presented by Sommerfield, Morris, Bond, and Gordon (1974) and by Hohmann, Smith, Tamor, and Kittle (1979) in their analysis and synthesis of events during 10 years of High/Scope Follow Through experience.

A variety of analysis of covariance designs were used in an attempt to adjust for differences between Follow Through and comparison groups in the national longitudinal evaluation (Stebbins *et al.*, 1977). Only the results of the "local" analysis of covariance designs are considered here, since they most closely parallel the analytic designs used by evaluators at the High/Scope Foundation. Decisions on whether mean differences were significant were based on the dual criteria of an alpha level of .05 and a magnitude of intergroup differences at least equal to .25 standard deviation units, which were established by researchers at Abt Associates, Inc. A number of the results reported from the national evaluation were labeled as "untrustworthy," due most frequently to either the magnitude of the covariance adjustments or to differences in the percentage of Follow Through and comparison children who had attended preschool.

Generally, the results of the national longitudinal evaluation indicated that there were no consistent patterns of differences between High/Scope Follow Through and comparison groups. No consistent mean differences were found in the scores that Follow Through and comparison students attained on either the Raven's test or the MAT. Among the six comparisons of Raven's scores declared "trustworthy," the results of five revealed no group mean differences and one was in favor of the comparison group. The majority of "trustworthy" mean differences on the MAT were also not statistically significant.

The general conclusion that appears to emerge from the results of a number of evaluation studies is that High/Scope Follow Through students and comparison non-Follow-Through students were performing at approximately the same levels on the standardized measures of aptitude and academic achievement. These findings are not necessarily surprising, since instruction in the Cognitively Oriented Curriculum Model is not of the direct, intensive sort that would reasonably be expected to produce disproportionately high scores on achievement tests during the primary years. It could be argued that these results may be interpreted as supporting the effectiveness of the High/Scope Model, since many students enrolled in High/Scope classrooms were known to be low performers. It also seems probable that the impact of the model may vary, depending on the level of implementation attained in each community.

NEED FOR ALTERNATIVE APPROACHES TO EVALUATION

During their first year of participation in Follow Through, the sponsor and members of his staff began to examine alternative approaches to evaluation. For example, they reviewed some Piagetian type instruments, but rejected their use because the purpose of the High/Scope model was to improve children's conceptual abilities in many areas, not to accelerate their passage through Piaget's stages of intellectual development. Because children in High/Scope Follow Through classrooms generate many of their own learning experiences, appropriate evaluation procedures must be consistent with the manner in which learning actually occurs. It was necessary that instruments yield information not only about educational outcomes but also about the educational environments in which the outcomes were produced. They also must provide information about the ability of children to develop products and to use learning processes either in classrooms or in circumstances that are similar to classrooms.

The evaluation procedures that eventually were developed were intended to reflect major curriculum goals of the model and learning experiences of children. Two of these approaches are described in the remainder of this section. The first approach was to study learning processes as they occurred in classrooms. These processes are sometimes referred to as the "climate" of classrooms, and they include the opportunities that children have to work with materials and to interact with peers and teachers. The effort to develop classroom observation procedures began in 1969 at the preschool level. Two observation instruments were completed for use in High/Scope Follow Through classrooms in 1973. The second approach was to study the productive language ability of children. This effort represents a "generative" approach to testing in which the children both create the questions to be answered and develop the responses to these questions. This approach to evaluation is useful for evaluating each child's capacity to establish control over the learning situation.

ASSESSING CLASSROOM CLIMATES—THE SCOPE AND SCOTE

The efforts of the High/Scope staff to develop observation procedures were strongly influenced by the results of previous work by Medley (1969), Flanders (1969), and Medley, Schluck, and Ames (1968a). The PROSE (Personal Record of School Experience), developed by Medley *et al.* (1968b) was particularly useful. This instrument was used by researchers to study the climates of preschool classrooms in the Curriculum Demonstration Project (Sheriff, 1971) and in the Planned Variation Head Start Project (Deloria, Dick, Hanvey, & Love, 1972). The PROSE was constructed to yield a range of information about classroom climates, including children's interactions with adults, peers, and materials, as well as their levels of physical activity and the nature of their activities in classrooms. The PROSE categories are presented in a decision tree format in Figure 6.2.

The experiences in using the PROSE revealed that some parts of the instrument were appropriate for assessing the High/Scope Cognitively

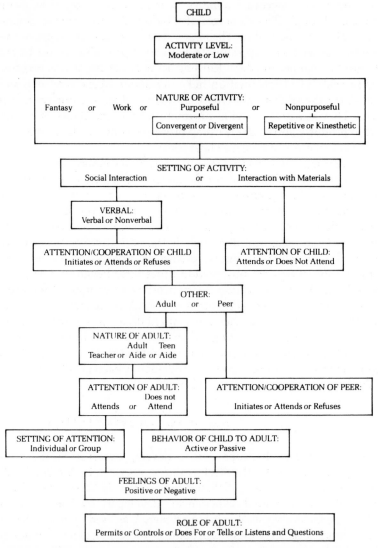

FIGURE 6.2 *PROSE, (Personal Record of School Experience) categories in decision tree format. When the behavior involves more than one category on the same horizontal line, the category on the far left takes precedence.*

Oriented Curriculum but that others were not. Consequently, researchers developed the Analysis of Classroom Interaction (ACI) instrument, which incorporated some categories and procedures from the PROSE along with other categories and procedures that were more attuned to major objectives of the Cognitively Oriented Curriculum. The ACI consisted of 13 categories that contained from 2 to 9 variables. This instrument was employed in a study conducted in a number of first and third grade classrooms during the 1972–1973 school year (Morris & Love, 1973).

The results of the administration of the ACI revealed the need for a number of changes in the instrument. For example, ambiguous definitions of some categories led to outcomes that were difficult to interpret. Furthermore, because the focus of the ACI instrument was primarily on children, the behavior of adults was recorded only when a target child interacted with an adult. Since teachers must engage in certain prescribed patterns of behavior in order to successfully implement the High/Scope Follow Through Model, it was decided that the ACI should be revised to permit observers to devote much more attention to recording details of teachers' behavior in classrooms. Another weakness of the ACI was that there were no categories that observers could use to record the specific object materials that children were manipulating. Finally, the classroom was the unit of analysis employed in both the PROSE and the ACI. Researchers concluded that they could develop procedures that also would yield individual profiles of children. Thus, it would be posible to examine changes over time in both classroom climates and in the behavior of individual children in those classrooms.

The revisions of the ACI resulted in two new observation instruments—the Systematic Classroom Observation of Pupil Experience (SCOPE) and the Systematic Classroom Observation of Teacher Experience (SCOTE). Both of these instruments represent further attempts to measure the range of classroom behaviors and interactions that occur in successfully implemented Cognitively Oriented Curriculum classrooms. The SCOPE and SCOTE may be used to perform systematic observations of the behaviors of children and teachers in educational settings. The categories of variables that comprise the two instruments, the procedures for administration, scoring, and data processing, and some representative research are presented in the following paragraphs.

Categories of Variables that Comprise the SCOPE and SCOTE

Tables 6.1 and 6.2 contain the categories of variables that are included in the SCOPE and SCOTE, respectively. The variables are behaviors of pupils and teachers that observers code. Additional information about the categories and about the linkage between the coded behaviors and the goals of the High/Scope Cognitively Oriented Curriculum Model is presented in the next two paragraphs.

The SCOPE consists of the six categories of variables that are stated in

TABLE 6.1
Categories of Variables that Comprise the SCOPE

	Category 1
1. ACTTLK	— Child and adult engaged in activity, child talking
2. ACTLIS	— Child and adult engaged in activity, child listening
3. ACTION	— Child and adult engaged in same activity, neither talking
4. TALK	— Child talking to adult
5. LISWAIT	— Child listening to adult and waiting for adult to talk
6. PLSWT	— Child looking at adult who is not looking at child
7. PLSWTOB	— Child watching observer
8. AGG	— Child verbally or physically abusive or aggressive toward adult

	Category 2
1. COOP	— Child interacting with peer, both contributing to effort
2. PARL	— Child interacting with peer, each in separate activity
3. 1T1W	— Child interacting with peer, only one engaged in activity
4. READLIS	— Child reading to peer, or listening to peer read
5. TALK	— Child interacting with peer, neither engaged in activity
6. LSWT	— Child listening to and watching peers who are not attending to child
7. UNCOOP	— Agressive behavior

	Category 3
1. READOWN	— Child reading own creation
2. READPR	— Child reading peer's creation
3. READOTH	— Child reading creation by someone other than child or peer
4. WRITOWN	— Child writing about own creation
5. WRITPR	— Child writing about peer's creation
6. WRITOTH	— Child writing about creation by someone other than child or peer

	Category 4
1. UNSTRMN	— Child manipulating materials that do not structure entire activity
2. UNSTRLK	— Child looking at materials that do not structure entire activity
3. UNSTRNU	— Child holding materials that do not structure entire activity
4. STRMN	— Child manipulating materials that do not structure entire activity
5. STRLK	— Child looking at materials that structure entire activity
6. STRNU	— Child holding materials that structure entire activity
7. LOOK	— Child not involved in activity, is looking at or manipulating materials
8. NONUSE	— Child not involved in activity, is holding materials
9. DESTR	— Child using materials destructively

	Category 5
1. LONE	— Child not interacting with adult, peer, or materials

	Category 6

Group Size	— One
	— Two
	— 3-5
	— 6-10
	— 11+

Table 6.1. The first four of these categories pertain to patterns of interactions between children on the one hand and adults, peers, reading and writing materials, and other types of material on the other. Children in High/Scope Follow Through classrooms are expected to engage in a predominately active mode in which they initiate communication with adults. Therefore, passive listening behaviors should occur at a comparatively low frequency. In their interactions with peers, which are coded in Category 2, the children are expected to engage in primarily self-selected activities that often may be completed through cooperative or parallel behaviors with peers. Aimless, bystanding, onlooking, or aggressive behavior should occur infrequently. Children are encouraged to write about the experiences they have during Work Time and to read to peers and adults about these experiences during Evaluation Time, and these writing and reading activities are coded in Category 3 of the SCOPE. Children's uses of materials included in High/Scope classrooms are coded in Category 4. Unstructured materials (those that do not structure an entire activity) are more preferred than materials that lend themselves to only one or a few uses. Obviously, children's uses of material in task-oriented behavior are more valued than simply looking at materials, involvement with materials in nonpurposeful activities, or destructive use of materials. Children's lack of interaction with adults, peers, or materials is coded in Category 5. Category 6 pertains to the size of the group in which the target child is participating. If the teacher's attention is focused only on the target child, the observer would code *One*. It is expected that the small group sizes would be coded most frequently in High/Scope classrooms.

The SCOTE consists of eight categories of variables that are stated in Table 6.2. Observers use the first three categories to code teacher's questions or statements to children. Categories 4 and 5 pertain to teacher's nonverbal behavior and to the materials that teachers and children use in joint activities, respectively. The teacher's attention to a child or a group of children, the number of children with whom the teacher is interacting, and the continuity of teacher's interactions across observed events are coded in Categories 6, 7, and 8, respectively. In the High/Scope Follow Through Model, teachers are encouraged to ask questions or to make statements that help children extend their own thought processes and to minimize evaluative or controlling comments that tend to hinder or block the flow of open communication in classrooms. The purpose of this emphasis is to enhance children's confidence in the use of their own abilities to identify and initiate activities, to solve problems, and to evaluate outcomes. Teachers are expected to encourage children to use materials of their own creation, to verbalize and represent their own thoughts, and to work cooperatively with other children. Teachers will have many brief interac-

TABLE 6.2

Categories of Variables that Comprise the SCOTE

Category 1	
1. QDVG	— Teacher asks divergent questions
2. CHOICE	— Teacher asks choice questions
3. QCVG	— Teacher asks convergent questions
4. STATEMENT	— Teacher makes statement
5. READ	— Teacher reads to or sings with children
6. DIRREQ	— Teacher gives directions or makes requests
7. CNTR	— Teacher makes controlling statements

Category 2	
1. OBJECT	— Teacher comments about object materials children are using
2. WRITPIC	— Teacher comments about written or pictorial materials children are using
3. OTHER	— Child not using materials, or teacher's statements not about materials

Category 3	
1. RESP	— Teacher's statements follow child's statements
2. NRESP	— Teacher's statements do not follow child's statements

Category 4	
1. DOWTHLIS	— Teacher and child participating in activity using similar materials, teacher listening to child
2. DOWTH	— Teacher and child participating in activity, but no verbal interaction or only teacher talking
3. LISTEN	— Teacher not participating in activity with child, but is listening to or waiting for child's response
4. DO4	—
5. SHOW	— Teacher is showing materials to child, or is demonstrating to child how to make something
6. PLSWT	— Teacher is watching or listening to child, but not interacting with child
7. NONTCH	— Adult participating in activity that is not child-oriented
8. PHYSREP	— Teacher is physically reprimanding child

Continued

tions with children during a day, but they will also spend concentrated, prolonged periods of time with each child. Therefore, it is expected that in well-implemented classrooms the coded teacher behaviors will reflect a preponderance of desirable behaviors that are consistent with the teaching–learning goals of the model.

Administration, Scoring, and
Data Processing Procedures

The SCOPE and SCOTE are administered by trained observers. Each observer is equipped with a portable tape cassette or specially designed

TABLE 6.2 *Continued*

	Category 5
1. OBJCH	— Teacher and child using materials made by child
2. TCHR	— Teacher and child using materials made by teacher
3. COMM	— Teacher and child using commercial materials
	Category 6
1. STAR	— Teacher gives individual attention
2. PART	— Teacher gives group attention
	Category 7
Group Size	— Zero
	— One
	— Two
	— 3–5
	— 6–10
	— 11–15
	— 16+
	Category 8
1. SAME	— Teacher interacting with same child or group of children as in previous coded event
2. DIFFERENT	— Teacher interacting with different child or group of children than in previous coded event

battery-powered timer that emits audible signals at fixed intervals into an earphone to designate successive intervals of 2 and 18 sec. During the 2-sec interval, the observer watches and listens to the target person (child or teacher) and anyone with whom the target person interacts. During the following 18-sec interval, the observer codes information obtained during the preceding 2-sec interval on an appropriate scoring form.

Scoring forms for the SCOPE and SCOTE are presented in Figures 6.3 and 6.4, respectively. Each 2-sec observation period, followed by an 18-sec period for recording data, represents an *event*, and five successive events constitute a *cycle*. A cycle is completed in 100 sec. Data gained during each event are coded in a separate column on the appropriate scoring form. For example, the first event in an observation of a child's behavior would be coded on the six categories of variables on the *SCOPE* scoring form in the first column of Cycle A. The second event would be coded in the second column of Cycle A, and so forth. Typically, children are observed during six complete cycles, or for a total of approximately 10 min, which are dispersed over an entire day. Teachers are observed continuously for as many cycles as possible.

Each SCOPE and SCOTE scoring form is assigned a unique identification number. All data are recorded on tape using a Texas Instrument ASR ter-

		CYCLE A					CYCLE B					CYCLE C				
1	ACTTLK	[1]	[1]	[1]	[1]	[1]	[1]	[1]	[1]	[1]	[1]	[1]	[1]	[1]	[1]	[1]
	ACTLIS	[2]	[2]	[2]	[2]	[2]	[2]	[2]	[2]	[2]	[2]	[2]	[2]	[2]	[2]	[2]
	ACTION	[3]	[3]	[3]	[3]	[3]	[3]	[3]	[3]	[3]	[3]	[3]	[3]	[3]	[3]	[3]
	TALK	[4]	[4]	[4]	[4]	[4]	[4]	[4]	[4]	[4]	[4]	[4]	[4]	[4]	[4]	[4]
	LISWAIT	[5]	[5]	[5]	[5]	[5]	[5]	[5]	[5]	[9]	[5]	[5]	[5]	[5]	[5]	[5]
	PLSWT	[6]	[6]	[6]	[6]	[6]	[6]	[6]	[6]	[6]	[6]	[6]	[6]	[6]	[6]	[6]
	PLSWTOB	[7]	[7]	[7]	[7]	[7]	[7]	[7]	[7]	[7]	[7]	[7]	[7]	[7]	[7]	[7]
	AGG	[8]	[8]	[8]	[8]	[8]	[8]	[8]	[8]	[8]	[8]	[8]	[8]	[8]	[8]	[8]
2	COOP	[1]	[1]	[1]	[1]	[1]	[1]	[1]	[1]	[1]	[1]	[1]	[1]	[1]	[1]	[1]
	PARL	[2]	[2]	[2]	[2]	[2]	[2]	[2]	[2]	[2]	[2]	[2]	[2]	[2]	[2]	[2]
	ITIW	[3]	[3]	[3]	[3]	[3]	[3]	[3]	[3]	[3]	[3]	[3]	[3]	[3]	[3]	[3]
	READLIS	[4]	[4]	[4]	[4]	[4]	[4]	[4]	[4]	[4]	[4]	[4]	[4]	[4]	[4]	[4]
	TALK	[5]	[5]	[5]	[5]	[5]	[5]	[5]	[5]	[5]	[5]	[5]	[5]	[5]	[5]	[5]
	LSWT	[6]	[6]	[6]	[6]	[6]	[6]	[6]	[6]	[6]	[6]	[6]	[6]	[6]	[6]	[6]
	UNCOOP	[7]	[7]	[7]	[7]	[7]	[7]	[7]	[7]	[7]	[7]	[7]	[7]	[7]	[7]	[7]
3	READOWN	[1]	[1]	[1]	[1]	[1]	[1]	[1]	[1]	[1]	[1]	[1]	[1]	[1]	[1]	[1]
	READPR	[2]	[2]	[2]	[2]	[2]	[2]	[2]	[2]	[2]	[2]	[2]	[2]	[2]	[2]	[2]
	READOTH	[3]	[3]	[3]	[3]	[3]	[3]	[3]	[3]	[3]	[3]	[3]	[3]	[3]	[3]	[3]
	WRITOWN	[4]	[4]	[4]	[4]	[4]	[4]	[4]	[4]	[4]	[4]	[4]	[4]	[4]	[4]	[4]
	WRITPR	[5]	[5]	[5]	[5]	[5]	[5]	[5]	[5]	[5]	[5]	[5]	[5]	[5]	[5]	[5]
	WRITOTH	[6]	[6]	[6]	[6]	[6]	[6]	[6]	[6]	[6]	[6]	[6]	[6]	[6]	[6]	[6]
4	UNSTRMN	[1]	[1]	[1]	[1]	[1]	[1]	[1]	[1]	[1]	[1]	[1]	[1]	[1]	[1]	[1]
	UNSTRLK	[2]	[2]	[2]	[2]	[2]	[2]	[2]	[2]	[2]	[2]	[2]	[2]	[2]	[2]	[2]
	UNSTRNU	[3]	[3]	[3]	[3]	[3]	[3]	[3]	[3]	[3]	[3]	[3]	[3]	[3]	[3]	[3]
	STRMN	[4]	[4]	[4]	[4]	[4]	[4]	[4]	[4]	[4]	[4]	[4]	[4]	[4]	[4]	[4]
	STRLK	[5]	[5]	[5]	[5]	[5]	[5]	[5]	[5]	[5]	[5]	[5]	[5]	[5]	[5]	[5]
	STRNU	[6]	[6]	[6]	[6]	[6]	[6]	[6]	[6]	[6]	[6]	[6]	[6]	[6]	[6]	[6]
	LOOK	[7]	[7]	[7]	[7]	[7]	[7]	[7]	[7]	[7]	[7]	[7]	[7]	[7]	[7]	[7]
	NONUSE	[8]	[8]	[8]	[8]	[8]	[8]	[8]	[8]	[8]	[8]	[8]	[8]	[8]	[8]	[8]
	DESTR	[9]	[9]	[9]	[9]	[9]	[9]	[9]	[9]	[9]	[9]	[9]	[9]	[9]	[9]	[9]
5	LONE	[1]	[1]	[1]	[1]	[1]	[1]	[1]	[1]	[1]	[1]	[1]	[1]	[1]	[1]	[1]
6	ONE	[1]	[1]	[1]	[1]	[1]	[1]	[1]	[1]	[1]	[1]	[1]	[1]	[1]	[1]	[1]
	TWO	[2]	[2]	[2]	[2]	[2]	[2]	[2]	[2]	[2]	[2]	[2]	[2]	[2]	[2]	[2]
	3 -5	[3]	[3]	[3]	[3]	[3]	[3]	[3]	[3]	[3]	[3]	[3]	[3]	[3]	[3]	[3]
	6 - 10	[4]	[4]	[4]	[4]	[4]	[4]	[4]	[4]	[4]	[4]	[4]	[4]	[4]	[4]	[4]
	11+	[5]	[5]	[5]	[5]	[5]	[5]	[5]	[5]	[5]	[5]	[5]	[5]	[5]	[5]	[5]

TEACHER:
OBSERVER:
DATE OF OBSERVATION:
CENTER:
SEX:
GRADE:
SUBJECT IDENTIFICATION

FIGURE 6.3. *Scoring form for SCOPE.*

minal. One feature of this machine is a tape mount device that allows the user to enter data onto a tape while the terminal is not connected to a computer. Both the creation of the files and corrections of the files can be made in this manner in order to eliminate the cost of computer time usually involved in this process. After the data printouts from the terminal are verified, corrections are made on the tape. The tape is then transmitted, via the tape mount device, to files on the IBM 360/67 computer at the University of Michigan Computing Center, thus making the data available for analysis.

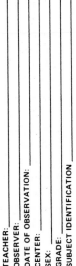

		CYCLE A					CYCLE B					CYCLE C				
1	QDVG	[1]	[1]	[1]	[1]	[1]	[1]	[1]	[1]	[1]	[1]	[1]	[1]	[1]	[1]	[1]
	CHOICE	[2]	[2]	[2]	[2]	[2]	[2]	[2]	[2]	[2]	[2]	[2]	[2]	[2]	[2]	[2]
	QCVG	[3]	[3]	[3]	[3]	[3]	[3]	[3]	[3]	[3]	[3]	[3]	[3]	[3]	[3]	[3]
	STATEMNT	[4]	[4]	[4]	[4]	[4]	[4]	[4]	[4]	[4]	[4]	[4]	[4]	[4]	[4]	[4]
	READ	[5]	[5]	[5]	[5]	[5]	[5]	[5]	[5]	[5]	[5]	[5]	[5]	[5]	[5]	[5]
	DIRREQ	[6]	[6]	[6]	[6]	[6]	[6]	[6]	[6]	[6]	[6]	[6]	[6]	[6]	[6]	[6]
	CNTR	[7]	[7]	[7]	[7]	[7]	[7]	[7]	[7]	[7]	[7]	[7]	[7]	[7]	[7]	[7]
2	OBJECT	[1]	[1]	[1]	[1]	[1]	[1]	[1]	[1]	[1]	[1]	[1]	[1]	[1]	[1]	[1]
	WRITPIC	[2]	[2]	[2]	[2]	[2]	[2]	[2]	[2]	[2]	[2]	[2]	[2]	[2]	[2]	[2]
	OTHER	[3]	[3]	[3]	[3]	[3]	[3]	[3]	[3]	[3]	[3]	[3]	[3]	[3]	[3]	[3]
3	RESP	[1]	[1]	[1]	[1]	[1]	[1]	[1]	[1]	[1]	[1]	[1]	[1]	[1]	[1]	[1]
	NRESP	[2]	[2]	[2]	[2]	[2]	[2]	[2]	[2]	[2]	[2]	[2]	[2]	[2]	[2]	[2]
4	DOWTHLIS	[1]	[1]	[1]	[1]	[1]	[1]	[1]	[1]	[1]	[1]	[1]	[1]	[1]	[1]	[1]
	DOWTH	[2]	[2]	[2]	[2]	[2]	[2]	[2]	[2]	[2]	[2]	[2]	[2]	[2]	[2]	[2]
	LISTEN	[3]	[3]	[3]	[3]	[3]	[3]	[3]	[3]	[3]	[3]	[3]	[3]	[3]	[3]	[3]
	DO4	[4]	[4]	[4]	[4]	[4]	[4]	[4]	[4]	[4]	[4]	[4]	[4]	[4]	[4]	[4]
	SHOW	[5]	[5]	[5]	[5]	[5]	[5]	[5]	[5]	[5]	[5]	[5]	[5]	[5]	[5]	[5]
	PLSWT	[6]	[6]	[6]	[6]	[6]	[6]	[6]	[6]	[6]	[6]	[6]	[6]	[6]	[6]	[6]
	NONTCH	[7]	[7]	[7]	[7]	[7]	[7]	[7]	[7]	[7]	[7]	[7]	[7]	[7]	[7]	[7]
	PHYSREP	[8]	[8]	[8]	[8]	[8]	[8]	[8]	[8]	[8]	[8]	[8]	[8]	[8]	[8]	[8]
5	OBJCH	[1]	[1]	[1]	[1]	[1]	[1]	[1]	[1]	[1]	[1]	[1]	[1]	[1]	[1]	[1]
	TCHR	[2]	[2]	[2]	[2]	[2]	[2]	[2]	[2]	[2]	[2]	[2]	[2]	[2]	[2]	[2]
	COMM	[3]	[3]	[3]	[3]	[3]	[3]	[3]	[3]	[3]	[3]	[3]	[3]	[3]	[3]	[3]
6	STAR	[1]	[1]	[1]	[1]	[1]	[1]	[1]	[1]	[1]	[1]	[1]	[1]	[1]	[1]	[1]
	PART	[2]	[2]	[2]	[2]	[2]	[2]	[2]	[2]	[2]	[2]	[2]	[2]	[2]	[2]	[2]
7	ZERO	[1]	[1]	[1]	[1]	[1]	[1]	[1]	[1]	[1]	[1]	[1]	[1]	[1]	[1]	[1]
	ONE	[2]	[2]	[2]	[2]	[2]	[2]	[2]	[2]	[2]	[2]	[2]	[2]	[2]	[2]	[2]
	TWO	[3]	[3]	[3]	[3]	[3]	[3]	[3]	[3]	[3]	[3]	[3]	[3]	[3]	[3]	[3]
	3 - 5	[4]	[4]	[4]	[4]	[4]	[4]	[4]	[4]	[4]	[4]	[4]	[4]	[4]	[4]	[4]
	6 - 10	[5]	[5]	[5]	[5]	[5]	[5]	[5]	[5]	[5]	[5]	[5]	[5]	[5]	[5]	[5]
	11 - 15	[6]	[6]	[6]	[6]	[6]	[6]	[6]	[6]	[6]	[6]	[6]	[6]	[6]	[6]	[6]
	16 +	[7]	[7]	[7]	[7]	[7]	[7]	[7]	[7]	[7]	[7]	[7]	[7]	[7]	[7]	[7]
8	SAME	[1]	[1]	[1]	[1]	[1]	[1]	[1]	[1]	[1]	[1]	[1]	[1]	[1]	[1]	[1]
	DIFFERNT	[2]	[2]	[2]	[2]	[2]	[2]	[2]	[2]	[2]	[2]	[2]	[2]	[2]	[2]	[2]

TEACHER: _____
OBSERVER: _____
DATE OF OBSERVATION: _____
CENTER: _____
SEX: _____
GRADE: _____
SUBJECT IDENTIFICATION

FIGURE 6.4 *Scoring form for SCOTE.*

Representative Research

During the 1973–1974 school year, the SCOPE and SCOTE were administered to a total of 96 randomly selected students and their teachers in 14 classrooms located in communities in Colorado, Florida, Michigan, and Mississippi. Six Follow Through students were selected from each of three second-grade classrooms and three third-grade classrooms. Using the same guidelines, a total of 36 non-Follow-Through students were also randomly selected from six classrooms located in the same communities. Only "well-implemented" Follow Through classrooms were selected, since one purpose of the study was to obtain criterion frequencies of teacher and child behaviors in well-implemented classrooms in the Cognitively Oriented Curriculum Model. In addition, a total of 24 other randomly selected students, 12 from a multiage Follow Through classroom and 12 from the High/Scope Training Development Center in Ypsilanti, Michigan, also were included in the study.

Detailed information about the design of the study, training of observers, data collection procedures, analyses of data, and results is presented by Morris (1974) and Bond, Smith, and Morris (1975). The representative findings that are cited in the next paragraph were obtained through comparisons of mean differences between Follow Through and non-Follow-Through students, and all of them were statistically significant at beyond the .02 level. In addition, interobserver reliabilities were at least .70 for the variables on which these significant mean differences occurred.

The results of the administration of the SCOPE and SCOTE in classrooms indicated that many important curriculum objectives for children and teachers had been attained in well-implemented High/Scope Follow Through classrooms. As compared to non-Follow-Through students, High/Scope Follow Through students engaged more frequently in interacting with adults on a one-to-one basis, working in small groups rather than in large groups, participating actively with other peers and adults, talking with teachers, writing and reading materials of their own creation, and manipulating objects. As compared to non-Follow-Through teachers, Follow Through teachers engaged more frequently in interacting with children (and less time in "management" activities), interacting with individual children rather than with groups of children, interacting with small groups rather than large groups, listening to children even when listening was not a requirement of the activity (as in drill), responding to previous statements made by children (dialogue versus lecturing), asking children questions to extend their thinking, and concentrating on materials constructed by children as the focus of their interactions with peers.

ASSESSING LANGUAGE PRODUCTION—THE PLAT

The Productive Language Assessment Tasks (PLAT) represent a "generative" approach to evaluating productive language. The PLAT may be used to measure children's ability to express their thoughts and feelings through written language (Bond, 1976). Standardized tests of language competence are oriented toward the assessment of the formal–mechanical characteristics of language, correct usage, and decoding rather than encoding, in a highly artificial test situation. During the administration of the PLAT, children structure and solve interesting problems that they design themselves in a relaxed situation that closely resembles their classroom environment. Thus, this approach is more compatible with the High/Scope approach to instruction in which students have an active–generating role and work in classroom settings that are intended to encourage individualized, divergent behavior and purposeful communication through the use of oral and written language as well as other media.

The PLAT procedures may be used to assess students' linguistic competence and communication competence in written language production. Linguistic competence pertains to the formal-mechanical characteristics of language that children produce independently of content and functional or interactional qualities. However, information on linguistic competence is derived from samples of students' discourse that is elicited in situations that stimulate divergent verbal behavior rather than from students' responses to convergent questions of the sort that are employed in standardized achievement tests. Communicative competence pertains to the content and to the functional quality of written language that is produced for the purpose of communicating meaning. It is not possible to investigate these dimensions of productive language through the administration of standardized tests. The materials and administration procedures, scoring and data processing procedures, and representative research for the PLAT are presented in the following sections.

Materials and Administration Procedures for the PLAT

The PLAT consists of two tasks—*reporting* and *narrating.* In the administration of the reporting task, children receive identical sets of unstructured materials and are asked to use the materials to construct "anything you want to make." The materials include the following: paper of different grades, colors, and shapes; plastic foam, crepe paper, double-knit fabric, plastic screen, paper fasteners, cotton, pipe cleaners, and a rubber band. Scissors, magic markers, and tape are also available for use. Children are allowed 20 min to complete the task. Then, they are given 35 min to describe "how they made" the products. The children are permitted to keep whatever they made and any materials that remain. They are free to interact with others during all phases of the task.

In the administration of the narrating task, children receive identical sets of unstructured materials and are asked to use the materials to make a "make-believe or pretend story." The materials include 12 1-in. colored cubes, a wooden "car" with bottle cap wheels, human figures made from wooden dowels of different lengths, two pieces of felt, and a cardboard box. After about 15 min of free play, which is often dramatic play, on a carpeted floor, children are asked to write "whatever make-believe or pretend story you want to write. You might want to begin with 'once upon a time.' " A maximum of 35 min is allowed for completion of this task. As in the reporting task, the children are permitted to interact with others during their playing and writing.

The individuals who administer the PLAT are hired in local communities and trained by members of the High/Scope staff. All examiners are required to have previous work experience with children of primary age. During the administration of the PLAT, examiners support the students, avoid making "right" or "wrong" judgments about children's products, and view their products and verbalizations as expressions of children's current levels of ability. Thus, students are permitted to express educational strengths in a supportive, nonthreatening environment. A detailed account of the instructions used in the administration of the PLAT are presented in a manual prepared by members of the High/Scope staff.

The PLAT may be administered to groups of no more than six children at one time. Both tasks should not be administered to a child during the same day. The time required to administer each task is approximately 1 hr. Before an examination period begins, Child Identification Forms are completed for each child, writing paper is prepared for each child by printing his or her name in the top right hand corner of the first page, and required materials are obtained for use by the children. The examination room should be relatively quiet and carpeted if possible. There should be enough chairs and table surface for six children to work comfortably with materials and to write their stories (approximately 10 sq. ft. of table surface per child). While the children use materials and write their stories, the examiners sit in locations that enables them to see and hear each child, but not so close as to distract them from completing their tasks. Examiners are responsive to children's questions, but they do not interact with or talk to them unnecessarily while they work.

Scoring and Data Processing Procedures for the PLAT

Analyses of children's writing samples yielded 32 first-order variables—16 for each of the two tasks. Eleven second-order variables were constructed from the two sets of 16 variables during subsequent computer analyses of data. All but 2 of these 11 variables (No. 8 and 9 in the following list) were derived by combining scores from both the reporting and narrating tasks. Brief descriptions of the 11 variables are presented here.

1. *Fluency:* an index of writing facility that is independent of writing quality. It is the mean number of words in the valid texts of reporting and narrating stories.

2. *Syntactic Maturity:* the average length of T-units in children's stories. A T-unit (Hunt, 1965) is a single independent predication (subject +

verb + object if verb is transitive) together with any subordinate clauses or phrases that may be grammatically related to it. It may be a simple or complex sentence but not a compound sentence. In conversation and written dialogue, elliptical constructions are accepted as T-units if missing grammatical elements are clearly implied by preceding T-units. The number of T-units in a language sample represents the number of grammatically complete statements. Average T-unit length is computed by dividing the total number of words in a language sample by the total number of T-units. Research by Hunt (1965) and O'Donnel, Griffin, and Norris (1967) indicates that average length of T-unit is a valid index of syntactic maturity in both oral and written language production.

3. *Vocabulary Diversity*: a measure of diversity in the vocabulary of a language sample that is adjusted for the length of sample (cf. type–token ratio in Carroll, 1964). It is computed for each task and then averaged across tasks according to the following formula:

$$\text{Vocabulary Diversity} = \frac{\text{number of different words}}{\sqrt{2 \text{ (number of decodable words)}}}$$

4. *Descriptive Quantity*: the total number of words and larger constructions that describe the attributes of and relationships between objects, persons, and events. It is computed for each task and then averaged across tasks.

5. *Descriptive Density*: the proportion of descriptive words among all decodable words in the text. Expressions of class relationship and similes–metaphors are excluded, since they are not expressed through single words.

6. *Descriptive Diversity*: a proportional measure of the diversity of descriptive words (excluding class relationship and simile–metaphor) that is adjusted for the total number of descriptive words in a language sample. It is computed for each task and then averaged across tasks according to the following formula:

$$\text{Descriptive Diversity} = \frac{\text{number of different descriptive words}}{\sqrt{2 \text{ (number of descriptive words)}}}$$

7. *Descriptive Scope*: the average number of descriptive categories (see No. 4) that is used in reporting and narrating stories, independent of how frequently each is used. It indicates the conceptual breadth of descriptions in reports and narratives.

8. *Reporting Quality*: derived from analysis of reporting stories and represents the extent to which a report describes "how" something was

made. The report may be irrelevant to the task, merely enumerate materials used, describe what was made but not how it was made, or it may describe how something was made.

9. *Narrative Orangization:* derived from analysis of narrating stories. It is a measure of the organizational quality of a narrative. The T-units in a narrative may be unrelated, related to one another logically and thematically but the story may lack closure, or they may be interrelated in a narrative that has closure.

10. *Explanatory Statements:* the average number of statements in reports and narratives that express cause, rationale, and purpose in order to explain relationships, attributes, decisions, and events.

11. *Decodability:* a measure of the extent to which a story can be decoded by experienced readers of children's writing according to the following formula:

$$\text{Decodability} = \frac{\text{number of decodable words in valid T-units}}{\text{total number of words in language sample}}$$

The denominator includes all decodable words in valid T-units, all nonsense words in valid T-units, and all words in extraneous material.

For the purpose of calculating interscorer agreement, 15 samples of writing from the reporting task and 15 from the narrating task were randomly selected and coded by all scorers. Ebel's intraclass correlation coefficient (Ebel, 1951) was used to estimate scoring reliability. It is similar to an average intercorrelation for all possible pairs of raters. Interscorer reliability coefficients were in the range of .90 to .99 for all variables.

Coding the written material obtained through the administration of the PLAT is accomplished in two stages. In the first stage, experienced scorers analyze and edit the text in order to identify T-units, which were defined in the definition of variable No. 2. Prior to entering the T-units at remote computer terminals, scorers also assess the text as a whole on those variables that pertain to global dimensions of the story or report (see Parts III, IV, and V of the *PLAT Coding Manual*).

An interactive computer program is used in the second stage of coding. The texts of stories or reports are entered by scorers in T-unit segments at remote computer terminals. The texts are then reprinted one word at a time allowing the scorers to attach number codes to words where appropriate. Correction procedures are used by scorers when necessary. Appropriate designated codes for global variables are entered in response to task-specific prompts, after the words in the text have been coded. Finally, the codes are tallied and printed in summary form by the computer beneath a clean copy of the text, which is attached to the original story or report. The segment of computer printout presented in the following illustrates the final product of the coding program.

1 *HOW TO MAKE A HOUSE
2 WHAT_YOU_NEED_IS_A_LITTLE_6 PIECE_7 OF_
   WHITE_1 PIPECLEANER_ AND_ SIX_7 SQUARES_1 A_
   GREEN_1 ONE_7 A_ WHITE_1 ONE_7 A_ RED_1 ONE_7
   A_ORANGE_1 ONE_7 AND_ A_ YELLOW_1 ONE_7 AND
   TWO_7 LIGHT_1 BLUE_1 TRIANGLES_1/

3 I_ TAPED_9 ALL_3 OF_ THE_ SQUARES_1 TOGETHER_4
   TO_ MAKE_ A_ CUBE_1/

4 AND_ THEN_ I_ TOOK_ A_ PAIR_7 OF_ SCISSORS_/

5 AND_ I_ CUT_9 A_ DOOR_ IN_4 THE_ GREEN_1
   SQUARE_1

6 AND_ THEN_ I_ PUT_ THE_ LITTLE_6 PIECE_7 OF_
   PIPECLEANER_ IN_4 THE_ DOOR_ FOR_ A_ DOORKNOB_
   TO_ OPEN_ IT_/

CHILD	T	C	DATE	S	T/W	D/W	N/W	T-U	DDW	*FS	*WD	SIM	LCS
106344	1	1	022776	4	080	080	000	005	043	000	000	000	000

TOTAL NUMBER OF	CLS	SUB	C-R	SPC	SER	P-Q	NUM	TIM	TRN	SUP
DIFFERENT WORDS	14		1	3		2	10		2	32
	11		1	2		1	5		2	22

I/D	I/S	STP
1	4	4

Representative Research

A number of studies have been conducted to examine students' performance on the PLAT. For example, intercorrelations among the 11 PLAT variables were computed for large samples of second graders, third graders, and the total sample of approximately 900 students by pooling data from both the reporting and narrating tasks. In addition, researchers have used a variety of approaches to explore the validity of the PLAT. The instrument appears to have high levels of content and face validity, since the test conditions are similar to those that occur during instruction and learning in High/Scope Follow Through classrooms. Furthermore, students' responses during the administration of the PLAT represent goals and competencies that are sought in those classrooms.

The construct validity of the PLAT was examined through studies of changes in the quality of children's written language production as they advance through the primary grades. It was assumed that students generally improve their performance in written language production as they grow older, but that the rate of improvement would be greater among students enrolled in High/Scope Follow Through classrooms than among those enrolled in non-Follow-Through classrooms. Bond (1976) reported that the results of a study conducted in the spring of 1975 indicated, as expected, that the PLAT scores of third graders ($N = 455$) were significantly higher ($p < .001$) than the PLAT scores of second graders ($N = 455$) on each of the 11 variables. In that same study, the PLAT scores of Follow Through and non-Follow-Through students were compared separately at second and third grade levels. Among second grade children, the mean scores of the Follow Through group were significantly higher on only 3 variables (Fluency, Vocabulary Diversity, and Decodability). But among third grade children, the scores of Follow Through children were significantly higher on 7 PLAT variables (see Table 6.3).

Intercorrelations among PLAT, aptitude, and achievement test scores for non-Follow-Through and Follow Through students were also studied by

TABLE 6.3
PLAT Variables:
Comparison of Third Grade Follow Through with Non-Follow-Through

PLAT variables	Follow Through			Non-Follow-Through			F ratio	Direction of significant effects
	Mean	SD	N	Mean	SD	N		
Fluency	64.92	39.07	270	48.40	29.97	175	30.90***	FT > NFT
Syntactic maturity	8.38	2.20	270	8.22	2.43	175	.735	NS
Vocabulary diversity	3.12	.625	270	2.76	.613	175	41.44***	FT > NFT
Descriptive quantity	9.39	7.93	270	7.74	6.62	175	10.22**	FT > NFT
Descriptive density	.119	.055	270	.136	.071	175	5.82*	NFT > FT
Descriptive diversity	1.38	.589	270	1.25	.594	175	6.84**	FT > NFT
Descriptive scope	3.21	1.69	270	2.84	1.66	175	8.77**	FT > NFT
Reporting quality	2.77	.876	265	2.69	.939	169	2.03	NS
Narrative organization	2.17	.535	287	2.07	.579	169	4.91*	FT > NFT
Explanatory statements	.419	.723	270	.460	.728	175	.043	NS
Decodability	.934	.119	270	.900	.166	175	6.99**	FT > NFT

[a]The treatment group main effect was tested within grade level in a multiple linear regression design, covarying on sex and site.
*$p < .05$
**$p < .01$
***$p < .001$

Bond (1976). These intercorrelations, which are presented in Tables 6.4 and 6.5, pertain to both the criterion-related validity and the construct validity of the PLAT. Attempts were made to match children in the non-Follow-Through and Follow Through groups as closely as possible on such variables as sex, ethnicity, economic status, and social mobility. It was expected that moderate intercorrelations would be found between students' performance on the PLAT and their scores on standardized aptitude and achievement tests. But it also was assumed that the PLAT could be used to assess some important dimensions of students' performance that were not measured by aptitude and achievement tests.

The results from Bond's study are presented separately for each community represented in Tables 6.4 and 6.5, since different aptitude and achievement tests were administered in the various communities. Among non-Follow-Through students, most of the intercorrelations between scores on the PLAT and the Stanford–Binet Intelligence Test were within the expected range (.45–.66). Among children in the Follow Through classrooms, however, the pattern of intercorrelations between scores on the two instruments was much lower (.08–.30). The patterns of intercorrelations between PLAT scores and achievement test scores were approximately the same for children in both groups.

Bond, Smith, and Kittle (1976) examined the effects of program implementation on students' performance on the PLAT. These authors reported that the magnitude of group mean differences on the PLAT varied according to the level of success attained in implementing the language arts components of the High/Scope Curriculum. When these components were well-implemented, Follow Through students' scores on the PLAT were significantly higher than non-Follow-Through scores, but when the implementation of these components was mediocre or low, the group mean differences on the PLAT diminished accordingly.

In summary, the PLAT is a generative instrument that appears to measure distinctive skills that children acquire in High/Scope Follow Through classrooms. It is a measure of students' ability to produce language. In that essential area of the High/Scope Cognitively Oriented Curriculum, Follow Through students appear to excell. More extensive accounts of the origins of the PLAT, its development through several iterations, and pertinent research results are presented in Love and Bond, 1975; Bond, 1976; Cazden, Bond, Epstein, Matz, and Savignon, 1977; Kittle, Smith, and Bond, 1977; and Hohmann *et al.*, (1979).

Lessons Learned

The High/Scope Cognitively Oriented Curriculum at both the preschool and elementary levels is an innovative, open-framework educational pro-

TABLE 6.4
Correlation of PLAT Scores with Aptitude and Achievement Test Scores at Third Grade—Non-Follow-Through[a]

Variable	Mississippi Missouri — Binet IQ N 95-100	Florida — SFTAA Verbal N=41	Florida — SFTAA Nonverbal N=42	Mississippi — CAT Reading N=39-43	Mississippi — CAT Language N=38-41	Mississippi — CAT Math N=38-41	Florida — CTBS Reading N=67	Florida — CTBS Language N=66	Florida — CTBS Math N=67	Missouri — ITBS Vocabulary N=49-51	Missouri — ITBS Reading N=49-50
Fluency	.47	.32	.26	.55	.25	.48	.28	.27	.24	.43	.35
Syntactic maturity	.18	.02	.02	-.08	-.05	-.17	.16	.17	.05	.18	.13
Vocabulary diversity	.56	.32	.27	.50	.35	.32	.35	.37	.29	.43	.33
Descriptive quantity	.60	.47	.28	.64	.41	.54	.41	.37	.33	.49	.40
Descriptive density	.48	.50	.17	.27	.23	.24	.37	.34	.33	.35	.20
Descriptive diversity	.66	.46	.15	.56	.41	.40	.39	.32	.34	.47	.37
Descriptive scope	.64	.47	.29	.55	.43	.34	.42	.43	.41	.41	.28
Reporting quality	.47	.40	.40	.35	.13	.12	.34	.29	.30	.37	.21
Narrative organization	.38	.06	.16	.56	.40	.30	.18	.09	.29	.26	.26
Explanatory statements	.45	.10	.24	.57	.20	.50	.07	.05	.17	.39	.26
Decodability	.31	.18	.20	.38	.21	.29	.35	.21	.28	.32	.35

[a]There was no non-Follow-Through group in New York City.

TABLE 6.5
Correlation of PLAT Scores with Aptitude and Achievement Test Scores at Third Grade—Follow Through

| | Mississippi Missouri | Florida | | Mississippi | | | Florida | | | New York City | | Missouri | |
| | Binet | SFTAA | | CAT | | | CTBS | | | CAT | | ITBS | |
Variable	IQ $N=164\text{-}165$	Verbal $N=40\text{-}41$	Nonverbal $N=40\text{-}41$	Reading $N=91\text{-}92$	Language $N=81\text{-}82$	Math $N=89\text{-}90$	Reading $N=77\text{-}79$	Language $N=77\text{-}79$	Math $N=77\text{-}79$	Vocabulary $N=30\text{-}32$	Reading $N=30\text{-}32$	Vocabulary $N=49$	Reading $N=49$
Fluency	.08	.46	.47	.01	-.20	-.04	.35	.44	.28	.30	.37	.41	.28
Syntactic maturity	.20	-.13	-.05	.29	.22	.31	-.04	-.11	-.13	-.01	.30	.33	.23
Vocabulary diversity	.12	.58	.48	.14	.16	.21	.39	.49	.37	.29	.62	.52	.43
Descriptive quantity	.19	.33	.28	.14	-.13	-.01	.27	.35	.24	.42	.48	.54	.48
Descriptive density	.19	-.04	-.01	.22	.08	.08	.09	.11	.11	.50	.36	.65	.66
Descriptive diversity	.17	.36	.38	.15	.07	.16	.28	.37	.30	.55	.58	.67	.58
Descriptive scope	.24	.44	.32	.14	-.06	.07	.29	.39	.30	.43	.56	.58	.49
Reporting quality	.21	.46	.24	.07	.03	.11	.32	.30	.20	.30	.16	.46	.55
Narrative organization	.30	.39	.21	.01	-.03	-.08	.17	.17	.16	.19	.47	.24	.36
Explanatory statements	.29	.14	.18	-.04	-.08	-.02	.12	.18	.17	-.15	.12	.46	.44
Decodability	.27	.27	.32	.19	.05	.07	.26	.26	.27	.34	.52	.40	.26

gram. It is innovative because the educational goals and teaching–learning processes are quite different from those in traditional approaches. Teachers in open-framework classrooms differ from those in programmed classrooms by encouraging active, generative, problem-focused learning, rather than passive, rote, nonfunctional learning. They differ from teachers in child-centered classrooms by encouraging frequent initiation behaviors by both students and teachers through the plan–work–represent–evaluate process rather than a preponderance of child control in learning environments. A central thesis of this chapter is that the evaluation procedures applied in an open-framework classroom must be appropriate and consistent with the educational experiences that children actually have in those classrooms.

DEVELOPING THE CURRICULUM

The guiding principle in the construction of the Cognitively Oriented Curriculum has been the adaptation of Piaget's developmental theory to instruction and learning in classrooms. During the first phase of this work, the focus was on Piaget's description of relational and quantitative concepts and the qualitatively different ways in which children comprehend these concepts in various developmental stages. The primary goal was to identify instruction–learning sequences that would support children's conceptual development in areas such as classification, seriation, spatial relations, time, and number. When this goal was accomplished, it was possible to concentrate on other educational implications of Piaget's writings.

Recent efforts in curriculum development have been directed toward defining and implementing the classroom arrangements and daily routine that permit children to have large blocks of time that they may use to select, design, and complete project activities. Carefully selected materials now are available to children in activity centers, and the use of these materials is an important part of the plan–work–represent–evaluate cycle. During the completion of this cycle, the children use materials and information to define problems, confront and resolve obstacles, organize and direct individual and group efforts, create products, and communicate the results of their work to others. Children's active involvement in tasks of their own choosing is the chief means for increasing their competence in academic, physical–motor, aesthetic, and interpersonal areas of development.

Even though the focus of curriculum development has changed somewhat over the years, the basic intent always has been to help children develop the underlying cognitive skills that they must have in order to be effective problem solvers. No attempt is made to teach Piagetian concepts directly. Instead, knowledge about logical, spatial, temporal, and quantitative concepts are used by curriculum developers and teachers to define in each content area those opportunities for problem solving that are appropriate for each child.

TRAINING TEACHERS

Changes in the approach to training teachers have been linked to changes in the focus of curriculum development. During the first phase of curriculum development, teachers received instruction in Piagetian theory. It was assumed, although the assumption appears naive in retrospect, that when teachers understood the theory about children's growth and development, they would use their own ingenuity to generate insights and procedures that would produce appropriate changes in their teaching practices. For example, at that time it seemed reasonable to expect that teachers would use information on how children form symbols to increase opportunities for children to explore objects and concrete materials and to link this knowledge to verbal and written symbols.

The instruction on Piagetian theory was received warmly by teachers, but it seemed to have litle impact on how instruction and learning occurred in classrooms (Weikart & Banet, 1975). It was clear that instruction in Piaget's theory alone would not evoke desirable changes in teachers' behaviors. Apparently, a complete restructuring of materials, furniture, and events in classrooms was required to implement the Cognitively Oriented Curriculum. Consequently, rows of desks were replaced with open-space environments in which activity centers contained carefully selected equipment and materials. The daily routine was changed to include not only instruction in small and large groups, but also the plan–work–represent–evaluate cycle. The implementation of this cycle was responsible for a major shift in the behavior of teachers and children in classrooms. Children no longer worked primarily with printed materials in reading or arithmetic; instead, they engaged in self-initiated and self-directed activities with a variety of materials. Accordingly, training materials and procedures were redesigned to help teachers develop competencies that were in line with the new characteristics and procedures in classrooms.

DEVELOPING NEW APPROACHES
TO EVALUATION

It is axiomatic that in education the power to test is the power to control the content of curriculum. The extensive use of standardized achievement tests of basic academic skills is a major obstacle to the success of efforts to reform traditional approaches to curriculum. Standardized tests actually measure only a limited subset of what children learn in school, but the content of the tests also strongly influence teachers' judgments about what each child must know and when it should be learned. Therefore, the pressure to teach students testlike content in language arts and mathematics is intense. Recommended content and procedures in the Cognitively Oriented Curriculum often contrasted with and competed for time with traditional materials and procedures that previously had been used for instruction in basic skills. Teachers sometimes found it difficult to accept the position that children enrolled in High/Scope Follow Through classrooms would master academic skills but not necessarily at the rate of one grade level per year during the primary grades.

Since standardized achievement tests have such a powerful influence in legitimizing what is taught in school, it seemed reasonable to develop instruments that could be used to assess the central goals of the Cognitively Oriented Curriculum. Effective productive writing is one such goal, and the Productive Language Assessment Tasks (PLAT) were devised to measure the impact of the curriculum on children's writing. It is unlikely that the current popular interest in improving children's skills in writing will have any substantial effect on instruction in language arts until new assessment procedures, such as the PLAT, require students to have composition skills per se rather than simply nonfunctional subskills such as punctuation, usage, and spelling.

Many new evaluation procedures must be constructed before changes in current educational programs can be accomplished. If the broad, lifelike educational experiences envisioned in the Cognitively Oriented Curriculum are to be provided for large numbers of students through their experiences in school learning, evaluation procedures must focus not only on isolated tasks but also on continuous assessment of meaningful work. Continuous assessment will probably require much more extensive use of computers and sophisticated software in education.

During the decade beginning in 1968, Follow Through evolved into a national longitudinal effort to develop and evaluate a range of innovative approaches for providing educational and other services to children and their parents. The project is important because it represents the first large-scale attempt to examine in detail the programmatic implications of diverse beliefs among educators and social scientists about children's growth and education. Developing and implementing educational models is extremely difficult and time-consuming work. It requires coping with a seemingly relentless succession of problems and frustrations. Nevertheless, most of the individuals who have worked in Follow Through share the belief that the project represents a truly creative response to the current crisis in education. The knowledge that has been gained about curriculum development, evaluation, parent participation, and the interface between education and the social sciences probably could not have been obtained through any other means. This fund of knowledge can be of great significance for the reform and improvement of education for many years to come.

Acknowledgements

The work described in this chapter would not have been possible without the participation of large numbers of teachers, principals, parents, and children in the 10 communities served by the High/Scope Follow Through Model. In addition, two members of the High/Scope Foundation staff made essential contributions to the preparation of this chapter. James T. Bond reviewed draft versions of the manuscript and made many helpful suggestions. Jeri Conroy coordinated many technical activities required to maintain communication among the authors and to produce the final version of the manuscript.

References

Bond, J. T. Research report: The Productive Language Assessment Tasks. *Bulletin of the High/Scope Foundation*, Winter, 1976, No. 3, 1–8.

Bond, J. T., Smith, A. G., & Kittle, J. M. *Evaluation of curriculum implementation and child outcomes.* Annual report (Vol. 2, Part 1). Ypsilanti, Mich.: High/Scope Foundation, 1976.

Bond, J. T., Smith, A. G., & Morris, M. *Historical summary of the High/Scope Foundation's Follow Through evaluation activities 1968–1975.* Annual report (Vol. 2). Ypsilanti, Mich.: High/Scope Foundation, 1975.

Braine, M. D., & Shanks, B. The development of conservation of size. *Journal of Verbal Learning and Verbal Behavior*, 1965, 4, 227–242.

Britton, J., Burgess, T., Martin, N., McLeod, A., & Rosen, H. *The development of writing abilities (11–18).* London: Macmillan Education, 1975.

Bruner, J. S. *Toward a theory of instruction.* Cambridge, Mass.: Harvard University Press, 1966.

Bruner, J. S., Oliver, R., & Greenfield, P. *Studies in cognitive growth.* New York: Wiley, 1966.

Carroll, J. B. *Language and thought.* Englewood Cliffs, N.J.: Prentice-Hall, 1964.

Cazden, C. B., Bond, J. T., Epstein, A. S., Matz, R. D., & Savignon, S. J. Language assessment: Where, what, and how. *Anthropology and Education Quarterly*, 1977, 8, 83–91.

Cicirelli, V. G., Cooper, W., & Granger, R. *The impact of Head Start: An evaluation of the effects of the Head Start experience on children's cognitive and affective development.* Athens, Ohio: Westinghouse Learning Corporation & Ohio University, 1969.

Deloria, D., Dick, C., Hanvey, R., & Love, J. *A classroom observation study of four cognitively oriented Head Start sites.* Ypsilanti, Mich.: High/Scope Foundation, 1972.

Ebel, R. L. Estimation of the reliability of ratings. *Psychometrica*, 1951, 16, 407–424.

Flanders, N. A. *Interaction analysis in the classroom: A manual for observers* (Rev. ed.). Ann Arbor: University of Michigan, School of Education, 1966.

Flavell, J. H. Stage-related properties of cognitive development. *Cognitive Psychology*, 1971, 2, 421–453.

Flavell, J. H. *The developmental theory of Jean Piaget.* Princeton, N. J.: Van Nostrand, 1963.

Furth, H. C. *Piaget and knowledge: Theoretical foundations.* Englewood Cliffs, N. J.: Prentice-Hall, 1969.

Hohmann, C. F., Smith, A. G., Tamor, L., & Kittle, J. A. Synthesis of 10 years' experience in Follow Through. *Annual report, Cognitively Oriented Curriculum, Project Follow Through (Vol. 2)* Ypsilanti, Mich.: High/Scope Foundation, 1979.

Hohmann, M. N., Banet, B., & Weikart, D. P. *Young children in action.* Ypsilanti, Mich.: High/Scope Foundation, 1979.

House, E. R., Glass, G. V., McLean, L. D., & Walker, D. F. No simple answer: Critique of the Follow Through evaluation. *Harvard Educational Review,* 1978, *48,* 128–160.

Hunt, K. W. *Grammatical structures written at three grade levels* (Research Report No. 3). Champaign, Ill.: National Council of Teachers of English, 1965.

Kennedy, M. M. Findings from the Follow Through planned variation study. *Educational Researcher,* 1978, *7,* No. 6, 3–11.

Kittle, J., Smith, A., & Bond, J. *Annual report, Cognitively Oriented Curriculum, Project Follow Through* (Vol. 2, Part 1). Ypsilanti, Mich.: High/Scope Foundation, 1977.

Kohlberg, L. Early Education: A cognitive–developmental view. *Child Development,* 1968, *39,* 1013–1062.

Lambie, D. Z., Bond, J. T., & Weikart, D. P. Framework for infant education. In B. Z. Friedlander, G. M. Sterritt, & G. E. Kirk (Eds.), *Exceptional infant* (Vol. 3). New York: Brunner/Mazel, 1975. Pp. 263–284.

Love, J. M., & Bond, J. T. *The High/Scope Productive Language Arts Test in the Cognitively Oriented Curriculum: Effects of Follow Through on the written language of second and third grade children.* Ypsilanti, Mich.: High/Scope Foundation, 1975.

Medley, D. M. *OScAR goes to nursery school: A new technique for recording pupil behavior* (Research Memorandum). Princeton, N. J.: Educational Testing Service, 1969.

Medley, D. M., Schluck, C. G., & Ames, N. P. *Assessing the learning environment in the classroom: A manual for users of the OScAR* (Research Memorandum 68–69). Princeton, N. J.: Educational Testing Service, 1968. (a)

Medley, D. M., Schluck, C. G., & Ames, N. P. *Recording individual pupil experiences in the classroom: A manual for PROSE recorders.* Princeton, N. J.: Educational Testing Service, 1968. (b)

Morris, M. *Classroom observation study of teacher and child interactions in three Follow Through sites.* Ypsilanti, Mich.: High/Scope Foundation, 1974.

Morris, M. E., & Love, J. M. *Progress report: Cognitively Oriented Curriculum, Project Follow Through* (Vol. 3). Ypsilanti, Mich.: High/Scope Foundation, 1973.

O'Donnel, R. C., Griffin, W. J., & Norris, R. C. *Syntax of kindergarten and elementary school children: A transformational analysis* (Research Report No. 8). Champaign, Ill.: National Council of Teachers of English, 1967.

Piaget, J. *Play, dreams, and imitation in childhood.* New York: Norton, 1962.

Piaget, J. Piaget's theory. In Mussen, P. H. (Ed.), *Manual of child psychology.* New York: John Wiley & Sons, 1970.

Raven, J. C. *Coloured Progressive Matrices,* Sets A, A_b, B. Dumfries, England: The Chrichton Royal, 1968.

Sheriff, F. *Comparison of classroom interactions in three different preschools.* Unpublished doctoral dissertation, University of Michigan, 1971.

Sigel, I., & Hooper, F. (Eds.). *Logical thinking in children.* New York: Holt, Rinehart & Winston, 1968.

Smedslund, J. The acquisition of conservation of substance and weight in children, III. Conservation of discontinuous quantity and the operations of adding and taking away. *Scandinavian Journal of Psychology,* 1962, *3,* 69–77.

Smilansky, S. *The effects of sociodramatic play on disadvantaged preschool children.* New York: John Wiley & Sons, 1968.

Sommerfield, D., Morris, M., Bond, J., & Gordon, S. *Standard tests of aptitude and achievement. Annual report* (Vol. 2). Ypsilanti, Mich.: High/Scope/Foundation, 1974.

Stauffer, R. *Directing the reading–thinking process.* New York: Harper & Row, 1975.

Stebbins, L. B., St. Pierre, R. G., Proper, E. C., Anderson, R. B., & Cerva, T. R. *Education as experimentation: A planned variation model. Volume IV–A: An evaluation of Follow Through.* Cambridge, Mass.: Abt Associates, 1977. (Also issued by the U.S. Office of Education as *National evaluation: Patterns of effects,* Volume II–A of the *Follow Through planned variation experiment series.*)

Van Allen, R. *Language experiences in communication.* Boston: Houghton, Mifflin, 1976.

Van Allen, R., & Van Allen, C. *An introduction to a language experience program.* Chicago: Encyclopedia Britannica Press, 1966.

Weikart, D. P. (Ed.). *Preschool intervention: Preliminary results of the Perry Preschool Project.* Ann Arbor, Mich.: Campus Publishers, 1967.

Weikart, D. P. Relationship of curriculum, teaching, and learning in preschool education. In J. C. Stanley (Ed.), *Preschool programs for the disadvantaged.* Baltimore, Md: Johns Hopkins University Press, 1972. Pp. 22–66.

Weikart, D. P., & Banet, B. A. Model design problems in Follow Through. In A. M. Rivlin & P. M. Timpane (Eds.), *Planned variation in education.* Washington, D.C.: Brookings Institution, 1975. Pp. 61–77.

Weikart, D. P. Curriculum for early childhood education. *Focus on Exceptional Children,* 1974, *6*, 1–8.

ELIZABETH C. GILKESON
LORRAINE M. SMITHBERG
GARDA W. BOWMAN
W. RAY RHINE

7

Bank Street Model:
A Developmental–Interaction Approach[1]

Overview

[1] Preparation of this chapter was supported by USOE Grant G00–7507237, but no endorsement of its content by the federal government should be inferred.

249

Overview

The Bank Street Follow Through Model is based upon a comprehensive theoretical position on early childhood education. Two basic beliefs are (*a*) children have predictable growth patterns that can be identified by teachers; and (*b*) children learn best when their interactions with adults are warm, supportive, and intellectually stimulating. The Bank Street approach to educating children has been applied and refined in many different educational settings over more than half a century. Teachers in the model seek to provide both experiences and information that foster children's capacities for knowing, thinking, and feeling without subordinating any one area of their growth to another.

This chapter contains a brief historical statement about the origins and orientation of Bank Street College, followed by a description of the rationale and goals of the Developmental–Interaction Approach. In the section on implementation (enactment) of the model in Follow Through, the topics include the characteristics of well-implemented classrooms, the curriculum components, and program components that make implementation possible. These program components include staff development, parent participation, and sponsor–community relations. Evaluation (assessment) is described as a tripartite activity consisting of program analysis, child assessment, and evaluation of program outcomes. Finally, the chapter concludes with the statement of some lessons that have been learned from participation in Follow Through.

Origins

In 1916, a group of men and women of varying academic and professional backgrounds founded the Bureau of Educational Experiments in New York City. Over the years, the Bureau developed into an institution now known as Bank Street College. Lucy Sprague Mitchell, the leader among the founders, and her colleagues conducted many interdisciplinary studies to explore how children learn and to identify the patterns of interaction that promote children's growth and development. The staff of the Bureau included a physician, a psychologist, a statistician, a social worker, health workers, and "teacher–scientists." The work of the Bureau's staff also was ably supported by many consultants in the social sciences, including Mitchell's husband, Wesley Clair Mitchell, an economist and professor at Columbia University.

Mitchell emphasized an interdisciplinary approach to education in order to bring many sources of information to bear on the development and education of children. She and her colleagues believed that the improvement of educational opportunities available in schools would be an important step toward elevating the character of human life and human societies. They also believed that striving to live democratically, in and out of schools, is the best way to advance the concept of democracy. The work of the Bureau of Educational Experiments was based on faith that human beings can improve the society they have created. Mitchell (1950) wrote, "It is imperative for all people who have social consciences to understand in what direction our schools are moving and to help schools move in the directions they believe make for cultural progress. Our very future depends upon our children and our schools [p. 434]."

Mitchell expressed views on the education of children that were innovative and markedly different from the authoritarian methods that were commonly practiced in the early decades of the twentieth century. Consequently, many changes in the training of teachers were necessary in order to implement her recommendations. She stated, "A shift in the conception of the kind of lives children should have in school would inevitably mean a shift in the kind of teachers they should have [Mitchell, 1950, p. 27]." She chose the term *teacher–scientist* to designate a new kind of professional educator who practiced experimental and clinical methods for both analyzing the characteristics of children and providing individualized educational experiences for them.

Many of the guidelines issued in the national Follow Through Project in 1968 already had been implemented in the Bureau of Educational Experiments. For example, school personnel and specialists in child development worked closely to improve education in both the Bureau and Follow Through. Other points of agreement included an emphasis on the role of the family in the education of children, the advocacy of an interdisciplinary approach to education, and the search for creative interactions between teaching and research in the schools. In 1917, the Bureau published a pamphlet that contained this statement, "The aims of the Bureau were made practical by having a school for our research staff, a school conducted in the spirit of experimentation, one that gives children a curriculum of experiences as well as information [Winsor, 1973, p. 9]."

Some landmarks in the history of Bank Street College are cited in this paragraph and the next one. In 1930, the Bureau's informal educational program for the preparation of teachers was reorganized as the Cooperative School for Teachers. In 1943, the New York City Board of Education invited that institution, located at 69 Bank Street and then known as the Bank Street School, to participate in a revision of the curriculum of the New York City public schools. In 1950, the corporate name of the institution was changed to Bank Street College of Education, and it was authorized to grant the degree of Master of Science in Education, and subsequently, postmaster's degrees. In 1958, the National Institute of Mental Health awarded a 5-year grant to Bank Street College for the purpose of analyzing the role of the school in coordinating comprehensive health and psychological services for children (Minuchin, Biber, Shapiro, & Zimiles, 1969). In 1968, the Bank Street Model was selected as one of the original 13 models that were implemented in Follow Through.

The facilities of the college include three laboratory centers that are used to provide research, training, and demonstration programs. In 1956, the Harriet Johnson Nursery School was reorganized as the Bank Street School for Children. This center serves as a laboratory school in which students are enrolled from preschool through eighth grade. In 1959, the Polly Miller Child Care Center was established to provide care and teaching services that support and strengthen the family life of children whose parents are either employed full-time or are economically disadvantaged. In 1966, the Early Childhood and Family Resources Center began serving low-income families by offering programs for parents and children, as well as training and consultation services for educators. (The latter two centers are still used for placement of students but are no longer used for research and demonstration purposes).

The faculty and staff of Bank Street College conduct teacher education, basic and action research, and field services, as well as a laboratory school and units for publication and media. Members of the faculty also engage in numerous research and dissemination projects with cooperating schools located throughout the United States and in many foreign countries. These projects include research in such areas as infancy, day care, bilingual education, leadership, and mainstreaming. Educators at Bank Street College continue to adhere to many of the beliefs and methods that were formulated by the founders of the Bureau of Educational Experiments. Like Mitchell and her colleagues, the members of the Bank Street faculty are guided by the "spirit of experimentation" as they develop programs pragmatically by analyzing their practical consequences.

The first three authors of this chapter collectively have more than 30 years of work experience at Bank Street College. Elizabeth C. Gilkeson served as the first director of the Bank Street Follow Through Model until 1976. Lorraine M. Smithberg has been director of the model since that time. Garda W. Bowman has fulfilled many key responsibilities, including program analysis and evaluation research.

Rationale

The two purposes of this section are (a) to describe the sources of knowledge that have contributed to the conceptual framework that underlies the Developmental–Interaction Model; and (b) to state the primary goals of the model for children and teachers.

CONCEPTUAL FRAMEWORK

Educators at Bank Street have incorporated and adapted knowledge from many sources in order to construct their approach to educating children. The three general sources that will be discussed briefly in this section are the following: the writings of Mitchell, information about children's growth and development drawn from several schools of psychology, and psychologically based concepts of pedagogy.

Writings of Mitchell

A number of excerpts from Mitchell's writings were cited in the previous section. One of Mitchell's most important statements was her description of the quality of life experience that educators should seek to provide for children. Mitchell (1950) wrote,

> What, then, is a good life for children? An active, a full, a rich life of meaningful experience at each stage of their development. A good life is a life in which one keeps growing in interests, in breadth of expressions, in depth and extent of human relations. Growth in all one's powers step-by-step up through the early stages toward maturity, leads on to an adulthood which is not static, completed, but still retains capacity and the eagerness to grow . . . Children's best chance to be learners, doers, creative constructive members in the society they live in as adults is to have lived lives which gave these qualities a chance to grow steadily from a child level to an adult level [p. 14]

Concepts from Several Schools of Psychology

Shapiro and Biber (1972), members of the Bank Street community, referred to the Bank Street Model as the Developmental–Interaction Approach. These authors stated,

> Developmental refers to the identifiable patterns of growth and modes of perceiving and responding which are characterized by increasing differentiation and progressive integration as a function of chronological age. Interaction refers, first, to the emphasis on the child's interaction with the environment—adults, other children, and the material world—and second, to the interaction between cognitive and affective spheres of development. The developmental–interaction formulation stresses the nature of the environment as much as it does the patterns of the responding child [pp. 59–60].

Shapiro and Biber (1972) also identified three sources that have influenced Bank Street's rationale for early childhood education:

> This approach flows from three main sources: (1) the dynamic psychology of Freud and his followers, especially those who have been concerned with the

development of autonomous ego processes, for example, Anna Freud, Erikson, Hartmann, Sullivan, and Rapaport; (2) the gestalt and developmental psychologists who have been primarily concerned with cognitive development, like Wertheimer, Werner, and Piaget, theorists who have, for the most part, been only incidentally interested in pedagogic issues per se; and (3) the educational theorists and practitioners who have themselves been influenced by these psychologists or who have developed a functional and/or psychodynamic approach of their own, for example, John Dewey, Harriet Johnson, Susan Isaacs, Lucy Sprague Mitchell [p. 60].

Additional information on the Developmental–Interaction Approach may be found in other publications by Biber (1955, 1961, 1977). Biber and Minuchin (1969), and Biber, Shapiro, and Wickens, 1971).

Psychologically-Based Concepts of Pedagogy

The development of instructional methods has been influenced by a number of psychologically-based concepts on how children learn. For example, educators at Bank Street agree with Piaget (1973) and others who have stated that as children interact with their environment, they construct models of the world in which they live. Their models consist of sets of ideas that serve to organize and give meaning to the children's experiences. These models include past experiences, present integrated world views, and future orientations. Models are the personal creations of the children, but the meaning of these models can also be understood by adults. Furthermore, teachers can use their knowledge about children's models to enhance their learning in classrooms. An important purpose of schooling is to provide experiences that encourage children to construct models that are desirable, both in terms of the goals of society and the goals of the individual.

Educators at Bank Street also agree with Bruner's (1966) position that each individual develops modes of coping and defending that reveal much about the quality of that person's total intellectual life. Consequently, children's learning should occur in environments in which feelings of threat are minimized and feelings of support are maximized. When children perceive schools as dull, depressing, or terrifying places, they are likely to develop avoidant and defensive attitudes toward school personnel and learning in general. But if their lives in school are filled with lively, challenging, and joyful experiences, they are likely to develop positive feelings about learning not only in school but in later adult life as well. Therefore, we feel that the quality of school life is both a means to an end and an end in itself.

Other comtemporary writers who have expressed views that appear to be consistent with the Developmental–Interaction Approach include Bettelheim (1960), Erikson (1963), Elkind (1971), Cazden (1972), Kohlberg and Mayer (1972), and Loban (1976).

GOALS OF THE MODEL

Educators at Bank Street College and members of local program staffs cooperated in the formulation of the goals for children and teachers that are stated next.

Goals for Children

The primary goal for children is to help them develop into adults who can maintain and enhance a free, democratic society. Thus, it is essential in the early years of schooling to establish the foundations that enable individuals to become *confident, inventive, responsive,* and *productive* human beings who can both adapt to and shape their society in meaningful ways. Such individuals possess a mastery of academic skills, but even more importantly, they are competent in the following broad intellectual, affective, social, and physical areas.

1. *Intellectual competence* includes developing interest and ability in inquiry, investigation, and problem solving; increasing the capacity to employ rational and logical processes for organizing meaning; achieving mastery of academic skills in reading, writing, mathematics, and communication; and using imagination and symbols to express thoughts and feelings.

2. *Affective competence* includes developing self-awareness and self-esteem as a person and as a learner; acquiring knowledge about and identification with one's own cultural heritage; actively participating in one's own learning process; demonstrating ego strength to cope with emotional stress; and responding to the beauty of life in its artistic, aesthetic interpretation.

3. *Social competence* includes communicating effectively with one's peers, empathizing and becoming involved with individuals of different social, economic, ethnic, religious, and age groups; interacting with others in a spirit of understanding, respect, trust, and cooperation; and growing in awareness of and ability to enact ethical values in day-to-day living.

4. *Physical competence* includes becoming aware of one's physical strengths and needs; demonstrating sequential development of motor skills in age-appropriate activities; and experiencing pleasure in exercising one's physical capabilities as a living person.

Goals for Teachers

The teacher is a person who teaches, whether fully credentialed professional or paraprofessional. Teachers are expected to understand and accept the Developmental–Interaction Approach and to use that understanding effectively when they serve as advocates and enablers for children's learning.

Their chief responsibility is to use knowledge about the Bank Street Model and about the thoughts and feelings of each child to build individualized curricula that provide both experiences and information for students.

The teaching strategies (adult interventions) listed here are recommended for teachers, but some of them also may be useful to other school personnel and to parents as well.

1. Create a classroom milieu that includes space for quiet study as well as movement, materials that invite experimenation, and a stimulating yet relaxed climate in which children are encouraged to trust and cooperate with each other.
2. Observe and study individual children systematically and with insight and sensitivity.
3. Impart knowledge and develop skills in a functional manner to build on individual strengths and to meet individual needs.
4. Elicit, accept, and extend children's ideas in order to encourage them to enter and live within an expanding world of fact, fancy, and logical reasoning.
5. Nurture and support an evolving selfhood for each child by communicating understanding and respect and by cultivating a belief in each child's capacity for growth and development.
6. Maintain a schedule of stimulating, wholesome activities and provide necessary assistance to children who have special physical or learning problems.

The Well-Implemented Model

The purpose of this section is to describe the implementation of the Follow Through Developmental–Interaction Approach in the 13 communities that are listed in Appendix B. Some school systems that adopted the model are large, urban, and complex; others are small and self-contained. The children in these communities represent a variety of cultures and ethnic backgrounds. The implementation characteristics presented in this section are described in greater detail by Gilkeson and Bowman (1976). These characteristics occur under optimal conditions; in practice, the operation of educational programs may vary somewhat according to local circumstances. This section also contains descriptions of the procedures that are employed in staff development, parent participation, and sponsor–community relations.

CHARACTERISTICS OF THE BANK STREET MODEL

Perhaps the best way to begin the description of the model is to contrast students' perceptions of events in "traditional" classrooms with students' perceptions of events in Bank Street classrooms. In traditional classrooms, children typically believe that an important part of learning is obeying teachers' directions or following instructions stated in standardized curriculum materials, even though they may have little comprehension of the reasons for those instructions and virtually no conception of learning as a "self-mission." In contrast to these authoritarian conditions, Bank Street classrooms are intended to be democratic life situations in which children learn to generate and evaluate alternatives and to initiate many of their own learning experiences. It also is important to emphasize that in the Bank Street Model, children's learning environments include not only classrooms but the whole community as well. Through their participation in field trips, students engage in many valuable individual and group experiences in learning. The four groups of characteristics described below denote a well-implemented Bank Street program.

The Classroom Setting

Students and teachers work together to create supportive and intellectually stimulating classroom environments that also are characterized by spontaneity, cooperation among peers, and energetic, self-initiated behaviors. Written labels, messages, job charts, and other signals are used to inform children of the events of the day, choices available to them, and work to be accomplished. A library in each classroom contains many types of reading materials. Students have easy access to books (some written by the students themselves), reference books, newspapers, magazines, and catalogues.

Students have many opportunities for motor and sensory experiences through frequent investigations and manipulations of objects and materials that are readily available in the work spaces. The science equipment includes scales, thermometers, and kits. Math materials include attribute blocks, geoboards, cuisenaire rods, and counters. There also will be many types of games, especially those that aid children in learning basic skills in language, reading, math, and spelling.

Structuring Group Life

The daily schedule is carefully structured but also has a high degree of flexibility that permits children to pursue unexpected opportunities for learning experiences generated by their explorations. Students often work independently or in small groups with or without the presence of adults, and many learning activities are conducted simultaneously. Teachers acquire valuable knowledge about the needs and abilities of children by observing them in both individual and group learning situations. The children meet as a whole group when their interests converge or when activities require participation by all. The rules and physical structure for the learning–teaching process are clearly defined. As students complete their work, they move about and talk freely to others. They make plans and complete them with a strong sense of responsibility and purpose, learn how to organize and record information, and learn how to solve problems. Most importantly, they learn how to learn.

Building the Curriculum

The main purpose of curriculum building in the Bank Street Model is to create integrated learning experiences based on children's abilities, needs, interests, and significant events that occur in their lives outside of school. Including a variety of content areas in each learning experience is the key to building an integrated curriculum, as opposed to the use of compartmentalized, nonfunctional, or drill approaches to learning. For example, an activity drawn from social studies, language, reading, writing, mathematics, or one of the expressive areas may serve as the starting point for an exercise in integrated learning. But information from a number of these curriculum areas may be incorporated before the completion of the total learning experience. Activities such as visits to the post office, supermarket, a nearby factory, park, or construction site can be arranged in local communities to provide opportunities for children to pursue their interests and to learn skills in reading, writing, mathematics, and research.

Integrated learning experiences probably can be developed with the greatest ease in social studies, because this broad curriculum area focuses on how people live within their environments. An example of cooperative, integrated learning in social studies is the project that students at P. S. 243 in Brooklyn, New York, completed on Weeksville—a community of former slaves located where the school now stands. The children dug up artifacts, read historical records, and recreated the clothing, tools, and activities of Weeksville. The results of the group's efforts were so impressive that the New York Metropolitan Museum of Art since has sponsored an annual, week-long display of this project. Much space would be required to enumerate the host of skills that students acquired through the completion of this one integrated learning experience.

The teaching of language processes permeates most activities in classrooms. Reading and written language skills are developed through both formal and informal instruction and through integrated learning experiences. Oral language is stressed. There are frequent opportunities for discussion and exchange of ideas, peer communication abounds, and literature or reference materials are often discussed. Adults listen to students express their thoughts, engage them in short discussions, and read to them daily. Adults also record children's dictated stories and charts, encourage them to read silently from self-selected books, and conduct frequent individualized instruction in reading skills.

Children learn to read at different ages and through a variety of decoding strategies. Bank Street teachers become observant and knowledgeable about helping students understand their particular decoding processes. They analyze each child's approach to reading and thus are prepared to respond to his or her preferred learning style. The first step in teaching reading is to help individuals understand that meaning is communicated through printed words. When children master this first step, adults seek to identify the most efficient decoding systems for each child. They then can proceed to enlarge the children's knowledge of vocabulary and syntax.

Progress in writing and reading are closely interconnnected throughout the elementary grades. Bank Street students prepare written records of their experiences in diaries and journals. This practice helps them understand that symbolic expression is useful in accomplishing their own goals, and it assists children in clarifying and organizing their experiences at deeper levels of meaning. In addition, it provides adults with another important method for understanding children's thought processes and their concepts of the world in which they live. The most important positive effect from this method of teaching language is that students not only learn to read, but they also *become readers*. They not only learn to write, but they also *become writers* in their own journals and stories.

The principles and practices described above also apply to building curriculum in the areas of mathematics and expressive activities. For example, children acquire much information about such topics as measurement, money, and time as by-products of integrated learning activities and projects in science and social studies. They also may acquire mathematical concepts functionally by learning that a trip to the supermarket or post office requires them to count change, or that cooking requires them to count time and measure ingredients. Students engage in integrated expressive activities through a variety of media and modes, such as music, art, paints, clay, and drawing materials. Younger children participate in dramatic play through which they grow along a number of dimensions as they learn to express the developing concepts of their world. Dramatic play among older children may take the form of presenting original scripts for invited audiences, thus enabling them to integrate and communicate their mastery of skills and concepts. Older children construct, and often reconstruct, their maps of the world by choosing from among various options for study, recording, and reporting.

The Teaching Role

The teaching team consists of a teacher and a paraprofessional. In order to become competent in analyzing students' learning styles and in the use of this information to plan individual and group instruction, teachers must acquire thorough knowledge about child development, teaching methods, and instructional materials. In addition, they must develop the ability to translate scholarly knowledge into appropriate teaching behavior. In both actions and words, teachers should express respect and high expectancies for students' abilities, desires to learn, and efforts to communicate. Furthermore, teachers are expected to be competent and trustworthy persons who are capable of presenting challenging opportunities for the mastery of essential academic and social skills.

The Interdisciplinary Team

The concept of the interdisciplinary team is useful for integrating the efforts of all professionals who provide instructional, psychological, health, and social services to children and their families. In the Bank Street Model, the aim is to support and integrate the children's learning experiences at school, at home, and in the neighborhood. Consequently, school administrators have important responsibilities to coordinate the services of appropriate professional personnel as members of the interdisciplinary team.

STAFF DEVELOPMENT

The staff development program in the Bank Street Model includes the following four components: creative experiences, child study, diagnostic teaching of academic skills, and problem solving.

Creative Experiences

Teachers are more likely to encourage self-expression in others when they possess that ability themselves. Therefore, frequent opportunities for creative experiences in language, music, art, media, and science are provided in the staff development program. Teachers often create their own materials for teaching children, and they are encouraged to engage in a number of activities that promote their own growth in self-expression.

The ideas for creative expressions are derived from many sources. For example, teachers are encouraged to maintain a small professional library, which should include publications by such authors as Cohen (1972), Goodman and Burke (1972), Jansky and de Hirsch (1972), Wilson and Hall (1972), Stauffer (1973), Gilkeson and Bowman (1976), Heilman (1976), Pasamanick (1976), Van Allen (1976), Graves (1978), and Hall (1978). Other recommmended publications contain guidelines for teaching social studies, language, and reading. In addition, filmstrips on reading, cooking, working with clay, and other topics are available to teachers in Bank Street Follow Through classrooms. A complete list of filmstrips and other teaching materials may be obtained by writing to the Bank Street Bookstore, 610 W. 112th Street, New York, N.Y. 10025.

Child Study

In the preservice education of teachers, the study of child development often is neglected or contained in a single course. Information on child development seldom is linked to the study of curriculum development, teaching behavior, or classroom management. In contrast, the study of child development is an integral part of all phases of teacher education at Bank Street College. The beliefs about how students learn and grow strongly influence educational practices and staff development procedures. Teachers are taught how to ask themselves important questions, such as "How does the child feel?" "How does the child perceive?" and "How does the child organize information?" The answers to these questions often suggest answers to the challenging "What to do?" and "How to do it?" questions that teachers must cope with in school settings.

Diagnostic Teaching of Academic Skills

Teachers are required to become competent in teaching academic skills. They learn about methods of instruction and how to select methods and materials that are appropriate to students' conceptual abilities and interests. In addition, educators at Bank Street have selected or constructed a number of diagnostic instruments that teachers may use to assist them in analyzing children's academic knowledge and skills. Many of these instruments are described below in the section on evaluation.

Problem Solving

Participants in Bank Street programs are expected to use the process of problem solving as a method for setting goals and resolving conflicts. In each phase of staff development, participants engage in problem solving tasks in which they review their experiences, evaluate the meaning of what they are learning, provide corrective feedback to each other, and set new goals. Small-group seminars are organized around the concepts of teams (e.g., staff of a school), roles (e.g., teachers or paraprofessionals), or functions (e.g., grade levels). Thus, all training activities are focused on issues and requirements of program development. The use of this approach makes it possible to assess the progress of local programs and how well they are responding to emergent needs in the communities they serve.

The aims of staff development in the Developmental–Interaction Approach were summarized by Mitchell (1950) when she described the purpose of teacher education as helping students develop a scientific attitude toward their work and toward life. To Mitchell, this meant that teachers would be eager, alert observers of children's behavior, constantly questioning older procedures in the light of current observations, using learning opportunities in the community as well as source materials, and keeping reliable records on the results of their teaching in order to base the future upon factual knowledge of the past.

In the 1931 catalogue of the Cooperative School for Teachers, Mitchell expressed what continues to be the approach at Bank Street College. Mitchell stated, "We are interested in imbuing student (teachers) with an experimental, critical, and ardent approach to their work, and to the social problems of the world in which they, as adults, must take an active part. If we can accomplish this we are ready to leave the future to them [p. 3]."

PARENT PARTICIPATION

Parent participation is essential to effective enactment of the Bank Street Model. Consequently, parents are encouraged to participate in four areas of the implementation process: teaching their children, making educational decisions, self-development activities, and action groups.

Teaching Their Children

When parents understand what the teaching teams are seeking to accomplish, they become more effective in teaching their children at home. Parents increase their awareness of the school's educational goals by participating in classrooms as observers, volunteers, or paid paraprofessionals. Thus, parents and teachers develop a shared understanding of children's needs and are therefore better able to provide continuity in their learning experiences. Moreover, when parents have an active role in the learning–teaching process, they not only gain direct knowledge about school programs and how students participate in them, but they also encourage children to trust and identify with members of the school staff (Gilkeson, 1960). When there is a spirit of mutual respect between parents and teachers, parents are more likely to give valuable assistance to teachers. They also are more likely to learn how to support and extend their children's learning at home and to encourage the integration of their experiences gained in school and at home.

Making Educational Decisions

Parents usually become more interested and effective in making educational decisions when they understand the school's approach to providing educational services. They also are more likely to express concerns about their children's education when school personnel listen, understand, and attempt to respond. Home visits and parent-to-parent contacts succeeded in increasing the number of parents who participated in making educational decisions in Follow Through programs, but it may not be realistic to expect that all parents will participate in such decision-making activities.

Self-Development Activities

Resource rooms (or houses) are maintained for parents in all Bank Street Follow Through programs. The parents and parent coordinators are responsible for maintaining these facilities and for organizing and planning meetings, social events, and other educational, vocational, and avocational activities. Care services are provided for infants and toddlers so that parents and their relatives may attend planned events. Fathers are urged to participate. In one community, parents planned a Father's Month in order to encourage fathers to visit classrooms and to attend meetings and other activities during the evening hours. Parents who choose to enroll in the Career Development Program may obtain academic credit for completion of in-service training programs from Bank Street College. Those credits may be applied toward the completion of the requirements for an associate or bachelor's degree at a local college or university.

Action Programs

Through their experiences as advocates for Follow Through and as members of the PAC, many parents participated effectively for the first time in programs for improving educational opportunities for children. For example, parents organized an intensive letter writing campaign and a network for disseminating information when they learned that Congress might enact legislation to phase out Follow Through kindergarten and first grade classrooms in September, 1976. These actions were among the important influences that persuaded Congress to continue funding for local Follow Through programs. In addition, parents often support Follow Through programs by participating in meetings of local boards of education and other community agencies and organizations. The confidence and motivation they gained from participation in these activities often encouraged parents to participate in other action programs for community improvement.

SPONSOR–COMMUNITY RELATIONS

Members of the Bank Street staff identified the following five steps in the successful implementation of the Developmental–Interaction Approach:

1. Communicate knowledge about the model and enlist support for it.
2. Establish channels of communication and participation among members of the sponsor's staff, school personnel, and parents to facilitate planning the program and setting goals.
3. Translate theory into practice through staff development acitivities.
4. Analyze the results of program implementation, provide quick feedback of results to participants, and restructure program operations when necessary.

5. Engage in demonstration and dissemination activities in Bank Street Follow Through communities and in school systems that do not have Follow Through programs.

In each community there are positive influences that facilitate change toward desired goals and negative influences that oppose it. The balance of these forces differs from one community to another. Facilitating factors include effective cooperation between Bank Street representatives and local leaders in planning programs and the evolution of staff development procedures that prepare trainers and trainees to create supportive environments for learners. The most frequent obstacles to progress are inflexible bureaucratic procedures, resistance to or insufficient knowledge about Bank Street's position on child development and education, conflicting value systems, and such unexpected events as strikes, budget cuts, and arbitrary changes in personnel at every level from paraprofessional to superintendent of schools. The activities of the Bank Street staff necessarily are focused on successfully enacting the model within the context of existing circumstances in each community.

Evaluation

The description of the Bank Street approach to evaluation is presented in six parts: orientation to evaluation, program analysis, child assessment, evaluation of program outcomes—results from standardized tests, the BRACE—a new process approach to evaluation, and results of independent evaluation studies.

ORIENTATION TO EVALUATION

Educators at Bank Street College view learning–teaching as a dynamic process in which members of the interdisciplinary teams must use their skills in observation and analysis to guide program development. Thus, in evaluation the concern is not only with *whether* a particular program is effective or ineffective, but also with *why* certain outcomes occur and how this knowledge may be used to improve the program. The ultimate goal of evaluation is to educate teacher–scientists who can effectively implement the Developmental–Interaction Approach to educating young children.

Existing instruments were generally not suitable for assessing numerous areas of learning–teaching that are essential in the model. These areas include children's critical thinking, the quality of interaction in classrooms, and the integration of intellectual, affective, and social competencies (Biber & Minuchin, 1969). Consequently, it was necessary to develop a variety of new instruments (See Table 7.1) and supporting materials. Not all the instruments in Table 7.1 are used in each community, but all are available as needed. In a few instances, existing instruments were selected for evaluation purposes.

The three most widely used components in the evaluation system are program analysis, child assessment, and evaluation of program outcomes. Program analysis and child assessment are two formative components that make essential contributions to program development. Evaluation of program outcomes is directed toward summative evaluation of the model's impact on participants. As shown in Table 7.1, some instruments were used in only one component of the evaluation system, but others were used in two or even three components. Each of the three evaluation components is discussed below, and representative characteristics of each are described. In addition, the characteristics of the BRACE and the results of independent evaluation studies will be presented.

PROGRAM ANALYSIS

Program analysis consists of continuing cycles of analysis, restructuring, and reanalysis of the implementation process in each Bank Street Follow Through community. The results are used to examine and improve the implementation of the model in each community. For example, teachers use the findings to analyze and improve their teaching behaviors, to formulate individualized curricula, and to make appropriate revisions in learning environments and curricula. Other uses of the results include improving staff development procedures, identifying and resolving conflicts before they become disruptive, and studying the usefulness of evaluation procedures. The remainder of this section contains a description of how program analysis is used in classrooms and an explanation of why various instruments were developed or selected.

The Use of Program Analysis in Classrooms

Program analysis begins in each classroom with a description of Bank Street's educational philosophy to those individuals who implement the program in local schools. Members of the teaching teams learn about basic principles, teaching strategies, dynamics of child behavior, and the application of this knowledge in teaching children. Teachers also are taught to be accurate observers of children's behavior, and they are encouraged to experiment by engaging in new teaching behaviors and carefully appraising the results. Eventually, teachers become adroit in developing individualized curricula, making self-assessments of their own effectiveness, and implementing Bank Street's analytic, clinical approach to teaching. A long-term goal of program analysis is to construct more effective communication systems among the teachers, parents, paraprofessionals, staff developers, ancillary personnel, and directors who conduct local programs.

TABLE 7.1
Representative Evaluation Instruments

Instruments	Purpose	Use[a]
A. Developed by Bank Street Staff		
1. Self-Study for Teaching Teams	To help teachers analyze their own performance and to encourage diagnostic teaching	PA
2. Checklist of Model Implementation	To assist the sponsor and school personnel in assessing model implementation	PA
3. Reading Assessment Form	To identify children's expected reading competencies at successive stages of learning	PA, CA
4. Roster Profile	To provide for each classroom an overview of children's competencies and growth potentials	PA, CA
5. Parent Interview	To study parents' understanding of and involvement in their children's learning	PA, EPO
6. Analysis of Communication in Education (ACE)	To observe and analyze child–adult and child–child verbal communication	PA, CA, EPO
7. Behavior Ratings and Analysis of Communication in Education (BRACE)	To observe and analyze verbal and nonverbal communication and other characteristics of educational settings	PA, CA, EPO
8. Individual Child Assessment Form	To provide a more detailed picture of each child's competencies and potential for growth	CA

9. Discussion Task	To study children's language production and thinking processes in a small-group situation	CA
10. Child Profiles	To summarize information about children obtained from many sources	CA
11. Analysis of Children's Oral Storytelling Task (ACOST)	To study children's language production and thinking processes in one-to-one situations	CA, EPO
12. Differentiated Child Behavior Form (DCB)	To observe and analyze children's verbal communication and nonverbal behavior	EPO
B. Selected/Adapted from Other Sources		
1. Screening Test of Academic Readiness (STAR)	To assess the strengths and needs of children when they enter school	CA
2. House–Tree–Person–Animal (HTPA)	To study the symbolic representations and thought processes that are revealed in children's drawings	CA
3. Jansky-deHirsch Battery	To study in greater detail the academic skills of those children who perform poorly on the STAR	CA
4. Spache Diagnostic Reading Test	To assess children's progress in reading at second and third grade levels	CA
5. Various standardized achievement tests	To evaluate children's progress in academic areas	EPO

---

[a] PA = program analysis, CA = child assessment, EPO = evaluation of program outcomes

Instrument Development

To facilitate the process of program analysis, members of the research and training teams developed a number of diagnostic instruments, including self-rating scales, reading assessment procedures, observation instruments for studying the behaviors of children and adults in classrooms, interview schedules to assess parents' perceptions and attitudes, and various checklists for studying the enactment of the model (see Table 7.1). Other supporting materials that were generated included curriculum guides, position papers, training films and videotapes, implementation criteria, and manuals that describe the rationales for the instruments, procedures for administering and scoring them, and ways to use the results for improving educational practices (Bowman *et al.* 1976). All instruments and supporting materials were developed to help individuals cope with various needs that were identified during the enactment of the Developmental–Interaction Approach in Project Follow Through. Three representative instruments employed in program analysis and their uses are briefly described in the following paragraphs.

Self-Study for Teaching Teams One urgent need that surfaced soon after Follow Through began in the fall of 1968 was to describe the characteristics of the Bank Street Model to school personnel in local communities and to help them use this knowledge to examine their own teaching behaviors. A number of new instruments were constructed to help adults assess their own progress toward conducting the model correctly. The Self-Study for Teaching Teams was one of those instruments. It is a 4-point rating scale that teachers and paraprofessionals use to rate the attainment of recommended educational objectives. The purpose of this instrument is to help members of teaching teams analyze their own performance more objectively and to identify areas in which staff developers or ancillary personnel may assist them to improve.

Reading Assessment Form This instrument was developed by Bank Street staff to assess each child's language development in many areas including comprehension, physical development skills that are linked to acquisition of reading skills, encoding skills, and decoding skills (Gilkeson, Sardo, & Garfinkle, 1970). In addition, the instrument consists of a checklist for assessing children's development through the various stages of learning to read. Teachers use the information from this instrument in diagnostic and prescriptive approaches to teaching reading. During the mid-1970s, reading programs were initiated in many communities that had already adopted the model. But the approaches to teaching reading in many of these newly mandated reading programs were not compatible with an individualized approach to teaching reading. These discrepancies created confusion for teachers who received conflicting messages. Consequently, Elizabeth C. Gilkeson and members of the field staff analyzed the mandated programs in order to identify the components that were or were not consistent with the Developmental-Interaction Approach. The results of these analyses then were used in negotiations with school administrators to make adjustments in their required procedures for teaching reading in local school districts.

Checklist of Model Implementation This checklist was developed to assist persons in local communities to analyze their level of success in enacting the model correctly. It has been used in all 13 of the Bank Street Follow Through programs to establish appropriate objectives and to correct discrepancies between local practices and those recommended by Bank Street (Smithberg, 1977). In many communities, staff members use this checklist to perform self-assessments of their performance in an annual review procedure. They use the results to set objectives for the coming year.

CHILD ASSESSMENT

The practice of the Bank Street individualized approach to education requires that a large amount of information concerning each child be obtained through the diagnostic procedures that comprise the child assessment component of the evaluation system. The purpose of this second evaluation component is to analyze children's competencies, learning needs, and patterns of behavior. The results are used for the following purposes: to identify children's strengths and interests, to identify children who have special problems, to help school personnel and parents establish appropriate educational goals for children, and to plan individualized curricula for all children in order to build on strengths and ameliorate problems. The instruments employed in child assessment may be divided into two groups: (*a*) those employed in school entry assessment; and (*b*) those employed in other components of child assessment. Some representative instruments in each group and their uses are briefly described as follows.

Instruments Used in School Entry Assessment

The purpose of school entry assessment is to perform continuing analyses of the strengths and needs of each entering child throughout the first year of schooling in order to provide early and appropriate interventions. Teachers make many informal observations of children's behavior in the first few weeks after school begins. During the second month, teachers administer the Screening Test for Academic Readiness (STAR) (Ahr, 1966) to assess each entering child's language development. If children's responses on the STAR indicate the need for additional inquiry, other instruments may be administered. For example, the House–Tree–Person–Animal (HTPA) test (Buck, 1948) may be administered to some students to study further the organization and integration of cognitive and affective areas that are revealed in their drawings. The Jansky-de Hirsch Battery for Kindergarten Screening (Jansky & de Hirsch, 1972) is another diagnostic instrument that is sometimes administered to assess a number of underlying learning abilities, including visual–motor organization, oral language, pattern matching, and pattern memory. In the third month, teachers administer the "Beginnings" portion of the Reading Assessment Form. The first phase of the data collection is completed when teachers collect language samples from each child.

Meetings are convened periodically throughout the year to review and interpret the findings from the school entry assessment procedures and to incorporate what has been learned into individualized instructional programs. Thus, members of the interdisciplinary teams make detailed studies of each child's characteristics in order to understand capabilities for performance and to provide appropriate learning experiences. When children appear to have special problems, the intent of school personnel in the model is to *prevent* failure rather than simply to *predict* it. Some children have special problems that require supportive and/or remedial programs and perhaps other types of educational or therapeutic services. Thus, school staff members representing social services, health services, as well as psychological and guidance services, often contribute in significant ways to school entry assessment.

Other Child Assessment Procedures

Members of the Bank Street evaluation staff constructed a number of instruments that are employed in the remainder of the child assessment component of the evaluation system. For example, a Roster Profile is used to record the particular strengths, needs, interests, learning styles, motivation, and social skills of children in each classroom. Periodic administration of this instrument reveals changing patterns of growth in students, and these results are valuable for planning instructional programs and for organizing small-group activities on the basis of common interests and needs. The Individual Child Assessment Form is used to record each child's preferences for activities and ways of using time at home and at school. This information is useful for in-depth studies of children and for making decisions on methods of classroom instruction.

The study of children as learners, doers, and thinkers often focuses on language development, and several instruments have been selected or developed for that purpose. For example, the Spache Diagnostic Reading Test (Spache, 1972) is administered to each child individually at the beginning of the second grade and again at the beginning of the third grade. It is used to measure children's decoding skills and comprehension skills. In addition, the three remaining portions (Initiation to Reading, Middle Reading, and Later Reading) of the Reading Asessment Form are administered to students at appropriate times to assess their continued progress through the developmental stages of learning to read.

Members of the evaluation staff developed two process-oriented instruments for use in analyzing language skills that cannot be studied through the administration of paper-and-pencil tests. The Analysis of Children's Oral Storytelling Task (ACOST) (Gould, 1974; Weissman, 1979) is employed to elicit oral stories from children and to record the organization, clarity, logical content, and use of imagination in each child's story. The content of each child's story also is analyzed on a number of other dimensions including the length of thought (T) units, number of words, and words per T-unit. In the administration of the Discussion Task, one adult presents a visual stimulus such as a picture and conducts a discussion about the object with two children. The children's performance on this task often reveals much about their cognitive processes, language competence, communication skills, critical thinking, and ability to express concepts and feelings in a small-group situation. In addition, the statements often contain important clues about children's self-concepts and about their models of the world. In both the ACOST Task and the Discussion Task, the role of the adult is to encourage children to make statements, not to direct the course of their thoughts and comments. Since the coding systems for both tasks are complex, the sessions are recorded on audiotape to facilitate transcription and coding of the responses.

Other sources of information about each child include anecdotal reports and statements made by parents during home visits and in parent conferences at school, as well as examples of the children's written work and art work completed at school. The contributions to what eventually becomes a comprehensive fund of data about each child begin when the school entry assessment procedures are administered during the first year of attendance in school. The knowledge that is obtained from the instruments and other sources stated previously eventually is organized into a *profile* for each child (Bowman, Gilkeson, Mayer, & Thacher, 1977).

Thus far, the focus of this description of the evaluation system for the model has been on the formative evaluation techniques that comprise program analysis and child assessment. The next three sections contain descriptions of the summative evaluation procedures included in the third component of the evaluation system, evaluation of program outcomes.

These procedures include (a) standardized tests; (b) the BRACE interaction analysis instrument, which was developed by the sponsor; and (c) research conducted by independent consultants.

EVALUATION OF PROGRAM OUTCOMES—RESULTS FROM STANDARDIZED TESTS

Standardized achievement tests were employed to assess Bank Street Follow Through programs in two approaches to evaluation—the national longitudinal evaluation of Follow Through and the sponsor's evaluation. Each of these approaches is discussed here.

The National Longitudinal Evaluation

There has been much heated debate about the national longitudinal evaluation of Follow Through. Educators at Bank Street share the concerns that have been expressed by many researchers and practitioners about the issues and problems that emerged in the national evaluation. The emphasis upon the use of standardized achievement tests as the primary indicators of program effectiveness seems extremely inadequate, since such tests yield only discrete pieces of information about limited areas of students' knowledge and skills. Moreover, standardized achievement tests do not even accurately assess the "basics" of academic performance when they are administered to children below the third grade level. Nevertheless, the results of children's performance on these tests are widely-accepted as sources of information about the effects of schooling. The specific issues in the national longitudinal evaluation of Follow Through have been formulated and discussed by House, Glass, McLean, and Walker (1978), Haney (1977), and others. Readers who wish to examine the results of the national evaluation that pertain to the Bank Street Follow Through Model are referred to Stebbins, St. Pierre, Proper, Anderson, and Cerva (1977) and House et al. (1978).

Sponsor's Evaluation

Researchers at Bank Street College frequently have expressed their concerns about the design of the national longitudinal evaluation of Follow Through. Consequently, the members of the research group chose to compare the achievement test scores of students enrolled in Bank Street Follow Through classrooms with national achievement test norms, rather than with the scores of the controversial comparison groups of low-income children employed in the national longitudinal evaluation (Weissman, 1978). Since the amount of testing conducted in the schools in order to meet the requirements of federal, state, and local educational programs already appeared to be excessive when Follow Through began, it seemed unwise to increase that burden. Therefore, the sponsor chose to utilize data from standardized achievement tests that were administered regularly in each school system, rather than to impose another uniform testing program.

The sponsor's entire approach to evaluation was intended to develop cooperative and facilitating relationships with local school districts. Accordingly, a number of services were performed by members of the sponsor's evaluation staff to assist local evaluators in collecting and analyzing data. These services included providing item analyses of various standardized tests, providing a form used for collecting and reporting demographic data, and preparing evaluation reports. The achievement test data used in the sponsor's evaluation were collected by persons employed in the school districts that were implementing Bank Street Follow Through classrooms. The instruments, procedures for collecting and analyzing data, and some representative results are presented in the following sections.

Instruments and Data Collection Procedures The instruments employed by the various districts to collect data included the California Achievement Test (CAT), Comprehensive Test of Basic Skills (CTBS), Gates-MacGinitie Reading Test, Metropolitan Achievement Test (MAT), and the Stanford Achievement Test (SAT). Information on the psychometric characteristics of these instruments is presented in the Mental Measurement Yearbook (Buros, 1963). In most instances, classroom teachers administered the tests under the supervision of local psychometrists and administrators. After the data were collected, they were presented to members of the Bank Street evaluation staff for analysis (Weissman, 1978).

Data Analysis Since data collection procedures varied among school districts, it was necessary to impose certain quality controls on the selection of data included in the analyses reported in this section. Consequently, data were analyzed only when procedures met the following criteria: (*a*) The Bank Street Model was enacted in classrooms under normal operating conditions during the period when data were collected; (*b*) data were obtained from at least two consecutive analytic cohorts enrolled in each participating school in the local community (an analytic cohort consists of children who entered Follow Through classrooms at the initial grade level, whether kindergarten or first grade, and had continuous attendance in the model through the completion of third grade); and (*c*) test scores for third graders were obtained in the spring of each year.

When the three criteria stated above were applied, data from eight school systems were acceptable for evaluating performance in reading, and data from five of these eight school systems were acceptable for evaluating performance in mathematics. The mean grade equivalent test scores were

calculated for each Bank Street Follow Through third grade classroom included in the analytic sample. The mean mathematics and reading scores of
those classrooms were then compared with: (a) the national norm for
mathematics and reading at the end of third grade—the characteristics of
children in the national norm group and the Bank Street Follow Through
analytic cohorts differed on several dimensions, including median annual
family income ($9590 versus $5800) and ethnic minority representation
(13% versus 51%); and (b) the expected score for low-income children,
which was 1 year below grade level. In addition, the mean scores at the
third grade level for Follow Through students in the analytic sample in one
school were compared with those of students enrolled in the entire school
district in which that school was located. The mean scores of these same
two groups were compared again, after the Follow Through students had
enrolled in regular grade classrooms and were nearing the completion of
the fourth and fifth grades. These three sets of analyses were performed to
provide answers to three important questions.

*Are the achievement levels in reading and mathematics attained by Bank
Street Follow Through students at the end of third grade commensurate
with national norms at that same level?* Inspection of Table 7.2 reveals that
among 20 Follow Through analytic cohorts, one-third had mean scores in
total reading that were at or above the national norm (*cohort* when used
hereafter refers to the analytic cohorts previously described), one-third of
those cohorts scored within 2 months of the national norm, and one-third
scored 3–6 months below the national norm. All Follow Through cohorts
had mean scores in total reading that were far above the mean score of 2.8
(1 year below grade level) that low-income students would have been expected to achieve.

TABLE 7.2

Mean Total Reading Scores of Follow Through Third Grade Students in Eight Communities[a]

| | Cohort | | |
| | III | IV | V |
Community	1971	1972	1973
A	4.0	3.7	3.7
B	3.5	4.3	
C	3.3	3.5	3.3
D	4.1	3.2	
E	3.6	4.0	3.7
F	4.0	3.6	
G		3.3	3.6
H	3.9	3.8	3.7

[a] National norm score = 3.8; expected score for low-income students = 2.8

Data presented in Table 7.3 compare the mean scores in total mathematics attained by Bank Street Follow Through third-grade students in this sample with the national norm group. More than two-thirds of the 13 Follow Through cohorts had scores that were equal to or above the national norm. Mean scores for the remaining cohorts were from 1 to 2 months below the national norm. All the cohorts attained mean scores that were far above the mean score of 2.8 (1 year below grade level) that would have been predicted for low-income students.

How does the percentage of Bank Street Follow Through students whose achievement levels in reading and mathematics are 1 year or more below grade level compare with that percentage for the national norm? Scores presented in the discussion of the previous question do not reveal the actual proportion of Follow Through students who were at least 1 year below grade level, which is deemed to be indicative of academic failure. The comparisons in Table 7.4 reveal that more than one-half of the cohorts had a lower percentage of academic failure (i.e., children falling 1 year or more below grade level) in total reading, as compared to the national norm group. The comparisons in Table 7.5 indicate that in total mathematics all Follow Through cohorts had a lower percentage of academic failure than in the national norm group.

Do students who have been enrolled in Bank Street Follow Through classrooms maintain their gains in reading and mathematics after they enroll in regular fourth and fifth grade classrooms? The answer to this question was pursued by comparing the mean total reading scores of the analytic sample of Bank Street Follow Through students who were enrolled in fourth and fifth regular grade classrooms in New York City Public

TABLE 7.3
Mean Total Mathematics Scores of Follow Through Third Grade Students in Five Communities[a]

	Cohort		
	III	IV	V
	1971	1972	1973
Community			
A	3.8	3.8	4.0
C	3.6	3.7	3.7
D	4.3	3.6	
F	4.8	3.9	
H	4.0	4.2	4.1

[a] National norm score = 3.8; expected score for low-income students = 2.8

TABLE 7.4

Percentage of Follow Through Third Grade Students in Seven Communities Whose Total Reading Scores Were 1 Year or More Below the National Norm[a]

		Cohort		
		III	IV	V
		1971	1972	1973
Community	Test			
B	SAT	17	10	
C	CAT	35	28	33
D	MAT	22	28	
E	SAT	20	14	18
F	MAT	9		
G	MAT		25	30
H	MAT	11	9	16

[a] Percentage of national norm group scores that were 1 year or more below grade level (SAT, 20%; CAT, 24%; MAT, 24%).

School 243 with the mean total reading scores for the entire population of fourth and fifth grade students enrolled in the school district in which P.S. 243 is located—District 16, New York City. Demographic data indicated that the Follow Through graduates and the District 16 population (located in Bedford Stuyvesant, Brooklyn) were closely equated on median annual family income (approximately $6000) and ethnic minority representation (approximately 95%). Inspection of Table 7.6 reveals that the mean total reading scores are consistently higher for the students who had been enrolled in the Follow Through classrooms. The superior performance of Follow Through graduates in both reading and mathematics at fourth and fifth grade levels also has been documented in four other communities where similar studies were conducted.

TABLE 7.5

Percentage of Follow Through Third-Grade Students in Four Communities Whose Total Mathematics Scores Were 1 Year or More Below the National Norm[a]

		Cohort		
		III	IV	V
		1971	1972	1973
Community	Test			
C	CAT	15	12	14
D	MAT	10	8	
F	MAT	0	6	
H	MAT	4	4	6

[a] Percentage of national norm group scores that were one year or more below grade level (MAT - 12%; CAT - 17%).

TABLE 7.6

Mean Total Reading Scores for Follow Through Students in P. S. 243 and All Students in District 16 in Grades 3, 4, and 5

Students	Comparisons for Cohort II			Comparisons for Cohort III		
	Grade 3 1970	Grade 4 1971	Grade 5 1972	Grade 3 1971	Grade 4 1972	Grade 5 1973
Follow Through students (P. S. 243)	3.9	4.6	7.0	3.6	5.3	5.8
All students in District 16	3.1	4.2	5.9	3.4	4.7	

THE BRACE—A NEW PROCESS APPROACH TO EVALUATION

As stated previously in this section, both standardized tests and instruments developed by researchers at Bank Street College were included in the summative evaluation of the Developmental–Interaction Model. As shown previously in Table 7.1, the instruments developed by members of the sponsor's staff included the Parent Interview (Martin, 1973), the Behavior Ratings and Analysis of Communication in Education (BRACE) (Bowman *et al.*, 1976), and the Differentiated Child Behavior (DCB) Form (Ross, Zimiles, & Gerstein, 1976). The most widely used of these instruments is the BRACE. The purpose, structural characteristics, administration and scoring procedures, and uses of the BRACE are discussed next.

Purpose

The purpose of the BRACE is to observe and analyze child–adult, child–child, and adult–adult interactions in educational settings. It was developed at Bank Street by Garda W. Bowman and Rochelle S. Mayer for several reasons. For example, paper-and-pencil achievement tests measure only a limited number of educational objectives in the model. The results of standardized tests are of little value in efforts to analyze and understand the process of teaching–learning in classrooms, particularly the quality of child–adult interaction, or to examine the integration of cognitive, emotional, and social areas of development. In order to implement the model effectively, teachers require much information about the strengths, needs, interests, and learning styles of students. Members of the sponsor's staff also require process information about the implementation of the model in order to improve its effectiveness in local school districts. Finally, there was a need for an instrument that could be used to study how children grow in autonomy, self-activation, inventiveness, cooperation, and a sense of personal responsibility through their educational experiences. The BRACE has evolved through many stages, but it is a developmental instrument that may require additional refinement before its complete potential for research and application is fully realized.

Structural Characteristics

The BRACE consists of two parts, Analysis of Communication in Education (ACE) (Bowman, 1972, 1973) and Behavior Observation Ratings in Settings (BORIS). The first part is used to analyze patterns of verbal communication during teaching–learning. The second part is used to study nonverbal communication and the characteristics of the setting in which children and adults interact. The dimensions of the two parts of the BRACE are represented in Figures 7.1 and 7.2.

Administration and Scoring

The observers who administer the BRACE are carefully selected and trained to insure that the data they collect are of high quality. Observers are trained in teams of two, and they are expected to attain an intercoder reliability of at least .80 before they administer the BRACE independently. It may be administered to children or adults, but the observer focuses on the behavior of one individual during each of 12 5-min observation periods that are spaced throughout an entire day. Further information about the BRACE is presented in Johnson's (1976) anthology of instruments for systematic observation.

The forms used to record data for the ACE and the BORIS are portrayed in Figures 7.1 and 7.2, respectively. Verbal behavior is scored according to the number of thought (T) units that are expressed during the observation period. A single T-Unit is represented by a tally mark that is recorded in the appropriate rectangular cell of the scoring sheet represented in Figure 7.1. Thus, the placement of each tally mark requires that the observer make judgements about the *flow* (to child, to group, to adult), *mode* (initiate, ask, respond), and *substance* (supportive, cognitive, affective, routine, harmful) of each T-unit. The observer describes nonverbal behavior and the characteristics of the teaching–learning setting after the completion of the observation period by making appropriate entries on the checklist presented in Figure 7.2.

The data pertaining to children's verbal communication that is collected through the administration of the BRACE yields scores on the following 11 dimensions:

1. Expression of unsolicited comments
2. Expression of unsolicited feelings
3. Expression of positive feelings
4. Expression of unsolicited ideas
5. Expression of critical thinking
6. Extending others' ideas

7. Peer communication
8. Support of others
9. Exhibiting a sense of responsibility
10. Use of information
11. Fluency (frequency of t-units)

SPEAKER (Subject): A Particular child □ (1) A child in rotation □ (2) Teacher □ (3) Para □ (4) Other □ (5) (Code ONE Speaker at time)

SUBSTANCE			FLOW → MODE	TO: CHILD (C)			TO: [?] (T)			TO: ADULT (A)			
				INITIATE (I) Card 1	ASK (A) Card 2	RESPOND (R) Card 3	INITIATE (I) Card 4	ASK (A) Card 5	RESPOND (R) Card 6	INITIATE (I) Card 7	ASK (A) Card 8	RESPOND (R) Card 9	
SUPPORTIVE	OF LEARNING		ACCEPTING, ENCOURAGING (ae)										[2/3]
			EXTENDING CLARIFYING (ec)										[4/5]
			RECOGNIZING SPECIFIC ACCOMPLISHMENT (r)										[6/7]
			STIMULATING SELF-CORRECTION (sc)										[8/9]
	OF PERSON		Showing WARMTH to others, AFFECTION (w)										[10/11]
			Showing HUMAN INTEREST in other's comfort, out-of-school life, etc. (hi)										[12/13]
	THROUGH MGMT.		REDIRECTING and/or GUIDING ACTIVITIES (rg)										[14/15]
			CALM, RATIONAL CONTROL of behavior (cc)										[16/17]
COGNITIVE			LOGICAL THOUGHT processes (lt)										[18/19]
			IMAGINATIVE THOUGHT processes (it)										[20/21]
			LOGIC & IMAGINATION COMBINED (li)										[22/23]
			THINKING with overtones of FEELING (tf)										[24/25]
			INFORMATION, FACTS, simple recall or recognition of facts (i)										[26/27]
AFFECTIVE			POSITIVE FEELINGS (Internal) (pf)										[28/29]
			NEGATIVE FEELINGS (Internal) (nf)										[30/31]
			HUMOR, Kidding (h)										[32/33]
			NEEDS, DESIRES (nd)										[34/35]
ROUTINE	MANAGEMENT		DIRECTING, PROCEDURAL (dp)										[36/37]
			PERMISSION (p)										[38/39]
	FEEDBACK		CORRECTING INFORMATION (c)										[40/41]
			GENERALIZED PRAISE (gp)										[42/43]
			ACKNOWLEDGEMENT without interest or encouragement (ak)										[44/45]
	OTHER		Indicating OWN LACK OF KNOWLEDGE/SKILL (lk)										[46/47]
			SOCIAL AMENITIES (sa)										[48/49]
			VAGUE comments (v)										[50/51]
HARMFUL			DEMEANING comments and/or HOSTILITY (dc)										[52/53]
			HARSH, PUNITIVE CONTROL of BEHAVIOR (hc)										[54/55]

Punch items in this frame on the 9th Card only

Single Code: Make entry below ONLY
PRESENTING INFORMATION (Pi) [56/57]
PRESENTING THOUGHT PROVOKING MATERIAL (Pt) [58/59]
READING ALOUD (1 PERSON) TO AUDIENCE (Ra-1) [60/61]
READING ALOUD TO SELF (Ra-s) [62/63]
NOT CODABLE (NC) [64/65]

Double Code: Make entry below AND in other appropriate place
SPEAKING OR READING IN CHORUS (SR-ch) [66/67]
SPEAKING TO SELF (S-s) [68/69]
INACCURATE STATEMENTS (IS) [70/71]
ONE WORD, MINIMAL COMMENT (OW) [72/73]
HIGHLY ELABORATED COMMENT (NE) [74/75]

Type of Adult present: Teach □ (1) Para □ (2) Both □ (3) Other □ (4) None □ (5) [76]
Position of Observation in Sequence (   ) [77/78]

Card | 1 | 2 | 3 | 4 | 5 | 6 | 7 | 8 | 9 | [79/80] (For key punch operator only)   (TURN PAGE AND CODE FOR SAME SITUATION)

FIGURE 7.1 Scoring for communication categories of BRACE.

Duration of Observation: 1′ ☐ (1) 1½′ ☐ (2) 2′ ☐ (3) 2½′ ☐ (4) 3′ ☐ (5) 3½′ ☐ (6) 4′ ☐ (7) 4½′ ☐ (8) 5′ ☐ (9) [35]

Time Observation Concluded a.m. (1) p.m. (2) [36] **Cumulative Time**

SIZE OF GROUP OBSERVED: 1 child ☐ (1) 2 ☐ (2) 3 ☐ (3) 4-6 ☐ (4) 7-12 ☐(5) 13-20 ☐ (6) Whole Class ☐ (7) [37]

ADULT ROLE

Check When Subject Is An Adult:	Role of Subject [38] Re: Major Contact	Role of Subject Re: Minor Contacts	Role of Other Adult [46] Re: Subject's Major Contact
Directs Activity Continuously	☐ (1)	1 2 3 4 5 6 7 8 9 [39]	☐ (1)
Gives Substantive Assistance: Contact Initiated By Adult	☐ (2)	1 2 3 4 5 6 7 8 9 [40]	☐ (2)
Gives Substantive Assistance: Contact Initiated By Child	☐ (3)	1 2 3 4 5 6 7 8 9 [41]	☐ (3)
Gives Procedural Assistance Only: Contact Initiated By Adult	☐ (4)	1 2 3 4 5 6 7 8 9 [42]	☐ (4)
Gives Procedural Assistance Only: Contact Initiated By Child	☐ (5)	1 2 3 4 5 6 7 8 9 [43]	☐ (5)
Is Basically A Participant Not A Leader	☐ (6)	1 2 3 4 5 6 7 8 9 [44]	☐ (6)
Observes Activity But Does Not Participate	☐ (7)	1 2 3 4 5 6 7 8 9 [45]	☐ (7)
Is Basically Unrelated To Activity	☐ (8)		☐ (8)

Check When Subject Is A Child:	Role of Teacher [47]	Role of Paraprofessional [48]
Directs Activity Continuously	☐ (1)	☐ (1)
Gives Substantive Assistance: Contact Initiated By Adult	☐ (2)	☐ (2)
Gives Substantive Assistance: Contact Initiated By Child	☐ (3)	☐ (3)
Gives Procedural Assistance Only: Contact Initiated By Adult	☐ (4)	☐ (4)
Gives Procedural Assistance Only: Contact Initiated By Child	☐ (5)	☐ (5)
Is Basically A Participant Not A Leader	☐ (6)	☐ (6)
Observes Activity But Does Not Participate	☐ (7)	☐ (7)
Is Basically Unrelated To Activity	☐ (8)	☐ (8)

CHILD ROLE IN SETTINGS

Form of Activity: [49]

Independent Activity (one child working alone)	☐ (1)
Adult/One Child Activity	☐ (2)
Parallel Activity: (children working individually in close proximity)	
with UNIFORM products	☐ (3)
with DIFFERENT products	☐ (4)
Joint Activity (children working cooperatively)	☐ (5)
Collective Activity (group with single focus)	☐ (6)

Content of Activity: [50/51]

Math	☐ (01)
Language Arts	☐ (02)
Reading	☐ (03)
Creative Writing	☐ (04)
Social Studies	☐ (05)
Science	☐ (06)
Graphic	☐ (07)
Manipulative	☐ (08)
Motor	☐ (09)
Fantasy	☐ (10)
Discussion	☐ (11)
Reading to Children	☐ (12)
Card or Board Games	☐ (13)
Music	☐ (14)
Integrated	☐ (15)
Other	☐ (16)

Base of Activity: [52]

Based on Child/Children's Real Experience	☐ (1)
Not Based on Child/Children's Real Experience	☐ (2)

Nature of Activity: [53]

Abstract Activity	☐ (1)
Manipulative Use of Material:	
Expressive Activity	☐ (2)
Structured Activity	☐ (3)

Choice of Activity: [54]

Adult Planned As To Content and Timing:	
with NO other options	☐ (1)
with other options	☐ (2)
Planned Jointly By Child/Children with Adult	☐ (3)
Self Selected As To Content Only	☐ (4)
Self Selected As To Timing Only	☐ (5)
Self Selected As To Both Content And Timing	☐ (6)
Not Enough Evidence	☐ (7)

Child Communication to Adult: [55]

Mostly Child Initiated	☐ (1)
Mostly Adult Solicited	☐ (2)
Frequently Choral	☐ (3)
Basically Listening	☐ (4)
None (adult present)	☐ (5)
None (no adult present)	☐ (6)

Peer Communication: [56]

Essential or Likely	☐ (1)
Unlikely But Not Prohibited	☐ (2)
Inappropriate	☐ (3)
Prohibited	☐ (4)
Impossible (no other child in close proximity)	☐ (5)

NONVERBAL BEHAVIOR RATINGS (check all that apply)

	To Child	To Group	To Adult
Subject Shows Friendliness, Affection, Support	☐ [57]	☐ [58]	☐ [59]
Subject Shows Hostility, Anger	☐ [60]	☐ [61]	☐ [62]

CHILD INVOLVEMENT IN ACTIVITY [63]

High Attention Or Involvement In Activity	☐ (1)
Mixture Or Moderate Involvement In Activity	☐ (2)
Low Attention Or Involvement In Activity	☐ (3)

BEHAVIOR RATINGS (check and discuss all that apply in the boxes below)

Subject misses opportunity to respond to, clarify, or extend a child's thinking ☐ [64]	Subject copes with stress situation ☐ (1) [65] Subject fails to cope with stress situation ☐ (2)	DESCRIPTION OF ACTIVITY [68/76]
Subject acts in way which contradicts own words ☐ [66]	Subject disrupts ongoing activity ☐ [67]	

Position Of Observation In Sequence ( )[77/78] Card [10] [79/80]

FIGURE 7.2 *Scoring for setting and behavior categories of BRACE.*

The first three dimensions pertain to children's attainment of affective competence. Dimensions 4, 5, and 6 pertain to competence in intellectual areas. Dimensions 7, 8, and 9 refer to social competence. The last two dimensions (10 and 11) have been interpreted as an index of productivity.

Uses of the BRACE

The BRACE has been used for purposes of program analysis, child assessment, and evaluation of program outcomes. Observation data may be used in program analysis to help teachers and paraprofessionals become more knowledgeable about their patterns of communication and management procedures in classrooms. Consequently, they are able to compare their teaching behaviors with those recommended for teachers in the Bank Street Model. The use of the BRACE in the child assessment component of the evaluation system provides valuable information on the language and behavior of children and on the nature of their interactions with peers and adults in learning situations.

The BRACE also has been used in a number of studies to compare events in Follow Through and non-Follow-Through classrooms in the evaluation of program outcomes. Detailed results of these studies are contained in a publication entitled *The BRACE Program for Systematic Observation* (Bowman *et al.*, 1976). Only a brief summary of some representative results can be presented here, due to the limited space available. As compared to non-Follow-Through students, children enrolled in Bank Street Follow Through classrooms have evidenced in numerous studies a significantly greater frequency of the following behaviors: self-activation; ability to reason, draw conclusions from evidence, and state rationales for their actions; ability to formulate and express original ideas, use imagination, and formulate concepts; peer communication; support of peers as learners and as persons; eliciting and extending others' ideas; and complex thought processes.

All or part of the BRACE has been used for data collection in research projects conducted in 34 states, the District of Columbia, Puerto Rico, Australia, Ireland, Israel, and Venezuela. The BRACE has been translated into Spanish and Hebrew. Researchers at Bank Street College have prepared a BRACE Training Package, which includes a manual, scoring forms, films, a system for data analysis, and reports that illustrate the various uses of the instrument. Presentations about the BRACE have been made at many annual meetings of professional organizations, including the National Association for the Education of Young Children (NAEYC), the American Society for Curriculum Development (ASCD), The National Association of Elementary School Principals (NAESP), the Elementary, Kindergarten, and Nursery Educators (EKNE), the American Educational

Research Association (AERA), and the American Orthopsychiatric Association (AOA).

RESULTS OF INDEPENDENT EVALUATION STUDIES

Two researchers conducted independent studies of the effects of the Bank Street Model. Victoria Seitz (1976) of Yale University designed a longitudinal study to investigate the long-term effects of the Bank Street Follow Through Model in Hamden/New Haven, Connecticut. She concluded,

> For certain groups of children (boys in one year's sample, girls in the second year's sample), effects of an intervention program (Hamden/New Haven Follow Through) were seen upon academic performance in mathematics, upon general information scores, and upon Peabody Picture Vocabulary Test IQ scores. Retesting of these children 4-5 years following completion of the intervention showed these children still performing higher than non-intervention children in these areas [p. 1].

In the second study, Joseph C. Grannis (1978) of Columbia University, investigated "Task Engagement and the Consistency of Pedagogical Controls" in 10 classrooms representing various Follow Through models, including 3 classrooms that were sponsored by Bank Street. He reported that children in Bank Street classrooms had the greatest number of "open options" for selecting learning activities. Children in all classrooms selected more open options from enrichment programs (such as science, social studies, art, cooking, fantasy, and play) than from basic skills areas (such as reading, writing, and math). As compared to children enrolled in the other 7 classrooms, those in the 3 Bank Street classrooms selected more open options from basic skills areas and they were more competent in performing self-paced activities. Grannis stated that these findings may have resulted in part because only Bank Street children helped each other frequently in parallel learning activities. These findings appear to support the conclusion that children in Bank Street classrooms develop the values and competencies that enable them to pursue their own cognitive development, cooperation with peers, and self-directed learning activities.

Lessons Learned: Old Concepts Reaffirmed And New Insights Gained

In the Bank Street Developmental–Interaction Approach, the focus is on educating individual children who can live creatively and constructively in a democratic society. The emphasis on educating the whole child necessarily requires a broad definition of both education and the role of schools in society. Therefore, the goals and teaching methods of the Bank Street Model are more comprehensive than those stated in many other Follow Through models. The purpose of this last section of the chapter is to describe some distinctive Bank Street perspectives on a number of important topics in the current national debate on education. Those topics include (a) the purpose of education; (b) accountability and the basics; and (c) the need for new evaluation procedures.

THE PURPOSE OF EDUCATION

It has been stated previously in this chapter that the aims of education necessarily are linked to children's natural patterns of development. Thus, the purpose of education is to stimulate and guide children's progress through successively higher stages of growth. In 1895, Dewey and McLellan stated that the school should be "a vital, effective institution" that engages "in the greatest of all constructions—the building of a free and powerful character" [Dewey & McLellan, 1964, p. 207]." Indeed, schools occupy a crucial role in the pursuit of this desirable goal of human development and education, since they may be used to exert great influence on both the course of human development and on the social organizations that free and powerful people create. Unfortunately, mandated educational procedures often are rigid and complex, thus inhibiting the potential usefulness of the services that schools provide for achieving the goal that Dewey and McLellan stated so eloquently.

Most educators want to understand and respond to the needs of children, and most children are eager to learn and to please their teachers and parents. Nevertheless, many adults and students become frustrated, bored, angry, and alienated by their experiences in schools. There are a number of reasons for the depersonalization that often characterizes educational settings. For example, school personnel at all levels often are assigned to their positions in order to serve organizational purposes, rather than to improve the quality of education. Moreover, decision makers frequently authorize procedural changes with little or no sensitivity to how the needs and feelings of children, their parents, or teachers may be affected. Appropriate inservice training and opportunities for staff development seldom are available for school personnel. Reductions in budgets may contribute to low priorities for and perhaps termination of guidance and other social services. Finally, principals often fail to provide effective educational leadership. For these and other reasons, educators, parents, and children often are disappointed with their school experiences.

The experiences in Follow Through have served to confirm and strengthen the belief that changing and improving school systems from within is extremely difficult. Thus, many of the model sponsors concluded that in order to implement their approaches successfully, they must become change agents in local school districts. As outside facilitators, the sponsors have helped local decision makers to define problems, develop educational services from a consistent set of principles, and evaluate and refine these services. The results of the Follow Through experience suggest that sponsorship can be an effective strategy for planning and implementing change in educational settings and therefore an important resource for personalizing and humanizing schools. Because they are based in universities, colleges, and research institutes, the sponsors and members of their staffs are independent agents. Thus, they are able to engage in cooperative educational planning and goal setting in ways that maintain both the autonomy of local decision makers and the integrity of the sponsors' educational models.

ACCOUNTABILITY AND THE BASICS

Educators at Bank Street College know that one of the priority purposes of schooling is to teach academic skills effectively to children. Nevertheless, they strongly oppose the narrow interpretations that frequently are derived from the current emphasis on concepts such as "accountability" and "back to the basics." An adequate definition of accountability must contain both a description of quality education and a prescription for educating each child accordingly. Teachers should be accountable for meeting the needs of children, for helping them to develop their potential for growth, and for supporting efforts by the children's parents to provide educational opportunities in their homes. When teachers feel accountable to children, classroom environments are more likely to be supportive, children are more likely to be treated with respect as individuals, and teachers are more likely to use functional and integrated methods for teaching subject matter. The teaching of academic skills is important, but *the true basics are the human basics,* which are the broad intellectual, affective, social, and physical competencies that were described previously in this chapter.

Educators at Bank Street believe that some current interpretations of accountability and teaching the basics are not consistent with the needs and best interests of children. For example, there is currently some support for the position that teachers should be held accountable for their students' scores on standardized achievement tests. Indeed, it is essential that students attain mastery of academic skills, but interpretations of accountability that are linked to narrow definitions of curriculum are not likely to support either the immediate or the long-term developmental needs of children. For example, the contention that mastery of academic skills will automatically produce positive self-images and the entire range of coping skills required in a complex society appears simplistic, shortsighted, and misleading. When educators adopt a restricted view of accountability and the basics, they are likely to lose sight of the basic developmental needs of children, including their needs for intimacy and responsiveness in their interactions with adults and peers. Children are naturally inclined to be learners when their school environments are adaptive and receptive to their unique needs and potentials for growth.

THE NEED FOR NEW EVALUATION PROCEDURES

The primary reliance on standardized, paper-and-pencil achievement tests in the national longitudinal evaluation of Follow Through was more appropriate for some models than others. Children enrolled in Follow Through models that are child-centered, individualized, and interactive are at a disadvantage in responding to standardized achievement tests, because they are not accustomed to right–wrong response formats or to working independently for a long period of time in a silent, large-group situation. For example, children in Bank Street classrooms work primarily in small groups where self-pacing and peer communication are encouraged. The rigid structure and time limits imposed in testing situations are unfamiliar to them and may therefore be perceived as intimidating and restrictive on performance. Furthermore, standardized achievement tests not only are inadequate for assessing higher-order cognitive processes, affective processes, and patterns of social interaction, but also they are inadequate for assessing even the academic skills of most young children in kindergarten and first and second grade. In the Bank Street Model, the focus is on developing productive language, oral, and written skills in discourse, and other communication skills. In order to improve the test-taking skills of primary-age students in Bank Street classrooms, it would be necessary for teachers to replace essential content in the curriculum with material that is believed to be comparatively less fundamental—even superficial. There may be some value in the results of achievement tests administered to third graders, since they are beginning to integrate many academic skills. But it probably is more appropriate to administer such tests to fourth graders.

One of the clearest lessons from the Follow Through experience is that new approaches to evaluating educational programs are needed. These efforts should be expanded to include procedures for assessing children's higher-order cognitive processes, affective processes, and oral language competencies. The encouraging results of the work with the BRACE instrument indicates that more attention should be directed toward developing systematic observation procedures that are appropriate for various educational models. In addition, the scope of evaluation efforts should include not only the behaviors of children, but also teacher behaviors, patterns of parent participation, and the characteristics of educational environments.

In conclusion, Follow Through has made it possible for school personnel, parents, sponsors, and officials at federal, state, and local levels of government to form a unique and effective coalition. This coalition has been a major, constructive force for generating hope, commitment, and a sense of purposeful growth in American public education since 1968 and can continue to serve that purpose during the remainder of this century. It is clear that educational achievement and life opportunities for children can be improved when they develop positive attitudes toward learning and a sense of self-direction. The Follow Through experience indicates that such attitudes and capabilities are fostered by well-planned, emotionally rewarding, intellectually stimulating learning experiences and by interaction with teachers and parents who understand each child's special strengths and developmental needs.

Acknowledgements

The authors gratefully acknowledge the participation of large numbers of teachers, principals, parents, and students in the 14 communities served by the Bank Street Follow Through Model. In addition, three members of the Bank Street staff made noteworthy contributions to the completion of this chapter. Carol Weissman analyzed the achievement test data, reported the results, and reviewed portions of the manuscript. Shirley McCall collected and coded some of the achievement test data and most of the BRACE data. Patty O'Brien displayed great patience and competence in performing the technical and support services that were necessary to collect, organize, and process materials through numerous draft versions of the manuscript.

References

Ahr, E. A. *Screening test for academic readiness (STAR)*. Skokie, Ill.: Priority Innovations, 1966.
Bettelheim, B. *The informed heart: Autonomy in a mass age*. Glencoe, Ill.: Free Press, 1960.
Biber, B. Schooling as an influence in developing healthy personality. In R. Kotinsky & H. Witmer (Eds.), *Community programs for mental health*. Cambridge, Mass.: Harvard University Press, 1955. Pp. 158–221.
Biber, B. Integration of mental health principles in a school setting. In G. Caplan (Ed.), *Mental disorders in children*. New York: Basic Books, 1961. Pp. 323–351.
Biber, B., & Minuchin, P. The role of the school in the socialization of competence. In B. C. Rosen, H. I. Crockett, & C. Z. Nunn (Eds.), *Achievement in American society*. Cambridge, Mass.: Schenkman Publishing, 1969. Pp. 260–282.
Biber, B., Shapiro, E., & Wickens, D. *Promoting cognitive growth from a developmental-interaction point of view*. Washington, D.C.: National Association for the Education of Young Children, 1971.
Biber, B. A developmental–interaction approach: Bank Street College of Education. In M. C. Day & R. K. Parker (Eds.), *Preschool in action* (2nd ed.). Boston: Allyn & Bacon, 1977. Pp. 423–459.
Bowman, G. W. Analysis of communication in education. In G. Bayer, A. Simon, & G.

Karafin (Eds.), *Measures of maturation: An anthology of early childhood observation instruments.* Philadelphia, Penn.: Research for Better Schools, 1973. Pp. 551–600.

Bowman, G. W. Team training in systematic observation in the Career Opportunities Program. *Journal of Research and Development in Education,* 1972, *5,* 106–148.

Bowman, G. W., Gilkeson, E. C., Mayer, R. S., & Thacher, S. *Program analysis system in Bank Street Follow Through: Focus on productive language and expression of thoughts and feelings.* Paper presented at the annual meeting of the American Educational Research Association, San Francisco, 1977.

Bowman, G. W., Mayer, R. S., Wolotsky, H., Gilkeson, E. C., Williams, J. H., & Pecheone, R. *The BRACE program for systematic observation.* New York: Bank Street Publications, 1976.

Bruner, J. S. *Toward a theory of instruction.* Cambridge, Mass.: Harvard University Press, 1966.

Buck, J. N. The H–T–P technique: A qualitative and quantitative scoring manual. *Journal of Clinical Psychology,* Monograph Supplement No. 5, 1948.

Buros, O. K. *Mental measurement yearbook.* Highland Park, N. J.: Bryphon Press, 1963.

Cazden, C. *Child language and education.* New York: Holt, Rinehart & Winston, 1972.

Cohen, D. *The learning child.* New York, Pantheon Books, 1972.

Dewey, J., & McLellan, J. The psychology of number (1895). In R. Archambault (Ed.), *John Dewey on education: Selected writings.* New York: Random House, 1964. Pp. 197–217.

Elkind, D. *A sympathetic understanding of the child six to sixteen.* Boston: Allyn & Bacon, 1971.

Erikson, E. H. *Childhood and society.* New York: Norton, 1963.

Gilkeson, E. C. *Teacher–child–parent relationships.* New York: New York State Association for Nursery Education, 1960.

Gilkeson, E. C., & Bowman, G. W. *The focus is on children.* New York: Bank Street Publications, 1976.

Gilkeson, E. C., Sardo, K., & Garfinkle, V. *Reading assessment form.* New York: Bank Street College, 1970. (mimeo)

Goodman, Y., & Burke, C. L. *Reading Miscue Inventory: A procedure for diagnosis and evaluation.* New York: Macmillan, 1972.

Gould, D. *Analysis of Children's Oral Storytelling Task.* Unpublished manuscript, Bank Street College, 1974.

Grannis, J. C. Task engagement in the consistency of pedagogical controls: An ecological study of differently structured classroom settings. *Curriculum Inquiry,* 1978, *8,* 3–36.

Graves, D. *Balance the basics: Let them write.* New York: Ford Foundation, 1978.

Hall, M. *Teaching reading as a language experience: A research perspective* (2nd ed.). Urbana, Ill.: ERIC/IRA, 1978.

Haney, W. *Analysis of interim Follow Through evaluation reports.* Cambridge, Mass.: Huron Institute, 1977.

Heilman, A. *Phonics in proper perspective* (3rd ed.). Columbus, Ohio: Charles E. Merrill, 1976.

House, E. R., Glass, G. V., McLean, L. D., & Walker, D. F. No simple answer: Critique of the Follow Through evaluation. *Harvard Educational Review,* 1978, *48,* 128–160.

Jansky, J., & de Hirsch, K. *Preventing reading failure.* New York: Harper & Row, 1972.

Johnson, O. G. *Tests and measurements in child development: Handbook II.* San Francisco: Jossey-Bass, 1976.

Kohlberg, L., & Mayer, R. S. Development as the aim of education. *Harvard Educational Review,* 1972, *42,* 449–496.

Loban, W. *Language development: Kindergarten–grade twelve.* Urbana, Ill.: National Council of Teachers of English, 1976.

Martin, B. *Report of parent survey: Bank Street Follow Through.* New York: Bank Street College, 1973. (mimeo)

Minuchin, P., Biber, B., Shapiro, E., & Zimiles, H. *The psychological impact of school experience.* New York: Basic Books, 1969.

Mitchell, L. S. *Our children and our schools.* New York: Simon & Schuster, 1950.

Pasamanick, J. *Talkabout: An early childhood language development resource* (Vols. 1 & 2). New York: Center for Media Development, 1976.

Piaget, J. *The child and reality.* New York: Grossman Publishing, 1973.

Ross, S., Zimiles, H., & Gerstein, D. *Children's interactions in traditional and non-traditional classrooms.* Grand Forks, N.D.: University of North Dakota Press, 1976.

Seitz, V. *Long-term effects of intervention.* New Haven, Conn.: Yale University, 1976. (mimeo)

Shapiro, E., & Biber, B. The education of young children: A developmental–interaction approach. *Teacher's College Record,* 1972, 74, 55–59.

Smithberg, L. M. *Checklist of model implementation.* New York: Bank Street College, 1977. (mimeo)

Spache, G. D. *Diagnostic reading scales.* Monterey, Calif.: McGraw-Hill, 1972.

Stauffer, R. *The language experience approach to the teaching of reading.* New York: Harper & Row, 1973.

Stebbins, L. B., St. Pierre, R. G., Proper, E. C., Anderson, R. B., & Cerva, T. R. *Education as experimentation: A planned variation model. Vol. IV–A: An evaluation of Follow Through.* Cambridge, Mass.: Abt Associates, 1977. (Also issued by the U.S. Office of Education as *National evaluation: Patterns of effects,* Vol. II–A of the *Follow Through planned variation experiment series).*

Van Allen, R. *Language experiences in communication.* Boston: Houghton Mifflin, 1976.

Weissman, C. *Technical proposal: Planning information for Follow Through experiments* (RFP 78-101, Section III. Submitted to the U.S. Office of Education, Washington, D.C., August, 1978, by Bank Street College Follow Through.)

Weissman, C. *A compendium of studies on the development of Bank Street Follow Through's Analysis of Children's Oral Storytelling Task (ACOST).* New York: Bank Street College, 1979.

Wilson, R., & Hall, M. *Reading and the elementary school child.* New York: Van Nostrand Reinhold, 1972.

Winsor, C. (Ed.). *Experimental schools revisited: Bulletins of the Bureau of Educational Experiments.* New York: Agathon Press, 1973.

Part III
The Impact of Follow Through

Head Start and Follow Through represent a monumental effort to show that the intellectual competence of vast numbers of children can be altered through mass education.

[BERGAN, J. R., & DUNN, J. A. *Psychology and education: A science for instruction.* New York: John Wiley & Sons, 1976, p. 39.]

The social scientist today relates to institutions less as an uninvolved scholar seeking for general truth, than as a participant whose concerns are close to the concerns of the practitioner.

[GLAZER, N. The disciplinary and the professional in graduate school education in the social sciences. In W. K. Frankena (Ed.), *The philosophy and future of graduate education.* Ann Arbor: University of Michigan Press, 1980. P. 161.]

The coupling between science and application is more reciprocal than many of us have realized. These two elements feed into and correct one another. It is this interactive mode of operation among application, development, and basic science that is to be encouraged for education.

[GLAZER, R. *Adaptive education: Individual diversity and learning.* New York: Holt, Rinehart & Winston, 1977. Pp. 137–138.]

W. RAY RHINE

8

Follow Through: Perspectives and Possibilities

Making Schools More Effective

The focus in this volume has been on describing the origins and innovative characteristics of Project Follow Through, and on portraying the features of five of the most visible and widely implemented models. When the comprehensive history of the project is written, the development of a variety of new, effective educational programs will probably be cited as its most impressive accomplishment. The planned variation experimentation in Follow Through was possible because the model sponsors were willing to persevere for many years in the difficult task of adapting the knowledge and methodology of the social sciences to the complex requirements of a large-scale intervention project. Since 1968, the efforts of sponsors and their coworkers have generated a unique fund of educational knowledge and capabilities that may be used to strengthen education during the remainder of this decade.

This chapter contains perspectives on four major areas of activity in Follow Through and comments on future possibilities. The discussion of planned variation and sponsorship is followed by an examination of issues in "across–models" and "within–model" approaches to evaluation. Then, a number of themes in implementation and dissemination are explored. Finally, recommendations for improving Follow Through are presented.

Planned Variation and Sponsorship

Rivlin (1971) described planned variation and sponsorship in Follow Through as representing an exciting new concept in the federal approach to developing educational programs. Prior to 1968, the USOE had encouraged "random innovation" by funding local school personnel to follow general guidelines in formulating programs, but educators never had been requested to engage in "systematic variation." Thus, John F. Hughes, Director of the Division of Compensatory Education in the USOE, wrote in an interoffice memo dated January 24, 1968, "The decision . . . to initiate a project (Follow Through) which will permit examination of the consequences of different program approaches holds promise of inaugurating what could be literally a new era in governmental support for educational and social ventures, i.e., an era in which the knowledge and technical expertise of the educational specialist, the systems engineer, and the behavioral scientist are brought into harmony with the pluralistic value structure of our society."

The planned variation experimentation conducted in Follow Through has produced a number of practical effects for education, and two of them will be discussed here. First, sponsorship emerged as a new force for change in the nation's schools. Second, the knowledge gained from Follow

Through constitutes an important contribution to the current national debate on education.

A NEW FORCE FOR CHANGE IN EDUCATION

In 1968, sponsorship of numerous local educational programs by proponents of innovative models was a new, untested approach to improving schooling. Few sponsors were prepared for the difficulties they encountered in meeting their responsibilities in Follow Through. They were stressed severely during the completion of tasks such as developing curriculum materials, training teachers, identifying and organizing classroom procedures, and coordinating program initiatives in schools and communities scattered throughout the country. In addition, most sponsors had to acquire much new knowledge about the requirements for conducting long-term intervention studies in public school systems. But the sponsors proved their persistence and adaptability by both defining their responsibilities in specific terms and learning "on the run" to fulfill them.

When the sponsors began working in Follow Through, they knew that providing instructional services was one of their major responsibilities. Nevertheless, many questions about sponsorship remained unanswered. For example, how could a sponsor maintain the integrity of an educational model and yet adapt it to the unique requirements of many communities that differed in population mix, size, and geographic location? Would sponsors' need for control over the formulation and implementation of curriculum, instruction, and evaluation conflict with the requirement that local school personnel and parents have meaningful participation in making decisions about children's education? Would school personnel and parents become engaged in disputes over control of educational decision making? Basically, most of the questions stemmed from one central concern, "What does it mean to intervene on a long-term basis in a public school system?"

The sponsors developed their models during the turbulent years of the late 1960s and early 1970s. The strong emphasis on ethnic minority representation and parent participation in Follow Through often appeared to transform the project into a lightning rod that attracted flashes of energy generated by expressions of discontent and demands for social justice that surged through the larger society. Rivlin and Timpane (1975) described the experiences of the sponsors during the first 5 years of Follow Through as "trials by the sword." Weikart and Banet (1975) wrote that in the midst of conditions that often appeared bewildering and at times overwhelming, "It was a credit to everyone that something happened, a project was born, and people worked extraordinarily hard to fit the pieces into a constantly changing jigsaw puzzle [p. 61]."

Sponsorship represents an important new approach in educational programming, dissemination, and change. Curriculum reform movements in the early 1960s, such as the School Mathematics Study Group (SMSG), usually were limited to the development of curricula for a single subject area such as mathematics or science. But the developers of these curricula were not responsible for implementing them in classrooms. In contrast, Follow Through sponsors derived complete instructional programs from their conceptual orientations. Furthermore, they accepted major responsibilities for planning and monitoring implementation and for program evaluation as well. Hodges, Sheehan, and Carter (1979) wrote, "Sponsors were no longer consultants, nor were they simply advocates. Sponsors were on-the-job adult educators who still had to consult and to advocate, but who could no longer ignore the problems of meshing an idealized program into the real world of schools and communities [p. 668]." The terms that these writers used to describe the activities of sponsors included "catalysts," "burrs under the saddle," and "intellectual brokers." Above all, they were change agents who were intent on using their expertise to help citizens in local communities improve educational services.

Elmore (1976) conducted a detailed study of the organization and management of Follow Through during the period from 1967 to 1974. He concluded that there were elements of "genius" in the "sponsored model mechanism," which he described as "the most important organizational feature of the Follow Through experiment, and the one that deserves closest scrutiny by designers of future experiments [p. 381]." One important advantage of sponsorship is that it enabled federal administrators to delegate the responsibilities for program development and implementation to the sponsors and individuals in local communities. The use of this procedure minimized controversies over control of school programs and yet permitted administrators at federal, state, and local levels to exert necessary influence over the management of Follow Through. In addition, the sponsored model mechanism also enabled most of the sponsors to maintain their presence in local school systems over a period of many years, which was a requirement for the success of the planned variation strategy.

The establishment of long-term working relationships among social scientists who served as model sponsors, school personnel, and parents distinguishes Follow Through from previous federally funded initiatives to improve education. The sponsors were able to develop the productive relationships with members of local communities that were necessary to implement their educational models, primarily due to two reasons. First, the USOE policy of providing joint funding for sponsors and local school systems encouraged cooperative approaches to problem solving. Second, the facilitating orientation of the sponsors enabled them to work with their partners in local communities in ways that avoided many of the divisive strivings and confrontations that probably would have resulted from more arbitrary patterns of interaction. Additional comments on the significance of sponsorship are interspersed in the remainder of this chapter.

CONTRIBUTIONS TO THE NATIONAL DEBATE ON EDUCATION

The knowledge gained from planned variation studies in Follow Through is a timely contribution to current discussions on such issues as the purpose of schooling, the variety of approaches to curriculum and instruction, preservice and in-service education of teachers, parent participation, and the outcomes of education. For example, what purposes should schools serve in our society? Evans and McCandless (1978) state that there is widespread agreement on two sets of goals for schools: (a) skills-training–cultural transmission; and (b) actualization. Citizens, educators, and researchers generally agree that students should become "culturally competent" by learning the basic academic skills in reading, writing, and arithmetic, and that they should acquire knowledge of content areas such as history and literature. There is also a consensus that children's sense of actualization through positive experiences in school should enhance their personal and interpersonal development, as well as their responsiveness in aesthetic areas of life.

The Follow Through sponsors represented in this volume generally agree on the importance of competence and actualization goals, but they disagree on the teaching–learning sequences and processes that are most likely to aid students in reaching those goals. For example, the proponents of the Bank Street Model: A Developmental–Interaction Approach, the High/Scope Cognitively Oriented Model, and the Parent Education Model advocate the guided growth of students through stages of intellectual, social, moral, and affective development as the most desirable approach to facilitating *functional* cultural competence and actualization goals among students. But the sponsors of the Behavior Analysis Model and the Direct Instruction Model emphasize the use of behavioral psychology to improve the effectiveness of teaching basic skills. They contend that students who master academic subjects also probably will develop positive affective characteristics in areas such as self-concept. The differences in stated beliefs about schooling reflect fundamental differences in philosophical and psychological perspectives on the growth, development, and education of children, which have been described by many writers (Bereiter, 1972; Bloom, 1971; Kohlberg & Mayer, 1972). In addition, increasing numbers of individuals believe that educational priorities should include community control of schools, parent participation in educational decision making, teaching ethnic heritage and values, and providing educational and job opportunities for adults.

As the number of stated purposes for schools has proliferated, the number of educational programs purporting to exemplify these purposes also has increased. Typically, advocates of various approaches to education are convinced that the one they represent is superior to all the others. But the amount of research conducted to study the characteristics and effects of the different approaches is small. Consequently, those individuals at federal, state, and local levels who make decisions about the funding of educational programs need more objective, empirical information that can provide a basis for comparing the characteristics and effects of the various programs.

Follow Through is the first longitudinal investigation in which qualified proponents of different perspectives on education have been encouraged to study the outcomes produced by their approaches. Consequently, the research in Follow Through probably has come closer than any previous effort to clarifying the issues that emerge from confrontations among different perspectives on education. This research also has made it possible for the selection of educational programs in local school districts to be based on the results of evaluation. In addition, this research has served to identify important issues on which existing data are meager or altogether lacking. Thus, the planned variation experimentation that has been performed in Follow Through appears to be a significant step toward identifying rational choices in education.

The worth of Follow Through ultimately will be assessed by its influence on educational practitioners and researchers. Consequently, generating a comprehensive literature in order to communicate the knowledge gained and the issues raised in the project should receive a high priority. To date, the literature on Follow Through may be grouped into five categories. These categories, and some contributors to each, are (a) accounts of the social, political, and legislative forces that supported the planning, organization, and continuation of the project (Elmore, 1976; Haney, 1977; Krulee, 1973; Rhine, 1973); (b) reports and critiques on the national longitudinal evaluation (Anderson, St. Pierre, Proper, & Stebbins, 1978; House, Glass, McLean, & Walker, 1978; Kennedy, 1978; Rhine, 1971; Rhine & Spencer, 1975; Soar & Soar, 1972; Stebbins, St. Pierre, Proper, Anderson, & Cerva, 1977); (c) in-depth analyses of the characteristics of a particular Follow Through model (Becker, 1977; Emrick & Peterson, 1980; Gordon & Breivogel, 1976); (d) long-term gains from early intervention (Seitz, Apfel, & Efron, 1978; Seitz, Apfel, & Rosenbaum, 1978); and (e) studies of a number of models to examine and compare advances in specific areas of activity, such as parent participation, teacher education, implementation, curriculum development, sponsorship, or evaluation (Judd, Beers, & Wood, 1975; Rath, O'Neil, Gedney, & Osorio, 1976).

Emrick and Peterson (1980) wrote, "The ambitious and unprecedented Follow Through effort has emerged as a fountainhead for knowledge and experience on how school systems can be improved [p. 1]." Unfortunately, many of the sources of information on the project are technical reports that are not readily available to interested individuals. Therefore, much of what has been learned has not been communicated effectively to educators and researchers. It is essential that this knowledge and experience be incorporated within the mainstream of thought about education in America. Thus, more effort should be directed toward accomplishing this goal.

Encouraging examples of how more information about Follow Through can be disseminated among practitioners and researchers have been provided by Patricia P. Olmsted, Roberta I. Rubin, and their colleagues at the University of North Carolina at Chapel Hill. They recently organized two conferences, "Parent Education and Public Policy" and "Teacher Education: Successes from the Follow Through Experience," which convened in Chapel Hill during March, 1980, and October, 1980, respectively. The information presented by representatives of a number of Follow Through models in both conferences will be published. Hopefully, there will be other similar initiatives that are intended not only to inform participating educators and researchers directly about the accomplishments of Follow Through, but also to stimulate the production of quality literature for a much larger audience. Thus, more information about Follow Through would be available to enrich the current national debate on ways to improve education.

Evaluation of Models

In Follow Through, the resources of the social sciences were directed toward the completion of two central tasks: developing a variety of educational models and evaluating their effects. Many sponsors have made significant progress in developing their models, but evaluating these models has been difficult and often controversial. When the attempt to conduct a large-scale "across-models" evaluation (the national longitudinal evaluation) encountered problems, USOE-Follow Through administrators provided increased funding to assist each sponsor in developing a "within-model" evaluation. Both approaches to evaluation are discussed in this subsection, but most of the comments pertain to the across-models evaluation.

NATIONAL LONGITUDINAL EVALUATION

The cost of this large, across-models evaluation and the controversies provoked by the results are two of the most obvious reasons that it has received so much attention. But a more fundamental reason for the visibility of this effort is the original justification for implementing planned variation and sponsorship in Follow Through. The project survived as one of the last initiatives of the War on Poverty because the planners described it as an "experimental program" that would aid in identifying educational approaches that "work best" with low-income children and their families. Thus, the outcomes of the evaluation of Follow Through were awaited with particular concern by many individuals who hoped that social reforms, which they believed to be justified on political and humanitarian grounds, also could be justified on scientific grounds.

The characteristics of the national longitudinal evaluation are described in Chapters 1 and 4 and elsewhere in this volume. Here, some problems in conducting that study are examined, followed by comments on the results of the national evaluation. Then there is a brief discussion of the evaluations performed by the sponsors of Follow Through models.

Problems in Conducting the National Evaluation

A number of writers have commented on the management, design, and measurement problems in the national longitudinal evaluation (Anderson et al., 1978; House et al., 1978; Rivlin & Timpane, 1975; Tucker, 1977; Wisler, Burns, & Iwamoto, 1978). There is general agreement that results of the national evaluation would have been more meaningful if goals of the Follow Through Project, and of many participating models, had been stated with greater clarity; each model had been subjected to a pilot phase of implementation and pretesting in a few communities before a large-scale field test was begun; children had been chosen randomly for enrollment in Follow Through and comparison classrooms; and more attention had been devoted to studies of implementation. Writers disagree on whether limits should have been placed on the duration of the study and the number of models included; the degree of similarity or dissimilarity of children's characteristics in Follow Through and comparison classrooms; and the appropriateness of instruments, classification of models, units of analysis (child, classroom, school, or community), data analysis techniques, and interpretation of results.

The reasons for the problems in the national evaluation are complex. Several members of the USOE attributed some responsibility to management deficiencies within their own agency. Wisler et al. (1978) wrote, "USOE must shoulder much of the blame for not clearly laying down the conditions of the experiment. Some conditions must be satisfied before a field experiment begins; one of the most important of them is agreement on the outcomes to be measured . . . the early difficulties with the Follow Through evaluation can be traced to lack of sound and strong direction from USOE . . . [p. 179]." According to Tucker (1977), "USOE's administrative role, from the perspective of this writer, was less than effective due in part to ambiguities about the goals of the program within USOE . . . [p. 12]."

Some writers who criticized the national longitudinal evaluation also praised it. House *et al.* (1978) commented, "The lessons that can be learned from the Follow Through evaluation are valuable ones [p. 130]." Tucker (1977) described the Follow Through evaluation as

> the most elaborate undertaken in social research. Were it not for the persistence of many people in and out of government our level of awareness relative to the difficulties of planned variation experiments in a social setting would not have been enhanced. What has been learned should place future researchers well ahead of the game. The ones who have endured this attempt will approach new challenges with a lot more savvy [p. 17].

Kennedy (1978) stated, "Because of the size, scope, and duration of the study, and because the study approximated an experimental paradigm, it was an important educational study. In spite of its weaknesses in design, the Follow Through study has produced new knowledge and has raised significant new research issues [p. 11]." Anderson *et al.* (1978) believe that their work in analyzing the data in the national longitudinal evaluation represents

> one of the first large-scale studies to use a strategy of multiple parallel analyses, incorporating several methodological innovations and addressing many problems that are usually ignored in evaluation research. We have achieved some success, for example, in obtaining answers to the following questions. Did differential attrition of pupils from treatment and comparison groups bias the evaluation results? Were the results dependent on the particular covariate set used? Did violation of the assumptions of the primary analyses bias the evaluation results? Would a nonparametric analysis yield results leading to the same conclusions as the results of the primary analyses? Did using the child as the unit of analysis invalidate our statistical-significance tests? Did the inclusion of pupils with particularly low pretest scores bias the results? Finally, did the use of a fallible covariate bias the results [p. 169–170]?

Many problems in the national longitudinal evaluation were linked to management decisions that federal project administrators made about the design of the project during the period from 1968 to 1971. Often these decisions were attempts to reconcile conflicts between those individuals who adhered to the rules of social science methodology and others who followed a pragmatic, political, bureaucratic approach to decision making.

For example, the goals of a scientific study should be coherent and stated clearly. However, the agencies that provided funding and administrative services for the project could not agree on whether the highest priority was to use parent activism in schools to stimulate community social action, to provide educational and other social services for children and members of their families, or to conduct an experimental study in order to obtain useful information for educational policymakers, planners, and administrators. The attempt to pursue these three disparate goals simultaneously often did produce uncertainty and confusion in planning and conducting many activities, including the national evaluation.

Another source of difficulty was the "let-all-flowers-bloom" approach to including a large number of model sponsors. It had the advantage of enlarging the project's public constituency and contributing to the organization of a national coalition that was extremely effective in increasing political support for Follow Through. But limiting participation to a smaller number of sponsors would have been more compatible with the requirements of an experimental study. The initial plan was to evaluate each model by administering two types of items: those that were appropriate for all models and those that were distinctive to each particular model. Whether this approach could have been applied successfully to a number as large as the original 13 models is doubtful; the initial plan clearly was not practicable when the number of models was increased to 22. [Tucker (1977) recommended that in future planned variation experiments, the number of sponsored models should be limited to less than 6.]

Elmore (1976) identified a third source of problems in Follow Through. He cited a substantial amount of primary documentation to support his thesis that ranking USOE–Follow Through administrators during the period from 1967 to 1971 had a number of competing motives. For example, he concluded that their interest in approximating a truly experimental approach in the project clearly was subordinate to their primary goal, which was to keep alive the possibility that eventually Follow Through could be converted into a major national service project on the scale of Head Start. Elmore contended that,if the federal administrators had placed a higher priority on defending the experimental characteristics of the project, they might have prevented some flaws in the design of the national longitudinal evaluation.

In defense of the federal project administrators, perhaps it should be stated that departures from accepted experimental procedures in Follow Through often were influenced by strong bureaucratic resistance to the enactment of a rigorous methodology. But focusing on methodological issues restricts perception of many essential components of planned variation experimentation in Follow Through. For example, large-scale social experiments are not laboratory studies conducted by a single experimenter; they are complex organizations of numerous groups of individuals who may agree on general statements of goals but often disagree intensely on specific objectives and means for achieving them. Thus, organizing and administering social intervention studies usually require much attention to building and maintaining effective coalitions of stakeholders whose interests often are diverse and competitive. In such circumstances, there may be frequent conflicts between methodological requirements and administrative requirements in decision making.

The politicization of evaluation research when it becomes an extension of public policy in large-scale intervention projects has been described by Timpane (1970), Weiss (1970, 1972), Rossi and Williams (1972), and others. Perhaps this politicization is inevitable and should be expected, since representative government itself thrives on, indeed depends on, advocacy and competition among groups to aid in the process of establishing priorities and allocating resources. The challenge for social scientists, then, is to learn how to use their expertise and professional skills with as much objectivity as possible in politicized environments.

It may be argued that the history of the national longitudinal evaluation is important because it illustrates the full array of problems that occurred when social scientists applied their disciplines within the context of complex political and bureaucratic pressures. Many individuals who participated in the national longitudinal evaluation believe that knowledge about these challenges now may be used to strengthen the contribution of the social sciences to the national welfare. Since the problems that occurred in Follow Through also may be encountered in future attempts to implement planned variation and sponsorship, anticipating them should make their resolution more likely. A number of recommendations for a new series of planned variation experiments are presented in the section entitled "Future Possibilities for Follow Through."

Results of the National Longitudinal Evaluation

There are a number of reports on major analyses of data from the national longitudinal evaluation of Follow Through (Bereiter & Kurland, 1978; Emrick, Sorensen, & Stearns, 1973; House *et al.*, 1978; Kennedy, 1978; Rhine, 1971; Stebbins *et al.*, 1977). Chapter 4 of this volume contains another report, which is based on the use of the Index of Significant Outcomes (ISO). Some of the reports have included noncognitive data, but the greatest emphasis has been on reporting the results of analyses of achievement test data from the administration of the Metropolitan Achievement Test (MAT). The MAT subtests include language, reading comprehension, math computations, and math problem solving.

One general conclusion is stated consistently in reports on the results of the national longitudinal evaluation. *The highest mean scores on the MAT subtests were attained by students enrolled in two models, the Direct Instruction Model and the Behavior Analysis Model.* Bereiter and Kurland (1978) wrote, "These two models are at or near the top on every achievement variable, regardless of the covariates used [p. 5]." Perhaps one of the more important observations on the pattern of findings was reported by Kennedy (1978): "Almost every model demonstrated lower effects in these two large cities [New York and Philadelphia] than in other project sites. It seems likely that these large urban systems are more impermeable than other school systems. The Direct Instruction Model was a notable exception to that rule, and did not display any diminution of effects in the large cities [p. 10]."

A number of qualifications may be stated for most interpretations of results from the national longitudinal evaluation. For example, speculations about the reasons for the comparatively higher performance on the MAT subtests by children enrolled in the Direct Instruction Model and the Behavior Analysis Model include the following:

1. Perhaps the sponsors of these models may have pursued more aggressive and effective implementation procedures. Or, in highly structured models such as the Direct Instruction Model and the Behavior Analysis Model, teachers may be able to learn their roles and responsibilities more quickly. In less-structured models, whose sponsors emphasize active–experiential learning, participation by children in planning their curriculum, and the role of teachers as facilitators of children's growth, effective inservice training of teachers may be more complex and therefore require more time.

2. The MAT may represent traditional goals of education, not the goals sought in innovative or unique curricula. The sponsors of the two highly structured models emphasize the teaching of basic skills and rote learning of factual knowledge of the sort measured by the MAT. Other sponsors may have devoted more time to accomplishing "nontraditional" educational goals, such as autonomy, problem-solving skills, productive language, and so forth. They also emphasize the learning of functional knowledge and its use in solving meaningful problems, which are not measured by the MAT. Thus, in many models the educational goals may have differed substantially from those measured by the MAT.

3. Students in highly structured classrooms may have had more experience during their daily classroom routines in working with both the workbook format of the test materials and the paper-and-pencil mode of response to the test items.

Gage and Berliner (1979) stated that the results of the Follow Through evaluation support the conclusion that basic academic skills were taught more effectively to Follow Through children through the use of direct instruction methods. Nevertheless, for many individuals the question of which Follow Through models "work best" has not been satisfactorily resolved by the results of the national longitudinal evaluation of Follow Through. The issue of "specificity of effects" among Follow Through models is a lively concern for many sponsors, and its implications for comparisons among the various models will receive further attention in the following discussion of the sponsors' evaluations.

SPONSORS' EVALUATIONS

Initial discussions about evaluation in Follow Through centered on the national longitudinal evaluation. Many sponsors wanted to use data from that source to monitor their program development activities, but they also complained that important educational goals in their models were not assessed by instruments included in the national evaluation. Evaluation researchers at the Stanford Research Institute attempted to select or develop appropriate instruments for the various models. Eventually, the sponsors themselves were invited to develop new approaches to assessing their models.

The range of measurement activities initiated by the sponsors is illustrated by the new instruments described in this volume. Attempts to measure many behaviors that occur in educational settings included parent teaching styles, home environments, vertical diffusion, children's non-cognitive characteristics, levels of consumer satisfaction, and patterns of interaction between teachers and students in classrooms. Examples of representative new instruments are Analysis of Children's Oral Story Telling Task (ACOST), Annual Consumer Evaluation (ACE), Behavior Ratings and Analysis of Communication in Education (BRACE), Checklist of Model Implementation (CMI), Home Environment Review (HER), Productive Language Assessment Tasks (PLAT), Systematic Classroom Observation of Pupil Experience (SCOPE), Systematic Classroom Observation of Teacher Experience (SCOTE), and Taxonomy of Classroom Behavior (TCB).

The major emphasis in sponsors' evaluations has been on developing observation scales. Evaluators have employed process data obtained from these instruments to study implementation procedures, the behavior of individual teachers and students, and outcomes of instructional programs. Many new instruments were included in the in-service education of teachers. Some sponsors taught teachers to administer checklists and observation schedules and to use this information for improving their own observation skills and for appraising their success in implementing a sponsor's model in the classroom.

The sponsors' evaluations of their own models have had a number of important effects. For example, evaluation has been established as an essential component of each model. Therefore, the entire Follow Through Project has been placed within a framework of accountability, one created by the sponsors themselves. In addition, there has been progress in obtaining more explicit definitions of desirable parent, teacher, and student behaviors, as well as such concepts as autonomy, productive language, and problem solving. These advances have increased possibilities for sponsors to use information gained through studies of implementation and evaluation to improve learning opportunities in classrooms and homes.

Another effect of the sponsors' evaluations has been to underscore a major challenge in planned variation experimentation—how to conceptualize and conduct a "fair" evaluation of models represented by different values and educational goals. If the intent of Follow Through had been to improve children's achievement test scores on the Metropolitan Achievement Test, the results of the national longitudinal evaluation would have established unequivocally that the Direct Instruction Model and the Behavior Analysis Model were the "winners." But the stated purpose of the project was to identify educational approaches that "work best" with low-income children and their families.

Disagreement among the sponsors on the definition of what works best in the education of children is at the center of the specificity of effects issue in Follow Through. The intent in the Direct Instruction Model and the Behavior Analysis Model was to improve students' rates of learning basic academic skills. But the priority goals of other models included increasing parents' teaching skills, increasing students' active–experiential learning, and increasing teachers' abilities to serve as facilitators of children's learning. Apparently, a number of Follow Through sponsors generally were successful in accomplishing their priority educational goals, which represent those sponsors' views on the characteristics of instructional approaches that work best. From this perspective, there were many "winners" in Follow Through.

Mosteller (1975) recognized that there are problems in comparing models when each one must be evaluated on a number of distinctive variables. He contended that ultimately decisions on educational approaches that work best must be made by consumers of educational services. He wrote,

> In the end, society should decide what it wants, not the researchers, not the teachers, and not even a panel of experts, though all these groups may advise—society must look at what happened to the several variables and notice

what progress has been made in such areas as language, mathematics, self-concepts, skills, ability to deal with people, or civil rights attitudes. After reviewing that whole set of measures, society will have to·assign weights to each measure or assess them as a whole, even though different progress is being made in different models at different times and on different variables. This is routine evaluation practice in other areas of inquiry. The idea that different schools produce different products is not an upsetting or new idea [p. 171].

Studies of Implementation

The discussion on implementation is presented in two parts: (a) the need for implementation studies in Follow Through; and (b) new conceptual approaches.

NEED FOR IMPLEMENTATION STUDIES IN FOLLOW THROUGH

During the past decade, many writers have recommended more research to examine the implementation of innovative programs within school districts. For example, Gross (1979) contended that many "failures" of educational innovations probably resulted from ineffective implementation, since evaluators "generally ignore whether an innovation has been implemented when they compare the performance of 'experimental' and 'control' groups. . . . Unless the innovation has been actually implemented, however, questions about its effectiveness are inappropriate [p. 6]." Similarly, Williams (1975) wrote, "Both the systematic study of implementation and the development of better techniques for such study are needed. . . . the most basic descriptive information is in short supply [p.565]."

Researchers who studied Follow Through often commented on the urgent need for investigations of implementation in order to clarify the meaning of evaluation data. For example, Emrick et al., (1973) wrote, "We view as one of the most serious gaps in the total Follow Through evaluation the absence of operational statements of the specific manipulations the sponsor intends to implement and the actual materials and procedures he employs to effect this implementation [p. 315]." Since local conditions were known to vary, sometimes dramatically, and to often have strong effects on the enactment of models, the outcomes of studies of a model's effectiveness could be interpreted with greater confidence when the degree of fidelity in program implementation was known.

There have been two general approaches to studying the implementation of Follow Through models. First, independent researchers used observation scales to analyze the implementation characteristics of selected models (Soar & Soar, 1972; Stallings, 1973). Second, implementation studies were initiated in many Follow Through models. The sponsors of the five models described in this volume directed substantial effort toward studying the characteristics of their programs in a number of communities to aid them in developmental activities. The chapters on Follow Through models contain descriptions of many new procedures that were developed to analyze and improve components of models, including materials, in-service training of teachers, participation of parents, consumer satisfaction, and instruction of students.

NEW CONCEPTUAL APPROACHES

Studies of implementation in Follow Through have been aimed at understanding and solving the daily problems that emerged from efforts to develop new educational models. But some sponsors are beginning to examine recent conceptual advances in the study of implementation. For example, Chapter 5 in this volume contains a brief description of three of the eight Levels of Use (Hall, Loucks, Rutherford, & Newlove, 1975; Loucks, Newlove, & Hall, 1975). This is an approach that focuses on stages of change that occur in the perceptions of individual practitioners during different phases of implementation. In addition, the Stages of Concern questionnaire was developed by Hall, George, and Rutherford (1977). Fullan and Pomfret (1977) described the two instruments developed by Hall and his colleagues as representing "the most sophisticated and explicit conceptualization of 'the fidelity' orientation to assessing degree of implementation [p. 355]."

The innovative approaches developed by Hall and his colleagues are among several recent promising advances toward the study of implementation. For example, intensive case studies have been used to study the dynamics of innovative change efforts in education (Bentzen, 1974; Gross, Giacquinta, & Bernstein, 1971; Sarason, 1971; Smith & Keith, 1971). Herriott and Gross (1979) believe that case studies can be used to examine the complex interactions between the characteristics of educational settings and the behaviors of internal and external change agents during the adoption of new practices and programs. Another promising formulation has been proposed by Fullan and Pomfret (1977). These writers suggest that changes during the implementation of an innovation occur along five dimensions: subject matter or materials, organizational structure, role–behavior, knowledge and understanding, and value internalization.

John A. Emrick has investigated implementation processes in five recent studies of educational dissemination and change (Emrick & Peterson, 1978); in the National Diffusion Network (NDN) (Emrick, 1977; Emrick &

Peterson, 1977); and in Project Follow Through (Emrick & Peterson, 1980). The goals of the latter study were (a) to examine events and issues that characterized the implementation of the Direct Instruction Follow Through Model in 42 kindergarten and first-grade classrooms located in seven schools in the City Schools of San Diego, California; and (b) to develop methodologies for assessing the status and quality of implementation. In this study, the researchers drew from a number of conceptual approaches that were described in the preceding two paragraphs in formulating their definition of three levels of implementation variables:

1. Macro variables—decision processes, control processes, obtaining resources, and relations with the environment
2. Intermediate variables—supervisory expectations, standard operating procedures, communication flow, work group norms, and technical characteristics of the innovation
3. Individual variables—knowledge, attitudes, and behaviors

The results of Emrick and Peterson's study illustrate the intricate pattern of interactions that occurs when an external change agent, in this instance a Follow Through sponsor, initiates new educational practices in a large urban school system. The results of the study indicate both the impressive accomplishments of the Follow Through intervention and the numerous challenges that had to be resolved during the adaptation of the Direct Instruction Model to the requirements of the host schools. Emrick and Peterson believe that there is increasing awareness of the complexities of program implementation and change in educational settings and that additional implementation studies are needed to produce information that may be used to improve the quality of learning and instruction in classrooms.

Dissemination of Follow Through Programs

The purpose of Follow Through was to develop effective educational programs. But the initial planning for the project did not include procedures for disseminating the elements of effective programs to other individuals who might want to replicate them in their schools. During the early 1970s, a number of individuals in the USOE recognized the need for mechanisms that could be used to identify and disseminate exemplary programs in many areas of education. To serve these purposes, the Joint Dissemination Review Panel (JDRP) and the National Diffusion Network (NDN) were created. Thus, dissemination of Follow Through programs has occurred through the JDRP and the NDN, as well as through direct contacts between sponsors and school districts.

JOINT DISSEMINATION REVIEW PANEL (JDRP)

Some characteristics of the JDRP were described previously in Chapter 5, "The Behavior Analysis Model." The JDRP originated in the fall of 1972, largely through the efforts of John W. Evans, then the head of the USOE's Office of Planning, Budgeting, and Evaluation (OPBE). The intent was to identify successful local educational programs that had been developed with federal funds and to evaluate them against rigorous performance criteria. The Dissemination Review Panel, which consisted of 11 ranking officials from the USOE, was established to validate "exemplary" programs. In 1975, the panel was expanded to include 11 additional members selected from the National Institute of Education (NIE), and the group was renamed the Joint Dissemination Review Panel (JDRP).

Members of the JDRP are selected for their expertise in research and evaluation and for their general ability to make informed judgments about the effectiveness of educational programs. Decisions about effectiveness are made on the basis of the quality of the evidence, the magnitude of educational effects, and the likelihood that the intervention can be replicated at other sites. The specific criteria used by the JDRP were described by Tallmadge (1977). Examples of positive effects that may establish the effectiveness of educational programs include improvements in academic achievement, attitudes toward school, self-concepts, mental or physical health, and quality of instruction in classrooms. According to Tallmadge (1977), "Positive impacts are probably as numerous and as varied as the goals of our educational system [p. 3]."

NATIONAL DIFFUSION NETWORK (NDN)

Educational programs that are validated as exemplary by the JDRP are disseminated to local schools through a nationwide system known as the National Diffusion Network (NDN). The purpose of the NDN is to provide the information, materials, and technical assistance that educators need to incorporate effective practices into their own schools. A complete listing of all exemplary programs disseminated through the NDN is presented in *Educational Programs That Work*, which is published annually by the Far West Laboratory for Educational Research and Development. The sixth edition (1979) of this publication listed approximately 250 exemplary programs in these twelve categories:

1. Adult Education
2. Alternative Schools/Programs
3. Bilingual/Migrant Education
4. Career/Vocational Education
5. Early Childhood/Parent Readiness/Parent Involvement

6. Environmental Education/Science/Social Science
7. Organizational Arrangements/Administration
8. Preservice/In-service Training
9. Reading/Language Arts/Mathematics
10. Special Education/Learning Disabilities
11. Special Interests: Arts/Communication/Technology
12. Special Interests: Gifted and Talented/Health/Human Behavior/ Physical Education

Among the first group of Follow Through programs submitted to the JDRP, 22 were validated as exemplary. Fourteen of these exemplary programs were produced by the five models described in this volume. Exemplary programs are supported as Follow Through Resource Centers by USOE–Follow Through. All Follow Through Resource Centers have facilities for responding to inquiries and receiving visitors. All have descriptive materials and all offer training at their own site or will negotiate off-site training. There have been no additional submissions of Follow Through programs to the JDRP since the initial applications in 1977. The consensus among Follow Through sponsors is that many other programs now would be able to meet the JDRP criteria for validation as exemplary programs.

The NDN provides resources for dissemination of exemplary programs through developer/demonstrators and state facilitators. The term *developer/demonstrators* refers to the exemplary programs that receive federal funds to provide training, materials, and technical assistance to those who adopt the programs. State facilitators (one or more in each state, the District of Columbia, Puerto Rico, and the Virgin Islands) are individuals who are employed by the USOE to serve as facilitators between the developer/demonstrators and individuals in school districts who want to adopt the exemplary programs. Thus far, there have been approximately 10,000 "adoptions" of the programs judged as exemplary by the JDRP. In addition, NDN has funded a number of studies in order to develop more knowledge about the conditions that assist or hinder the dissemination of exemplary programs to new educational environments.

DISSEMINATION BY SPONSORS

Some dissemination activities by sponsors have been unintentional; others have been intentional. Many sponsors have suspected that a number of their practices were assimilated informally by teachers of students enrolled in non-Follow-Through comparison classrooms, thus possibly reducing the group mean differences in performance reported in the national longitudinal evaluation. If indeed this happened, it illustrates a form of unintentional dissemination that sponsors would have preferred to avoid.

Nevertheless, this type of dissemination probably cannot be prevented entirely in large-scale, longitudinal intervention research.

Most of the intentional dissemination activities by sponsors have occurred through the adoption of their models in additional schools located within communities in which Follow Through services already were provided. However, some sponsors have been requested to implement their models in new communities. For example, educators in the public schools of San Diego, California, requested in the fall of 1978 that the Direct Instruction Model be implemented in many classrooms. Similarly, the sponsor of the Behavior Analysis Model was requested in the fall of 1979 to initiate that model in many classrooms in the public schools of Compton, California. Reportedly, representatives of other communities recently have contacted a number of Follow Through sponsors to express interest in adopting their models.

Future Possibilities for Follow Through

Planning for Follow Through generally has focused on developing practical solutions for immediate problems. The atmosphere that prevailed during the late 1960s and during the decade of the 1970s required that attention be focused primarily on maintaining the survival of the project. These circumstances seldom permitted the luxury of quiet contemplation and reflection on alternative futures for Follow Through. But recent meetings and discussions have led to major decisions on Follow Through. The purpose of this section is to summarize a number of recommendations from model sponsors, representatives of the USOE, and representatives of the NIE that may shape the future of the project.

RECOMMENDATIONS FROM THE MODEL SPONSORS

The literature on Follow Through contains a number of recommendations that sponsors have made for improving the planning and evaluation of the project. The chapters in Part II of this volume contain many suggestions, and they will not be repeated here. Some suggested changes from other sources pertain to one or a few details, but others encompass comprehensive plans for the use of planned variation and sponsorship to initiate a new series of experiments in Follow Through. Four sets of recommendations are described here.

Rivlin and Timpane (1975) commented that Follow Through sponsors and other participants in the conference on sponsorship and planned variation conducted by the Brookings Institution generally endorsed the basic intent of Follow Through. The conferees supported the development of more effective educational programs by commiting the necessary time and resources in a systematic approach, one that would include a major effort to develop new instruments for measuring both educational processes and products. There also seemed to be a consensus for the assignment of approximately equal numbers of communities to each model, the placement of each model in communities representing each major geographic region of the country, and the enrollment of students from all major population groups in each model. In addition, they supported the random assignment of students to Follow Through and comparison classrooms, and the inclusion of fewer models to ensure that only those that had reached a mature stage of development were included in the study.

Weikart and Banet (1975) described a procedure for developing educational models that consisted of five phases: research, development, demonstration, dissemination, and regional dissemination and implementation. These authors wrote, "In future studies it is essential that adequate time and resources be devoted to preparation. The more complex the proposed ideas and the more they diverge from current practice, the greater the need for preparation [p. 76]." Weikart and Banet proposed the use of planned variation and sponsorship to create new educational systems that would more effectively stimulate and support the growth and development of children. They urged that Follow Through be perceived as "just the beginning of an extended process of development, not a completed demonstration of what exists [p. 76]."

Becker, Gersten, and Carnine (1979) examined a number of design and measurement issues in research on Follow Through. They contended that the knowledge gained during the Follow Through experience provides the basis for a new, improved series of demonstration studies conducted within the format of planned variation and sponsorship. The purpose of these studies would be to identify effective systems of curriculum design, classroom management, and parent involvement. Thus, recommendations were presented on such basic issues as the design of studies, analysis of data, and measurement of outcomes.

Becker and his associates believe that planned variation studies can be improved in a number of ways. But they reluctantly concluded that an improved quasi-experimental design may be the most feasible approach within the political, social, and ethical constraints on the random assignment of children to treatment and comparison groups, which would be required in a true experimental design. They suggested separate analyses of data, using first the *child* and then the *site* as units of analysis. Other priority goals were to minimize the need for covariate adjustments by ensuring that students in Follow Through and comparison classrooms have similar characteristics and to improve the measurement of students' entry skills.

Finally, they proposed a plan for increasing knowledge about implementation by employing checklists and direct observation to study both the quantity and quality of instruction provided for Follow Through and comparison groups.

In their discussion of outcome measures, Becker's group advised that all instruments should be examined carefully in order to verify that content, test formats, and instructions were appropriate for the students tested. Their choice for the basic achievement test battery was the Metropolitan Achievement Test (MAT), including the reading instructional tests, even though they criticized some characteristics of the MAT. They recommended that additional instruments be selected to measure oral reading, reading comprehension, and word knowledge. For the measurement of oral language, self-concept, and written expression, they urged the use of a number of innovative techniques in small-scale longitudinal studies.

Finally, a recent monograph entitled *Follow Through: Forces For Change in the Primary Schools* (Hodges, Branden, Feldman, Follins, Love, Sheehan, Lumbley, Osborn, Rentfrow, Houston, & Lee, 1980) contains the perceptions and recommendations of Walter L. Hodges, the sponsor of a Follow Through model, and a number of his associates. These writers believe that Follow Through is an extremely important source of information about problems and possibilities for success in the pursuit of more effective educational programs for young children, and particularly for children from low-income backgrounds. Because their comments about the Follow Through experience and their recommendations for the future represent many years of participation in the project, as well as careful reflection on their observations, a number of their conclusions are summarized here:

1. Information from the Follow Through models now can be used to provide more complete descriptions of effective educational programs for economically disadvantaged children.
2. Instructional models alone cannot enable economically disadvantaged children to perform academically at levels attained by their more advantaged peers.
3. More field studies should be conducted to examine the processes that promote educational change.
4. Communities differ radically, and more information is required to identify and index these differences.
5. Broader outcome criteria should be included in evaluations.
6. Both internal and external evaluation should be included in educational intervention studies and funded adequately.
7. The field of educational evaluation would benefit from a systematic collation, field testing, and validation of some promising research instruments developed in various Follow Through models.

8. Information on the characteristics of school systems should be analyzed prior to the initiation of intervention programs.
9. Model sponsorship should be studied carefully.
10. Communities should receive information and assistance that aid in selecting appropriate educational models.
11. Much more information should be obtained on patterns of parent involvement and ways to encourage it.
12. It is possible to develop support for parent participation in education at state and local levels.
13. Participation by state educational agencies in educational changes in schools should be more meaningful.
14. Federal decision making concerning large-scale projects such as Follow Through should be more timely and better coordinated.

RECOMMENDATIONS FROM THE U.S. OFFICE
OF EDUCATION (USOE)

During the 6-month period from March to August in 1979, a team from the Office of the USOE Assistant Secretary for Planning and Evaluation (ASPE) conducted an exploratory evaluation of Follow Through. The effort was directed by Joseph S. Wholey, Deputy Assistant Secretary for Evaluation, and it was intended to assist in formulating new objectives, regulations, and directions for the project (Wholey, 1979). The exploratory evaluation included an extensive review of documentation on Follow Through and interviews with congressional staff members, the USOE policymakers, Follow Through staff members, and Follow Through sponsors. Conclusions drawn from the findings of the exploratory evaluation included (a) the status quo in Follow Through was unsatisfactory; (b) members of Congress perceived Follow Through as a service program with a social-action–antipoverty emphasis and close links to Head Start, but the USOE policymakers believed that the emphasis should be on research, development, and demonstration; (c) existing procedures for producing effective services and knowledge about effective services were inadequate; and (d) changes were required in the organizational structure and staffing of the project.

The members of the exploratory evaluation team identified five possible policy–management objectives for Follow Through:

1. Compliance with laws and regulations
2. Providing specific services according to specific performance standards
3. Achieving intended results of services for children, parents, and school systems
4. Producing knowledge about successful early childhood educational practices and educational change strategies

5. Disseminating–diffusing knowledge about early childhood practices and educational change strategies

After the findings, policy–management objectives, and information options were reviewed by the USOE policymakers and managers, the exploratory evaluation team then outlined implications of a number of policy, management, and evaluation options. Wholey (1979) listed the following implications as among the most important.

1. Service Projects
   a. Continue most existing Follow Through Local Education Agencies (LEAs) at least through school year 1981–1982 or 1982–1983, although programs would be permitted to select another sponsor (or be self-sponsored).
   b. Formulate performance indicators (types of evidence) on which Follow Through service programs would be held accountable.
   c. Develop and implement a system for monitoring the compliance status and the performance of Follow Through service programs on the performance indicators.
   d. Cease funding State Education Agencies to provide technical assistance for Follow Through programs.

2. Knowledge Production (Pilot) Projects
   a. Allocate 15–20% of Follow Through appropriations for a series of studies/experiments designed to develop and test new approaches or methods that further the development of low-income children and their parents. The goal of such studies/experiments should be to produce knowledge about early childhood educational practices and change strategies that are effective in producing intended results in children, parents, and schools systems; and the conditions under which those practices and change strategies are effective.

3. Dissemination
   a. The primary vehicle for dissemination of successful practices should be the National Diffusion Network (or another agency-wide program).
   b. Since the dissemination objectives should not be stressed in Follow Through, less funding will be required for resource centers.

4. Evaluation and Research Activities
   a. Develop and implement performance indicators and systems for monitoring the compliance status and performance of Follow Through service programs in producing intended services and

achieving intended results for children, parents, and school systems.
  b. Perform a short-term evaluation to assist in selecting "effective" sponsors and designing a system for monitoring sponsor performance.
  c. Design and evaluate pilot projects/experiments to test the effectiveness of alternative approaches for achieving intended results for children, parents, and school systems.
  d. Perform a short-term evaluation to assist in selecting "effective" resource centers and designing a system for monitoring the performance of resource centers.

5. Staffing
  a. Establish a research and evaluation branch in Follow Through that would assume responsibility for all research, evaluation, and monitoring activities whether conducted in-house or through grantees or contractors.
  b. Add a total of five positions and two or three Intergovernmental Personnel Act detailees to the Division of Follow Through in order to expedite the new emphasis on outcome-oriented program performance and evaluation of pilot projects.
  c. Monitor/evaluate Follow Through service programs on the new set of performance indicators/performance standards, evaluate pilot projects/experiments, and use data on program effectiveness in refunding decisions in order to improve the effectiveness of Follow Through.

After the Assistant Secretary for Education, Mary Berry, met with representatives of a number of the USOE agencies in August, 1979, to consider the new array of objectives for Follow Through, the following decisions were made

1. Follow Through should achieve two sets of objectives: service and knowledge production. Approximately 80% of local programs should be managed to provide effective comprehensive services to Follow Through children. Approximately 20% of the local programs should be managed to produce knowledge about services that are effective.
2. A task force should be created to help begin the implementation of the new directions for Follow Through.
3. LEAs should be permitted to select the sponsor of their choice.
4. A research and evaluation branch should be established within Follow Through, but overall evaluation of the project must be conducted by an outside agency.

5. A number of studies should be conducted to:
   a. Develop and test performance indicators and systems for monitoring the compliance status and performance of Follow Through programs.
   b. Design studies/pilot projects/experiments to (a) test the relative effectiveness of alternative parental involvement strategies; (b) test successful Follow Through models in entire schools (K–6); (c) test successful models at alternative levels of services; and (d) test the ability of local education agencies to design, implement, and evaluate effective Follow Through programs.
   c. Accelerate collection of information on Follow Through resource centers.
6. The task force should recommend roles and funding levels for state education agencies and resource centers.

The members of the Follow Through Task Force confirmed and restated the overall objectives of Follow Through: "The Follow Through program of the future will have two clear purposes: first, it will provide effective comprehensive services to poor children in elementary schools in the nation: and second, it will fund activities designed to improve our understanding of the ways that comprehensive educational services may be most effectively delivered to financially needy elementary school children [Wholey, 1979, p. 1]." The members of the task force also made the following recommendations: (a) Service project sponsors should continue to receive funds only if they are selected by a certain minimum number of LEAs (the minimum number was to be established by USOE–Follow Through); (b) in unsponsored programs, funds will be provided directly to the LEA to construct its own Follow Through model and contract for teacher training and other assistance from any source; (c) state education agencies may participate in pilot projects but should no longer be funded to provide technical assistance and conduct dissemination activities; and (d) the role of resource centers should be modified to provide information to the LEAs (especially Follow Through LEAs) about LEA effectiveness in providing both instructional and noninstructional services, and the funding level for resource centers should be reduced.

Late in September, 1979, the USOE executive deputy commissioners met with the members of the Follow Through Task Force and approved their recommendations on Follow Through service programs, knowledge production (pilot) programs, sponsors, unsponsored programs, State Education Agencies, and resource centers. Many of these recommendations are now in preliminary stages of implementation. For example, the Applied Management Sciences, Inc. (AMS) in Silver Springs, Maryland, contracted with USOE–Follow Through to develop a range of performance indicators and to construct a monitoring system for the project. In addition, the Boone-Young Associates in Washington, D.C., contracted to develop a range of models for implementation and evaluation of pilot programs.

RECOMMENDATIONS FROM THE NATIONAL
INSTITUTE OF EDUCATION (NIE)

In June, 1980, representatives of the NIE agreed with representatives of the USOE Assistant Secretary for Elementary and Secondary Education (ASESE) to accept $400,000 in Follow Through funds for the purpose of planning a new series of research and pilot activities (Schiller, Stalford, Rudner, Kocher, & Lesnick, 1980). This initiative is part of the new knowledge production component in Follow Through that now receives 20% of the total project funding. (The plan to restructure Follow Through by allocating 80% of Follow Through funds to *service* and 20% to *knowledge production* was stated in the preceding section on "Recommendations from the U.S. Office of Education"). Completion of the new research and pilot project activities will require at least 5 years and a projected total expenditure of approximately $12½ million. Under the terms of the NIE–ASESE agreement, NIE will provide a range of leadership and technical services to produce knowledge for use in improving the effectiveness of local Follow Through programs. This section contains preliminary descriptions of the research strategy for the new endeavor, two principal strands of activities and plans for implementing them, and uses of information obtained from knowledge production activities in Follow Through.

Research Strategy

The intent in the two strands of new activities is to establish in Follow Through a capability for continuous renewal through the infusion of new research based knowledge to improve services. Eventually, the project may serve as a source of new concepts and validated educational practices that will be used to stimulate desirable changes in a variety of federal educational projects. The plan is to develop and study several cohorts of new Follow Through approaches that may be implemented over a period of 5-10-20 years. Representatives of stakeholder groups including parents, teachers, administrators, researchers, Follow Through staff members, Follow Through model sponsors, and State education agencies will participate at all levels of discussion and decision making on policy, planning, and operations. The new effort will be managed as part of NIE's Teaching and Learning Program, which is currently directed by Lois-Ellin Datta. Support services will be provided through other NIE programs including Educational Policy and Organization, and Dissemination and Improvement of Practice. In the remainder of this section, current descriptions of the two principal strands of activity and plans for implementing them will be presented.

Strand One: The First Wave of New Approaches

The goal in Strand One is to develop the guidelines for funding the first cohort of new Follow Through approaches to be tested beginning in the 1981–1982 school year. Rather than developing new curricula or theories about learning, which occurred during the previous history of Follow Through, the purpose of the first wave of new Follow Through approaches is to improve schooling by identifying and solving the obstacles to effective management of instruction and implementation of educational programs. Thus, the intent in the first strand of activities is to build upon the successes of existing Follow Through models in such areas as direct instruction, humanistic, and bilingual approaches to education. The results of cross-model analyses and studies of implementation may prove useful. In addition, the first cohort of new approaches probably will incorporate such research-based concepts and practices as engaged academic-learning time, reduction of distractions in daily schooling routines, and effective parent involvement in children's learning. Specific examples of processes that may be used to generate the first cohort of innovative approaches are included in the following list:

1. Increasing instructional time and reducing distractions in Follow Through classrooms through improved management services.
2. Preparing teachers to better utilize existing knowledge, including cooperative in-service agreements between schools and teacher education programs in colleges and universities.
3. Systematically involving parent and community groups in planning and conducting Follow Through programs.
4. Using information systems, including testing and evaluation results, to develop improved diagnostic and prescriptive information for use in Follow Through classrooms.
5. Coordinating services for students that are provided both by Follow Through and other sources in local communities.

The plan for expediting the first strand of activities includes obtaining the best available thinking about the value of Follow Through and desirable characteristics of new approaches. This goal has been pursued by commissioning a series of 26 focused papers on a variety of pertinent topics, and by planning several conferences and public hearings in which many other individuals will express their beliefs about and aspirations for Follow Through. The topics that will be addressed in the papers and conferences include the following:

1. Knowledge gained from previous efforts to systematically change and improve the management of instruction in Follow Through classrooms and other settings.
2. Promising new approaches to systematically changing and improving the management of instruction, including evidence for their effectiveness and descriptions of their primary characteristics.
3. Contextual analyses of influences that either may support or oppose systematic change and improvement in the management of instruction and suggestions for using this information in the preparation of the new models.
4. Procedures for incorporating parents and other stakeholder groups in communities in the development and implementation of systematic change efforts.
5. Procedures for assessing the implementation and outcomes of efforts to improve schools at both local and national levels.
6. Procedures for developing new models for changing school environments that may be disseminated successfully in many other locations.

The authors of the 26 commissioned papers represent the range of stakeholder groups in Follow Through. These papers will be designed either to assist in the selection and programmatic development of new Follow Through approaches or to assist in methods for studying and evaluating the new approaches. Two conferences will be convened to discuss programmatic issues, one in Philadelphia and the other in Portland, Oregon. A third conference on methods for studying and evaluating the Strand One approaches will convene in Austin, Texas. Approximately 100 individuals will participate in these conferences. The participants in the conferences will include authors of the commissioned papers and many other individuals who possess the range of knowledge about Follow Through that is required to analyze and synthesize the content of the various papers into a specific plan for initiating the first cohort of new models in fiscal year 1981.

Strand Two: The Search for Future Follow
Through Approaches

The goal in Strand Two is to develop the second wave of approaches for eventual funding in 5 years. Many possibilities for improving educational services for low-income children through programmatic activities in Follow Through will be explored. In addition to inquiries in educational areas of practice and research, other areas of inquiry may include: the effects of media and new technology on early childhood learning; broad societal and environmental influences on early childhood education; and extrapolation of results of research in many areas for use in formulating new Follow

Through approaches. The products eventually will be channeled into the construction of practical approaches for improving schooling and learning. Thus, the guiding intent is to identify as much creative and productive thinking as possible, and then assess the feasibility of converting these ideas into operational programs. Finally, Strand Two also will encompass opportunities for conducting research on issues of persisting interest in Follow Through. These issues include methodological questions, program topics, and secondary analyses of existing Follow Through data.

The plan for implementing Strand Two includes commissioning a total of 18 individuals to write papers on relevant topics. These authors also will serve as resources at two conferences in which alternative futures for Follow Through will be explored. One conference will convene in Atlanta, Georgia; the location of the second conference has not yet been established.

The intent in Strand Two is to examine many promising ideas at the beginning and to identify the most productive through successive waves of review. In addition to educators and researchers, the participants in Strand Two will include representatives from the arts, journalism, public interest groups, and the media. The 18 papers commissioned for Strand Two will be designed for two purposes—to assist in developing future program approaches and to assist in identifying required supporting research. Issues that will be addressed in these papers include:

1. The use of media for learning in schools and homes and the implications for future Follow Through approaches.
2. A view of ghettos as examples of "extreme environments" for learning and implications for future Follow Through programs in inner-city areas.
3. Effects of single-parent families and other social changes, including increased numbers of working mothers, on desirable characteristics of curricula, social development of students, and extended services of Follow Through programs.
4. Potential uses of technology in Follow Through classrooms during the 1980s.
5. Characteristics of home learning and parent education approaches that should be expanded in Follow Through programs during the 1980s.

In addition to the commissioned papers and conferences planned for Strand Two, an advisory group of nine qualified individuals will consult with NIE and USOE–Follow Through during fiscal year 1981. The members of this group will work in part independently on different alternatives for future Follow Through approaches and also meet as a group to critique and organize their ideas. They also will serve as resources at the Strand Two conferences on alternative futures for Follow Through, which will be attended by a total of approximately 50 persons. Another conference on future needs for supporting research, particularly focusing on methodological procedures for studying the new Follow Through approaches and conducting associated research, will convene approximately 25 participants in Pittsburgh. The proceedings of Strand Two conferences will be published and thus available to the public.

Uses of New Research

There are many potential uses for new information generated through Strand One and Strand Two activities. For example, the information will be disseminated through existing Follow Through programs and resource centers, the National Diffusion Network (NDN), Teacher Centers, Teacher Corps, and other appropriate channels. The information also may be used to improve existing Follow Through programs, to plan new concepts of operational programs, and to assist in the search for acceptable performance indicators for Follow Through models. The management focus of the Strand One approaches should assist in developing procedures that improve the prospects for disseminating Follow Through models on a large scale. The efforts to improve instruction by removing barriers to effective teaching and learning also may reduce the cost of implementing the Follow Through models in local communities. The results of the supporting research on methodological and programmatic issues and the secondary analyses of Follow Through data will benefit directly the present models as well as the new approaches.

The content of this chapter indicates that Follow Through has become a unique national resource for developing effective educational programs for children in kindergarten and the primary grades. The project now appears to represent the nation's most aggressive and tenacious commitment to reforming elementary education and to educating children from low-income families more effectively. The current enthusiasm for identifying and reinforcing successes in the project and for developing new directions is further evidence of the remarkable vitality and capacity for adaptation that has characterized the entire history of Follow Through.

References

Anderson, R. B., St. Pierre, R. G., Proper, E. C., & Stebbins, L. B. Pardon us, but what was the question again? A response to the critique of the Follow Through evaluation. *Harvard Educational Review*, 1978, *48*, 161–170.

Becker, W. C. Teaching reading and language to the disadvantaged: What we have learned from field research. *Harvard Educational Review*, 1977, *47*, 518–543.

Becker, W. C., Gersten, R. M., & Carnine, D. W. *Design and measurement issues in Follow Through research.* Unpublished manuscript, University of Oregon, 1979.

Bentzen, N. M. *Changing schools: The magic feather principle.* New York: McGraw-Hill, 1974.

Bereiter, C. Schools without education. *Harvard Educational Review,* 1972, *42,* 390–413.

Bereiter, C. A., & Kurland, M. *Were some Follow Through models more effective than others?* Paper presented at the annual meeting of the American Educational Research Association, Toronto, Ontario, Canada, March 1978.

Bloom, B. S. Learning for mastery. In Bloom, B. S., Hastings, T. J., & Madaus, G. F. (Eds.), *Handbook on formative and summative evaluation of student learning.* New York: McGraw-Hill, 1971. Pp. 43–57.

Elmore, R. E. *Follow Through: Decision making in a large-scale social experiment.* Unpublished doctoral dissertation, Harvard University, 1976.

Emrick, J. A. *Evaluation of the National Diffusion Network. Vol I: Findings and recommendations.* Menlo Park, Calif.: Stanford Research Institute, 1977.

Emrick, J. A., & Peterson, S. M. *Evaluation of the National Diffusion Network. Vol. II: Technical supplement.* Menlo Park, Calif.: Stanford Research Institute, 1977.

Emrick, J. A., & Peterson, S. M. *A synthesis of five recent studies in educational dissemination and change.* San Francisco: Far West Laboratory for Educational Research and Development, 1978.

Emrick, J. A., & Peterson, S. M. *San Diego implementation study: Case study report and first-year measurement development.* Los Altos, Calif.: John A. Emrick & Associates, 1980.

Emrick, J. A., Sorensen, P. H., & Stearns, M. S. *Interim evaluation of the national Follow Through program 1969–1971.* Menlo Park, Calif.: Stanford Research Institute, 1973.

Evans, E. D., & McCandless, B. R. *Children and youth: Psychosocial development* (2nd ed.). New York: Holt, Rinehart & Winston, 1978. Far West Laboratory for Educational Research and Development. *Educational programs that work.* San Francisco: 1979.

Fullan, M., & Pomfret, A. Research on curriculum and instruction implementation. *Review of Educational Research,* 1977, *47,* 335–397.

Gage, N. L., & Berliner, D. C. *Educational psychology* (2nd. ed.). Chicago: Rand McNally, 1979.

Gordon, I. J., & Breivogel, W. G. (Eds.). *Building effective home/school relationships.* Boston: Allyn & Bacon, 1976.

Gross, N. Basic issues in the management of educational change efforts. In R. E. Herriott & N. Gross (Eds.). *The dynamics of planned educational change.* Berkeley, Calif.: McCutcheon, 1979. Pp. 20–46.

Gross, N., Giacquinta, J. B., & Bernstein, M. *Implementing organizational innovations: A sociological analysis of planned educational change.* New York: Basic Books, 1971.

Hall, G. E., George, A. A., & Rutherford, W. L. *Measuring stages of concern about the innovation: A manual for use of the SoC questionnaire.* Austin: University of Texas, R & D Center for Teacher Education, 1977.

Hall, G. E., Loucks, S., Rutherford, W. L., & Newlove, B. W. Levels of use of the innovation: A framework for analyzing innovation adoption. *Journal of Teacher Education,* 1975, *26,* 52–56.

Haney, W. *The Follow Through evaluation: A technical history* (Vol. 5). Washington, D.C.: Office of Education, U.S. Department of Health, Education, and Welfare, 1977.

Herriott, R. E., & Gross, N. (Eds.). *The dynamics of planned educational change.* Berkeley, Calif.: McCutchan, 1979.

Hodges, W. L., Branden, A., Feldman, R., Follins, J., Love, J., Sheehan, R., Lumbley, J., Osborn, J., Rentfrow, R. K., Houston, J., & Lee, C. *Follow Through: Forces for change in the primary schools.* Ypsilanti, Mich.: High/Scope Press, 1980.

Hodges, W. L., Sheehan, R., & Carter, H. Educational intervention: The role of Follow Through sponsors. *Phi Delta Kappan*, 1979, *60*, 666–669.

House, E. R., Glass, G. V., McLean, L. D., & Walker, D. F. No simple answer: Critique of the Follow Through evaluation. *Harvard Educational Review*, 1978, *48*, 128–160.

Judd, D. E., Beers, C. D., & Wood, S. E. *Project Follow Through: A description of sponsor implementation processes*. Portland, Oreg.: Nero and Associates, 1975.

Kennedy, M. M. Findings from the Follow Through planned variation study. *Educational Researcher*, 1978, *7*, No. 6, 3–11.

Kohlberg, L., & Mayer, R. S. Development as the aim of education. *Harvard Educational Review*, 1972, *42*, 449–496.

Krulee, G. K. *An organizational analysis of Project Follow Through, final report*. Evanston, Ill.: Northwestern University, 1973. (ERIC Document Reproduction Service No. 093 446).

Loucks, S. F., Newlove, B. W., & Hall, G. E. *Measuring levels of use of the innovation: A manual for trainers, interviewers, and raters*. Austin: University of Texas, R & D Center for Teacher Education, 1975.

Mosteller, F. Comment by Frederick Mosteller. In A. M. Rivlin & P. M. Timpane (Eds.), *Planned variation in education*. Washington, D.C.: Brookings Institution, 1975. Pp. 169–172.

Rath, S. W., O'Neil, B. B., Gedney, B. D., & Osorio, J. *Follow Through: A resource guide to sponsor models and materials*. Portland, Oreg.: Nero and Associates, 1976.

Rhine, W. R. *Issues in noncognitive measurement: Interim report on Project Follow Through 1969–1971*. Menlo Park, Calif.: Stanford Research Institute, 1971, 403 pp.

Rhine, W. R. Strategies for evaluating Follow Through. In R. M. Rippey (Ed.), *Studies in transactional evaluation*. Berkeley, Calif.: McCutchan, 1973. Pp. 157–180.

Rhine, W. R., & Spencer, L. M. Effects of Follow Through on school fearfulness among black children. *Journal of Negro Education*, 1975, *44*, 446–453.

Rivlin, A. M. *Systematic thinking for social action*. Washington, D.C.: Brookings Institution, 1971.

Rivlin, A. M., & Timpane, P. M. (Eds). *Planned variation in education*. Washington, D.C.: Brookings Institution, 1975.

Sarason, S. B. *The culture of the school and the problem of change*. Boston: Allyn & Bacon, 1971.

Schiller, J., Stalford, C., Rudner, L., Kocher, T., & Lesnick, H. Plans for Follow Through research and development. Interdepartmental memorandum, National Institute of Education, Washington, D.C., October 1, 1980.

Seitz, V., Apfel, N. H., & Efron, C. Long-term effects of early intervention: The New Haven Project. In B. Brown (Ed.), *Found: Long-term gains from early intervention (AAAS 1977 Selected Symposium 8)*. Boulder, Colo.: Westview Press, 1978. Pp. 79–109.

Seitz, V., Apfel, N. H., & Rosenbaum, L. K. Projects Head Start and Follow Through: A longitudinal evaluation of adolescents. In M. J. Begab, H. Garber, & H. C. Haywood (Eds.), *Proceedings of the NICHD Conference on the Prevention of Retarded Development in Psychosocially Disadvantaged Children, July, 1978*. Madison, Wis.: University of Wisconsin Press, 1979.

Smith. L. M., & Keith, P. M. *Anatomy of educational innovation: An organizational analysis of an elementary school*. New York: John Wiley & Sons, 1971.

Soar, R. S., & Soar, R. M. An empirical analysis of selected Follow Through programs: An example of a process approach to evaluation. In I. J. Gordon (Ed.), *Early childhood education* (seventy-fifth yearbook of the National Society for the Study of Education). Chicago: University of Chicago Press, 1972. Pp. 229–259.

Stallings, J. A. *Follow Through program classroom observation evaluation*. Menlo Park, Calif.: Stanford Research Institute, 1973.

324   W. RAY RHINE

Stebbins, L. B., St. Pierre, R. G., Proper, E. C., Anderson, R. B., & Cerva, T. R. *Education as experimentation: A planned variation model. Vol. IV-A: An evaluation of Follow Through*. Cambridge, Mass.: Abt Associates, 1977. (Also issued by the U.S. Office of Education as *National evaluation: Patterns of effects*, Vol. II-A of the *Follow Through planned variation experiment series*.)

Tallmadge, G. K. *Ideabook: The Joint Dissemination Review Panel*. Mountain View, Calif.: RMC Research Corporation, 1977.

Timpane, P. M. Educational experimentation in national social policy. *Harvard Educational Review*, 1970, *40*, 547–566.

Tucker, E. *The Follow Through planned variation experiment: What is the pay-off?* Paper presented at the annual meeting of the American Educational Research Association, New York, April 1977.

Weikart, D. P., & Banet, B. A. Model design problems in Follow Through. In A. M. Rivlin & Timpane (Eds.), *Planned variation in education*. Washington, D.C.: Brookings Institution, 1975. Pp. 61–77.

Weiss, C. A. The politicization of evaluation research. *Journal of Social Issues*, 1970, *26*, 57–68.

Weiss, C. A. *Evaluating social action programs*. Boston: Allyn & Bacon, 1972.

Wholey, J. S. *New directions for Follow Through*. Interdepartmental memorandum, U.S. Office of Education, Washington, D.C., December 14, 1979.

Williams, W. Implementation analysis and assessment. *Policy Analysis*, 1975, *1*, 531–566.

Wisler, C. E., Burns, G. P., & Iwamoto, D. Follow Through redux: A response to the critique by House, Glass, McLean, and Walker. *Harvard Educational Review*, 1978, *48*, 171–185.

W. RAY RHINE　　　**9**

Follow Through: Implementation Awareness and Its Implications

The decision to organize this volume was based on two premises: (*a*) the linkage between the social sciences and education that flourished during the past 2 decades is likely to continue; and (*b*) many of the problems, accomplishments, and future prospects of this initiative are illustrated in the events of Project Follow Through. The lessons learned through both the implementation of Follow Through and the preparation of this book about the project have implications for two central issues that are discussed in this chapter—utilization of the social sciences in problem-focused research and production of literature on large-scale intervention research.

325

Utilization of the Social Sciences

Follow Through represents a major example of the utilization of the social sciences in a national research and development project. Consequently, the experiences of the professionals who worked in that effort are pertinent to a discussion of conflicting perspectives on appropriate roles for social scientists in problem-focused research. The use of the strategies of planned variation and sponsorship to strengthen future efforts to solve social problems also will be considered in this section.

ROLES FOR SOCIAL SCIENTISTS IN
PROBLEM-FOCUSED RESEARCH

How should social scientists contribute in efforts to solve social problems? Moynihan (1970) cited difficulties that social scientists encountered in attempts to use their expertise in community action programs during the 1960s. He described certain problems that occurred during that effort and cautioned that similar results from further ill-advised attempts might persuade social scientists to conclude that the world is indeed a poisoned oyster. He stated that conceptual schemes derived from the social sciences often were weak and therefore susceptible to becoming pawns in the struggle between competing social and political ideologies. Accordingly, Moynihan recommended that social scientists restrict themselves to the task of evaluating social change. Writing from the perspective of a sociologist, Hauser (1970) also recommended that social scientists limit their involvement in efforts to solve social problems. He advised that they resist the temptation to turn activist and, instead, devote their energies to research, the construction of theory, and the development of their disciplines.

Other social scientists contended that the positions stated by Moynihan and Hauser were unnecessarily conservative. For example, Rossi (1970) and Rossi and Williams (1972) insisted that social scientists could bridge the gap between research findings and practical applications of social value. These writers proposed that social scientists gain greater "implementation awareness" by formulating, critiquing, and evaluating alternative solutions to social problems. Glaser (1973) also supported the participation of social scientists in a broad range of social problem-solving activities. He stated, "The behavioral and social sciences are at a point in their development where they absolutely require the direction and disciplining effects that come from contact with real-world problems [p. 557]." Glaser affirmed that the relation between basic science and technology is reciprocal rather than a one-way street, and he urged that the functions of application, technology, and basic science be perceived as interactive and mutually interdependent.

Glazer's (1974, 1980) views on the utilization of the social sciences are similar to those expressed by Rossi, Williams, and Glaser. Glazer (1980) wrote, "They [social scientists] have moved from a stance toward the world that emphasizes detached observation and analysis . . . to a stance in which observation is increasingly mixed with participation, analysis with judgment and advice [p. 161]." He described three areas of change that have contributed to a rapid increase in "professional" interests in the social sciences: (a) many government-funded intervention programs are influencing social change processes; (b) the pace of change has become more rapid in institutions such as schools, hospitals, prisons, and social work agencies; and (c) social scientists have become more interested in examining, critiquing, and shaping social change processes.

Glazer believes that the fundamental reorientation of the social sciences has enhanced both disciplinary and professional interests. One effect is a reduced effort to create "theoretical" knowledge, which contributes solely to the development of disciplines, and an increased effort to create "practical" knowledge, which is intended for use in solving social problems. Another effect is a heightened inclination to approach the study and amelioration of social problems on their own terms and to consider the total context of these problems in order to contribute analyses and recommendations that are more relevant to the missions of social institutions. He wrote, "I think a necessary adaptation of the social science disciplines to a changing world is taking place . . . . On the whole this is a healthy development [p. 171]."

The experiences of social scientists who worked in Follow Through provide strong support for the views stated by Rossi, Glaser, and Glazer. To be sure, difficult problems were encountered in Follow Through, but the participants displayed remarkable tenacity and resourcefulness in developing working solutions. These accomplishments both contributed to the strength of educational programs in local communities and reinforced the confidence of the participants that through their cooperative efforts they would be able to identify and surmount future obstacles. The social scientists who contributed to this volume probably are representative of the total group of their colleagues who participated in Follow Through. Taken as a whole, their perceptions of what has happened in the project are positive and optimistic. Generally, the participants appear to share a strong conviction that productive efforts to explore the practical applications of the social sciences in education should be continued.

POTENTIAL OF PLANNED VARIATION AND SPONSORSHIP

The use of planned variation and sponsorship in Follow Through has yielded results that are important for their own value, but the significance of these two strategies extends beyond the project for two reasons. First, they represent a framework for using knowledge about human and organizational behavior in problem-focused research to improve the development and delivery of a broad range of services to increase life opportunities for citizens. Second, planned variation and sponsorship are relatively inexpensive procedures for systematically examining new projects on a small scale. The results of these studies then may be used to decide whether the projects should be made available for wider dissemination.

Many social scientists have believed that their disciplines were social innovations that, when they eventually reached a sufficient level of maturity, could be useful for improving the social conditions in which people live. The conduct of Follow Through during the past 12 years indicates that in an imperfect way that goal has been achieved. Social scientists who formerly had been employed in universities and research centers made long-term commitments to working with citizens in local communities. The successful use of planned variation and sponsorship in Follow Through suggests that these strategies could be used to study alternative models at all levels of education.

The revised, scaled-down version of Follow Through was launched in 1968 as an accommodation to the end of an era of strong support for the development of new, large-scale social intervention projects. Thus, planned variation and sponsorship were, in part, an adaptation to new budgetary restraints that eventually resulted in a lower level of funding for efforts to change and improve schools and other social institutions. During the decade of the 1970s, the administrators of these projects adapted their goals to the realities of reduced funding, closer scrutiny by congressional committees of the results from such projects, and increased attention to cost-effectiveness analyses within a framework of accountability.

Current political, social, and economic trends do not appear to support an increase in the allocation of funds for the initiation of untested social intervention projects, especially for large-scale projects of the sort that were begun in the 1960s. Nevertheless, the need to make schools and other social institutions more effective and to adapt them to changing requirements will continue and perhaps become even more urgent during the years ahead. Therefore, efforts to change and improve these social institutions probably will continue in some form. In these circumstances, the use of planned variation and sponsorship to plan, implement, evaluate, and refine social-change initiatives on a small scale before they are made available for dissemination appears to have many advantages.[1]

[1]Federal funding for "directed development" projects such as Follow Through, that are characterized by sponsors who engage in longitudinal program development activities, has diminished in recent years in favor of "local problem-solving" approaches for changing and

Production of Literature on Large-scale
Intervention Research

During the past 20 years, our country has invested a significant amount of resources in large-scale educational intervention projects. As Horowitz and Paden (1973) predicted, "The final question must eventually be asked: can children be brought to a productive level of functioning by [intervention] programs? If the answer is yes, we keep on doing what we are doing. If the answer is no, the social and educational implications are enormous [p. 385]." The final decision on the value of projects such as Follow Through will be strongly influenced by the literature about these endeavors. A comprehensive literature, not simply descriptive statements of a polemical or hortatory nature, is required if the results of problem-focused research projects are to be properly critiqued and assimilated into the mainstream of thinking about the reform and improvement of education and effective utilization of the social sciences. The sources cited in this volume indicate progress toward generating a comprehensive literature on Project Follow Through. This book represents an effort to contribute to this literature by providing statements from a number of model sponsors, information that previously had not been available.

---

improving educational services provided by schools. One major contribution to this change in federal policy is the strong preference for local problem-solving initiatives that researchers employed by the Rand Corporation (Berman & Berman, 1977, 1978; McLaughlin, 1975; Berman & Pauly, 1975; and Greenwood, Mann, & McLaughlin, 1975) stated in their series of reports, "Federal Programs Supporting Educational Change (FPSEC)." But Datta (1980) concluded after a careful analysis of these reports, "rather than being evidence against the components of the directed development approach (e.g., educational technologies, experts, additional resources, and specific focus) as they are so often claimed to be, the FPSEC data actually present a case against local problem-solving approaches to change [p. 102]."

Apparently, comprehensive educational models produced through systematic development and evaluation procedures, such as those represented in Follow Through, were not included in the FPSEC studies. Datta stated that recent reports from a number of projects conducted in the Bureau of Education for the Handicapped, the Fund for the Improvement of Postsecondary Education, Experience Based Career Education, and the state facilitator networks of the National Diffusion Network (NDN) "are suggesting considerable impacts of change programs varying substantially in directedness [p. 114]." I concur with Datta's conclusion, "Learning from others and 'inventing it here' could both have their honorable place in educational improvement [p. 115]."

Actually, the use of metaphors such as "directed development" or "local problem solving" may be inappropriate and misleading in discussions about Project Follow Through. The model sponsors, educators, parents, and other participants in local communities are more likely to perceive their decade of cooperation as an example of the meshing of the knowledge, skills, and emergent leadership of many individuals in sustained efforts to improve the effectiveness of schools. Thus, the events of Follow Through indicate that "directed development" and "local problem solving" are complementary, not opposing, strategies for changing and improving educational environments.

Many of the central issues that emerged during the completion of this volume are likely to surface in any attempt to describe programmatic activities and outcomes of large-scale longitudinal research and development projects in education. Thus, perhaps some comments about the experiences in preparing this volume will encourage discussion about ways to increase the amount, variety, and quality of published materials on large-scale research projects. Three issues will be discussed here—selecting the audience for the volume, organizing the content of the volume, and editing the manuscripts for the chapters on Follow Through models.

SELECTING THE AUDIENCE

The content of written materials on complex research and development projects must be selected carefully to meet the needs of the intended audience. For example, many technical reports were prepared to describe progress in developing the Follow Through models and the results of the national longitudinal evaluation. These reports assisted federal administrators, members of Congress, and congressional staff members in making decisions about funding activities in the project. However, these reports frequently had limited value for professional educators and researchers, audiences whose distinctive needs for information about Follow Through have received limited attention.

The effort to organize a volume on a large-scale project such as Follow Through also must be disciplined by selecting a target audience, both to sharpen the focus of the content and to identify potential readers. The task in the preparation of the present volume was to decide whether it would be designed for educational practitioners or researchers. Eventually, the decision was to address the interests of members of the research community and their students. But the authors concluded that the content also probably would appeal to educational practitioners and policymakers who valued a research orientation to the improvement of education.

To some extent, the needs of educational practitioners for knowledge on the application of the information gained through the various Follow Through models is being met by the activities of both the Follow Through resource centers and the National Diffusion Network (NDN). But a number of Follow Through sponsors also are preparing manuscripts for books intended primarily for teachers, administrators, members of local boards of education, parents, and other interested citizens. Eventually, appropriate materials may be available for each of the audiences interested in Follow Through.

The value of large-scale projects such as Follow Through and their contributions to the national welfare can be communicated to the general public through a variety of publications that indicate how the professional and research interests of education and the social sciences have been strengthened. Public knowledge about the worth of such efforts is crucial if they are to receive continued support and funding. Obviously, claims of accomplishment for large-scale intervention research projects should be scrutinized. Nevertheless, the maintenance of high standards of critical analysis and objectivity also may be accompanied by the recognition of successes when they occur, particularly when the results encourage optimism about future prospects for additional advances. But the production of more literature on the multifaceted characteristics of projects such as Follow Through is essential if their strengths, weaknesses, and prospects for future success are to be properly understood.

ORGANIZING THE CONTENT

I contended previously in Chapter 1 that reports by evaluation researchers often fail to include significant information about the accomplishments of large-scale intervention research. But, for a variety of reasons, the individuals who develop intervention programs also seldom provide comprehensive written accounts of their efforts. Indeed, when the production of this volume began, a search did not discover satisfactory examples of previous literature that effectively communicated comprehensive reports about research and development activities in large-scale longitudinal research. Thus, it was necessary to generate an acceptable format for reporting the results of the model sponsors' work in Follow Through.

Three decisions were especially important in shaping the content of the present volume. The first key decision was to organize a volume comprised of chapters written by a number of authors who had extensive experience in Follow Through, rather than a volume authored by one or a few individuals. Source materials on Follow Through models were not readily available, since most of the information, including evaluation data, was unpublished and in the files of the program sponsors. There were many obstacles, logistical and otherwise, to gaining access to these materials, reviewing their contents, and selecting appropriate information for inclusion in descriptions of the models. In addition, statements about the models appear to have more credibility when they are presented by individuals who created them.

The second key decision concerned the perspective, or format, that authors would adopt for describing the Follow Through models. One option was to employ a retrospective, "stream of consciousness" approach to selecting the most important among the multitude of moment-by-moment events that occurred during "a decade in the life of a Follow Through model." The second option was to describe the operational characteristics of the various service components in each model. The third option, and the one finally chosen, was to depict each Follow Through model as a quasi-experiment in education and to focus on the origin, rationale, implementation, evaluation, and lessons learned from a decade of developmental work on each of the five models.

The third key decision was on the guidelines that authors would follow in selecting the content of sections that composed the manuscripts on the models. The basic issue was whether the same set of guidelines would be used in preparing the descriptions of all models, or whether a different set would be generated for each model. After considerable discussion, it was agreed that: (a) the primary purpose of the volume was to communicate information that readers could use to examine and compare the characteristics of the various models; and (b) this purpose was most likely to be accomplished if all authors followed the general guidelines stated in the last section of Chapter 2. It also was agreed that the length of manuscripts would be in the range of 55–60 double-spaced pages, not including references, tables, and figures, and that at least one-third of each chapter would be assigned to reporting evaluation techniques and results.

The agreement to devote one-third of each chapter on Follow Through models to the description of evaluation techniques and results had two important implications for shaping the content of the volume. First, authors carefully selected the content of each evaluation section in order to communicate their most important programmatic emphases, since the space available was insufficient to report all possible outcomes of implementation procedures. Second, authors strived to gain internal consistency among statements about evaluation and the content of the other sections in order to produce a cohesive chapter. These decisions about priorities and internal consistency were extremely difficult and time-consuming in the preparation of each chapter. But the consensus among the writers is that the completion of the chapters served to sharpen their perception of priorities, as well as the possibilities for strengthening their models.

EDITING THE MANUSCRIPTS

After the initial drafts of the manuscripts on Follow Through models were completed, a number of issues emerged during the editing process, and two of these are discussed here. First, the initial drafts were characterized by expression of the strong feelings and commitment that developed during the authors' decade of experience in Follow Through. But the drafts also contained many polemical and defensive statements that reflected the stressful, and at times stormy, atmosphere in which the Follow Through sponsors had developed and refined their models. Thus, an essential task for the editor was to help the authors develop manuscripts that were characterized by a less subjective and more positive tone. But the intent was to accomplish this goal in ways that preserved the flavor of involvement that was reflected in the initial drafts of the manuscripts.

The second issue in the editing process pertained to the "compressed" forms of verbal and written communication that sponsors and members of their staffs evolved over a period of many years in order to communicate quickly among themselves on concepts, components, and activities in their models. Apparently, certain "in-house" terms, phrases, and statements were gradually coined and adopted as standard forms of communication because they conveyed a great deal of meaning in a minimum number of words. These compressed forms of communication were adaptive for individuals employed in the various models, since they reduced the amount of time required to discuss or write about issues in circumstances where pressures for performance often were intense. But when these expressions were incorporated into manuscripts, individuals who were not well-informed about the models could not readily comprehend many statements made about them. Therefore, a major challenge for the editor was to assist the authors to communicate the meaning of their compressed statements about the characteristics of the various models in more conventional language.

The implementation of planned variation and sponsorship in Follow Through required the participation of many social scientists during more than a decade. This adventure in implementation awareness provides a unique opportunity to examine the contributions of the social sciences to the national welfare in a large-scale longitudinal effort to improve educational services for large numbers of children and their parents. The intent in this volume has been to describe accomplishments and knowledge generated in Project Follow Through and to pursue the difficult but fascinating task of producing literature on problem-focused research.

References

Berman, P. *Federal programs supporting educational change. Vol. VIII: Implementing and sustaining innovations, R-1589/8-HEW.* Santa Monica, Calif.: Rand Corporation, 1978.

Berman, P., & McLaughlin, M. W. *Federal programs supporting educational change, R-1589/HEW.* Santa Monica, Calif.: Rand Corporation, 1975.

Berman, P., & Pauly, E. W. *Federal programs supporting educational change. Vol. II: Factors affecting change agent projects, R-1589/2-HEW.* Santa Monica, Calif.: Rand Corporation, 1975.

Datta, L. E. Changing times: The study of federal programs supporting educational change and the case for local problem solving. *Teachers College Record, 82,* (No. 1: Fall 1980), 101–116.

Glaser, R. Educational psychology and education. *American Psychologist,* 1973, *28,* 557–566.

Glazer, N. The schools of the minor professions. *Minerva*, 1974, *12*, 346–364.

Glazer, N. The disciplinary and the professional in graduate school education. In W. K. Frankena (Ed.), *The philosophy and future of graduate education*. Ann Arbor: University of Michigan Press, 1980. Pp. 160–176.

Greenwood, P. W., Mann, D., & McLaughlin, M. W. *Federal programs supporting educational change. Vol. III: The process of change, R-1589/3-HEW*. Santa Monica, Calif.: Rand Corporation, 1975.

Hauser, P. M. On actionism in the craft of sociology. In L. A. Zurcher & C. M. Bonjean (Eds.), *Planned social intervention*. Scranton, Penn.: Chandler, 1970. Pp. 20–31.

Horowitz, F. D., & Paden, L. Y. The effectiveness of environmental intervention programs. In B. M. Caldwell & H. N. Ricciuti, *Review of child development research. Vol. 3: Child development and social policy*. Chicago: University of Chicago Press, 1973. Pp. 331–402.

Moynihan, D. P. *Maximum feasible misunderstanding*. New York: Free Press, 1970.

Rossi, P. H. No good idea goes unpunished: Moynihan's misunderstanding and the proper role of social science in policy making. In L. A. Zurcher & C. M. Bonjean (Eds.), *Planned social intervention*. Scranton, Penn.: Chandler, 1970. Pp. 74–84.

Rossi, P. H., & Williams, W. (Eds.). *Evaluating social programs: Theory, practice, and politics*. New York: Seminar Press, 1972.

Parent-Supported Diagnostic Model (2)
  Department of Early Childhood Education
  Georgia State University
  Atlanta, GA 30303

Prentice-Hall Personalized Learning Model (1)
  Prentice-Hall Developmental Learning Center
  P.O. Box 655
  Andrews Drive
  West Paterson, NJ 07424

Responsive Educational Model (15)
  Far West Laboratory for Educational Research and Development
  1855 Folsom St.
  San Francisco, CA 94103

Tucson Early Education Model (20)
  College of Education
  University of Arizona
  Tucson, AR 85721

Appendix B:
Communities Served by
Five Follow Through Models

Parent Education Model
_____

1. Chattanooga, TN
2. Fairfield County, SC
3. Hillsborough County, FL
4. Houston, TX
5. Jacksonville, FL
6. Jonesboro, AR
7. Lac du Flambeau, WI
8. Lawrenceberg, IN
9. Philadelphia, PA
10. Richmond, VA
11. Yakima, WA

Direct Instruction Model
_____

1. Brooklyn, NY
2. Cherokee, NC
3. Chicago, IL
4. Dayton, OH
5. Dimmitt, TX
6. E. Las Vegas, NM
7. E. St. Louis, IL
8. Flint, MI
9. Flippin, AR
10. Grand Rapids, MI

11. Providence, RI
12. Racine, WI
13. Rosebud, SD
14. Smithville, TN
15. Todd County, SD
16. Tupelo, MS
17. Uvalde, TX
18. Washington, DC
19. W. Iron County, MI
20. Williamsburg County, SC

Behavior Analysis Model

1. Bronx, NY
2. Hopi Reservation, AZ
3. Indianapolis, IN
4. Kansas City, MO
5. Louisville, KY
6. Meridian, IL
7. New Madrid County, MO
8. North Cheyenne Reservation, MT
9. Philadelphia, PA
10. Pittsfield, MA
11. Trenton, NJ
12. Waukegan, IL

High/Scope Cognitively Oriented Curriculum Model

1. Central Ozarks, MO
2. Chicago, IL
3. Denver, CO
4. Greeley, CO
5. Harlem, NY
6. Leflora County, MS
7. Okaloosa County, FL
8. Riverton, WY
9. Seattle, WA
10. Trinidad, CO

Bank Street Model: A Developmental-Interaction Approach

1. Boulder, CO
2. Brattleboro, VT
3. Brooklyn, NY
4. Cambridge, MA
5. Elmira, NY
6. Fall River, MA
7. Hamden–New Haven, CT
8. Honolulu, HI
9. Huntsville, AL
10. Macon County, AL
11. Plattsburg, NY
12. Rochester, NY
13. Wilmington, DE

Author Index

Numbers in italics refer to the pages on which the complete references are listed.

Subject Index

EDUCATIONAL PSYCHOLOGY

continued from page ii